Laura A. Janda (Ed.)
Cognitive Linguistics: The Quantitative Turn

Cognitive Linguistics: The Quantitative Turn

The Essential Reader

edited by
Laura A. Janda

De Gruyter Mouton

ISBN 978-3-11-033388-6
e-ISBN 978-3-11-033525-5

Library of Congress Cataloging-in-Publication Data

A CIP catalog record for this book has been applied for at the Library of Congress.

Bibliographic information published by the Deutsche Nationalbibliothek

The Deutsche Nationalbibliothek lists this publication in the Deutsche Nationalbibliografie; detailed bibliographic data are available in the Internet at http://dnb.dnb.de.

© 2013 Walter de Gruyter GmbH, Berlin/Boston

Cover image: Caroline Sale/Flickr/Getty Images
Printing: Hubert & Co. GmbH & Co. KG, Göttingen
∞ Printed on acid-free paper

Printed in Germany

www.degruyter.com

Table of contents

Publication sources vii

Quantitative methods in *Cognitive Linguistics*: An introduction 1
Laura A. Janda

Constructional preemption by contextual mismatch:
A corpus-linguistic investigation 33
Anatol Stefanowitsch

Corpus evidence of the viability of statistical preemption 57
Adele E. Goldberg

Embodied motivations for metaphorical meanings 81
Marlene Johansson Falck and Raymond W. Gibbs, Jr.

The acquisition of the active transitive construction in English:
A detailed case study 103
*Anna L. Theakston, Robert Maslen, Elena V. M. Lieven and
Michael Tomasello*

Discovering constructions by means of collostruction analysis:
The English Denominative Construction 141
Beate Hampe

Phonological similarity in multi-word units 177
Stefan Th. Gries

The acquisition of questions with long-distance dependencies 197
Ewa Dąbrowska, Caroline Rowland and Anna Theakston

Iconicity of sequence: A corpus-based analysis of the positioning of
temporal adverbial clauses in English 225
Holger Diessel

Cognitive Sociolinguistics meets loanword research:
Measuring variation in the success of anglicisms in Dutch 251
Eline Zenner, Dirk Speelman and Dirk Geeraerts

What constructional profiles reveal about synonymy:
A case study of Russian words for SADNESS and HAPPINESS 295
Laura A. Janda and Valery D. Solovyev

The papers are reprinted with permission. They appear in their original form except for the following changes: adjusted pagination, removal of DOI. The article by Zenner, Speelman and Geeraerts features the latest De Gruyter typography.

Publication sources

Anatol Stefanowitsch
2011 Constructional preemption by contextual mismatch: A corpus-linguistic investigation. *Cognitive Linguistics* 22(1): 107–129.

Adele E. Goldberg
2011 Corpus evidence of the viability of statistical preemption. *Cognitive Linguistics* 22(1): 131–153.

Marlene Johansson Falck and Raymond W. Gibbs, Jr.
2012 Embodied motivations for metaphorical meanings. *Cognitive Linguistics* 23(2): 251–272.

Anna L. Theakston, Robert Maslen, Elena V. M. Lieven and Michael Tomasello
2012 The acquisition of the active transitive construction in English: A detailed case study. *Cognitive Linguistics* 23(1): 91–128.

Beate Hampe
2011 Discovering constructions by means of collostruction analysis: The English Denominative Construction. *Cognitive Linguistics* 22(2): 211–245.

Stefan Th. Gries
2011 Phonological similarity in multi-word units. *Cognitive Linguistics* 22(3): 491–510.

Ewa Dąbrowska, Caroline Rowland and Anna Theakston
2009 The acquisition of questions with long-distance dependencies. *Cognitive Linguistics* (20)3: 571–597.

Holger Diessel
2008 Iconicity of sequence: A corpus-based analysis of the positioning of temporal adverbial clauses in English. *Cognitive Linguistics* 19(3): 465–490.

Eline Zenner, Dirk Speelman and Dirk Geeraerts
2012 Cognitive Sociolinguistics meets loanword research: Measuring variation in the success of anglicisms in Dutch. *Cognitive Linguistics* 23(4): 749–792.

Laura A. Janda and Valery D. Solovyev
2009 What constructional profiles reveal about synonymy: A case study of Russian words for SADNESS and HAPPINESS *Cognitive Linguistics* 20(2): 367–393.

Quantitative methods in *Cognitive Linguistics*: An introduction*

Laura A. Janda

1. Introduction

Both the field of cognitive linguistics as a whole and the journal *Cognitive Linguistics* have taken a quantitative turn in recent years. The majority of conference presentations, articles, and books in our field now involve some kind of quantitative analysis of language data, and results are often measured using statistical methods. This does not mean that other types of contributions (theoretical, introspective) are in any way less welcome in cognitive linguistics, but the quantitative turn in our field is now a fact to be reckoned with.

This book presents some of the people and the statistical methods that have played a leading role in defining the current state of the art in cognitive linguistics, focusing specifically on researchers and methods that have appeared prominently in our journal in the past five years. The ten articles gathered here showcase recent achievements of the following individuals (plus coauthors) who have made quantitative contributions repeatedly in the pages of *Cognitive Linguistics*: Ewa Dąbrowska, Holger Diessel, Dirk Geeraerts, Raymond W. Gibbs, Adele E. Goldberg, Stefan Th. Gries, Beate Hampe, Laura A. Janda, Elena V. M. Lieven, Caroline Rowland, Anatol Stefanowitsch, Anna L. Theakston, and Michael Tomasello. Collectively these researchers have done much to shape contemporary practice in statistical analysis in cognitive linguistics, addressing issues at all levels of language, including phonology, morphology, syntax, semantics, acquisition, sociolinguistics, etc. Other significant leaders in quantitative analysis in our field include Ben Ambridge, Antti Arppe, Harald Baayen, Jeremy Boyd, Steven Clancy, William Croft, Dagmar Divjak, Dylan

---

* I would like to thank: the CLEAR (Cognitive Linguistics: Empirical Approaches to Russian) group (Anna Endresen, Julia Kuznetsova, Anastasia Makarova, Tore Nesset, and Svetlana Sokolova), Ewa Dąbrowska, Ludmila Janda, and Francis Tyers for their comments on this article; and the University of Tromsø and the Norwegian Research Council for their support of this research.

Glynn, Martin Hilpert, Willem B. Hollmann, Irraide Ibarretxe, Vsevolod Kapatsinski, Maarten Lemmens, John Newman, Sally Rice, Dominiek Sandra, Hans-Jörg Schmid, Doris Schönefeld, Dan Slobin, Dirk Speelman, Javier Valenzuela, and Stefanie Wulff.

The methods represent those that have proven useful and versatile in linguistic analysis: chi-square, Fisher test, binomial test, ANOVA, correlation, regression, and cluster analysis. Each of these methods, with their advantages and limitations, will be discussed in turn and illustrated by highlights from the articles in this collection. Additional methods that are gaining popularity and may become part of standard use are also presented in that section, and suggestions are made for best practices in the management and sharing of data and statistical code.

Based on a study of articles published in *Cognitive Linguistics*, the time period 2008–2012 emerges as a noticeably different era in our history. As described in section 2, the year 2008 marks the quantitative turn for our journal, and the past five years have been substantially different from the two decades that preceded them. It seems unlikely now that we will ever turn back, so this is an appropriate time to take stock of the situation, how it came about, and what it means for our future.

2. How we got here, where we are now, what challenges lie ahead

There are many reasons why cognitive linguists have become increasingly attracted to quantitative methods. A combination of theoretical and historical factors has facilitated the quantitative turn.

Unlike most other modern theories of linguistics, cognitive linguistics is a usage-based model of language structure (Langacker 1987: 46; 2008: 220). In other words, we posit no fundamental distinction between "performance" and "competence", and recognize all language units as arising from usage events. Usage events are observable, and therefore can be collected, measured, and analyzed scientifically (Glynn 2010: 5–6). In this sense, cognitive linguistics has always been a "data-friendly" theory, with a focus on the relationship between observed form and meaning. Linguistic theories that aim instead to uncover an idealized linguistic competence have less of a relationship to the observation of usage, though there are of course notable exceptions. For overviews of the use of corpus linguistics across various theoretical frameworks, see Gries 2009 and Joseph 2004.

Even the question of what constitutes data in linguistics is controversial, and largely dependent upon the theory that one uses. Many researchers in formal theories refer to constructed examples and individual intuitions as data, while others prefer to use corpus attestations or observations from acquisition or experiments. While introspection does play an important role in linguistic analysis, reliance on introspection to the exclusion of observation undermines linguistics as a science, yielding claims that can be neither operationalized nor falsified. It may seem attractive to assume that language is a tightly ordered logical system in which crisp distinctions yield absolute predictions, but there is no a priori reason to make this assumption, and usage data typically do not support it. Instead we find complex relationships among factors that motivate various trends in the behavior of linguistic forms. A usage-based theorist views language use as the data relevant for linguistic analysis, and this gives cognitive linguistics a natural advantage over other theories in applying quantitative methods, an advantage that we have been steadily realizing and improving upon over the past quarter century.

It is crucial to distinguish between the linguist's own intuitions about data (or intuitions solicited from a few colleagues) and judgment experiments involving the systematic study of the intuitions of naive informants under experimental conditions (which is a legitimate scientific method that normally involves quantitative analysis). There is a difference between these two uses of introspection in that the former does not yield reliable, replicable results, whereas the latter can. The linguist's intuitions present numerous problems in that there are disagreements between linguists (cf. Carden and Dietrich 1980, Cowart 1997); intuitions about mental phenomena are often inaccurate (Gibbs 2006); and last but not least, linguist's intuitions may be biased by their theoretical commitments (Dąbrowska 2010).

Computational linguists have made remarkable progress in developing technological applications for language in recent years. In terms of digital manipulation of language data, on the whole they have more experience than we typically find among cognitive linguists. The goals of computational linguists and cognitive linguists of course differ, but this opens up considerable opportunity for collaboration. We bring to the table a strong focus on foundational theoretical issues. Joining forces with computational linguists can help us to realize the potential that digital resources provide for investigating linguistically interesting questions. And hopefully computational linguists will inspire us to put our research results to work in developing language technology.

Recent history has impacted the practice of linguistics through the development of language corpora and statistical software. Today we have access to balanced multi-purpose corpora for many languages, often containing hundreds of millions of words, some even with linguistic annotation. Modern corpora of this kind became widespread only a little over a decade ago, but have already become the first resource many linguists turn to when investigating a phenomenon. At approximately the same time, statistical software likewise became widely available, in particular "R", which is open-source and supports

UTF-8 encoding for various languages. Thus we now have access to both vast quantities of data and the means to explore its structure.

Cognitive linguists are on the leading edge in terms of implementing data analysis in the context of a theoretical framework and we may well have a historic opportunity now to show leadership not only within cognitive linguistics, but in the entire field of linguistics. We can establish best practices in quantitative approaches to theoretical questions. Best practices should include acknowledgement of the most valuable kinds of statistical methods and significance measures, as well as public archiving and sharing of data and statistical code. This will help to move the field forward by providing standards and examples that can be followed. It is also a means of reducing the risk of fraud. Most academic fields in which researchers report statistical findings have experienced scandals involving fudged data or analyses, and current pressures to publish present an incentive to falsify results in hopes of impressing reviewers at a prestigious journal. Data sharing and best practices (see section 2.2) can help us to protect our field from this kind of dishonor.

2.1. *The quantitative turn in the pages of* Cognitive Linguistics

In this book I use the journal *Cognitive Linguistics* as a microcosm for the entire field, and here I present the quantitative turn as it has unfolded on our pages. Of course it would in principle be possible to undertake a comprehensive investigation, including other journals such as *Corpus Linguistics and Linguistic Theory*, and books such as Glynn and Fischer 2010, Gries and Stefanowitsch 2007, Schmid and Handl 2010, and Stefanowitsch and Gries 2007. However I justify this choice on the grounds that the journal gives us the most consistent longitudinal perspective available on this development.

I have surveyed all of the articles published in the journal *Cognitive Linguistics* from its inaugural volume in 1990 through the most recent completed volume in 2012. The numbers here represent the findings of this survey as an overview of the situation rather than a scientifically exact account. If we exclude review articles, book reviews, overviews, commentaries, replies, squibs, CLiPs (surveys of recent publications), and introductions to special issues, we find a total of 331 articles published in the journal in that interval. If we define a "quantitative article" as an article in which a researcher reports numbers for some kind of authentic language data, then we find 141 quantitative articles in that period, and they are distributed as shown in Figure 1.

In order to put all the data on the same scale, Figure 1 reports percentages of quantitative articles for each year. A thick line marks 50% to make this visualization clearer. On the basis of this distribution we can divide the history of *Cognitive Linguistics* into two eras, 1990–2007 – when most articles were not quantitative, and 2008–2012 – when most articles were quantitative.

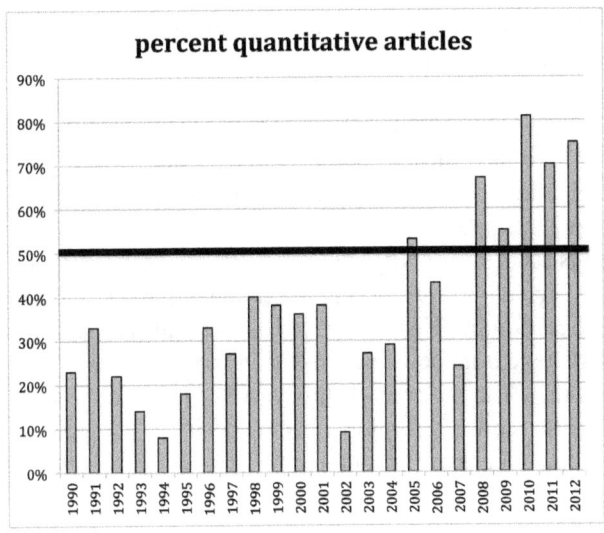

Figure 1. *Percent quantitative articles in* Cognitive Linguistics 1990–2012

In 1990–2007, twelve out of eighteen volumes had 20–40% quantitative articles. The lowest points were 1994, with one out of twelve articles, and 2002, with one out of eleven articles. 2005 reached in the other direction, with ten out of nineteen articles.

It is important to note that quantitative articles have always been with us; no year has ever been without quantitative studies. Three quantitative articles appeared already in the very first volume: Goossens 1990 (with a database of metaphorical and metonymic expressions), Delbecque 1990 (citing numbers of attestations in French and Spanish corpora), and Gibbs 1990 (presenting experimental results). However 2008 is the year in which we definitively crossed the 50% line, and it is unlikely that we will drop below that line again in the foreseeable future. Over half (75 out of 141 = 53%) of all quantitative articles published in *Cognitive Linguistics* have appeared in 2008–2012.

The majority of quantitative articles in our journal report corpus data (34%) or experimental data (48%) or a combination of the two (6%), and acquisition data (which can involve both corpus and experimental data) is also steadily represented (12%). 54 articles (38%) reported only raw and/or percent frequencies in the absence of any statistical test. The most popular statistical measure is by far the chi-square test (40 articles), but an accompanying effect size (Cramer's V) is reported only in 3 articles. The remaining measures that appear more than once are given here in descending order of frequency with the number of relevant articles (note also that some articles report several kinds of tests): ANOVA (26), t-test (13), correlation (11), regression (of various types, also including both fixed and mixed effects models; 8), clustering (5), Fisher test (4), binomial test (2). Visualization of data was spotty in the first decade of the journal, with only four graphs appearing before 2000 (in Hirschberg and Ward 1991, Sanders et al. 1993, Sandra and Rice 1995, and Hudson 1997). Between 2000–2007 the number of graphs ranges from zero (in 2002 and 2004) to five (in 2005), but becomes frequent in 2008–2012 when half or more of the quantitative articles appear with graphs.

We can thus securely identify 2008–2012 as a distinct period in the history of *Cognitive Linguistics*. During this period quantitative analysis emerges as common practice, dominating the pages of our journal. The selection of articles, authors, and statistical models represented in this anthology are motivated by these observations. The purpose of this book is to explicitly acknowledge the norms that we are implicitly forging as a community. In the next subsection we consider what this means for our future.

2.2. *The road beyond the quantitative turn*

Now that we have started off down a path dominated by quantitative methods, it is worth asking ourselves where we are headed. We have much to look forward to, but some words of caution are also in order.

It is essential for the legitimacy of our field to secure and maintain the status of linguistics as a science. In applying quantitative measures we are developing linguistics as a discipline, following psychology and sociology in bringing the scientific method best known from the natural sciences to the fore. However, we face two challenges, one involving the relationship between introspection and observation and the other involving the archiving and sharing of data and code.

Although I maintain that exclusive reliance on introspection can be problematic, especially in the presence of unfounded assumptions, it is important to remember that there always has been and always should be a place for introspection in linguistics. Our journal has always published both quantitative and non-quantitative articles, and there is no reason to expect that this should cease to be the case even after the quantitative turn. In other words, it is not the case that we are dealing with an S-curve in which a phenomenon was initially absent, there was an innovation, and then the innovation will necessarily reach 100% (cf. Blythe and Croft 2012). While it is not infallible as a method, introspection has a place in our field. There should be a healthy balance between introspection and observation in any scientific inquiry. Introspection is a source of inspiration for hypotheses, which are then tested via observation. When it comes to analysis, we need introspection again in order to interpret the results and understand what they mean for both theory and facts of language.

Introspection is irreplaceable in the descriptive documentation of language. In fieldwork a linguist interacts with speakers and posits the structure of a grammar based on a combination of observations and insights. The foundational role of descriptive work and reference grammars is not to be underestimated, for without this background we would have no basis for stating any hypotheses about languages at all. Linguists who pursue quantitative methods should never forget that they stand with one foot on the shoulders of descriptivists. Although it is not strictly within the mission of *Cognitive Linguistics* to publish purely descriptive work, contributions that present a previously unknown language phenomenon as attested by authentic data (whether quantitative or not) are welcome on our pages.

The other foot of quantitative linguists should be on the shoulders of theorists. Whereas theory should of course be informed by data, theoretical advances owe much to introspection and are often presented without recourse to new findings or in the context of summaries over multiple studies. It would be foolish to banish theoretical polemics from our journal and our field. Reducing our theoretical perspective would hinder our ability to pose linguistically interesting questions, both in quantitative and non-quantitative studies.

Both theoretical and descriptive components have long been common in the training of linguists, but now we should ask how much statistics should be added to our graduate programs and our professional expectations. The answer depends in part upon the goals of programs and individuals, however we have reached a point at which all programs should offer some quantitative component, and all linguists should have at least some passive statistical literacy. Relevant handbooks are available (King et al. 2010, Johnson 2008, Baayen 2008, Gries 2013, Cohen et al. 2003), and this book gives illustrations of how several statistical methods can be successfully applied to pertinent linguistic questions.

One important step we should take as a community is to make a commitment to publicly archive both our data and the statistical code used to analyze it. The goal should be to create an ethical standard for sharing data and code in a manner explicit enough so that other researchers can access the data and re-run the models. This can be done by creating designated websites for public access using standard and preferably open-source software. For example, Janda et al. 2013 presents a series of studies using chi-square, Fisher test, and logistic regression. Any visitor to this site http://emptyprefixes.uit.no/book.htm can find all the relevant data in csv (comma-separated-values) files and open-source annotated R scripts. The website gives instructions on how to access R, run the scripts, and interpret the results, and explains how the datasets are organized and what the values stand for. The annotations in the scripts describe every step needed to set up the model for analysis. Similarly Baayen et al. forthcoming presents a series of case studies comparing the results yielded by logistic regression, classification and regression trees and random forests, and naive discriminative learning, and all of the data and code are already housed at this site: http://ansatte.uit.no/laura.janda/RF/RF.html. De Gruyter Mouton has the facility to archive supplementary materials associated with the works it publishes, and this can include data, code, graphics, and sound files. To date, no author in *Cognitive Linguistics* has yet made use of this opportunity, perhaps because it is not widely known. I strongly encourage linguists to publicly archive data and code, for it has important implications for the advancement of the field and for its integrity.

Publicly archived linguistic data and statistical code have great pedagogical value for the community of linguists. As anyone who has attempted quantitative analysis of linguistic data knows, one of the biggest challenges is to match an appropriate statistical model to a given dataset. Access to examples of datasets and corresponding models will help us all over the hurdle of choosing the right models for our data. We can help each other and bring our whole field forward much more efficiently if we pool our experience. I think it is quite misguided to be overprotective of one's data and code. This does not need to be a race with winners and losers; it can instead be a collective learning experience. A shared pool of data and code will also have a normative effect on the use of statistics in linguistics, further clarifying the trends that I try to identify in this book.

While transparency does not guarantee integrity, it does make some kinds of fraud easier to detect, and it always improves the quality and depth of scholarly communication. It has long been the case in natural sciences, medicine, and psychology that authors are routinely requested to submit their data along with their manuscripts when seeking publication in a journal. I expect similar requests to become more common in connection with submissions to *Cognitive Linguistics* in the future. In many cases funding agencies also require researchers to share their data with any colleagues who ask for it (this is particularly common in medicine), and it is not unthinkable that such conditions could be placed upon grant funding for linguistics as well. For the researcher, both public archiving and submission of data can be accomplished via the same task, preparing annotations for datasets and code that facilitate the work of peer reviewers and colleagues.

Lastly I would like to make an appeal for elegance in analysis. We should not engage in an arms race to find out who can show off the most complex statistical models. It is usually the case that the simplest model that is appropriate to the data is the best one to use, since the results will be most accessible to readers. Sometimes the structure of the data dictates a more complex model, but some models carry with them the problem that they are well understood only by the statisticians who developed them. Overuse of "black box" methods will not enhance the ability of linguists to communicate with each other. Recall from section 2.1 that over one-third (38%) of the quantitative studies published in *Cognitive Linguistics* did not use any statistical test at all: the goals of the authors were achieved by reporting frequencies and ratios that are easy for everyone to interpret. I refer the reader also to Kuznetsova 2013 for several examples of how to find linguistic insights in quantitative studies without invoking heavy statistical machinery.

3. Methods

A research question must of course come first, along with some kind of hypothesis. Next the researcher can consider what kind of data can be collected in order to address the question. The design of a study inevitably involves some compromise between accessing an ideal dataset and the limitations of what is realistically obtainable. Already in the design, decisions must be made about what to collect, how to code it, etc. and these decisions will impact the choice of the statistical model. The choice of a model is very much dependent upon the structure and type of data involved. Ideally the researcher will be familiar with some possible statistical models and take this into consideration when designing a study.

This section presents the articles in this anthology organized according to the statistical models they use. First some information is given about each model and then the relevant articles are discussed, with focus on the theoretical linguistic issue that the author has posed, the type of data examined, and reasons why the given model is appropriate. The purpose of this discussion is not to serve as a textbook on applying statistical models, but rather to illustrate how the models are being used and provide sufficient orientation for readers who want to gain confidence in reading and understanding such articles.

3.1. Chi-square: Finding out whether there is a significant difference between distributions
Stefanowitsch 2011, Goldberg 2011, Falck and Gibbs 2012, Theakston et al. 2012

The chi-square test is very common and popular, so it is worth giving some detail about how it works, what it means, and what kinds of data it is appropriate for. This test is usually appropriate when you have a matrix of data and you want to explore the relationship between two variables. One factor is assigned to the rows and another to the columns. The matrix must have at least two rows and two columns, each column and row represents a given value for a variable, and each cell in the matrix has a number of observations. The chi-square test evaluates the distribution of observations in relation to what would be expected in a random distribution given the totals for the rows and the columns. If the distribution is very uneven, and this unevenness cannot be attributed to chance, then there is probably a relationship between the two variables. The chi-square test gives a p-value (probability value) that tells you the likelihood that you could get a distribution that is as uneven as the one observed (or even more extreme) if your observations are a sample from a (potentially infinite) population of data points in which there is no relationship between the factors and no difference in distribution. A very low number indicates a low likelihood that you could get this distribution by chance, and this is a measure of statistical significance. Usually the largest p-value that is acknowledged as significant is 0.05 (often signaled by one asterisk *), while more significant values are p < 0.01 (**) and p < 0.001 (***).

Here is a concrete example to illustrate how the chi-square test can be used. Dickey and Janda (2009) wanted to challenge the traditional definition of allomorphy, suggesting that allomorphy should be recognized as a gradient rather than all-or-nothing phenomenon because there are cases where the distribution of morpheme variants fails the classical criterion of complementary distribution, but displays a strong relationship akin to allomorphy. To this end, Dickey and Janda presented the distribution of Russian verbs derived with two semelfactive markers, the suffix -*nu* and the prefix *s*-, across the morphological classes of verbs. This distribution supports their argument that -*nu* and *s*- behave much like allomorphs. Here is the raw data:

Table 1. *Distribution of semelfactive markers across Russian verb classes from Dickey and Janda 2009*

		verb classes					
		-aj	non-prod	-*ě	-ova	-i	-*ěj
semelfactive	-nu	185	57	20	17	16	0
markers	s-	1	0	1	18	38	36

The two variables are the semelfactive markers and the verb classes. There are 185 verbs in the -*aj* class with the -*nu* marker, 57 verbs in the non-productive class with the -*nu* marker, etc. The chi-square test returns these values for this distribution: chi-squared = 269.2249, df = 5, p-value < 2.2e-16. 2.2e-16 is a very low number (0.00000000000000022), in fact it is the lowest p-value that R reports for the chi-square test, so it tells us there is almost no chance that we could have taken a sample with this distribution (or one even more extreme) from a hypothetically infinite population of verbs in which there is no relationship between the two variables. In other words, this result is statistically significant (***).

In addition to the chi-square test, Dickey and Janda report the effect size (Cramer's V), which measures the chi-square value against the total number of observations. Cramer's V ranges from 0 to 1, and it is generally acknowledged that 0.1 is the minimum threshold for a reportable though small effect size, 0.3 is the threshold for a moderate effect size, and 0.5 is the threshold for a large effect size. The Cramer's V in this study is 0.83, indicating a large effect. While effect sizes are not yet commonplace in linguistic studies, I strongly encourage all researchers to measure effect sizes when reporting p-values, especially when the number of observations is large (thousands or more). In a large dataset the chi-square test will find even infinitesimal differences in distribution to be statistically significant. For instance, Janda and Lyashevskaya 2011 is a study of the distribution of verb forms across aspect and aspectual markers for nearly 6 million observations from the Russian National Corpus. The p-values for all distributions were found to be significant, but only the p-value for the aspectual difference (perfective vs. imperfective) was confirmed by a robust Cramer's V effect size of 0.399, whereas effect sizes for differences in aspectual markers (prefixes vs. suffixes) were 0.076 and 0.037, an order of magnitude too small to be considered reportable. Thus a measure of effect size can be used to distinguish between effects that are worth our attention and ones that are not.

Some words of caution are in order with regard to the use of the chi-square test. Note that the input for this test must always be raw frequencies, not percentages. The chi-square test has a lower limit on the quantity of data needed: no cell in a matrix should have an expected value of five or less. While there are some lower values in Table 1, the expected values (based on the row and column totals) for all cells are greater than 5. If there is a large matrix and/or very uneven distribution of data, this will result in a paucity of data for chi-square, which gives error ("unreliable") messages in R. The chi-square test is also founded upon an assumption of independence of observations. In other words, no two observations should be related to each other, for example by having the same source. For corpus data this usually means that one should not have more than one example from any given author in order to avoid biasing the data according to individual preferences of authors, unless one is sampling within a population of utterances or using the author/utterer as one of the variables; see the discussion of Theakston et al. 2012 below. Note also that mixed effects regression models are designed to deal with such factors; see section 3.6.

Stefanowitsch 2011

The linguistic issue addressed is: How do children learn that a given syntactic structure, such as the English ditransitive, is ungrammatical for some verbs in the absence of negative evidence? Does the ungrammatical ditransitive get preempted when the child gets as input the prepositional dative in contexts that should otherwise prefer the ditransitive (see Pinker 1984)? Stefanowitsch uses corpus data (from the British Component of the International Corpus of English = ICE-GB) to address this issue, and analyzes this data by means of chi-square tests. The first variable in all tests is verb class, which can be either alternating (appearing in both the ditransitive and the prepositional dative constructions, like *read* and *tell*) or non-alternating (appearing only in the prepositional dative constructions, like *explain* and *mention*). The second variable was selected from a set of factors relevant to the information structure of these verbs. There were three such variables coded with reference to both the recipient and the theme: givenness (referential distance), syntactic weight (number of orthographic words), and animacy. Stefanowitsch extracts 50 sentences each for alternating and non-alternating verbs; all examples are of the prepositional dative construction. In nearly all tests of the first variable in relation to one selected from the second set of variables, the chi-square test yields a p-value too high to suggest statistical significance. Further tests show that the differences between verbs belonging to the same class are often greater than other differences. Stefanowitsch concludes that preemption is an unlikely explanation since corpus data do not support the relevant inferences.

Goldberg 2011

Goldberg addresses the same question as Stefanowitsch, namely whether preemption gives sufficient evidence for learners of English to understand that some verbs can only take the prepositional dative construction, as opposed to other verbs that can appear in both the prepositional dative construction and the ditransitive construction. For Goldberg the most important issue is whether the alternative constructions are actually in competition, and for this reason her data reflects use of both constructions, not just the prepositional dative. Goldberg argues that Stefanowitsch's sample of data (100 sentences, all of the prepositional dative construction) is too small and too restricted, and that the hypothesis is also too narrow. Goldberg takes a different sample from a corpus (Corpus of Contemporary American English = COCA), with over 15,000 examples of alternating verbs and over 400 examples of non-alternating verbs (the latter are of overall lower frequency), representing both the prepositional dative construction and the ditransitive construction with a pronominal recipient and a full NP for the theme. Goldberg shows that the probability of using the prepositional dative (ratio of prepositional dative/ditransitive uses) is very low (0.04 on average) for alternating verbs, but very high (0.83 on average) for non-alternating verbs. Goldberg compares the overall distribution of the two constructions across the two classes of verbs using the chi-square test. The first variable is the same as we see for Stefanowitsch: the class of verb as alternating vs. non-alternating. The other variable is the construction as prepositional dative vs. ditransitive. The p-value reported for this chi-square test is $p < 0.0001$, indicating a very significant result. Goldberg thus argues that the different distributions are indeed sufficient to give learners evidence for preemption. Several additional arguments are also adduced, such as frequency, experimental data (reported in other studies on use of adjectives) and a variety of other alternative hypotheses involving more complex sets of competing constructions and lexemes.

Falck and Gibbs 2012

Falck and Gibbs present a combination of experimental and corpus data addressing the question of how bodily experiences motivate metaphorical meanings. Their study focuses on differences between the use of the English words *path* and *road* both in reference to physical experience and to metaphorical understanding of other kinds of experience. Twenty-four undergraduates at UC Santa Cruz participated in an experiment by answering fourteen questions about their experiences of paths vs. roads. This questionnaire showed that the subjects expected paths to be more likely to involve problematic terrain and aimless pedestrian movement, whereas roads were judged more likely to be wide, paved and straight and traveled by vehicles. A chi-square test was performed for each question with one variable being the choice of *path* vs. *road*, and the other relating to each given question (e.g. more likely to have obstacles vs. not). The result for one question was significant at the $p < 0.05$ level, the result for one other question was significant at the $p < 0.01$ level, the results for ten questions were significant at the $p < 0.001$ level, and the results for two questions (involving presence of obstacles and which would be more used for biking) were not significant. These experimental results were compared to dictionary entries and to corpus examples. 1000 examples each for *path* and *road* were extracted from the *British National Corpus* (BNC) and the Pragglejaz Metaphor Identification Procedure was used to identify and classify all metaphorical uses in the sample. At an abstract level all of the metaphors were similar in that they used travel as the source domain, and had various life experiences as the target domain. However, at a more fine-grained level, the distribution of metaphorical uses was very different for the two words. While *path* was often used to describe courses of action and ways of living, *road* (with overall far fewer metaphorical uses) was more likely to be associated with purposeful activity and political or financial matters. A second set of chi-square tests, with the same first variable, but different second variables involving choice of metaphorical types, showed these results to be significant at the $p < 0.001$ level. Falck and Gibbs take this as evidence that people's understanding of their physical experiences with paths and roads also informs their metaphorical choices, making *path* more appropriate for descriptions of personal struggles, and *road* more appropriate for straightforward progress toward a goal.

Theakston et al. 2012

A twelve-month sample (from age 2;0 to 3;0) of acquisition data representing both the output of a child (Thomas) and the input of his mother was analyzed to track the use of SVO transitive constructions. The question motivating this research is whether children have preliminary biases favoring learning the expression of prototypical transitive events or they instead gradually build up competence based on previous use of the same verbs in SV and VO constructions. Chi-square tests are used in this study to show that there are significant differences across several types of distributions. For example, it is shown that Thomas's use of SVO constructions are different from his mother's use. When the first variable is Thomas vs. his mother (input) and the second variable is the form of the subject or object (pronoun/omitted, noun, or proper noun), the difference is significant at $p < 0.001$ at 2;6. Overall Thomas shows a propensity for expressing subjects as proper nouns and objects as pronouns (*it*), contrary to the input pattern of using pronouns for subjects and noun phrases for objects, which conforms to preferred argument structure. During the second half of the study phase (2;7 to 3;0) the proportional use of SVO (vs. SV vs. VO) is significantly different from month to month for most of the sample, with $p < 0.01$. However, even though these changes bring Thomas closer to the adult model, even at 3;0 his proportional use of SVO is significantly different from that of his mother, with $p < 0.001$. Thomas also shows more use of "Old" verbs (attested before 2;7) than "New" verbs (attested at or after 2;7) in the SVO construction ($p = 0.006$ at 2;9 and $p = 0.017$ at 2;11). Theakston et al. take this as evidence that children do not come to the acquisition task equipped with preliminary biases, but instead acquire the SVO construction via a complex process that involves different stages of development for different verbs (those acquired early vs. those acquired late), gradual abstraction of patterns, and integration of various semantic types.

3.2. Fisher test: Finding out whether a value deviates significantly from the overall distribution
Hampe 2011

The Fisher test is useful to evaluate the relationships among variables when data is very unevenly distributed and/or sparse. Like the chi-square test, the Fisher test takes into account the overall distribution of values in a matrix, and yields p-values. The difference is that a Fisher test can be applied to each cell, where it can tell us the probability that each value could deviate even more from the expected value, given the overall distribution. If the expected value is less than the observed value, we calculate a right-sided p-value, which indicates the probability that we would get this many items or more in the cell given the overall distribution of items. If the expected value is greater than the observed value, we calculate a left-sided p-value, which indicates the probability that we would get this many items or fewer in the cell given the overall distribution of items. In order to compute the Fisher test probability, four values are needed. These values relate the value in the cell to the sum for the row, the sum for the column, and the sum for the entire table.

This website http://emptyprefixes.uit.no/semantic_eng.htm gives a link to a Fisher Test calculator and shows how the Fisher test is applied to data relating the use of Russian verbal prefixes to the semantic tags assigned for verbs in the Russian National Corpus (Janda et al. 2013). For example, 51 verbs are found with the prefix *pro-* and the semantic tag "sound & speech", there are a total of 65 verbs prefixed by *pro-* (the column total), there are a total of 106 verbs with the "sound & speech" tag, and there are a total of 382 verbs in the study. Table 2 shows the values used for computing the Fisher test probability for *pro-*/"sound & speech":

Table 2. *An example of values used as input for a Fisher test (boldfaced)*

a = (value in the given cell) = **51**	b = (row total) – (value in the given cell) = 106 – 51 = **55**
c = (column total) – (value in the given cell) = 65 – 51 = **14**	d = (table total) – (value in the given cell) = 382 – 51 = **331**

Based on this array of values we can apply the Fisher test and we calculate a right-sided p-value of 5.7e-25 (an extremely low number, with twenty-four zeroes after the decimal point followed by the digits 57). This value indicates a strong relationship between the prefix *pro-* and the semantic tag "sound & speech" since there is an extremely small chance that we could get 51 or more verbs in that cell if we took another sample of the same size from a potentially infinite population of verbs in which there was no relationship between the prefix and the semantic class.

Hampe (2011) turns her attention to the family of complex transitive argument structures. She observes that whereas both generativists and cognitivists have paid considerable attention to both the caused-motion construction with a prepositional phrase (*John pushed Sally into the hole*) and the resultative construction with a predicate adjective (*John hammered the metal flat*), there has been less focus on a similar construction with a predicate noun phrase that Hampe calls the "denominative construction" (*Schoolmates called John a hero*). Hampe argues that the denominative construction deserves a place among complex transitive constructions and seeks support in corpus data from the ICE-GB. Following Stefanowitsch and Gries (2003, 2005), Hampe uses the Fisher test in collostruction analysis to measure the attraction of lexemes to constructions. She reports the p-values log-transformed on base 10, so that the number corresponds to the number of decimal places in the p-value (0.001 = 3, for example). Thus higher log-transformed numbers reflect lower p-values and stronger attractions, and Hampe arranges lists of verbs that appear in the relevant constructions according to their attraction to each construction. This results in distinctive lists that are very different from each other, supporting Hampe's claim that the denominative construction should be recognized as a construction in its own right. Hampe also finds that the denominative construction is attracted to the active voice, whereas the resultative construction is attracted to the passive voice.

3.3. Exact Binomial test: Finding out whether the distribution in a sample is significantly different from the distribution of a population
Gries 2011

Like the chi-square test and the Fisher test, the exact binomial test gives a p-value that reflects the chance that you could get a given distribution in a sample. The difference is that this test is appropriate when you have values for only two alternatives, provided that you also know the relative frequency of the two alternatives in the total population. In other words, if you know that there are ten white balls and ten red balls in an urn, you can calculate the chance of drawing three red balls when four total balls are drawn (and replaced each time) as p = 0.3125, or nearly a one in three chance (this example adapted from Gries 2001: 497–498). The exact binomial test is handy when you know the overall frequency of two alternatives in a corpus and want to know whether your sample differs significantly from what one would expect given the overall distributions in the corpus. For example, one could use the exact binomial test to compare the frequency of a given lexeme in a certain context with its overall frequency in the corpus to see whether there is an association between the context and the word.

Gries (2011) investigates the hypothesis that phonological similarity as realized in alliteration contributes to the cohesiveness of idiomatic expressions. Is the alliteration we see in phrases like *bite the bullet* and *turn the tables* just a random fact or does alliteration play a significant role in the formation of idioms? Gries undertakes two studies to find evidence in support of his hypothesis. The first study involves 211 high-frequency fully lexically specified idioms with a verb and a direct object. These idioms include 35 alliterations like the two cited above, but many others without any alliteration, like *spill the beans*. Gries makes several computations of baseline frequencies involving all allowable initial phonemes in English and their occurrence in the ICE-GB corpus and uses the binomial test to show that the frequency of alliteration in lexically-specified idioms is significantly above chance, with all p-values <0.001. Gries' second study is of the partially lexically specified *way*-construction as in *wend one's way*, where the direct object *way* is specified, but the verb can vary (since it can be replaced by *make*, *find*, and many other verbs). The question here is whether the verbs that fill the unspecified slot also have a tendency to alliterate with *way*. Again Gries undertakes a series of calculations to determine relevant baseline measures in the ICE-GB corpus and uses the exact binomial test to show that the alliteration in the *way*-construction is highly significant, again with p-values < 0.001.

3.4. T-test and ANOVA: Finding out whether group means are significantly different from each other
Dąbrowska et al. 2009

In order to understand ANOVA, it is helpful to start by tackling the t-test on which ANOVA is based. The t-test is useful for determining whether distributions of scores, for example from psycholinguistic experiments, are indeed different from each other. Let's say that we do an experiment collecting word-recognition reaction times from two groups of subjects, one that is exposed to a priming treatment that should speed up their reactions (the test group), and one that is not (the control group). The mean scores of the two groups are different, but the distributions overlap since some of the subjects in the test group have reaction times that are slower than some of the subjects in the control group. Do the scores of the test group and the control group represent two different distributions, or are they really samples from a single distribution (in which case the difference in means is merely due to chance)? The t-test can answer this question by giving us a p-value.

The t-test can only handle a simple comparison of two groups. ANOVA takes the t-test to a further dimension by making it possible compare more than two groups or more than one variable across the groups. ANOVA stands for "analysis of variance", and to understand ANOVA, one must first come to terms with variance. Variance is a measure of the shape of a distribution in terms of deviations from the mean. Since the sum of the deviations from the mean in any distribution is necessarily zero (half of the deviations will be positive and half will be negative), variance is measured by summing the squared deviations (all of which are rendered positive) and dividing them by the number of scores in the distribution. The square root of the variance gives us the standard deviation of the distribution. What ANOVA does is to divide the total variation among scores into two groups, the within-groups variation, where the variance is due to chance vs. the between-groups variation, where the variance is due to both chance and the treatment effect (if there is any). The F ratio has the between-groups variance in the numerator and the within-groups variance in the denominator, so if the F value is 1 or less, the inherent variance is greater than or equal to the between-groups variance, meaning that there is no treatment effect. But if F is greater than 1, higher values show a greater treatment effect and ANOVA can yield p-values to indicate significance. ANOVA can also handle multiple variables, for example priming vs. none and male vs. female and show whether each variable has an effect (called a main effect) and whether there is an interaction between the variables (for example if females respond even better to priming).

Generative linguists account for long-distance dependencies (LDDs) such as *What$_1$ do you think _____$_1$ is in the box?* and *Who$_1$ did Mary hope that Tom would tell Bill that he should visit _____$_1$?* in terms of abstract syntactic representations and iterate-able WH movement operations. If speakers really have such representations, they should perform equally well on simple, ordinary examples as on ones that are complex and deeply embedded. However, in a study of the BNC spoken corpus Dąbrowska discovered that 67% of LDD questions follow the lexically specific templates *WH do you think S-GAP?* or *WH did you say S-GAP?*, where S-GAP is a subordinate clause with a missing constituent, and the majority of the remaining attestations are minimal variations on these patterns. In other words, spontaneously produced LDD questions are highly stereotypical and might best be accounted for by means of these two lexically specific templates than by abstract schemas. Dąbrowska et al. (2009) tested this hypothesis in experiments on both children and adults. The results of an initial experiment with children were ambiguous since they could have been influenced by different frequencies of words. The design of the experiment was adjusted and both children and adults were asked to repeat four examples each of four types of questions using all the same lexemes (here only one example of each is given):

Prototypical LDD question: *What do you think the funny old man really hopes?*
Prototypical declarative: *I think the funny old man will really hope so.*
Unprototypical LDD question: *What does the funny old man really hope you think?*
Unprototypical declarative: *The funny old man really hopes I will think so.*

The children were stratified according to age: about half of them were five-year-olds and half of them were six-year-olds. For the children the results were analyzed using a $2 \times 2 \times 2$ ANOVA with the first variable as construction (declarative, question), the second variable as prototypicality (prototypical, unprototypical), and the third variable as age (5-year-olds, 6-year-olds). Both construction ($p = 0.016$) and prototypicality ($p = 0.021$) were found to be main effects, but not age. However, there was a significant interaction between construction and age ($p = 0.01$); five-year-olds performed better on questions than declaratives, but six-year-olds were equally good on both constructions. For adults a 2 × 2 ANOVA was used with the variables construction and prototypicality. Neither of the variables was significant as a main effect, but there was a significant interaction between construction and prototypicality (p = 0.021), suggesting that even adults make use of lexically specific templates for LDD questions, but not for declaratives. Overall, the results reported by Dąbrowska et al. indicate that children rely on lexically specific templates for both LDD questions and declaratives as late as age 6, and that even adults are more proficient with LDD questions that match these templates. These results support the usage-based approach, according to which children acquire lexically specific templates and make more abstract generalizations about constructions only later, and in some cases may continue to rely on templates even as adults.

3.5. Correlation and Regression: Finding significant relationships among values
Diessel 2008

Correlation refers to the degree of relationship between two variables, such that the greater the correlation, the better we are able to predict the value of one variable given the value of the other. Let's say, for example, that we want to explore the relationship between the corpus frequency of a word and reaction time in a word-recognition experiment. A likely outcome would be that there is a correlation, such that the higher the frequency of a word, the shorter the reaction time, and this relationship can be quantified as a coefficient. If this correlation exists, given the frequency of a word one would be able to use the coefficient to predict the reaction time, and conversely given the reaction time associated with a word one would be able to predict its frequency. There are two main ways to calculate correlation, also known as r, using Pearson's coefficient (which is appropriate for ordinary numerical scores) and Spearman's coefficient (which is appropriate for rank-ordered scores), and the two are very similar. Both involve calculations based on the deviations of individual data points from the mean and both yield measures that range from $r = +1$ (perfect positive correlation) to $r = 0$ (no correlation) to $r = -1$ (perfect negative correlation). In our example with frequency and reaction time we would expect to find a negative correlation since a higher value for frequency should give a lower value for reaction time. If the relationship is weak the value will be closer to zero, but if the relationship is strong it will be closer to -1. The value of the coefficient is an indication of how closely the data points come to approximating a straight line of best fit: if the data points follow a straight line the coefficient will be close to $+1$ or -1, but if the data points are scattered at random the coefficient will be close to zero.

Two caveats are important when using correlation. The first caveat is that the correlation coefficients assume that the relationship in question is linear, when in fact there are infinitely many other possible kinds of relationships (with various curves and clumps of data points) and indeed even for any given r value there is an infinite number of distributions of data points that it might describe. While correlation is handy for data that is perhaps a bit scattered but otherwise reasonably well behaved, in more complex cases the correlation coefficient might hide more structure than reveals. In some cases various transformations of the data can correct for the problem of non-linearity.

The second caveat is that the presence of a correlation does not mean that there is any causal relationship involved. There might be a causal relationship, but it cannot be inferred from a correlation. So while it might be the case that high frequency causes low reaction times, this is not proved by a correlation. The correlation would be just as likely (or unlikely) to prove the opposite: that low reaction times cause high frequency. For a perspective from another domain, it has long been known that there is a strong positive correlation between the wealth of a country and its cancer rate, but it would be very strange to assert that money gives people cancer. This correlation is probably due to other variables that are related to both wealth and cancer, such as for example that people in wealthy countries live longer and thus have more opportunity to eventually get cancer, and that they also have more access to doctors who can diagnose cancer, etc. Similar hidden variables can also lurk in linguistic data.

While correlation is not used as a measure in the articles in this anthology, it is worth understanding for two reasons: one reason is that correlation is well-represented in recent articles in *Cognitive Linguistics* (see Ambridge and Goldberg 2008, Ambridge and Rowland 2009, Chandler 2010, Ghesquière and Van de Velde 2011, Akita 2012, and Kraska-Szlenk and Żygis 2012) and the other reason is that the line of best fit described by correlation is the basis for regression models.

The line of best fit is called the regression line, and the equation that locates that line is called the regression equation. Like the correlation coefficient, the regression equation can predict the value of one variable given the value of the other variable, but this regression equation fits the data exactly only when the correlation is perfect ($+1$ or -1). Because the correlation is generally not perfect, there is a difference between the predicted values and the actual values, and this difference is referred to as the "error". The standard error of estimate (which is a kind of standard deviation of the actual scores from the predicted scores) gives us a measure of how well the regression equation fits our data.

Because regression is based upon the same calculations as correlation, it also inherits the same drawbacks, namely that it assumes a linear relationship (which may or may not be true), and that it cannot tell us anything about causation. Regression models come in a variety of types and all involve the prediction of a dependent variable based upon one or more independent variables (also called predictor values). Ideally the independent variables should be independent not just of the dependent variable, but also of each other (avoiding what is called collinearity). In logistic regression (named after the logistic function used to divide all values into a categorical choice between two levels) the dependent variable has only two values, and this is particularly useful for linguistic phenomena that involve a choice between two forms. For example, the locative alternation involves a choice between two constructions, the theme-object construction as in *load the boxes onto the cart*, and the goal-object construction as in *load the cart with boxes*. This website http://emptyprefixes.uit.no/constructional_eng.htm presents the data and R script for a logistic regression analysis of the locative alternation in Russian where the dependent variable is the construction (theme-object vs. goal-object) and the independent variables are the prefix on the verb, the status of the construction as full (with both theme and goal overt) vs. reduced, and the use of an active construction vs. a passive one (with a participle). (Note that multinomial extensions of logistic regression are also possible, allowing more than two choices.)

A regression analysis allows you to consider the relationship between an independent variable and a dependent variable, while making it possible to take into account the effects of additional independent variables. A regression model specifies the change in the group means when going from one variable level to another. The goal of a logistic regression model is to predict the probability that a given value (X, or alternatively, Y) for the dependent variable will be used. This is achieved by means of the logarithm of the odds ratio of X and Y. The odds ratio is the quotient of the number of observations supporting X and the number of observations supporting Y. This ratio is negative when the count for Y is greater than the count for X. It is zero when the counts are equal. It is positive when the counts for X exceed the counts for Y.

Like the chi-square test, the binomial test, and ANOVA, regression will also give you p-values. Usually there will be an overall p-value to indicate the significance of the data sample (the likelihood that we would find a sample with this strong a deviation from a random pattern or even stronger if there were no pattern at all in a potentially infinite population of examples), as well as p-values indicating the significance of each of the variables in the model. A series of other measures come with a regression model, among them r in a new guise as r^2 (often written as R^2), which indicates the amount of the variance that is accounted for by the model and its variables. Like r, the maximum limit for this measure is 1, and higher numbers indicate a better model. Another common measure is C, the index of concordance, which should have a value of 0.8 or higher if a model is performing well. Measures of the performance of the model are important because it is usually necessary to undertake some trial-and-error in fitting a model to the data, and each model has to be evaluated in order to arrive at the optimal one, while avoiding overfitting (see section 3.8). Usually this is done by first putting all of the variables (and interactions) into the regression formula and then gradually trimming away variables that are not found to be significant, and chi-square, ANOVA, or AIC (Akaike Information Criterion) can be used to compare models and see whether subsequent ones are significantly better than previous ones.

Diessel (2008) sets out to test the hypothesis that there is an iconic relationship between the position of a temporal adverbial clause (which can come before or after the main clause) and the order of the event reported in the adverbial clause as prior, simultaneous, or posterior to the event in the main clause. In other words, Diessel's question is: Is there a tendency for the linear order of clauses to reflect the order of the reported events such that adverbial clauses reporting prior events are more likely to precede the main clause, whereas adverbial clauses reporting posterior events are more likely to follow the main clause? In terms of examples, the prediction would be that a speaker is more likely to produce *After I fed the cat, I washed the dishes* than *I washed the dishes after I fed the cat* and more likely to produce *I fed the cat before I washed the dishes* than *Before I washed the dishes, I fed the cat* (since feeding the cat is conceptually prior in all these cases). Diessel conducts two studies based upon corpus data from the ICE-GB, with samples of clauses beginning with *when*, *after*, *before*, *once*, and *until*. A chi-square test shows that there is a relationship between conceptual order and the linear order of clauses, with $p < 0.001$. However, there are certainly many examples of sentences that violate the iconic order and there are many differences among the sampled clauses that cannot be accounted for by iconicity, so it seems necessary to include more variables in the study. These additional variables include: 1) the meaning of the clause (which may account for the distributional differences between *once*-clauses, which are frequently conditional and *after*-clauses, which are frequently causal), 2) the length of the clause (since long clauses tend to occur sentence-finally), and 3) the syntactic complexity of the clause (since complex clauses tend to occur sentence-finally). Thus Diessel's logistic regression model has the position of the adverbial clause (initial vs. final) as the dependent variable, and has as independent variables conceptual order (iconicity), meaning, length, and syntactic complexity. Whereas syntactic complexity did not turn out to be significant and was removed from the model, all of the other variables were indeed significant. Quite a bit of detail is revealed by the regression model, for example that meaning is significant only for the positioning of conditional *once*- and *until*-clauses, and that length is significant only for *once*- and *until*-clauses. The analysis supports Diessel's hypothesis concerning iconicity and gives us much information about other factors that are involved in the order of clauses as well.

3.6. Mixed effects: Adding individual preferences into a regression model
Zenner et al. 2012

The variation found in data can have many sources. Hopefully the variables that you are testing are a major source of differences in the data, showing that the variables you have identified are indeed relevant. These independent variables are sometimes referred to as fixed effects since they have a fixed set of values. In Diessel's logistic regression model described above, all of the independent variables are fixed effects: syntactic complexity was coded with two values (simple, complex), meaning was coded with three values (purely temporal, temporal with implicit conditional meaning, temporal with causal or purposive meaning), and length was a continuous variable measured by dividing the number of words in the adverbial clause by the total number of words in the complex sentence (theoretically ranging from 0 to 1).

However, individual preferences or tendencies can also come into play, and since these are keyed to individuals sampled randomly from a potentially infinite population, they are called random effects. Recall our example of the correlation between corpus frequency and reaction time. If we ran this experiment, we would likely discover that each individual subject has a personal range of reaction times, since some people are just naturally faster than others. This is a well-known problem, and in fact in many psychological studies it turns out that the random effects of personal preferences are actually more pronounced than the effect that the researcher is trying to measure. Imagine, for example that the average baseline difference in reaction times between participant A and participant B in the experiment is 100 milliseconds, but the frequency effect is only 50 milliseconds. If you don't know and cannot account for the individual differences, the frequency effect will be overwhelmed by the random effects of the participants.

Mixed effects models can combine both fixed effects and random effects in a single regression model by measuring the random effects and making adjustments so that the fixed effects can be detected. In addition to use in psycholinguistic experiments, mixed effects models can be useful in various ways in corpus research too. For example, if a corpus has multiple data points from a set of authors, each author can serve as a random effect in order to take into account the fact that different authors will have different preferences for use of various linguistic forms. The source of random effects need not necessarily be human beings. For example, lexemes might also act as random effects in a model, since they can have individual patterns of behavior. For example, Nesset et al. (2010) and Nesset and Janda (2010) apply a mixed effects model to a historical change underway in Russian verbs; in this model the individual verbs are a random effect since each verb has its own tendencies in relation to the ongoing change. Note also that Baayen et al. forthcoming includes a mixed effects model for an experiment in which subjects (as a random effect) chose between Russian prefix allomorphs *o-* vs. *ob-* and all the data and R code associated with this model are available at this site: http://ansatte.uit.no/laura.janda/RF/RF.html.

Zenner et al. (2012) bring a quantitative perspective to a sociolinguistic study of anglicisms in Dutch. Several possible factors in the success of loanwords have been suggested by previous research, but very little empirical work has been undertaken, and no prior studies use a multivariate approach. Corpus data (from two newspaper corpora), along with a host of other measures are collected in relation to 149 lexemes with human reference such as *manager*. An onomasiological profile shows the relative distribution of the English loanword and its Dutch equivalents (if any). For example, English *backpacker* is attested 425 times in the corpus, while its Dutch equivalents *rugzakker*, *rugzaktoerist* are attested 941 times, and thus the success rate of *backpacker* is $425/(425 + 941) = 31\%$, which serves as the dependent variable. Zenner et al. investigates the variables that have been proposed as factors in the penetration of English loanwords, namely: 1) relative length of the anglicism vs. Dutch equivalent; 2) lexical field (media & IT; sports & recreation; etc.); 3) era of borrowing (up to 1945, 1945–1989, after 1989); 4) luxury vs. necessary borrowing (where necessary borrowing occurs when there is no Dutch equivalent); 5) concept frequency (how often the concept was named by either a Dutch or an English word, for example, the concept frequency for BACKPACKER cited above is $425 + 941 = 1366$, however these figures were log transformed in order to reduce the effects of extreme numbers, so in this case $\log(1366) = 7.23$); 6) date of measurement (a diachronic corpus factor); 7) register (popular vs. quality newspapers); and 8) region (Belgian Dutch vs. Netherlandic Dutch). In addition to all of these fixed effects, because several measuring points were used for each concept and those data points would therefore not be independent observations, the concept expressed was taken as a random variable. In other words, the mixed effects model took into account any individual preferences associated with the concepts themselves. The model found both main effects and interactions. The regional, register, and diachronic variables were not found to be significant. The two strongest main effects, both with $p = 0.000$, were a negative correlation between concept frequency and the success of an anglicism, and a significantly lower success rate for borrowings from the most recent era (after 1989) than from the earlier eras. Both of these findings make sense because highly frequent concepts are likely to have well entrenched Dutch expressions that would be resistant to borrowing and loanwords from the most recent era have had less time to become established as successful. The interactions in the model give more nuance to the study, for example showing that concept frequency is a factor only when the anglicism is also the shortest lexicalization, and that the difference between luxury and necessary borrowings is strongest in the 1945–1989 era.

3.7. Cluster analysis: Finding out which items are grouped together
Janda and Solovyev 2009

All of the models discussed so far have involved testing whether a value is significant or not. In other words, the question we have asked has always been, given the value X that we obtain in this data, what is the probability that X reflects a meaningful property in a potentially infinite population, rather than being merely a chance artifact of the sample? Cluster analysis asks a different kind of question, namely: Given a set of items, which of them are grouped closest together and which are farthest apart? Another way to state this question is: What is the distance between the items in the set? If each item in a set has an array of values associated with it, it is possible to use mathematical means such as squared Euclidean distances to calculate the distances between the arrays of values. A cluster analysis does just this, yielding a proximity table that shows the distances between each pair of items in the set from which a graph of the clusters can be derived.

Janda and Solovyev (2009) approach the relationships within two sets of Russian synonyms, six words meaning 'sadness', and five words meaning 'happiness', by introducing the constructional profile method. The constructional profile of a word is the relative frequency distribution of the grammatical constructions that a word appears in, as measured in a corpus. The assumption is that the constructional profile is a possible measure of a word's meaning, since there should be a relationship between the meaning of a word and its behavior. Although a Russian noun can appear in seventy constructions involving prepositions and case endings, for most nouns fewer than ten such constructions occur regularly. Each noun has a unique constructional profile, and there are stark differences in the constructional profiles of words that are unrelated to each other. For the two sets of synonyms in this study, only six grammatical constructions are regularly attested, and these are the basis for the constructional profiles of these words. Within the set of 'sadness' synonyms, for example, there were significant differences in the constructional profiles (a chi-square test gives $p < 0.001$ and a Cramer's V effect size of 0.305), but this does not tell us which of the synonyms are closer to each other and which are further apart. The constructional profile for each noun, with the frequency found in each construction, is the array of values that serves as input for the cluster analysis. The output shows us which nouns behave very similarly as opposed to which are outliers in the sets. The clusters largely confirm the introspective analyses found in synonym dictionaries, giving them a concrete quantitative dimension, but also pinpointing how and why some synonyms are closer than others. There appear to be asymmetries between metaphorical uses of grammatical constructions and concrete ones. For example, metaphorically sadness can function as a pit and while the constructions for falling into and being in sadness are quite common, the construction for getting out again is exceedingly rare; by contrast, nouns denoting physical pits appear robustly in all three constructions.

3.8. Other alternatives: tree & forest, naive discriminative learning, multidimensional scaling, correspondence analysis

In addition to the models described here and illustrated in the articles in this anthology, there are many other statistical models that might be applied to linguistic data. Here we review a few additional models that the reader is likely to encounter. These can be divided into two groups: 1) alternatives to regression models, and 2) alternatives to cluster models.

Alternatives to regression

In addition to the weaknesses that follow from correlation cited above (assumption of linearity and lack of causal implication), regression rests on two assumptions that are often violated by linguistic data. One is that because regression is a parametric model, it assumes that data should follow the bell curve of what statisticians call a normal distribution. Corpus data is however usually highly skewed, thus rendering regression less appropriate. The other assumption is that all of the combinations of the various levels of all variables should be represented in the dataset. However, linguistic data often involves paradigmatic gaps where certain combinations of the relevant variables are necessarily absent. For example, in evaluating the distribution of certain suffixes in Russian, both the factors of form (with levels finite, gerund, participle) and prefixation (prefixed, unprefixed) are relevant, but it is categorically impossible to find examples of unprefixed gerunds (see Baayen et al. forthcoming).

There are two alternatives that can be used for similar data that avoid both the parametric assumption and the assumption concerning combinations of values: 1) classification and regression trees in combination with random forests (here called "tree & forest"; Strobl et al. 2009), and 2) naive discriminative learning (Baayen 2011, Baayen et al. 2011). The tree & forest model uses recursive partitioning to yield a classification tree, showing the best sorting of observations separating the values for the dependent variable. It can literally be understood as an optimal algorithm for predicting an outcome given the predictor values, and Kapatsinski (2013) suggests that from the perspective of a usage-based model, each path of partitions along a classification tree expresses a schema (see also Kyröläinen 2013 for an application of tree & forest modeling in cognitive linguistics). Naive discriminative learning is a quantitative model for how choices can be made between rival linguistic forms, making use of a system of weights that are estimated using equilibrium equations.

Baayen et al. (forthcoming) tests the performance of regression against tree & forest and naive discriminative learning models across four datasets and finds that the three models perform very similarly in terms of accuracy and measurement of the relative importance of variables. Note that all of the data and R code for these analyses are available at this site: http://ansatte.uit.no/laura.janda/RF/RF.html. In addition to avoiding the two assumptions inherent in regression mentioned above, the tree & forest and naive discriminative learning models come with several additional advantages. One is that the researcher does not have to struggle to build and fine-tune the model, because it is possible to just put all the variables into the formula and leave it to the model to ignore variables that are not significant. Another is that both models offer a means for validation that does not involve collecting any further data. Once one has built a model for how various independent variables influence a dependent variable for a dataset (a training set), it would be ideal to test that model out on a new, independent sample of data (a validation set). If the model performs equally well on a new sample of data, then we would be quite confident that it reflects the behavior of the population at large, not just the sample that it was built for. But often it is not possible to get another sample that is comparable in terms of size and structure. In the case of corpus data, the linguist has usually exhausted all the resources of the largest available corpus, and in the case of an experiment, the researcher has usually collected the only sample that funding and other logistics will permit. The tree & forest model uses repeated bootstrap samples drawn with replacement from the dataset such that in each repetition some observations are sampled and serve as a training set and other observations are not sampled, so they can serve for validation of the model. Naive discriminative learning partitions the data into ten subsamples, nine of which serve as the training set, reserving the tenth one to serve for validation. This process is repeated ten times so that each subsample is used for validation.

Alternatives to cluster models

Two common options to cluster models are multidimensional scaling and correspondence analysis. Like clustering, both of these methods begin with arrays of data associated with a set of items and use various mathematical techniques to sort the items into a "space" of two or more dimensions. Multidimensional scaling has been used in various ways in cognitive linguistics, for example to map out the functions of grammatical case in Slavic languages (Clancy 2006) and to map the relations of aspect and expressions for spatial location (Croft and Poole 2008; see also Janda 2009).

Correspondence analysis can yield similar results but works differently. Whereas the goal of clustering and multidimensional scaling is to divide the data into groups, the goal of correspondence analysis is to discover the smallest number of abstract mathematical factors that account for the variance in the data, with the first factor being the one that accounts for the highest percentage of the variance. The value for factor 1 (and all other factors) of each item can be used to make a map of the items and can show how far apart the items are.

This website – http://ansatte.uit.no/laura.janda/OCSGPs/OCSGPs.html – houses both the data and the R code for a correspondence analysis of Old Church Slavonic verbs described in Eckhoff and Janda forthcoming, which can serve as an illustration of how correspondence analysis can be used in cognitive linguistics. Dostál (1954) claimed that Old Church Slavonic verbs can be classified as perfective vs. imperfective, a claim that has since been challenged. With the grammatical profiles of verbs extracted from the Pragmatic Resources in Old Indo-European Languages (http://foni.uio.no:3000/) corpus as input, a correspondence analysis identifies a factor 1 that sorts the verbs according to Dostál's classification with 96% accuracy and also gives essentially the same results as a cluster analysis. In other words, Dostál was probably right.

4. Conclusion

Approximately five years ago, the community of cognitive linguists collectively and definitively turned in the direction of quantitative studies. Today we can already identify some leaders on this path, as well as some models that are common in analysis of linguistic data. The purpose of this book is to orient the reader to these leaders and models, and illustrate them with some exemplary articles that have appeared in *Cognitive Linguistics*. At the very least, this book should help linguists to become confident in their ability to read and interpret quantitative studies in their field, and perhaps it will inspire some to undertake new quantitative studies themselves. There is also room for communication among scholars with different theoretical perspectives in developing common ground in quantitative analysis. It is my hope that this volume will contribute to establishing best practices in our profession for the analysis, management, and sharing of data and statistical code using venues for public archiving and open-source formats. If this can be accomplished, we will have much more to look forward to in terms of linguistic discoveries and theoretical insights.

References

Akita, Kimi. 2012. Toward a frame-semantic definition of sound-symbolic words: A collocational analysis of Japanese mimetics. *Cognitive Linguistics* 23. 67–90.

Ambridge, Ben & Adele E. Goldberg. 2008. The island status of clausal complements: Evidence in favor of an information structure explanation. *Cognitive Linguistics* 19. 357–389.

Ambridge, Ben & Caroline F. Rowland. 2009. Predicting children's errors with negative questions: Testing a schema-combination account. *Cognitive Linguistics* 20. 225–266.
Baayen, R. Harald. 2008. *Analyzing linguistic data: a practical introduction to statistics using R*. Cambridge : Cambridge University Press.
Baayen, R. Harald. 2011. Corpus linguistics and naive discriminative learning. *Brazilian Journal of Applied Linguistics* 11. 295–328.
Baayen, R. Harald, P. Milin, D. Filipovic Durdjevic, P.Hendrix, & M. Marelli. 2011. An amorphous model for morphological processing in visual comprehension based on naive discriminative learning. *Psychological Review* 118. 438–482.
Baayen, R. Harald, Anna Endresen, Laura A. Janda, Anastasia Makarova, Tore Nesset. Forthcoming. Making Choices in Russian: Pros and Cons of Statistical Methods for Rival Forms. *Russian Linguistics*.
Blythe, Richard A. & William Croft. 2012. S–curves and the mechanisms of propagation in language change. *Language* 88. 269–304.
Chandler, Steve. 2010. The English past tense: Analogy redux. *Cognitive Linguistics* 21. 371–417.
Clancy, Steven J. 2006. The Topology of Slavic Case: Semantic Maps and Multidimensional Scaling. *Glossos* 7. 1–28 http://www.seelrc.org/glossos/issues/7/
Cohen, Jacob, Patricia Cohen, Stephen G. West & Leona S. Aiken. 2003. *Applied Multiple Regression – Correlation Analysis for the Behavioral Sciences (3rd Edition)*. Mahwah, NJ: Lawrence Erlbaum.
Cowart, W. 1997. *Experimental Syntax: Applying Objective Methods to Sentence Judgements*. Thousand Oaks, CA: Sage Publications.
Croft, William & K. T. Poole. 2008. Inferring universals from grammatical variation: multidimensional scaling for typological analysis. *Theoretical Linguistics* 34. 1–37.
Dąbrowska, Ewa. 2010. Naive v. expert competence: An empirical study of speaker intuitions. *The Linguistic Review* 27. 1–23.
Dąbrowska, Ewa, Caroline Rowland & Anna Theakston. 2009. The acquisition of questions with long-distance dependencies. *Cognitive Linguistics* 20. 571–597.
Delbecque Nicole. 1990. Word order as a reflection of alternate conceptual construals in French and Spanish. Similarities and divergences in adjective position. *Cognitive Linguistics* 1. 349–416.
Dickey, Stephen M. & Laura A. Janda. 2009. *Xoxotnul, sxitril*: The relationship between semelfactives formed with *-nu-* and *s-* in Russian. *Russian Linguistics* 33. 229–248.
Diessel, Holger. 2008. Iconicity of sequence: A corpus-based analysis of the positioning of temporal adverbial clauses in English. *Cognitive Linguistics* 19. 465–490.
Dostál, Antonín. 1954. *Studie o vidovém systému v staroslověnštině*. Prague: Státní pedagogické nakladatelství.
Eckhoff, Hanne M. & Laura A. Janda. Forthcoming. Grammatical Profiles and Aspect in Old Church Slavonic. *Transactions of the Philological Society*.
Falck, Marlene Johansson & Raymond W. Gibbs, Jr. 2012. Embodied motivations for metaphorical meanings. *Cognitive Linguistics* 23. 251–272.

Ghesquière, Lobke & Freek Van de Velde. 2011. A corpus-based account of the development of English such and Dutch zulk: Identification, intensification and (inter)subjectification. *Cognitive Linguistics* 22. 765–797.
Gibbs, Raymond W. Jr. 1990. Psycholinguistic studies on the conceptual basis of idiomaticity. *Cognitive Linguistics* 1. 417–452.
Gibbs, Raymond W. Jr. 2006. Introspection and cognitive linguistics: Should we trust our own intuitions? *Annual Review of Cognitive Linguistics* 4. 135–151.
Glynn, Dylan. 2010. Corpus-driven Cognitive Semantics. Introduction to the field. In Dylan Glynn & Kerstin Fischer (eds.) *Quantitative Methods in Cognitive Semantics: Corpus-Driven Approaches (= Volume 46 of Cognitive Linguistics Research Series)*, 1–42. Berlin: Mouton de Gruyter.
Glynn, Dylan & Kerstin Fischer (eds.). 2010. *Quantitative Methods in Cognitive Semantics: Corpus-Driven Approaches (= Volume 46 of Cognitive Linguistics Research Series)*. Berlin: Mouton de Gruyter.
Goldberg, Adele E. 2011. Corpus evidence of the viability of statistical preemption. *Cognitive Linguistics* 22. 131–153.
Goossens, Louis. 1990. Metaphtonymy: the interaction of metaphor and metonymy in expressions for linguistic action. *Cognitive Linguistics* 1. 323–342.
Gries, Stefan Th. 2009. What is corpus linguistics? *Language and Linguistics Compass* 3. 1–17.
Gries, Stefan Th. 2011. Phonological similarity in multi-word units. *Cognitive Linguistics* 22. 491–510.
Gries, Stefan Th. 2013. *Statistics for Linguistics with R*. Berlin: Mouton de Gruyter.
Gries, Stefan Th. & Anatol Stefanowitsch (eds.). 2007. *Corpora in Cognitive Linguistics: Corpus-based Approaches to Syntax and Lexis. (= Mouton Select Series. Volume 172 of Trends in Linguistics)*. Berlin: Mouton de Gruyter.
Hampe, Beate. 2011. Discovering constructions by means of collostruction analysis: The English Denominative Construction. *Cognitive Linguistics* 22. 211–245.
Hirschberg, Julia & Gregory Ward. 1991. Accent and bound anaphora. *Cognitive Linguistics* 2. 101–122.
Hudson, Richard. 1997. Inherent variability and linguistic theory. *Cognitive Linguistics* 8. 73–108.
Janda, Laura A. 2009. What is the role of semantic maps in cognitive linguistics? In Piotr Stalmaszczyk & Wieslaw Oleksy (eds.) *Cognitive approaches to language and linguistic data. Studies in honor of Barbara Lewandowska-Tomaszczyk*, 105–124. Frankfurt am Main: Peter Lang Publishers.
Janda, Laura A. & Valery D. Solovyev. 2009. What constructional profiles reveal about synonymy: A case study of Russian words for SADNESS and HAPPINESS. *Cognitive Linguistics* 20. 367–393.
Janda, Laura A. & Olga Lyashevskaya. 2011. Grammatical profiles and the interaction of the lexicon with aspect, tense and mood in Russian. *Cognitive Linguistics* 22. 719–763.
Janda, Laura A., Anna Endresen, Julia Kuznetsova, Olga Lyashevskaya, Anastasia Makarova, Tore Nesset & Svetlana Sokolova. 2013. *Why Russian aspectual prefixes aren't empty: prefixes as verb classifiers*. Bloomington, IN: Slavica Publishers.

Johnson, Keith. 2008. *Quantitative methods in linguistics.* Malden, MA : Blackwell.
Joseph, Brian. 2004. On change in Language and change in language. Language 80. 381–383.
Kapatsinski, Vsevolod. 2013. Conspiring to Mean: Experimental and Computational Evidence for a Usage-Based Harmonic Approach to Morphophonology. *Language* 89. 110–148.
King, Bruce M., Patrick J. Rosopa & Edward W. Minium. 2010. *Statistical reasoning in the behavioral sciences*, 6th ed. Hoboken, NJ: John Wiley & Sons.
Kraska-Szlenk, Iwona & Marzena Żygis. 2012. Phonetic and lexical gradience in Polish prefixed words. *Cognitive Linguistics* 23. 317–366.
Kuznetsova, Julia. 2013. *Linguistic Profiles: Correlations between Form and Meaning.* PhD Dissertation. University of Tromsø.
Kyröläinen, Aki-Juhani. 2013. Reflexive space. A Constructionist Model of the Russian Reflexive Marker. PhD Dissertation. University of Turku.
Langacker, Ronald W. 1987. *Foundations of cognitive grammar. v. 1. Theoretical prerequisites.* Stanford, Calif.: Stanford University Press.
Langacker, Ronald W. 2008. *Cognitive grammar: A basic introduction.* Oxford: Oxford University Press.
Larson-Hall, Jenifer. 2010. *A Guide to Doing Statistics in Second Language Research Using SPSS (Second Language Acquisition Research Series).* New York: Routledge.
Nesset, Tore, Laura A. Janda & R. Harald Baayen. 2010. Capturing Correlational Structure in Russian Paradigms: a Case Study in Logistic Mixed-Effects Modeling. *Corpus Linguistics and Linguistic Theory* 6. 29–48.
Nesset, Tore & Laura A. Janda. 2010. Paradigm structure: evidence from Russian suffix shift. *Cognitive Linguistics* 21. 699–725.
Pinker, Steven. 1984. *Language learnability and language development.* Cambridge, MA: Harvard University Press.
Sanders, Ted J. M., Wilbert P. M. Spooren, Leo G. M. Noordman. 1993. Coherence relations in a cognitive theory of discourse representation. *Cognitive Linguistics* 4. 93–134.
Sandra, Dominiek & Sally Rice. 1995. Network analyses of prepositional meaning: Mirroring whose mind—the linguist's or the language user's? *Cognitive Linguistics* 6. 89–130.
Schmid, Hans-Jörg & Susanne Handl (eds.). 2010. *Cognitive foundations of linguistic usage patterns.* Berlin: Mouton de Gruyter.
Stefanowitsch, Anatol. 2011. Constructional Preemption by Contextual Mismatch: A Corpus-Linguistic Investigation. *Cognitive Linguistics* 22. 107–129.
Stefanowitsch, Anatol & Stefan Th Gries. 2003. Collostructions: Investigating the interaction between words and constructions. *International Journal of Corpus Linguistics* 8. 209–243.
Stefanowitsch, Anatol & Stefan Th Gries. 2005. Covarying Collexemes. *Corpus Linguistics and Linguistic Theory* 1. 1–43.
Stefanowitsch, Anatol & Stefan Th. Gries (eds.). 2007. *Corpus-based Approaches to Metaphor and Metonymy.* Berlin: Mouton de Gruyter.

Strobl, C., G. Tutz & J. Malley. 2009. An introduction to Recursive Partitioning: Rationale, Application, and Characteristics of Classification and Regression Trees, Bagging, and Random Forests. *Psychological Methods* 14. 323–348.

Theakston, Anna L., Robert Maslen, Elena V. M. Lieven & Michael Tomasello. 2012. The acquisition of the active transitive construction in English: A detailed case study. *Cognitive Linguistics* 23. 91–128.

Zenner, Eline, Dirk Speelman & Dirk Geeraerts. 2012. Cognitive Sociolinguistics meets loanword research: Measuring variation in the success of anglicisms in Dutch. *Cognitive Linguistics* 23. 749–792.

Constructional preemption by contextual mismatch: A corpus-linguistic investigation

Anatol Stefanowitsch

Abstract

The seeming absence of negative evidence in the input that children receive during language acquisition has long been regarded as a serious problem for non-nativist linguistic theories. Among the solutions that have been suggested for this problem, preemption by competing structures is doubtless the most intensively researched and widely accepted. However, while preemption works well in the domain of morphology, it cannot apply categorically in the domain of syntax, as this would preclude the existence of semantically overlapping constructions, such as the ditransitive and the prepositional dative, which can be used alternatively with many, but not all, verbs of literal or metaphorical transfer. This paper investigates one specific version of preemption briefly entertained by Pinker (1984), which would account both for the existence of semantically overlapping constructions and for the fact that these constructions may preempt each other in the case of individual verbs. Typically, such pairs of grammatical constructions differ in their information-structural restrictions and speakers tend to choose the construction that best fits a given discourse context; when speakers use a construction even though there is an alternative that fits the discourse context better, children may take this as evidence that the alternative is not available for the specific verb in question. Two corpus studies are presented, comparing the information-structural profile of prepositional dative constructions containing verbs that may alternate between the dative and the ditransitive with the information structural profile of verbs that are restricted to the prepositional dative. For Pinker's preemptive mechanism to be feasible, there should be a clear and systematic difference in the information-

---

* I would like to thank Juliana Goschler, Adele Goldberg, one anonymous reviewer and the participants of the first ISLE conference in Freiburg, where an early version of this paper was presented, for comments and insightful discussions. Email: <anatol.stefanowitsch@ uni-hamburg.de>

structural profile of these two classes of verbs. However, no such difference can be found in actual usage.

Keywords: negative evidence, dative alternation, preemption, information structure, corpus linguistics

1. Introduction

The seeming absence of negative evidence in the input during language acquisition is one of the most intriguing problems in linguistic theorizing. Put simply, children may assume that (the large majority of) the linguistic structures they encounter in the input are grammatical. However, they cannot assume that structures they do *not* encounter are ungrammatical: the grammar of any language can generate an open-ended set of grammatical sentences, most of which the child will never hear simply because there is no reason for anyone to produce them. Since it is generally assumed that children receive little or no explicit feedback about the grammaticality of their own output, the question is how they learn to distinguish between the grammatical and ungrammatical sentences of their language.

Many answers have been proposed to this question, ranging from the idea of subtle cues in the feedback over preemption by competing structures and statistical learning to claims of innate linguistic knowledge. In this paper, I will discuss one specific version of preemption first suggested by Pinker (1984), which I will refer to as "preemption by contextual mismatch". The basic idea of this type of preemption is as follows. Many grammatical constructions have information-structural restrictions that determine the discourse contexts in which they may occur. When the discourse context does not fit, speakers have to use alternative constructions. If they fail to use an alternative construction even though the discourse-context calls for it, the language learner will take this as evidence that the alternative is not available in this case.

In Section 2, I will introduce the problem of negative evidence in more detail and give an overview of the most important types of potential solutions that have been proposed. I will then discuss the notion of preemption by contextual mismatch in depth, focusing on the way in which the input would have to be structured in order for this type of preemption to work.

In Section 3, I will present two corpus studies comparing the information-structural profile of prepositional dative constructions containing verbs that may alternate between the dative and the ditransitive with the information structural profile of verbs that are restricted to the prepositional dative. For preemption by contextual mismatch to be a feasible source of evidence, there should be a clear difference in the information-structural profile of these two classes of verbs.

My analysis shows, however, that there is no reliable difference in the information-structural profile of alternating and non-alternating verbs, making preemption by contextual mismatch an unlikely source of evidence.

2. Theoretical background

2.1. *The "no negative evidence" problem*

Researchers across a wide variety of frameworks agree that in order to acquire the grammar of a language, learners must somehow arrive at a mental representation of the general properties of that grammar. Current syntactic theories differ in how they view the nature of such generalizations—for example, whether they view them as rules, as constraints or as complex form–meaning associations ("constructions")—but they seem to agree that these representations must enable the language learner to produce and comprehend all grammatical utterances of a language and to avoid producing ungrammatical utterances.[1]

There also seems to be widespread agreement that children acquiring a first language are able to arrive at such generalizations on the basis of a limited corpus of actually occurring utterances without instruction from caretakers. Thus, a reasonable starting hypothesis would be that children generate hypotheses about possible generalizations on the basis of the available input and then construct their own novel utterances based on these hypotheses.

For example, children might come across utterances such as those in (1a, 1b) and (2a, 2b) (cf. Baker 1979; Bowerman 1988):

(1) a. *John told a story to Mary.*
    b. *John told Mary a story.*
(2) a. *John gave a book to Mary.*
    b. *John gave Mary a book.*

On the basis of this input, they might hypothesize that all verbs that occur in the pattern [NP_{subj} V NP_{obj} to NP_{obj}] (the prepositional dative construction) can also occur in the pattern [NP_{subj} V NP_{obj} NP_{obj}] (the ditransitive construction). This will allow them to produce, correctly, (3b) after having heard (3a), but it will also lead them, incorrectly, to produce (4b) after hearing (4a):

(3) a. *John sang a song to Mary.*
    b. *John sang Mary a song.*

---

1. A possible exception is the version of "Emergent Grammar" proposed by Hopper (e.g. 1998), in which linguistic competence is viewed in terms of "an open-ended collection of forms that are constantly being restructured and resemanticized during actual use" (Hopper 1998: 159).

(4) a. *John said goodnight to Mary.*
　　b. **John said Mary goodnight.*

　　The problem for language learners is that, on the basis of the input, they have no way of knowing that (3b) is a successful application of their generalization, while (4b) is not. In other words, generalizing over the available input solves one half of the language-learning task (it allows the learner to produce and comprehend grammatical utterances) but it does not solve the other half (it does not allow the learner to avoid producing ungrammatical utterances). This problem, generally known as the "no-negative evidence" problem was formulated forcefully by Gold (1967). What makes it central to any linguistic theory is the simple observation that children clearly *do* learn to avoid producing such ungrammatical utterances, and they also learn to recognize them as ungrammatical (i.e. as not forming part of their language) when they hear someone else producing them. The question that needs to be answered, therefore, is how children can do something that they should not be able to do.

　　There are two seemingly obvious potential solutions to this problem. First, children might assume that if an utterance never occurs in the input, it is ungrammatical; thus, they will not produce (3b) until they have heard it at least once, and they will never produce (4b). Second, children who produce ungrammatical utterances may receive explicit negative feedback from caretakers. However, neither solution is likely to provide a complete account of how language learners limit the application of their generalizations.

　　The first solution is based on the idea that children do not actually generalize beyond the input at all, i.e. that their output consists exclusively of verbatim repetitions of structures they have already heard. But this is evidently not the case. A number of recent studies have shown that imitation plays a larger role in early language acquisition than is traditionally assumed (e.g. Tomasello 2003: 238–239) and that children are generally quite conservative in extending grammatical structures to new words (Tomasello 2003: 117–222). However, children obviously produce novel utterances and it is well known that these utterances sometimes involve errors of exactly the kind expected if they were overgeneralizing from the input. For example, in the following excerpt from the Manchester Corpus, the child (Anne, age 2 years, 7 months) uses *say* with the recipient as the direct object (as in [4b]):

(5)　Mother:　*He is climbing up the hill. He says it's a long way up this hill. Oh.*
　　　Anne:　*Whee.*
　　　Mother:　*Oh. I didn't like that. He says he didn't like it.*
　　　Anne:　*He did.*
　　　Mother:　*No. He says he didn't.*
　　　Anne:　<u>*He . . . he said me he did.*</u>

Mother: *He told you he did?*
[Manchester Corpus, anne26a]

In addition to the empirical argument against imitation as the sole driving force behind the acquisition of grammatical structures, there is a long-standing theoretical argument: if our mental grammars consisted exclusively of representations of utterances encountered in the input, we would have no way of distinguishing grammatical sentences that simply have not occurred yet because no-one had any reason to utter them from sentences that have not occurred because they violate some aspect of the grammar of the language in question and therefore will not occur. Chomsky (1957: 15–16) makes a forceful case for keeping apart ungrammaticality and non-occurrence: speakers of English are unlikely to have heard the strings *I saw a fragile whale* and *I saw a fragile of* before, yet they can recognize the first as a grammatical and the second as ungrammatical. It should be noted that Chomsky and others who have followed his reasoning are oversimplifying matters considerably: the difference between accidental non-occurrence and ungrammaticality may not be as clear as they assume (cf. e.g. Sampson 2001; Stefanowitsch 2007), and the conclusions they draw are premature (cf. e.g. Stefanowitsch 2005, 2007), but their basic point seems relatively uncontroversial: speakers can mostly distinguish between grammatical utterances that they simply have not heard before and ungrammatical utterances. Therefore, they cannot have acquired their mental grammars by simply storing everything they have heard.

The second suggestion mentioned may initially seem more plausible, as it would be compatible with our observation that children generalize over their available input and produce, on occasion, ungrammatical utterances on the basis of these generalizations. However, it is widely agreed that caretakers do not usually point out the ungrammaticality of those utterance to children (and a quick look at any corpus of child language will confirm this). Of course, there are less obvious ways in which adults may provide feedback from which children can deduce that they have said something ungrammatical. For example, in (5), Anne's mother immediately reformulates Anne's ungrammatical use of *say* with a semantically similar verb that *does* allow the ditransitive—a correction that the child may recognize as such and take as evidence that her hypothesized ditransitive use of *say* is ungrammatical. However, the fact that a reformulation is offered cannot by itself be sufficient evidence of ungrammaticality, as caretakers also reformulate grammatical utterances (as in [6]) and repeat ungrammatical utterances (as in [7]):

(6) Mother: *What was her present?*
    Child: *It was a . . . a drink.*
    Mother: *A drink in a box, was it?*
    [Manchester Corpus, anne26a]

(7) Child: *I don't sure don't like it.*
    Mother: *You don't sure you don't like it.*
    [Manchester Corpus, anne26a]

There is no way for the child to realize that the reformulation in (5) is a correction while the one in (6) is simply a communicative uptake of what she has said. And of course the fact that the mother repeats the utterance in (7) would be wrongly taken as evidence that this utterance is grammatical.

Of course, individual examples do not prove or disprove the possibility that feedback may play a role in language acquisition. In fact, a number of studies suggest that caretakers tend to react differently to children's ungrammatical utterances than to grammatical ones. For example, Hirsh-Pasek et al. (1984) find that mothers repeat ungrammatical utterances of two-year olds (but not of older children) more frequently than grammatical ones (but see Pinker 1988: 105 for criticism of their methodology), Demetras et al. (1986) show that caretakers ask for clarification more frequently after children's ungrammatical utterances, and Bohannon and Stanowicz (1988) show—unsurprisingly, but nevertheless importantly—that adults tend to repeat grammatical utterances verbatim while repeating ungrammatical utterances with modifications (as in [5]). However, it is unclear whether children actually use the feedback they receive (see, for example, Marcus [1993], who argues that they ignore it); and in any case, the adult communicative behavior in these studies is typical only of certain speech communities; generally, adult responses to children's utterances range from a complete lack of uptake to elaborated reformulations (cf. e.g. Ochs 1991: 48–51), yet children in all these speech communities learn to discover the limits of their hypothesized generalizations. Thus, while adult feedback may aid this process, it cannot play a crucial role, and a as far as I am aware, neither generative nor cognitive-functional researchers currently assume that it does.

2.2. *Potential solutions to the "no-negative evidence" problem*

Before I turn to a discussion of the kinds of solution offered in the research literature to the "no-negative evidence" problem, let me briefly sketch out why the usage-based model in cognitive linguistics as it currently stands (cf. Langacker 1991, 2000) does not offer a solution to this problem (in doing so, I will follow closely the discussion in Stefanowitsch 2008: 515–516).

In the usage-based model, grammaticality is treated as a graded phenomenon. It is assumed that linguistic knowledge is represented in the form of linguistic units that emerge from recurrent usage-events. Such units may differ in their degree of schematicity, ranging from fully specified linguistic expressions over relatively concrete multi-morphemic expressions with one or two open slots to highly schematic configurations of abstract linguistic categories (see also Hoffmann and Trousdale this volume). As these units emerge from and are maintained by concrete usage-events, they may also differ in their degree of entrenchment. As Langacker puts it:

Every use of a structure has a positive impact on its degree of entrenchment, whereas extended periods of disuse have a negative impact. With repeated use, a novel structure becomes progressively entrenched, to the point of becoming a unit; moreover, units are variably entrenched depending on the frequency of their occurrence ... (Langacker 1987: 59)

Once a unit with a particular degree of entrenchment and schematicity is established in the system, it may serve to sanction further usage events to a greater or lesser extent:

To the extent that a target structure accords with the conventional units in the grammar, these units are said to sanction this usage. It is crucial to realize that sanction is a matter of degree and speaker judgment. It is a measure of an expression's well-formedness, i.e. how closely it conforms to linguistic convention, in all its aspects and dimensions. (Langacker 1987: 66)

The mechanisms of entrenchment and sanction explain straightforwardly how speakers are able to distinguish degrees of grammaticality (or conventionality, in Langacker's terms) among those utterances and utterance types that *do* occur. These degrees of grammaticality simply reflect the degree to which an utterance conforms to one or more established units and to the degree to which these units are entrenched. However, it does not explain how speakers are able to distinguish degrees of grammaticality among utterances and utterance types that *do not* occur. If a particular configuration of linguistic elements is never instantiated, speakers will not derive a schema corresponding to this configuration. Therefore, when faced with an utterance that does not correspond to an established unit, they should reject it categorically.

Of course, matters are slightly more complex: speakers do have the option of comparing the utterance in question to schemas to which it corresponds partially. This is referred to as "partial sanction" (Langacker 1987: 69). However, the mechanism of partial sanction itself must be restricted in some way, since many utterances correspond partially to established schemas but are unacceptable all the same. For example, (4b) is partially sanctioned by (and can be interpreted in relation to) the ditransitive construction and the utterance pairs in (1 to 3)—which is, of course, precisely the reason why Anne uses such a structure in (5)—yet it is categorically unacceptable to speakers of English.

There are three general kinds of solution to the "no-negative evidence" problem. First, a number of proposals that are based on the idea that the child brings innate knowledge about possible structures to the acquisition process (cf. Chomsky 1965 as well as the more specific proposals found, for example, in Baker 1979; Berwick 1985 and Berwick and Weinberg 1984). Second, there are a number of proposals based on the idea that language learners make use of statistical information in the input (e.g. Elman 1993; Stefanowitsch 2006, 2008). Third, there are a number of approaches based on the notion of preemption, i.e. on the idea that the presence of a particular form in the input preempts generalizations from other forms to cover the function served by that form (cf. e.g. Clark 1982 for a useful exposition). Let us briefly look at each of these three approaches.

The idea of innate knowledge may be attractive in theory and it is not inherently incompatible with a cognitive-linguistic approach to grammar. However, it shares the central problem of all nativist approaches to knowledge and learning: it is currently purely speculative, as it seems to be impossible to specify in detail the properties of a mechanism capable of constraining the learner to the relevant class of generalizations and to show that such a mechanism actually exists in humans (or at least, that it could have evolved in the history of our species). The most recent proposals on the nature of Universal Grammar (Hauser et al. 2002) offer nothing in this respect. This does not mean that no appropriate mechanism will ever be found, but until it is, it seems plausible to focus on more empirically tangible explanations. Thus, all current usage-based grammars take an agnostic (Langacker 1987: 13, 1991: 1, 8–9) or apathetic (Croft and Cruse 2004: 4–5) position on innateness or view it as a hypothesis to be considered only if empiricist, usage-based explanations fail (Goldberg 2006: 95).

The idea that negative evidence may be derived from statistical information in the input has been denied categorically by Chomsky (1957: 15–17), and many researchers, even corpus linguists (McEnery and Wilson 2001: 11–12) agree. However, I have argued recently (Stefanowitsch 2008) that negative evidence can be inferred from the positive evidence in the linguistic input if we assume a sufficiently sophisticated model of frequency. Using an extension of collostructional analysis (Stefanowitsch and Gries 2003; Gries and Stefanowitsch 2004), I have shown how the corpus linguist, and, by analogy, the language learner, can discriminate between combinations of linguistic items that are accidentally absent from a given corpus and combinations whose absence is statistically significant, by comparing the absence to the baseline expectation that the combination should occur. I have also shown that this kind of negative corpus evidence correlates with degrees of acceptability in judgment tasks (Stefanowitsch 2008), adding at least some initial plausibility to the idea that statistical evidence not only can be used, but actually is used by language learners to figure out grammatical constraints.

The theory of preemption is the most prominent attempt to construct a theory of negative evidence that is based exclusively on the input. Preemption is a simple but powerful mechanism based on the idea that children assume that exact synonyms do not exist and therefore take the existence of a particular form in the input as evidence against the existence of synonymous forms that could be derived by a particular rule or set of rules. For example, the child will derive the morphological rule/construction [V-*ed*]/PAST on the evidence of forms like *walked, crawled* and *danced*. This might lead the child to realize that *goed* is a highly likely potential form for the past tense of *go*. Hearing the word *went* in the input, the child will then take this as evidence that the rule [V-*ed*]/PAST does not apply to *go* (cf. e.g. Clark 1995: 81). If preemption could be shown to work not only in the acquisition of word forms but also in the acquisition of constructions, it would go a long way towards solving the "no-negative" evidence problem. However, despite initial evidence that it may play a role (cf. e.g. Brooks and Tomasello 1999 or Brooks and Zizak 2002), there is an important difference between words and constructions that needs to be taken into account.

2.3. *A closer look at preemption*

While preemption by alternative forms is a plausible strategy in the domain of inflectional morphology, it clearly cannot apply, in this simple version, in the domain of syntax: while alternative forms for the same or a similar meaning are almost unheard of in inflectional morphology, they are the norm in grammar.

Consider again the example of *went* vs. *goed*: the overwhelming majority of English verbs has one, and only one past tense form.[2] It is only this property of inflectional systems that allows children to infer, upon hearing the form *went*, that the predicted *goed* does not exist. In contrast, the overwhelming majority of English verbs occur in more than one construction, some of which, like the ditransitive and the prepositional dative, are similar enough in meaning to be exchangeable in many, if not most, contexts. If preemption worked in the same way in syntax as it does in inflectional morphology, upon hearing sentences like (1a)–(4a) often enough, the language learner would conclude that (1b)–(4b) respectively do not exist. However, while this inference would be correct in the case of (4b), it is clearly wrong in the case of (1b)–(3b). For preemption by alternative forms to work in the domain of syntax, at the very least the frequencies of potential alternative forms would have to be taken into account: One could argue (cf. Goldberg 2006, this volume; Stefanowitsch 2008), that a

---

2. There are always exceptions, of course, as verbs may be in the process of changing from an irregular past tense to a regular one or, much more rarely, vice versa (as in the case of *sneaked* replaced by *snuck* (especially in American English) or *shrieked* by *shruck* and *showed* by *shew* (in the traditional dialect of Norfolk, see Sampson et al. [2009: 105–106]).

potential structure is preempted by an alternative form only if that alternative form occurs in the input with a certain frequency.

Alternatively, one could argue that it is not the occurrence of alternative forms as such that has a preemptive effect, but that the context within which those forms occur plays a crucial role. Note that functional similarity is not functional identity: even synonymous or near-synonymous constructions are rarely randomly interchangeable; instead, they often differ in terms of the information-structural contexts in which they are typically occur.

On the basis of this observation, Pinker (1984) constructs a more refined notion of preemption. He begins by suggesting that:

the child [may] hypothesize a paradigm dimension differentiating the discourse-relevant aspects of alternative forms—for example, goal-focus versus theme-focus for the *to*-object and double-object forms of the dative, respectively ... or for alternative forms of figure-ground verbs. Presumably, the child would need such features as indexes to the various verb forms in order to select the form in speech production that is appropriate to his or her communicative intentions. (1984: 400)

In the specific case of the ditransitive (Pinker's "double" object form) and the prepositional dative (Pinker's "*to*-form"), Pinker follows Erteschik-Shir's (1979) account of the information-structural properties of the two constructions: the idea is that both constructions present the second postverbal NP as discourse-dominant. This means that the ditransitive would be chosen when the theme is dominant, while the prepositional dative is chosen when the recipient (Pinker's "goal") is dominant. Subsequent work has shown that the choice between the prepositional dative and the ditransitive is indeed influenced by phenomena that are plausibly related to the notion of dominance, namely discourse givenness (Thompson 1990), length/syntactic complexity (Thompson 1990; Wasow 1997a) and animacy (Thompson 1990): the ditransitive is chosen when the recipient (realized by the first object) is more given, shorter, and/or more animate than the theme (realized by the second object); the prepositional dative is chosen when the theme (realized by the object) is more given, shorter and/or more animate than the recipient (realized by the *to*-phrase).

Pinker then argues that once the child has recognized these differences in the information-structural profile of the two constructions, systematic violations of information-structural appropriateness may provide a crucial insight to the child:

Furthermore, it is at least conceivable that the child could use such a paradigm dimension to learn exceptions to lexical rules in circumstances where the exceptional verb is used and the child can predict from the context which argument the speaker wishes to focus. If the context demands that the theme be focused, for example, and the speaker uses the *to*-dative form, the child could enter that form in the theme-focus cell of that verb's paradigm. Since both the theme-focus and goal-focus cells are filled with the *to*-dative form, the child has in effect learned that the verb does not undergo dativization. (Pinker 1984: 400; cf. also Goldberg 1995: 124).

Abstracting away from Pinker's notion of lexical rules and an information-structural paradigm dimensions with "cells" that contain entries for the appropriate construction, the proposal is simply that if the child hears one construction (for example, the prepositional dative) in an information-structural context that normally calls for an alternative construction (for example, the ditransitive), the child may interpret this as evidence that this alternative is not available in this particular case (for example, because the verb in question cannot occur in the alternative construction). In effect, the occurrence of one construction in a context typical for the alternative construction would preempt this alternative.

As an example of how this preemption by contextual mismatch might work, consider the following passage from Charles Dickens' novel *Dombey and Son* (the pronouns are indexed for their referents, PD refers to the novel's protagonist, Paul Dombey, WG to his son-in-law, Walter Gay):

(8) *One time when Walter was in his$_{PD}$ room, he$_{PD}$ beckoned him$_{WG}$ to come near, and to stoop down; and pressing his$_{WG}$ hand, <u>whispered an assurance to him$_{WG}$</u> that he$_{PD}$ knew he$_{PD}$ could trust him$_{WG}$ with his$_{PD}$ child when he$_{PD}$ was dead.* (Charles Dickens, *Dombey and Son*, Chapter 61).

At the point in the narrative where the verb *whisper* occurs, the information-structural status of its arguments in terms of discourse givenness is as follows: the referent of the recipient NP (*Walter*) is highly discourse-given (the distance to its last mention is 1, as it is referred to in the preceding clause by the possessive pronoun *his*), while the theme NP (*an assurance*) is new (its referent has not been mentioned before this point). This discourse context normally calls for a ditransitive construction, thus, the expected form would be *whispered him an assurance*. In terms of animacy, the referent of *him* is animate, that of *an assurance* is inanimate abstract: again, the ditransitive would be the preferred choice. Finally, in terms of length, the recipient NP consists of a single word, *him*, while *an assurance* is part of the highly complex, discontinuous 16 word noun phrase *an assurance that he knew he could trust him with his child when he was dead*. Again, the ditransitive would be the preferred choice, with the additional advantage that the theme NP would not have to be split up. In other words, all three factors that are known to condition the choice between the prepositional dative and the ditransitive should influence the writer's choice in the direction of the ditransitive—the fact that instead the writer chooses the prepositional dative might very well suggest to the reader that the ditransitive is simply not available for the verb *whisper*.[3]

3. A corpus study of preemption by contextual mismatch

In order for preemption by contextual mismatch to provide evidence to the language learner, the input must be structured accordingly, i.e., it must contain a sufficient number of examples such as that in (8). More generally, the information-structural profile of non-alternating verbs in the prepositional dative should differ from the information-structural profile of alternating verbs such that the latter should always occur in the construction that best matches the appropriate discourse constraints, while the former necessarily occur in the construction that they are restricted to, regardless of whether or not this construction matches the information-structural constraints at the relevant point in the discourse.

Applying this perspective to a given construction, the prediction would be that the majority of instances of this construction containing an alternating verb will conform to its information-structural constraints while those instances containing non-alternating verbs should be distributed randomly across information-structural conditions. The following two studies test this prediction with respect to the prepositional dative.

3.1. Study 1

3.1.1. *Aims and method.* The best way of testing this prediction is to extract from a representative corpus all cases of a given construction with non-alternating verbs and compare their information-structural profiles to those of a matched sample of the construction with alternating verbs. Therefore, all tokens of the prepositional dative with non-alternating verbs were extracted from the British Component of the International Corpus of English (ICE-GB).[4] It

---

3. Note also that it would have been easy to avoid the prepositional dative here, either by choosing a verb that does allow the ditransitive, e.g. *gave him an assurance that . . .* (or, if the act of whispering has to be included (*speaking in a whisper, gave him an assurance that . . .*) or by choosing a transitive construction, e.g. *(speaking in a whisper), assured him that. . . .* The fact that the prepositional dative violates information-structural constraints in a situation where alternatives are readily available might give the reader additional evidence that this violation is syntactically necessary.
4. Only those cases of the prepositional dative construction were included where the verb involved a sense of transfer, either metaphorically or literally. The resulting data set includes cases where the use of a ditransitive would be highly anomalous even if the verb in question could occur in the ditransitive; for example, there are six cases with locative arguments which can never occur in the ditransitive. Goldberg (this volume, Section 7) criticizes the data set

turned out that non-alternating verbs are not very frequent in this construction: there were only fifty cases. While such a small data set will, of course, affect the reliability of any results derived from it, information-structural effects can usually be observed on the basis of data sets of similar size (cf., for example, Stefanowitsch 2003). Therefore, fifty tokens with non-alternating verbs of similar frequencies were extracted from the same files of the ICE-GB corpus, resulting in a data set of 100 examples. The recipient and theme arguments of each example were then coded for *givenness, syntactic weight* and *animacy* using the following criteria:

- Givenness was measured in terms of referential distance, defined by Givon (1983: 13) as "the gap between the previous occurrence in the discourse of a referent and its current occurrence in the clause . . . expressed in the terms of the number of clauses to the left".
- Syntactic weight was measured simply as *number of orthographic words*; although more complex measures have been proposed, Wasow (1997b) shows that all measures of syntactic weight are so highly correlated with each other that it does not matter which one is used.
- Animacy was measured by determining for each referent whether it was animate, non-animate concrete or abstract; while more sophisticated animacy hierarchies exist (see, for example, Silverstein 1976), those hierarchies tend to conflate animacy with other semantic and pragmatic features.

As all of the operational definitions in this annotation scheme can be applied unambiguously and objectively, the annotation was performed by a single annotator (the author himself).

The prediction for this annotated data set is as follows:

- For the instances of the prepositional dative constructions containing alternating verbs, the theme-NP (THM) should be more given, syntactically lighter, and higher up on the animacy scale than the recipient NP (REC) in the majority of cases;
- For the instances of the prepositional dative constructions containing non-alternating verbs, (a) there should be no systematic difference between THM and REC along any of these parameters; or at least (b) the differences should be less pronounced than for alternating verbs;

---

because of this and suggests that these examples should be removed. However, the examples are in the set of non-alternating cases anyway, so it does not actually matter that there are additional reasons for why they cannot alternate. In fact, the violations of information structure that are predicted for the prepositional dative extend naturally to complex transitives with locative *to*-phrases (or other PPs).

- In order for these potential differences to serve as a guide to the child learning to avoid ungrammatical alternatives, the difference between the alternating and the non-alternating verbs should be statistically significant, regardless of whether situation 2(a) or 2(b) holds.

3.1.2. *Results.* The results show that prepositional datives with alternating and non-alternating verbs do not differ significantly in terms of their information structural profiles, regardless of the measure applied.

Givenness. There are three potential information-structural conditions with respect to givenness: The theme NP can be more given (i.e., have a lower referential distance) than the recipient NP, or vice versa, or the two NPs can have the same referential distance. The distribution of the alternating and non-alternating instances of the prepositional dative across these three conditions is shown in Figure 1.

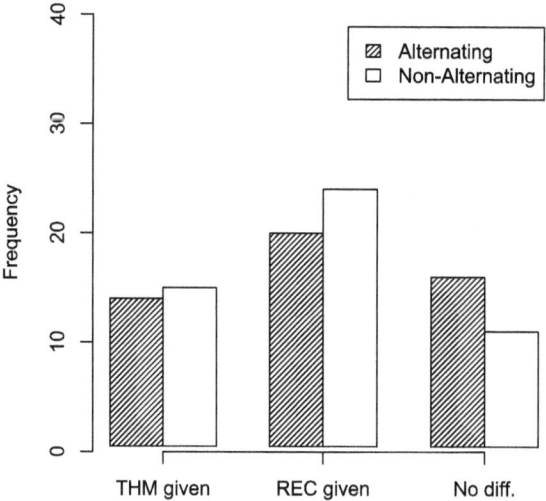

Figure 1. *Givenness of the theme NP and the recipient NP in the prepositional dative for alternating and non-alternating verbs (ICE-GB, n = 100).*

The distribution of both the alternating and the non-alternating cases contradicts the information-structural configuration expected for the prepositional dative: there are fewer cases where the theme is more given than the recipient than vice versa. This difference is not statistically significant for either class of verbs, although it is marginally significant in the case of non-alternating verbs (p = 0.1, Binomial test). The difference between the two classes of verbs is not significant either, regardless of whether the two conditions where theme and recipient differ are compared directly ($\chi^2 = 0.06$ (df = 1), p > 0.81, n.s.) or whether the cases where there is no difference are also taken into account ($\chi^2 = 1.32$ (df = 2), p > 0.51, n.s.).

Syntactic weight. As in the case of givenness, there are three potential information-structural conditions for syntactic weight: The theme NP can be heavier than the recipient NP, or vice versa, or the two NPs can have the same syntactic weight. The distribution of the alternating and non-alternating instances of the prepositional dative across these three conditions is shown in Figure 2.

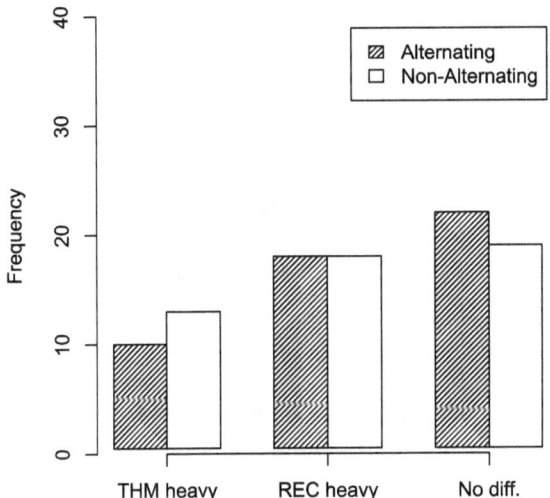

Figure 2. *Syntactic weight of the theme NP and the recipient NP in the prepositional dative for alternating and non-alternating verbs (ICE-GB, n = 100).*

The distributions of both the alternating and the non-alternating cases conform to the information-structural configuration expected for the prepositional dative: there are more cases where the recipient is heavier than the theme than vice versa. This difference, however, is not statistically significant for either class of verbs, although it is marginally significant in the case of alternating verbs (p = 0.09, Binomial test). The difference between the two classes of verbs is not significant either, regardless of whether the two conditions where theme and recipient differ are compared directly ($\chi^2 = 0.05$ (df = 1), p > 0.82, n.s.) or whether the cases where there is no difference are also taken into account ($\chi^2 = 0.61$ (df = 2), p > 0.74, n.s.).

Animacy. Again, there are three potential information-structural conditions: The theme NP can be more animate than the recipient NP, or vice versa, or the two NPs can have the same degree of animacy. The distribution of the alternating and non-alternating instances of the prepositional dative across these three conditions is shown in Figure 3.

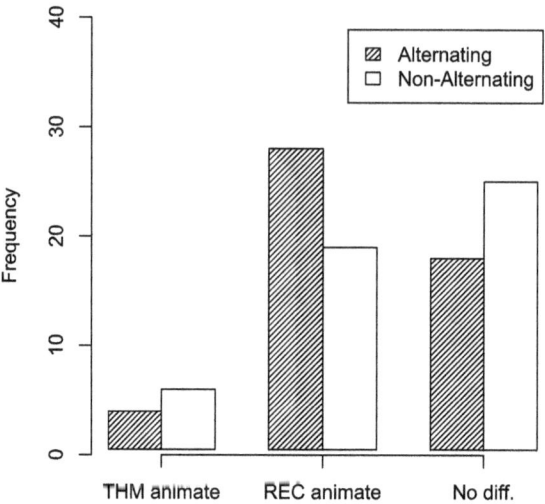

Figure 3. *Animacy of the theme NP and the recipient NP in the prepositional dative for alternating and non-alternating verbs (ICE-GB, n = 100).*

The distribution of both the alternating and the non-alternating cases contradicts the information-structural configuration expected for the prepositional dative: there are more cases where the recipient is more animate than the theme than vice versa. This conforms, of course, to a general semantically-based expectation that themes are less likely than recipients to be animate; the difference is statistically significant for both classes of verbs ($p < 0.001$ for the alternating verbs and $p < 0.01$ for the non-alternating verbs). As in the case of givenness and syntactic weight, however, the difference between the two classes of verbs is not significant, regardless of whether the two conditions where theme and recipient differ are compared directly ($\chi^2 = 0.61$ (df = 1), $p > 0.43$, n.s.) or whether the cases where there is no difference are also taken into account ($\chi^2 = 3.26$ (df = 2), $p > 0.19$, n.s.).

3.1.3. *Discussion.* The results of all three corpus analyses show that there are no significant differences in the information-structural profile of alternating and non-alternating verbs in the prepositional dative, making it unlikely that such differences could serve as a source of information to the language learner as to what verbs may alternate between the prepositional dative and the ditransitive and which ones may not.[5]

As mentioned, it is possible that the failure to reach statistical significance is due to the small size of the sample investigated here. I will address this possibility in Study 2, but there are good reasons to believe that the sample size is not the problem. Note that the differences do not just fail to reach significance, they also have extremely small effect sizes. Leaving aside the cases where theme and recipient do not differ in terms of the factor under investigation, Cramér's V is 0.0277 for givenness, 0.0637 for weight and 0.15 for animacy. Of course, such small effect sizes would become statistically significant in a sufficiently large corpus, but this would not change the fact that the effect is very small and therefore unlikely to serve the function envisioned by Pinker.

3.2. Study 2

3.2.1. *Aims and method.*
It is possible, that the data set in Study 1 is not just too small to yield significant results, but that it is not actually representative of the prepositional dative construction at all: In a small data set, individual examples that happen to be anomalous in some way influence the result more strongly than in a large data set. An investigation of a larger set of selected alternating and non-alternating verbs may yield a very different picture. Goldberg (cf. this volume, Section 7) sketches out such an investigation: she looks at a particular type of information-structure violation, namely prepositional datives with a lexical theme (which is assumed to be discourse-new) and

---

5. Note that for two out of the three criteria the information-structural profile of the prepositional dative seems to contradict my summary of the literature on information-structure and the dative alternation in Section 2.3. The literature is in agreement about the influence of information structure such that speakers are more likely to use the ditransitive if the recipient is more given, shorter, and/or more animate and the prepositional dative if the theme is more given, shorter, and/or more animate.

However, the results presented here do not actually contradict this claim. As the results from Thompson's (1990) study clearly show, the statements about the probability of choosing the prepositional dative or the ditransitive are correct, but they also show that these probabilities must be understood in the context of a baseline whereby the recipient is more likely to be given ("active" in Thompson's terms), short, and animate in both constructions. This distribution is more pronounced in the ditransitive than in the dative, and this is where the difference in probability comes from, but both constructions have the same general information-structural profile. This profile, incidentally, makes perfect sense from a semantic point of view: recipients are likely to be human, while themes are likely to be inanimate or abstract, simply because humans tend to give inanimate or abstract "things" to other humans, not vice versa. Human/animate referents, in turn, are more likely to be discourse-given (cf. the contributions in Givón 1983 for cross-linguistic evidence of this fact).

a pronominal recipient (which is assumed to be discourse-given) with two verbs, alternating *tell* and non-alternating *explain*. She finds that, in the *Corpus of Contemporary American English*, this structure accounts for 0.02 percent of all occurrences of *tell* and 0.3 percent of all occurrences of *explain*. This difference is statistically significant and, if the results are typical, would suggest that information-structure violations are more typical for non-alternating verbs than for alternating ones after all. However, one potential problem with this conclusion is that is only justified if the information-structural distribution of *tell* and *explain* is typical of alternating and non-alternating verbs in general and if the specific case of lexical theme and pronominal recipient is typical of the general information-structural profile of these two verbs. A second potential problem is that Goldberg evaluates the frequency with which the two verbs occur in the structure [V NP$_{lexical}$ to PRN] with the overall frequency of the two verbs in the corpus; however, both verbs are used in a range of constructions that are irrelevant in the present context (for example, simple transitives, prepositional datives with clausal direct objects, direct speech, etc.).

To provide a more reliable picture of the kind of result that the analysis of a large data set would yield, four verbs were selected, two alternating ones (*tell* and *read*) and two non-alternating ones (*explain* and *mention*).[6] For all four verbs, all canonical (active, non-topicalized) prepositional dative uses were extracted manually from the British National Corpus and coded for two criteria: givenness and length (animacy was not coded because communication verbs almost categorically have abstract themes and animate recipients, so there is no room for variation between the verb classes). As in Study 1, length was operationalized as "number of orthographic word forms", but givenness was operationalized, following Goldberg (this volume), on the basis of the form of the NP, with "proper name" included as a category in between pronouns and lexical NPs ("pronoun > proper name > lexical NP"). As in Study 1, it was then determined how many of the examples followed the information-structural restrictions of the prepositional dative (i.e., for how many of them the theme was shorter/more given), how many violated them (i.e., for how many cases the recipient was shorter/more given), and for how many of them were information-structurally neutral (i.e., for how many of them there was no difference between theme and recipient).

---

6. The verbs *tell* and *explain* were included for the obvious reason that Goldberg uses them, but also because collostructional analyses have shown that they are good examples of alternating and non-alternating verbs (Gries and Stefanowitsch 2004; Stefanowitsch 2006). *Read* and *mention* were chosen because Study 1 had shown them to be the most frequent communication verbs in the alternating and non-alternating category respectively, with the exception of *say*, which was not included because its overall frequency in the BNC is too high to extract the relevant uses manually.

3.2.2. *Results.* The results for givenness show that there is no systematic difference between alternating and non-alternating verbs in the prepositional dative with respect to information-structure violations, the results for length show weak significant difference. However, there are strong significant differences between the verbs within each category for both factors.

Givenness. The results for givenness are shown in Figure 4.

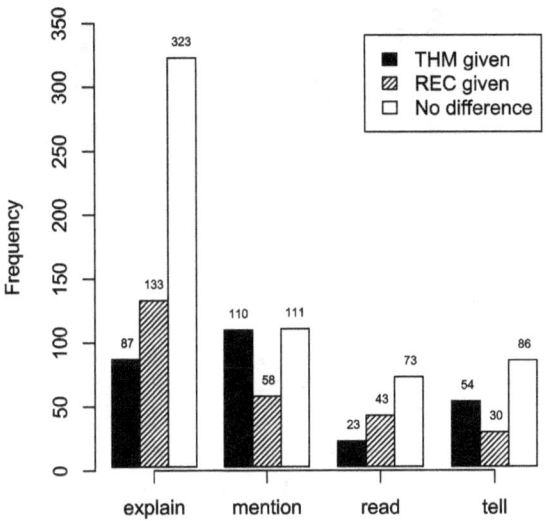

Figure 4. *Givenness of the theme and the recipient in the prepositional dative for two alternating and two non-alternating verbs in the BNC (n = 1131)*

The difference between the combined alternating and combined non-alternating verbs is not significant, regardless of whether the cases with no difference are included ($\chi^2 = 0.18$ (df = 2), $p > 0.05$) or not ($\chi^2 = 0.1$ (df = 1), $p > 0.05$). The differences within the classes are highly significant (*explain* vs. *mention*: $\chi^2 = 25.6$ (df = 1), $p < 0.001$ or $\chi^2 = 56.7$ (df = 2), $p < 0.001$; *read* vs. *tell*: $\chi^2 = 12.8$ (df = 1), $p < 0.001$ or $\chi^2 = 12.9$ (df = 2), $p < 0.01$). A direct comparison of *tell* and *explain* or of *read* and *mention* would also be significant, but a comparison of *tell* and *mention* or *read* and *explain* would not, and there is, of course, no reason to choose one pair of verbs over another for a cross-category comparison.

Length. The results for length are shown in Figure 5.

The difference between the combined alternating and combined non-alternating verbs is marginally significant if the cases with no difference

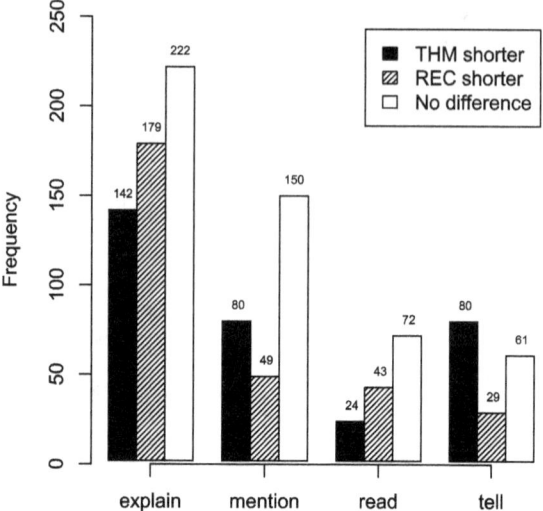

Figure 5. Length of the theme and the recipient in the prepositional dative for two alternating and two non-alternating verbs in the BNC (n = 1131)

between theme and recipient are included ($\chi^2 = 5.4$ (df = 3), p = 0.069), and very significant if the cases with no difference are excluded ($\chi^2 = 4.83$ (df = 1), p < 0.05), and the observed results deviate from the expected ones in the right direction: there are slightly more cases of information-structure violation than expected for the non-alternating verbs and slightly fewer for the alternating verbs. However, the differences within the categories are highly significant, both with and without the cases where there is no difference between theme and recipient (*explain* vs. *mention*: $\chi^2 = 11.6$ (df = 1), p < 0.001 or $\chi^2 = 22.95$ (df = 2), p < 0.001; *read* vs. *tell*: $\chi^2 = 24.23$ (df = 1), p < 0.001 or $\chi^2 = 30.99$ (df = 2), p < 0.001).

3.2.3. *Discussion.* The results for both length and givenness show that the differences between verbs within the verb classes are larger than those between the classes for the four verbs investigated. While the non-alternating verbs *explain* has a large number of information-structure violations and the alternating *tell* has a comparatively small number, the situation is reversed for *mention* and *read*, where the alternating verb has a large number of violations while the non-alternating one has a small number. This suggests that individual verbs differ with respect to the degree with which they adhere to the information-structural constraints of the constructions they occur in, but that this degree does not depend on whether alternative constructions are available to them or not.

4. Conclusion

The studies presented here are limited to a single pair of constructions, so they cannot invalidate the idea of preemption by contextual mismatch in general. However, they show that it is highly unlikely that this type of preemption plays a role in learning the restrictions on the ditransitive and the prepositional dative.

There are at least two possible interpretations of this result. First, the result may be specific to the dative alternation. Note that although information structure may play a role in the choice between the prepositional dative and the ditransitive, it is probably not the primary influencing factor. There are clear semantic differences between the two constructions (cf. e.g. Thompson and Koide 1987; Goldberg 1995; Gries and Stefanowitsch 2004), and information structure can play a role only where those semantic differences are neutralized. Perhaps a more detailed corpus analysis limited to neutralized contexts would show a difference in the information-structural profile of alternating and non-alternating verbs. Also, an investigation of grammatical alternatives that are more clearly governed by information structure, such as particle placement (cf. Chen 1986; Gries 2003) may well uncover the kinds of information-structural mismatches that could provide evidence that one or the other of the alternatives is not available for particular verbs.

Second, however, the results of the present study might point to a deeper problem of preemption by contextual mismatch. Pinker himself ultimately rejects his idea (1988: 16), arguing that statistical differences in the contextual appropriateness of alternative constructions are probably too weak to provide reliable evidence to the language learner. The present study would certainly seem to support this argument: Information-structure is just one of many factors governing the choice of a particular construction for a particular verb in a particular communicative context and while violations of information-structure may well provide information about the constructional preferences of a given verb, they do not reliably point to the non-availability of alternative constructions and thus are unlikely to be used as a source of negative evidence by children in the process of language acquisition.

Received 15 February 2010 *Universität Hamburg*
Revision received 6 August 2010

Data sources

International Corpus of English (British Component). 1998. Survey of English Usage, University College London.
Manchester Corpus. 2004. Elena Lieven, Julian Pine, Caroline Rowland, Anna Theakston (eds). Childes Data Repository. URL: http://childes.psy.cmu.edu/data/Eng-UK/Manchester.zip

References

Baker, Charles L. 1979. Syntactic theory and the projection problem. *Linguistic Inquiry* 10(4). 533–581.
Berwick, Robert. 1985. *The acquisition of syntactic knowledge*. Cambridge, MA: MIT Press.
Berwick, Robert & Amy Weinberg. 1984. *The grammatical basis of linguistic performance. Language use and acquisition*. Cambridge, MA: MIT Press.
Bohannon, John Neil & Laura Stanowicz. 1988. The issue of negative evidence: Adult responses to children's language errors. *Developmental Psychology* 24(5). 684–689.
Bowerman, Melissa. 1988. The 'no negative evidence' problem: How do children avoid constructing on overly general grammar? In John A. Hawkins (ed.), *Explaining language universals*, 73–101. Oxford: Blackwell.
Brooks, Patricia J. & Michael Tomasello. 1999. How young children constrain their argument structure constructions. *Language* 75(4). 720–738.
Brooks, Patricia J. & Otto Zizak. 2002. Does preemption help children learn verb transitivity? *Journal of Child Language* 29(4). 759–781.
Chen, Ping. 1986. Discourse and particle movement in English. *Studies in Language* 10(1). 79–95.
Chomsky, Noam. 1957. *Syntactic structures*. The Hague: Mouton.
Chomsky, Noam. 1965. *Aspects of the theory of syntax*. Cambridge, MA: MIT Press.
Clark, Eve. 1982. The young word maker: A case study of innovation in the child's lexicon. In Eric Wanner & Lila R. Gleitman (eds.), *Language acquisition: The state of the art*, 390–427. Cambridge, UK: Cambridge University Press.
Clark, Eve. 1995. *The lexicon in acquisition*. Cambridge, UK: Cambridge University Press.
Croft, William & D. A. Cruse. 2004. *Cognitive linguistics*. Cambridge, UK: Cambridge University Press.
Demetras, Marty J., Kathryn N. Post & Catherine E. Snow. 1986. Feedback to first language learners: The role of repetitions and clarification questions. *Journal of Child Language* 13(2). 275–292.
Dickens, Charles. 1848. *Dealings with the firm of Dombey and Son: Wholesale, retail and for export*, No. 19/20. London: Bradbury & Evans.
Elman, Jeff L. 1993. Learning and development in neural networks: The importance of starting small. *Cognition* 48. 71–99.
Erteschik-Shir, Nomi. 1979. Discourse constraints on dative movement. In Talmy Givón (ed.), *Discourse and syntax* (Syntax and semantics 12), 441–467. New York: Academic.
Givón, Talmy. 1983. Topic continuity in discourse: An introduction. In Talmy Givón (ed), *Topic continuity in discourse: A quantitative cross-language study*, 1–41. Amsterdam & Philadelphia: John Benjamins.
Gold, E. Mark. 1967. Language identification in the limit. *Information and Control* 10(5). 447–474.
Goldberg, Adele E. 1995. *Constructions: A construction grammar approach to argument structure*. Chicago: University of Chicago Press.
Goldberg, Adele E. 2006. *Constructions at work: The nature of generalization in language*. Oxford: Oxford University Press.
Gries, Stefan Th. 2003. *Multifactorial analysis in corpus linguistics: A study of particle placement*. London: Continuum.
Gries, Stefan Th., & Anatol Stefanowitsch. 2004. Extending collostructional analysis: A corpus-based perspective on 'alternations'. *International Journal of Corpus Linguistics* 9(1). 97–129.
Hauser, Marc D., Noam Chomsky & W. Tecumseh Fitch. 2002. The faculty of language: What is it, who has it, and how did it evolve? *Science* 298. 1569–1579.

Hirsh-Pasek, Kathy, Rebecca Treiman & Maita Schneiderman. 1984. Brown and Hanlon revisited: Mothers' sensitivity to ungrammatical forms. *Journal of Child Language* 11(1). 81–88.
Hopper, Paul. 1998. Emergent grammar. In Michael Tomasello (ed.), *The new psychology of language: Cognitive and functional approaches to language structure*, 155–176. Mawah, NJ: Erlbaum.
Langacker, Ronald W. 1987. *Foundations of cognitive grammar*. Vol. 1: *Theoretical prerequisites*. Stanford: Stanford University Press.
Langacker, Ronald W. 1991. *Foundations of cognitive grammar*. Vol. 2: *Descriptive application*. Stanford: Stanford University Press.
Langacker, Ronald W. 2000. A dynamic usage-based model. In Michael Barlow & Suzanne Kemmer (eds.), *Usage-Based Models of Language*, 1–63. Stanford: CSLI.
Marcus, Gary F. 1993. Negative evidence in language acquisition. *Cognition* 46. 53–85.
McEnery, Tony & Andrew Wilson. 2001. *Corpus linguistics*. 2nd edition. Edinburgh: Edinburgh University Press.
Ochs, Elinor. 1991. Misunderstanding children. In Nikolas Coupland, Howard Giles & John M. Wiemann (eds.), *"Miscommunication" and problematic talk*, 44–60. Newberry Park, CA: Sage.
Pinker, Steven. 1984. *Language learnability and language development*. Cambridge, MA: Harvard University Press.
Pinker, Steven. 1988. Learnability theory and the acquisition of a first language. In Frank S. Kessel (ed.), *The development of language and language researchers: Essays in honor of Roger Brown*, 97–119. Hillsdale, NJ: Lawrence Erlbaum.
Sampson, Geoffrey. 2001. *Empirical linguistics*. London & New York: Continuum.
Sampson, Geoffrey, David Gil & Peter Trudgill. 2009. *Language complexity as an evolving variable*. Oxford: Oxford University Press.
Silverstein, Michael. 1976. Hierarchy of features and ergativity. In Robert M. W. Dixon (ed.), *Grammatical categories in Australian languages*, 112–171. Canberra: Australian Institute of Aboriginal Studies.
Stefanowitsch, Anatol. 2003. Constructional semantics as a limit to grammatical alternation: The two genitives of English. In Günter Rohdenburg & Britta Mondorf (eds.), *Determinants of Grammatical Variation in English*, 413–441. Berlin & New York: Mouton de Gruyter.
Stefanowitsch, Anatol. 2005. New York, Dayton (Ohio), and the raw frequency fallacy. *Corpus Linguistics and Linguistic Theory* 1(2). 295–301.
Stefanowitsch, Anatol. 2006. Negative evidence and the raw frequency fallacy. *Corpus Linguistics and Linguistic Theory* 2(1). 61–77.
Stefanowitsch, Anatol. 2007. Linguistics beyond grammaticality (A reply to Sampson). *Corpus Linguistics and Linguistic Theory* 2(3): 57–71.
Stefanowitsch, Anatol. 2008. Negative evidence and preemption: A constructional approach to ungrammaticality. *Cognitive Linguistics* 19(3). 513–531.
Stefanowitsch, Anatol, & Stefan Th. Gries. 2003. Collostructions: Investigating the interaction of words and constructions. *International Journal of Corpus Linguistics* 8(2). 209–243.
Thompson, Sandra A. 1990. Information flow and 'dative shift' in English. In Jerrold Edmondson, Katherine Feagin & Peter Mühlhäusler (eds.), *Development and diversity. Linguistic variation across time and space*, 239–253. Dallas, TX: Summer Institute of Linguistics.
Thompson, Sandra A. & Yuka Koide. 1987. Iconicity and 'indirect objects' in English. *Journal of Pragmatics* 11(3). 399–406.
Tomasello, Michael. 2003. *Constructing a language*. Cambridge, MA: Harvard University Press.
Wasow, Thomas. 1997a. End-weight from the speaker's perspective. *Journal of Psycholinguistic Research* 26(3). 347–361.
Wasow, Thomas. 1997b. Remarks on grammatical weight. *Language Variation and Change* 9(1). 81–105.

Corpus evidence of the viability of statistical preemption*

Adele E. Goldberg

Abstract

The present paper argues that there is ample corpus evidence of statistical preemption for learners to make use of. In the case of argument structure constructions, a verb$_i$ is preempted from appearing in a construction A, CxA, if and only if the following probability is high: P(CxB|context that would be suitable for CxA and verb$_i$). For example, the probability of hearing a preemptive construction, given a context that would otherwise be well-suited for the ditransitive is high for verbs like explain *that overwhelmingly appear in the dative, and low for verbs like* tell *that readily appear in the ditransitive. Strength of statistical preemption is determined both by this probability, and by the* frequency (ln (F)) *of a verb in a preemptive construction when the context is at least as well suited to the preempted construction. The critiques of preemption by Stefanowitsch (2008, this volume) are countered by arguing that the relevant probabilities were not considered. Moreover, we find evidence that constructions are somewhat less constrained when yoked to non-alternating verbs, as Stefanowitsch (cf. this volume) suggests should be the case.*

Keywords: construction learning, dative, ditransitive, statistical preemption

---

* I am grateful to Lisa Goldman for checking the COCA corpus data I collected in order to remove misclassified instances of the dative or ditransitive. I would also like to thank Anatol Stefanowitsch for graciously sharing his paper and his data set with me, and Graeme Trousdale, Thomas Hoffmann, and an anonymous reviewer for helpful comments on an earlier draft. I am grateful to Laura Suttle and Devin Casenhiser for helpful discussions. Finally, I owe Mark Davies a special debt of gratitude for making large and easily searchable corpora such as COCA available for free. The research was supported by NSF grant # 0613227. Email <adele@princeton.edu>

1. Introduction

How do speakers learn what not to say? Sentences do not come marked as unacceptable. Nonetheless, there are perfectly sensible formulations that are judged ill-formed by native speakers. These include examples such as (1)–(3):

(1) ??*She explained her the news.*
    (cf. *She told her the news.*)

(2) ??*She considered to go to the farm.*
    (*She wanted to go to the farm.*)

(3) ?*She saw the afraid boy.*
    (*She saw the scared boy.*)

We should acknowledge at the outset that expressions such as those in (1)–(3) certainly do occasionally occur in corpus data (e.g. Fellbaum 2005). But it is clear to native speakers and it can be demonstrated with corpus evidence as explained previously that *explain* strongly prefers the prepositional dative (4), *consider* prefers a gerundive verb phrase (5) and *afraid* prefers a predicative rather than attributive use (6):

(4) *She explained the news to her.*

(5) *She considered going to the farm.*

(6) *She saw the boy who was afraid.*

Semantic considerations (Ambridge et al. 2009) do not provide an explanation of the ill-formedness of (1)–(3), since the meanings of the words are perfectly semantically compatible with the constructions, as indicated by the paraphrases provided in parentheses (cf. also Pollard and Sag 1987). In fact (1)–(3) illustrate just the sort of errors that advanced non-native speakers often make. How do native speakers learn to systematically avoid such formulations?

It might be tempting to believe that the simple non-occurrence of a verb in an argument structure construction is sufficient to rule it out (Braine and Brooks 1995). This proposal, that formulations are only acceptable if they are heard with some regularity—are *entrenched*—faces a problem once we recognize that many verbs are well entrenched in only one argument structure construction and yet they are freely available for use in a different one. This is clear in examples (7)–(10).

(7) *I actually had a moth go up my nose once. I . . . coughed him out of my mouth."* [bikeforums.net/archive/index.php/t-292132, accessed 28 October 2010]

(8) *"Sarah ... winked her way through the debates."* [pcneedtogo.blogspot.com, accessed 28 October 2010]

(9) *"She'd smiled herself an upgrade."* [Douglas Adams, Hitchhiker's Guide to the Galaxy, 1979: 11]

(10) *"Tim ... sneezed the milk out of his nose."* [www.zoackkennel.com/tims-story.html, accessed 28 October 2010]

Each of these verbs, *cough, wink, smile,* and *sneeze* is very frequent (entrenched) in the intransitive construction, and only exceedingly rarely, if ever, witnessed in the various transitive constructions in (7)–(10). Therefore an account based on entrenchment would seem to inappropriately rule out the sentences in (7)–(10) as unacceptable (Goldberg 2006). Stefanowitsch's (2008) proposal for addressing this issue is discussed in section 4, where we see that it falls prey to the same sort of counterexamples given in (7)–(10).

For challenges faced by other attempts to explain examples like (1)–(3), see excellent overviews by e.g. Bowerman (1996), Pinker (1989) and Stefanowitsch (this volume). Boyd and Goldberg (to appear) also review issues related to (a) entrenchment, (b) direct negative evidence, (c) underlying features, (d) the semantic proposal of Ambridge et al. (2009), and (e) the role of recasts or reformulations (e.g. Saxton 1997; Chouinard and Clark 2003).

2. Statistical preemption

Consider for a moment, the more easily tractable case of morphology. How is that we know we should use *went* instead of **goed*? Clearly it is because we consistently hear *went* in contexts where *goed* would have been at least as appropriate: this is statistical preemption. The preemption process is straightforward in these cases because the actual form serves the identical semantic/pragmatic purpose as the preempted form.

Notice that speakers do not avoid forms simply because an alternative form is highly entrenched. If we invent a new verb, *kleb,* meaning "to wash" and for some pragmatic reason (say it is learned at camp), it is only used in the future tense (e.g. *I will kleb my face later*). Intuitions are clear that as soon as the situation arises in which the past tense is appropriate, speakers will be perfectly comfortable using it (*yes, I've klebbed*!). The past tense is not preempted by the more entrenched future use, because the future was not used in contexts that were at least as appropriate for the past tense.

The role of statistical preemption when considering phrasal forms requires discussion, since distinct phrasal constructions are virtually never semantically and pragmatically identical, the way *went* and the hypothetical *goed* are. Any two phrasal constructions differ either semantically or pragmatically (or both)

(Bolinger 1977; Clark 1987; Goldberg 1995), and so both constructions often happily coexist for particular lexical items.

For example, the dative and ditransitive have overlapping, but distinct semantic and information structure properties. The differences have been documented time and again by many researchers (Arnold et al. 2000; Bresnan et al. 2005; Collins 1995; Erteschik-Shir 1979; Goldberg 1995; Goldberg 2006; Green 1974; Hovav and Levin 2005; Oehrle 1975; Thompson 1995; Wasow 2002). The differences are subject to some dialect differences and gradability, yet it is possible to predict with high probability which construction will be preferred in a given context, for a given dialect (Bresnan and Hay 2008; Bresnan and Ford 2010). Different formulations of the differences between the two constructions have been used; often, the emphasis has been on the greater restrictiveness of the ditransitive. For example, the dative is preferred when conveying caused motion to a place instead of a recipient (11a to 11b), and the dative is preferred in standard dialects of American and British English if the theme is a third person pronoun (12a to 12b):

(11) a. ??*She sent the moon a package*[1]. ditransitive
     b. *She sent a package to the moon.* dative

(12) a. ??*She sent him it.* ditransitive
     b. *She it to him.* dative

But knowledge that the prepositional paraphrase is licensed as in (13), based on positive evidence, should not in any simple way prevent the use of the ditransitive in (14), because a large number of verbs do freely appear in both constructions (Bowerman 1996; Pinker 1989):

(13) *She explained the story to someone.*

(14) ??*She explained someone the story.*

A statistical form of preemption can play an important role in learning to avoid expressions such as (1)–(3) in the following way (Goldberg 1993; 1995; 2006; cf. also Pinker 1984: 400). In a situation in which a construction A (CxA) might have been expected to be uttered with a given verb, $verb_i$, the learner can infer that CxA is not after all appropriate for that verb, if a different construction, CxB, is consistently witnessed instead. That is, CxB statistically preempts CxA for $verb_i$, to the extent that the probability in (15) approaches 1. I address the important factor of *confidence* of statistical preemption in section 4.

---

[1]. This sentence is only acceptable if *the moon* is construed to refer to some people at the moon.

(15) The probability of CxB statistically preempting CxA for a particular verb, $verb_i$:

P(CxB | a discourse context in which the learner might expect to hear CxA[$verb_i$])[2]

This probability is equivalent to the following:

P(CxB | a discourse context at least as suitable for CxA, and $verb_i$)

For example, if we assume that *explain* does not readily occur in the ditransitive construction because it is statistically preempted by the dative construction, we predict the probability in (16) to be high:

(16) P(dative | a discourse context at least as suitable for the ditransitive and *explain*)

As researchers, we need to operationalize how to count "discourse contexts that are at least as suitable for the ditransitive". It turns out there is a simple proxy for this number: the total number of ditransitive *and* dative uses of a given verb, when the semantics and information structure of the ditransitive are satisfied. That is,

(17) P(dative | context at least as suitable for ditransitive and $verb_i$)
$\approx$
P(dative | $verb_i$ and [dative$_{\text{with relevant restrictions}}$ *or* ditransitive])

In order to calculate the probability in (17), we need to find contexts in which the ditransitive is at least as appropriate as the dative construction. The particular well-known restrictions on the ditransitive just mentioned do not suggest such contexts. Instead, they provide contexts where a learner might expect to hear a dative rather than a ditransitive. One clear context in which the ditransitive *is* preferred over the dative is when the recipient is pronominal and the theme is not. The dative is certainly *allowed* in such contexts, but if we look at corpus data, we find the following preference quite clearly:

(18) a. *She told me the news.*
b. *#She told the news to me.*

The Corpus of Contemporary American English (COCA) is a 400 million word tagged corpus, freely available on-line at http://view.byu.edu/, thanks to Mark Davies. Table 1 shows that the probability of witnessing a dative construction in this corpus, given a pronominal recipient and a non-pronominal theme, is only, on average, .04, for verbs that alternate:

---

2. Recall that the conditional probability P(B|A) is the probability of B, given A: P(B&A)/P(A).

Table 1. Verbs that alternate: comparison of number of dative and ditransitive occurrences when the recipient argument is pronominal and the theme is not. COCA corpus.[3]

Alternating verbs	A Dative:[4] [v] [lexical NP] to [definite pronoun]	Ditransitive: [v] [definite pronoun] [lexical NP]	P (dative | dative$_{\text{with relevant restrictions}}$ + ditransitive)
Tell	36	3713	<.01
Give	111	7982	.01
Show	35	932	.04
Send	146	1098	.12
Sell	40	152	.21
Bring	111	415	.21
Read	81	275	.23
Lend	7	176	.04
Total	567	14743	.04 (Average)

We should note that dative uses with pronominal recipients and non-pronominal themes are at times fully acceptable. There are interacting factors that lead to the use of one construction over another, including focus structure and structural priming (e.g. Bates and MacWhinney 1987; Bresnan 2007). For example, if the recipient argument is contrastive, the dative is perfectly natural as in (19):

(19) *She told the news to ME.*

Nonetheless, Table 1 demonstrates that the ditransitive is generally preferred over the dative in contexts of pronominal recipients and non-pronominal themes when a verb alternates.

---

3. It might be tempting to think that these numbers indicate that the *ditransitive* construction should actually preempt the dative construction, for alternating verbs on the basis of Table 1, but in order to conclude that, we would need to calculate, for each verb:

    P(ditransitive | dative is at least as appropriate) ≈
    P(ditransitive | ditransitive $_{\text{with relevant restrictions}}$ + dative)

    As the relevant restrictions on the dative are not the same as those on the ditransitive, this is not equal to 1-P(dative | dative$_{\text{with relevant restrictions}}$ + ditransitive).

4. Searches were performed on COCA as follows:

    [v] [pp*] [a*] [n]   Ditransitive
    [v] [a*] [n] to [pp*] Dative

    [v] allows for all forms of the verb, pp* searches for all definite pronouns, a* searches for articles and n searches for all nouns. These formulas do not capture every non-pronominal noun (since bare nouns are non-pronominal), but they were used for ease of replication. We also removed by hand examples in which the second noun phrase was an adjunct or the first NP returned from a "ditransitive" search was an inanimate pronoun (*it*): (e.g. *I wish I could explain it the way Mary did.* was not counted as a ditransitive).

Table 2. Non-alternating verbs: comparison of number of dative and ditransitive occurrences when the recipient argument is pronominal and the theme is not. Data from the COCA corpus.

Non-alternating verbs	Dative: [v] [lexical NP] to [definite pronoun]	Ditransitive: [v] [definite pronoun] [lexical NP]	P (dative | dative$_{\text{with relevant restrictions}}$ + **ditransitive**)
Explain	120	1	.99
Whisper	16	1	.94
Transfer	20	0	1.0
Return	74	11	.88
Entrust	13	0	1.0
Deliver	33	18	.65
Present	43	37	.53
Repeat	26	0	1.0
Total	345	69	.83 (Average)

Many researchers have noted that some verbs are less available for the ditransitive construction than others (e.g. Pinker 1989; Levin 1993; Goldberg 1995). "Non-alternating" verbs should have a higher probability of occurring in the dative than alternating verbs, given an information structure that favors the ditransitive. In just this way, we find that verbs traditionally classified as non-alternating display a quite different distribution (Table 2) than alternating verbs.

Thus the data required for statistical preemption to work is readily available in corpora of sufficient size. For 6 out of 8 of the non-alternating verbs, more than 85% of the time that a ditransitive might have been expected, a dative is witnessed instead. Collectively, the distribution of alternating and non-alternating verbs is statistically distinct χ^2 (1) = 4678.24, p < .0001.

The astute reader might notice that two of the verbs, *deliver* and *present* appear almost half as often in the ditransitive as they do in the dative when there is a pronominal recipient and non-pronominal theme. This would seem to predict that ditransitive uses of these verbs would be relatively more acceptable than ditransitive uses of other verbs in Table 2, and this might well be the case. Whether a verb alternates is a matter of degree, and it is possible that verbs traditionally classified as non-alternating were in fact misclassified. At the same time, the distribution of even *deliver* and *present* is distinct from the average distribution of verbs that are well-known to alternate: *deliver*: χ^2 (1) = 503.95, p < .0001; *present*: χ^2 (1) = 523.65, p < .0001. This indicates that these verbs are at least more disfavored for the ditransitive than the average verb in Table 1. Moreover, there is a different preempting construction that is overwhelmingly preferred to either the dative or the ditransitive in the case of *present*. We return to a discussion of this in section 7.2.

3. Challenges to statistical preemption

Stefanowitsch has argued against preemption being an operative notion in two recent papers (2008, this volume). Both analyses are worth revisiting.

Stefanowitsch (this volume) states his critique as an argument against "preemption by contextual clues," but all preemption is via contextual clues since the basic idea is that construction B preempts another construction A by systematically appearing in discourse contexts that would be at least as suitable for construction A.

Stefanowitsch considers a data set of 100 sentences, and aims to investigate whether corpora contain the statistics necessary for statistical preemption on the basis of discourse functions to be viable. He suggests that there is no evidence that corpora do contain the relevant information. Specifically, he considers the probability of particular information structure distributions, given the dative construction, for verbs that alternate with the ditransitive and those that do not. That is, he investigates the probability of certain information structure properties, given the dative, as represented in (20).

(20) P(context at least as well suited to the ditransitive | dative)

Only dative examples are considered, not the combination of dative and ditransitive examples. But as we saw, the relevant probability is actually the probability of a dative, given certain information structure properties.

(21) P(dative | context at least as well suited to the ditransitive)

To understand the difference between the two conditional probabilities in (20) and (21), it is helpful to think of a concrete situation. Only rarely when it has rained does a rainbow appear; therefore the probability of a rainbow, given rain (22) is low. At the same time, however, every time a rainbow occurs, there has been rain. Therefore the probability of rain, given a rainbow (23) is very high.

(22) Probability (rainbow | rain)

(23) Probability (rain | rainbow)

Since Stefanowitsch (this volume) does not provide data on the number of contexts in which a ditransitive construction is used, his data do not directly address whether learners have the relevant evidence for statistical preemption to be viable. We have already seen that such evidence is available to learners in corpus data of sufficient size.

We return in section 7 to the secondary but intriguing question that Stefanowitsch's paper (this volume) raises, which is whether the dative construction is used with fewer restrictions when appearing with non-alternating verbs than when it appears with alternating verbs.

4. Strength of preemption

Stefanowitsch (2008) aims to correlate the "strength" of statistical preemption with speakers' judgments of ill-formedness. Finding only a non-significant correlation between the two measures, he concludes that evidence for statistical preemption is lacking.

He suggests measuring the strength of preemption by simply determining how strongly a given verb is associated with a particular preempting construction. In particular, he assumes that preemption should be stronger when the verb *only* or predominantly occurs in a potentially preempting construction. Thus for example, *consider* used with a gerundive VP (*considered going*) would only weakly preempt *consider* appearing with an infinitive VP (**considered to go*) if it were found that the majority of uses of *consider* did not involve a VP complement at all, but were instead, for example, simple transitives.

However, the prediction is inaccurate, and in fact the proposal misses the point of preemption: only the contexts in which the semantic and information structure properties satisfy the potentially preempted construction are relevant for statistical preemption. In the case of *consider*, only contexts in which the infinitive VP would be appropriate, but the gerundive VP is used instead are relevant. The verb may appear more often in some other context and corresponding construction(s), but these contexts are not relevant to the strength of preemption. **Two forms must compete for being used in the same context for one to preempt the other.**

The notion, strength of preemption, makes sense, but it does not depend on how associated a verb is with the preempting construction. Instead, two factors are relevant. Strength of preemptive evidence can be determined by how close the probability in (15) comes to being equal to 1, together with the frequency of preemptive expressions.

4.1. *Strength of preemption: Probability and frequency of a verb in a preemptive construction*

Suppose that the first time a learner hears *explain*, she has reason to expect to hear it used ditransitively, but instead hears it datively. At that moment, the probability of witnessing *explain* in a preemptive context is 1, but only a single case has been witnessed. Clearly, the learner should not infer from a single exposure that the ditransitive was preempted for *explain*. On the other hand, if a learner hears *explain* used datively 100 times without ever hearing it used in the ditransitive, the probability hasn't changed—it is still one—but the *confidence* of preemption should clearly be increased. Frequency plays a role in the process of statistical preemption exactly because preemption is statistical. Only upon repeated exposures to one construction in lieu of another related construction can the speaker learn that the second construction is not conventional. This requires that a given pattern occur with sufficient frequency.

We should note that the confidence of one construction preempting another is not a simple linear function of frequency: it is not likely that confidence doubles when a person hears their second example, or that their confidence increases two-fold when exposed to 2000 as opposed to 1000 examples. We can capture the fact that confidence grows more slowly by appealing to the natural log function.

Thus we can separate the two factors that determine the strength of preemption as follows:

Probability of CxB statistically preempting CxA for $verb_i$:
(24) P(CxB | contexts in which CxA is at least as appropriate)

Confidence of statistical preemption for $verb_i$:
(25) ln F(CxB when CxA would be at least as appropriate)

As represented in (25), confidence can be determined by the natural log of the frequency of CxB appearing when CxA would be appropriate. Thus the probability and confidence of statistical preemption for the verbs in Table 3 is as follows:

Table 3. *Strength of statistical preemption: a function of probability and confidence (based on frequency) of the preempting construction.*

Non-alternating verbs	P (dative | context appropriate to ditrans)	Confidence of statistical preemption
Explain	.99	ln(120) = 4.78
Whisper	.94	ln(16) = 2.77
Transfer	1.0	ln(20) = 2.99
Return	.88	ln(74) = 4.30
Entrust	1	ln(13) = 2.56
Deliver	.65	ln(33) = 3.49
Present	.53	ln(43) = 3.76
Repeat	1.0	ln(26) = 3.26

To summarize, we have seen that evidence that can be used by speakers to statistically preempt a non-occurring construction is available in corpora. However, the availability of the relevant data does not tell us that speakers actually make use of it. In fact, there is experimental evidence that they do.

5. Experimental evidence of statistical preemption in the domain of syntax

Statistical preemption of phrasal patterns has not received a great deal of attention in the experimental literature, except in a few notable studies. For example, Brooks and Tomasello (1999) found that children aged six or seven were less than half as likely to productively produce a novel verb in a transitive frame when the verb had been modeled in both an intransitive and periphrastic causative construction, than when it was only modeled in the simple intransitive. For example, if the child had heard both *The ball is tamming*, and *He's making the ball tam*, then they were less likely to respond to "what's the boy doing"? with *He's tamming the ball*, than they were if only the simple intransitive had been witnessed.

It seems that hearing the novel verb used in the periphrastic causative provided a readily available alternative to the causative construction, statistically preempting the use of the latter. That is, hearing a periphrastic causative in a context in which the transitive causative would have been at least equally appropriate led children to avoid generating a transitive causative in a similar contextual situation (cf. also Brooks and Zizak 2002).

Boyd and Goldberg (to appear) extend the experimental study of preemption via an investigation of the case of "a-adjectives." *A*-adjectives are adjectives that begin with an unstressed schwa and can be morphologically segmented into *a*- plus a semantically related stem (e.g. *a-live*, *a-sleep*). Relevantly, these adjectives disprefer appearing prenominally as shown in (3) and (26):

(26) ??*the asleep boy*.

The distribution is motivated by the fact that the majority of *a*-adjectives historically were prepositional phrases, and as prepositional phrases, they could not be expected to appear prenominally. However, speakers today are generally unaware of the historical facts and so the question arises as to how the restriction can be learned. Boyd and Goldberg examined adult naturalistic production in three experiments, all of which required participants to describe scenes in which one of two animals with different adjective labels moved to a star. We used four classes of adjectives: real *a*-adjectives; nearly synonymous real non-*a*-adjectives; nonsense *a*-adjectives, and nonsense non-adjectives.

The task resulted in either a relative clause or prenominal (attributive) use of the target adjective (e.g. 27 or 28).

(27) Prenominal: *The sleepy/??asleep/?adax fox.*
      (judgments based on data from Experiment 1 of Boyd and Goldberg)

(28) Relative Clause: *The fox that's sleepy/asleep/adax.*

The first experiment established that real *a*-adjectives (e.g. *asleep*) strongly disprefer prenominal use relative to non-*a* adjectives (e.g. *sleepy*). In addition, *novel a*-adjectives (e.g. *adax*) disprefer prenominal use relative to non-*a* adjectives (e.g. *chammy*) to a significant extent as well. This indicates that participants tentatively assimilate never-before-seen *a*-adjectives to the category of familiar *a*-adjectives. Categorization was tentative insofar as real *a*-adjectives were much less likely to occur prenominally than novel *a*-adjectives were.

A second experiment investigated the role of statistical preemption. It was found that in fact witnessing two of the four novel *a*-adjectives used in a preemptive relative clause context just three times each dramatically decreased prenominal uses so that *all* four novel *a*-adjectives behaved indistinguishably from familiar *a*-adjectives in avoiding prenominal uses. Non-*a*-adjectives were unaffected. This result is striking because it not only demonstrates the effectiveness of preemption, but it also indicates that speakers are able to generalize evidence gleaned from statistical preemption to other members of the same category. In the context of the present work, this suggests, for example, that strong evidence that verbs of manner of speech are statistically preempted in the ditransitive might be generalized to new verbs of manner of speech, without having to witness the new verbs themselves in a preempting construction.

A final experiment showed that learners rationally disregard *pseudo*-preemptive input. Speakers did not display an increased avoidance of prenominal uses when exposed to pseudo-preemptive contexts like (29), presumably because they rationally attributed *adax*'s appearance in the relative clause to the complex adjective (cf. 30), rather than to *adax*.

(29)   *The hamster, adax and proud of itself, moved to the star.*

(30)   **The proud of itself hamster moved to the star.*

Productions in the last experiment patterned like those in the first experiment where no preemptive context was provided. Fillers were used to obscure the goal of the experiment and to guard against the effects being a simple result of structural priming. Debriefing confirmed that speakers were unaware of the manipulations.

Collectively, the Boyd and Goldberg (to appear) experiments go some way toward establishing how speakers are able to learn arbitrary distributional restrictions in their language—i.e., how they learn what not to say. Learners categorize their input, tentatively generalizing restrictions to new members of a category. Familiar formulations can statistically preempt other formulations that have at least as appropriate functions in a given context. Providing more evidence that speakers categorize restrictions, results demonstrated that speakers extended the information gained from preemptive contexts to other instances of the same category. At the same time, speakers use statistical preemption wisely: they are impressively adept at ignoring alternative formulations when those formulations can be attributed to some irrelevant factor.

6. Limits of statistical preemption

Proponents of statistical preemption have emphasized that it cannot be the only mechanism by which we learn to avoid certain formulations. For example, Goldberg (1995: 126) points out that low frequency or novel non-alternating verbs are not addressed by statistical preemption since preemption presupposes hearing the verb multiple times. As noted, the Boyd and Goldberg (to appear) finding that speakers can generalize evidence from statistical preemption to other words of the same category is intriguing, but more work needs to be done to determine if this provides a general solution for low-frequency or novel words.

Statistical preemption does not provide a solution for cases where the target construction is so low frequency that it could not be expected to appear, or cases in which there is no construction that is closely enough related to the target construction (Goldberg 1995: 127). For this reason, *categorization* (in particular semantic and morpho-phonological classes, similarity, and type variability) has been invoked as an additional mechanism (Goldberg 1995: 126–140, 2006: Chapter 5; Suttle and Goldberg, to appear). As Boyd and Goldberg (to appear) emphasize, a combination of categorization and statistical preemption may provide a general solution to semantically arbitrary restrictions of the sort we set out to address, as exemplified by (1)–(3).

7. Are non-alternating verbs more free in their distribution?

At the same time that Stefanowitsch's (this volume) critique fails to undermine the existence of corpus evidence for statistical preemption, it does raise a very intriguing question. Almost all, if not all of the work comparing the information structure of the dative and ditransitive has focused on verbs that alternate, insofar as there has been an attempt to control for semantic differences (e.g. Bresnan et al. 2005; Goldberg 2006; Wasow 2002). Analyses have become quite sophisticated in determining which of two alternates actually appear (Bresnan et al. 2005). But what is a poor verb to do if it is not allowed to alternate?

Stefanowitsch (this volume) suggests the following hypothesis:

(A)   The single construction that non-alternating verbs occur in should be used in a wider range of contexts than it is for verbs that alternate.

Although Stefanowitsch ultimately argues that this prediction is unsupported, the hypothesis is informally confirmed by a comparison of (31a) and (31b):

(31) a. *She explained the problem to me.*
     b. *#She told the problem to me.*

Intuitively, 31a is completely natural while 31b sounds somewhat odd in a neutral context.

In order to systematically investigate (A), we can ask, if we consider only instances of the dative construction, do we find a greater proportion of contexts otherwise well suited to the ditransitive for verbs that do not alternate than for those that do?

We will see that there is in fact evidence supporting (A). But Stefanowitsch goes further and claims that the single construction that a non-alternating verb occurs in "should be distributed randomly across information-structural conditions" (Stefanowitsch, this volume, page 118), as if constructions with non-alternating dative verbs should have no information structure constraints whatsoever. We will see that this secondary claim does not follow from (A), because non-alternating verbs generally have other possibilities available.

In order to investigate the claim in (A), we need to consider dative uses of alternating and non-alternating verbs, as Stefanowitsch does. But we need to ask, do we find relatively more dative uses *that would be at least as suitable for the ditransitive* when a verb does not have the option of appearing in the ditransitive?

7.1. A closer look at Stefanowitsch's 100-sentence corpus (Stefanowitsch, this volume)

Stefanowitsch analyzes 50 sentences that include 8 alternating verbs and another 50 sentences that include 14 non-alternating verbs, culled from the ICE-GB corpus of one million words of spoken and written British English from the 1990s. He finds no significant differences in the factors he examines including animacy, givenness, or heaviness when comparing the dative arguments of alternating verbs to those of non-alternating verbs.

Because the data set is so small, it is well worth taking a close look to be sure all of the examples are relevant. In particular, we want to see whether there are relatively more instances of the dative with properties that would otherwise be well suited for the ditransitive in the case of non-alternating verbs when compared with alternating verbs.

It turns out that seven examples do not convey the semantics of "transfer" so they do not satisfy the semantic constraints on the ditransitive; these all involve non-alternating verbs, and are listed in (32a to 32g):

(32) a. *she can also introduce you to the Parish Council.*
     b. *I'll introduce you to them then.*
     c. *to entrust all their savings to the ups and downs of equity investment.*
     d. *pushing himself to the limit.*

e.   transfer the load directly to the pier.
   f.   Transfer your hands back to A and B and repeat.
   g.   Transfer your hands to C and D and repeat Steps 1–4.

Notice 32a and 32b (with *introduce*) do not involve intended or metaphorical transfer, and the rest involve locative goals, not animate recipients.

There are therefore 50 − 7 = 43 relevant examples of non-alternating verbs and 50 examples of alternating verbs. We know that in the case of alternating verbs, the ditransitive construction is preferred over the dative construction when the recipient argument is pronominal and the theme is not (recall Table 1). This is also consistent with Stefanowitsch's data set in that only 2 out of 50 examples (4%) of alternating verbs appear with this information structure. These two examples are provided in 33a and b:

(33) a.   *send the demand to me for checking.*
      b.   *she used to read Keats to herself.*

We have seen that non-alternating verbs more freely appeared in the dative when they had this same information structure (recall Table 2). This is also confirmed in Stefanowitsch's data in that seven of the 43 relevant non-alternating examples—16%—appear with a pronominal recipient and a non-pronominal theme:

(34) a.   *does that convey anything to you.*
      b.   *return the papers to me.*
      c.   *who was saying all these outrageous things to you.*
      d.   *I'm not saying anything to you about . . .*
      e.   *said this to you.*
      f.   *he didn't say anything to me.*
      g.   *he presents his feelings to us.*

That is, verbs that do not alternate are four times more likely to appear in a dative with a pronominal recipient and a non-pronominal theme than verbs that do alternate, when sample size is controlled for in Stefanowitch's data set. The small numbers make a chi-square test inappropriate, but Fisher's exact test (1 tailed) demonstrates a marginal effect, $p = .08$, indicating a trend toward a different information structure profile of dative for verbs that do not alternate as compared with verbs that do. This is consistent with the intuitive judgments offered in (31) and repeated:

(35) a.   *She explained the problem to me.*
      b.   *#She told the problem to me.*

The facts become even more clear when one considers a larger data set. We can consult the COCA corpus, and compare the single case of *tell* vs. *explain*, since this case allows us to hold general semantics roughly constant: both are

Table 4. *Comparison of number of dative uses when the information structure suits the ditransitive (i.e., recipient argument is pronominal and the theme is not.) COCA corpus.*

	Dative: [v] <lexical NP> [to <definite pronoun>]	Other uses (assuming three argument sense)	Overall frequency of V
Tell	36	166,591	166,627
Explain	120	31,766	31,886

verbs of communication, and both are routinely expressed with agent, content and recipient roles expressed or understood.

Despite the fact that *tell* is five times more frequent overall in the COCA corpus (166K vs. 31K), it is *explain* that is almost four times more likely to appear in the dative with pronominal recipient and non-pronominal theme (120 vs. 36).

Here we see that the distribution of datives is significantly different for *tell* and *explain*: $\chi^2(1) = 428.91$, $p < .0001$. Thus the hypothesis that Stefanowitsch set out to test appears to be true, at least as indicated by his own data, and confirmed for the case of *tell* vs. *explain* when the larger COCA corpus is used.

An anonymous reviewer suggests that I perform the same searches reported in Table 4 for all of the verbs in Tables 1 and 2, but this is not easy to do, because we are only interested in uses of each verb that involve a theme and a recipient, since again, the semantic properties of the ditransitive have to be satisfied. Yet many of the verbs in Tables 1 and Table 2 are frequently used without an animate recipient. For example, in order to compare *transfer* and *send*, we would need to know the *relevant* base-rates of these verbs. Note that *transfer* can readily occur intransitively, or transitively with an inanimate goal (*She transferred (the box) to Chicago*), and *send* can be used transitively with an inanimate goal (*She sent the box to Chicago*). These uses are not relevant to the proportion of datives used despite conditions being better suited to the ditransitive, because these uses don't fit the semantic requirements on the ditransitive construction. But to categorize all uses of each verb in a 400 million-word corpus by hand was prohibitively time consuming.[5]

---

5. It would certainly be worth investigating how general this phenomenon is. I find the following contrasts to pattern the same as *explain* vs. *tell*. In doing a more thorough investigation, one needs to be careful to control for pragmatic felicity. Word frequency is also a issue, since we know that higher frequency words are generally judged better; this factor would work against the hypothesis, since alternating verbs tend to be higher frequency verbs.

  a. *She returned the shirt to me.*
  b. *#She gave the shirt to me.*

  a. *They transferred the film rights to her.*
  b. *#They sent the film rights to her.*

Note that in the case of *explain* and *tell* I have assumed that the overwhelming majority of both verbs involve a theme (something told or explained) and an animate recipient of the information. This assumption allows the data in Table 4 to be usefully analyzed.

8. Other options are available to non-alternating verbs

Notice that instances of (V NP PP) datives, with pronominal recipients and non-pronominal themes, are relatively rare (Table 3). And yet since recipients are animate and animates are often pronominal, and since themes are typically inanimate and inanimates are somewhat less likely to be pronominal, it is likely that the relevant contexts are themselves not altogether uncommon.

We know that English speakers overall are much more likely to produce shorter arguments before longer arguments, animate arguments before inanimate arguments, and pronominal arguments before non-pronominal arguments (Wasow 2002; Bresnan et al. 2005). Non-alternating verbs *do* appear relatively more often in the dative than alternating verbs in ways that buck these trends, but these verbs are not renegades entirely in their distribution: V NP PP datives, even with non-alternating verbs, are fairly rare in this circumstance.

8.1. *"Heavy NP shift"*

Interestingly, English offers speakers a reasonable alternative solution when speakers are faced with a pronominal recipient, a non-pronominal theme, and a non-alternating verb. Speakers may order the arguments using a "heavy NP shifted" version of the dative construction to produce: V PP NP. This allows the general trends of the language to be respected. It turns out that the heavy NP shifted version of the dative is more common among verbs that do not alternate, when the information structure would otherwise suit the ditransitive.

For example, as shown in Table 5, despite the fact that *tell* is overall more than five times as likely to occur as *explain* overall, it is *explain* that is 53 times more likely to occur with a pronominal recipient in heavy NP shift construction (106 vs. 2).

Table 5. *Comparison of alternating* tell *with non-alternating* explain *in the "heavy NP shifted" dative. COCA corpus.*[6]

	Heavy NP shift Dative: [v] [to <definite pronoun>] <lexical NP>	Overall frequency of V (assuming three argument sense)
Tell	2	166,627
Explain	106	31,886

It turns out that non-alternating verbs have other options as well. In fact, there are three other logical possibilities that present themselves beyond the situation already considered in (A):

(A) The single construction that non-alternating verbs occur in should be used in a wider range of contexts than it is for verbs that alternate.
(B) There may be a third (fourth or fifth) construction that is used when the non-occurring alternant construction would otherwise be preferred.
(C) Non-alternating verbs may fail to be appropriate in the situations that would strongly prefer the alternant construction, due to a semantic restriction on their meaning.
(D) A different verb may be used in the appropriate construction instead.

These possibilities are not mutually exclusive, and in fact there is reason to believe that each factor plays a role. We consider them each in turn.

8.2. *Another preempting construction*

Completely monogamous verbs are quite rare. Dative verbs that do not combine with the ditransitive often appear in still other constructions. For example, many "non-alternating" verbs, including *present, provide, entrust*—which are among the ones Stefanowitsch (this volume) considers—readily appear with a direct object recipient and a prepositional theme as in the following examples from the COCA:

(36) *These findings present us with the challenge of making these activities*

(37) *provide them with the tools to perform confidently when interviewed.*

(38) *If you entrust me with the presidency, I will fight for you.*

The "provide with" construction potentially offers evidence of statistical preemption in exactly the way that the dative does. The only difference is that only the dative has traditionally been assumed to "alternate" with the ditransitive construction. But traditional alternations such as the dative-ditransitive need not take on an outsized role in our theorizing (Goldberg 2002). The data in

---

6. The probabilities of a shifted *or* non-shifted dative, given that the context would otherwise be as suitable for a ditransitive should ultimately be combined to provide evidence of statistical preemption, as follows:

P (dative (shifted or not) | context at least as suitable for the ditransitive)

This would yield a probability of .99 for *explain* (240/241) and a probability of .01 for *tell* (72/3782).

Table 6 provide straightforward evidence that the "provide with" construction statistically preempts the ditransitive construction, insofar as the probability of witnessing the "provide-with" construction when a ditransitive would otherwise be appropriate approaches 1 for these verbs.

Table 6. *Comparison of the "provide with" and ditransitive constructions when the recipient is pronominal and the theme is not.*

"non"-alternating verbs that alternate with "provide with" construction	A. "Provide with": [v] [definite pronoun] with [lexical NP] e.g. "she provided him with a pencil"	B. Ditransitive [v] [definite pronoun] [lexical NP] e.g. ?"she presented him a pencil"	C. P(A | A or B)
provide	1541	7	.99
entrust	46	0	1
present	613	37	.94

8.3. Non-occurrence of the ditransitive for semantic reasons

Option C raised another possibility. Some verbs do not alternate because their semantics is inappropriate. For example, once we recognize that the prepositional dative is part of a broader "caused-motion" construction, it is clear that many verbs that convey motion, but not transfer or means of transfer, only occur in the "caused-motion" construction. *Put* is such a case:

(39) a. *She threw the blanket to Paul.*
 b. *She threw the blanket to the pole.*
 c. *She threw the blanket on the pole.*
 d. *She put the blanket on the pole.*

(40) **She put the pole the book.*

Speakers do not require preemptive evidence to learn not to produce (40), because the semantics of *put* makes it ill-suited for the ditransitive. The semantic properties of the verb must be compatible with the semantic constraints on the construction in order for the verb to appear in the construction (Ambridge et al. 2009; Goldberg 1995; Gropen et al. 1991). The "restriction" on *put* is not semantically arbitrary, so it is a different type than we set out to address (cf. 1 to 3).

8.4. Another verb statistically preempts a particular verb in a given construction

There is one final situation to be considered, that outlined in option (D). Another verb may be used if a particular construction is appropriate in a given discourse but a particular verb does not occur in that construction. It is difficult to quantify how often this happens, since it is hard for both researchers and learners to tell when a particular verb is not used but would have been appropriate. At the same time, this surely does happen, and when it does, it provides evidence relevant for statistical preemption. For example, it is widely accepted that *kill* preempts the causative use of *die*, because *kill* is consistently heard in the transitive construction when one might have otherwise expected to hear *die* (McCawley 1978).

(41) **The man died the duck.*

(42) *The man killed the duck.*

That is, the probability of witnessing *kill*, given contexts in which someone is understood to die by means of direct causation—i.e., contexts where the simple causative and the verb *die* would otherwise be appropriate—is quite high:

(43) P(transitive *kill* | direct causation and *die*)

9. Conclusion

To conclude, just the sort of corpus evidence that would be required for statistical preemption to be viable is available to learners. This is clear once we recognize that the relevant probability for construction CxB to preempt construction CxA is:

P(CxB | context that would be at least as suitable for CxA)

When this probability is high, there is evidence for statistical preemption. Learners' *confidence* that CxB statistically preempts CxA increases logarithmically, as the frequency increases of CxB being witnessed in a context that would otherwise be at least as suitable for CxA. Boyd and Goldberg (to appear), moreover, find that speakers may be able to extend evidence gleaned from statistical preemption to other members of the same morpho-semantic-phonological class.

Future research is required to determine whether confidence must merely be above some threshold, or whether confidence actually continues to increase logarithmically as the number of tokens increases. We also need to know how stable the probability and relative confidence levels are across corpora. Ultimately it will be important to determine how probability and confidence combine to yield speaker judgments of ill-formedness. Another question concerns the age at which learners receive sufficient input to make statistical preemption viable. A non-trivial amount of data is required, and so we might expect the effects of statistical preemption of words in particular constructions to emerge relatively late (see Brooks and Tomasello 1999 for relevant age effects).

As Stefanowitsch (this volume) suggests should be the case, there *is* evidence that verbs that are arbitrarily yoked to a single construction display a greater willingness to exploit that single construction in a broader range of discourse contexts. But constructions do not end up varying *dramatically* in their information structure properties because "non-alternating" verbs generally have other options that allow them to avoid extending a construction much beyond its normal comfort zone. In particular, there are sometimes ways to use a target construction without violating its general constraints (e.g. "heavy NP" shifted version of the dative); there often exists a third construction that can be used instead (e.g. the "provide with" construction); and speakers sometimes use a distinct verb that *can* readily appear in the better-suited construction (e.g. causative *kill* instead of *die*). Thus languages tend to find reasonable solutions to multiple interacting constraints.

While much of language is semantically and historically motivated, there remain pockets of idiosyncrasy that speakers must learn. An important fact about language is that constructions are often in competition with one another when speakers produce (and comprehend) utterances (Bates & MacWhinney 1987). Statistical preemption of one construction by one or more other constructions provides an important factor in the learning of arbitrary distributional restrictions.

Received 21 May 2010   *Princeton University*
Revision received 27 July 2010

References

Adams, Douglas. 1979. *Hitchhiker's guide to the Galaxy.* Harmony Books.
Adams, Douglas. 1993. *Mostly harmless.* Hitchhiker's Trilogy, No. 5. New York: Ballantine Books.
Ambridge, Ben, Julian M. Pine, Caroline F. Rowland, Rebecca L. Jones & Victoria Clark. 2009. A Semantics-Based Approach to the "No Negative Evidence" Problem. *Cognitive Science* 33(7). 1301–16.
Arnold, Jennifer E., Thomas Wasow, Anthony Losongco & Ryan Ginstrom. 2000. Heaviness vs Newness: The effects of structural complexity and discourse status on constituent ordering. *Language* 76(1). 28–55.
Bates, Elizabeth & Brian MacWhinney. 1987. Competition, variation, and language learning. In Brian MacWhinney (ed.), *Mechanisms of language acquisition.* 157–193. Hillsdale, NJ: Lawrence Erlbaum Associates.
Bolinger, Dwight. 1977. *Meaning and form.* London: Longman.
Bowerman, Melissa. 1996. Argument Structure and Learnability: Is a Solution in Sight? In Jan Johnson, Matthew L. Juge & Jeri L. Moxley (eds.), *Proceedings of the twenty-second annual meeting of the Berkeley Linguistics Society: General session and parasession on the role of learnability in grammatical theory*, 454–468. Berkeley: Berkeley Linguistics Society.
Boyd, Jeremy K. & Adele E. Goldberg. to appear. Learning what not to say: Categorization and preemption in a-adjective production. *Language*.

Braine, Martin D. S. & Patricia Brooks. 1995. Verb argument structure and the problem of avoiding an overgeneral grammar. In Michael Tomasello & William Edward Merriman (eds.), *Beyond names for things: Young children's acquisition of verbs*. 353–376. Hillsdale, NJ: Lawrence Erlbaum.

Bresnan, Joan. 2007. Is syntactic knowledge probabilistic? Experiments with the English dative alternation. In Sam Featherston and Wolfgang Sternefeld (eds.), *Roots: Linguistics in search of its evidential base* (Studies in Generative Grammar 96), 75–96. Berlin & New York: Mouton de Gruyter.

Bresnan, Joan & Marilyn Ford. 2010. Predicting syntax: Processing dative constructions in American and Australian varieties of English. *Language* 86(1). 186–213.

Bresnan, Joan & Jennifer Hay. 2008. Gradient grammar: An effect of animacy on the syntax of *give* in New Zealand and American English. *Lingua* 118(2). 245–259.

Bresnan, Joan, Anna Cueni, Tatiana Nikitina & R. Harald Baayen. 2005. Predicting the dative alternative. Paper presented at the KNAW Academy Colloquium: cognitive foundations of interpretation, Amsterdam.

Brooks, Patricia J. & Michael Tomasello. 1999. How children constrain their argument structure constructions. *Language* 75(4). 720–738.

Brooks, Patricia & Otto Zizak. 2002. Does preemption help children learn verb transitivity? *Journal of Child Language* 29(4). 759–781.

Chouinard, Michelle M. & Eve V. Clark. 2003. Adult reformulations of child errors as negative evidence. *Journal of Child Language* 30(3). 637–669.

Clark, Eve V. 1987. The principle of contrast: A constraint on language acquisition. In Brian MacWhinney (ed.), *Mechanisms of language acquisition*. 1–33. Hillsdale, NJ: Lawrence Erlbaum Associates.

Collins, Peter. 1995. The indirect object construction in English: An informational approach. *Linguistics* 33(1). 35–49.

Erteschik-Shir, N. 1979. Discourse constraints on dative movement. In Suzanne Laberge & Gillian Sankoff (eds.), *Syntax and semantics*. 441–467. New York: Academic Press.

Fellbaum, Christiane. 2005. Examining the constraints on the benefactive alternation by using the World Wide Web as a Corpus. In Marga Reis & Stephan Kesper (eds.) *Linguistic evidence: Empirical, theoretical and computational perspectives*. Mouton de Gruyter, 209–240.

Goldberg, Adele E. 1993. Another look at some learnability paradoxes. Paper presented to the Proceedings of the 25th Annual Stanford Child Language Research Forum. Stanford, 1993.

Goldberg, Adele E. 1995. *Constructions: A construction grammar approach to argument structure*. Chicago: Chicago University Press.

Goldberg, Adele E. 2002. Surface generalizations: An alternative to alternations. *Cognitive Linguistics* 13(4). 327–356.

Goldberg, Adele E. 2006. *Constructions at work: The nature of generalization in language*. Oxford: Oxford University Press.

Green, Georgia M. 1974. *Semantics and syntactic regularity*. Bloomington, Indiana: Indiana University Press.

Gropen, Jess, Pinker Steven, Michelle Hollander & Richard Goldberg. 1991. Syntax and semantics in the acquisition of locative verbs. *Journal of Child Language* 18(1). 115–151.

Hovav, Malka Rappaport & Beth Levin. 2005. Are dative verbs polysemous? Paper presented to the Linguistics Colloquium, Princeton University, February 17, 2005.

Levin, Beth. 1993. *English verb classes and alternations*. Chicago: Chicago University Press.

McCawley, James. 1978. Conversational implicature and the lexicon. In Peter Cole (ed.) *Syntax and semantics 9: Pragmatics*. 245–259. New York: Academic Press.

Oehrle, Richard. 1975. The Grammatical Status of the English Dative Alternation. Cambridge, MA: MIT PhD dissertation.

Pinker, Steven. 1984. *Language learnability and language development*. Cambridge, MA: Harvard University Press.

Pinker, Steven. 1989. *Learnability and cognition: The acquisition of argument structure*. Cambridge, MA: MIT Press.

Pollard, Carl Jesse & Ivan Sag. 1987. *Information-based syntax and semantics*. Stanford: CSLI.

Saxton, Matthew. 1997. The Contrast Theory of negative input. *Journal of Child Language* 24(1). 139–161.

Stefanowitsch, Anatol. 2008. Negative entrenchment: A usage-based approach to negative evidence. *Cognitive Linguistics* 19(3). 513–531.

Suttle, Laura and Adele E. Goldberg. to appear. The partial productivity of constructions as induction. *Linguistics*.

Thompson, Sandra. 1995. The iconicity of "dative shift" in English: Considerations from information flow in discourse. In Marge E. Landsberg (ed.), *Syntactic iconicity and linguistic freezes: the human dimension* (Studies in Anthropological Linguistics 9). 155–175. Berlin & New York: Mouton de Gruyter.

Wasow, Thomas. 2002. *Postverbal Behavior*. Stanford: CSLI.

Embodied motivations for metaphorical meanings*

*Marlene Johansson Falck and
Raymond W. Gibbs, Jr.*

Abstract

This paper explores the relationship between people's mental imagery for their experiences of paths and roads and the metaphorical use of path and road in discourse. We report the results of two studies, one a survey examining people's mental imagery about their embodied experiences with paths and roads, with the second providing a corpus analysis of the ways path and road are metaphorically used in discourse. Our hypothesis is that both people's mental imagery for path and road, and speakers' use of these words in metaphorical contexts are strongly guided by their embodied understandings of real-world events related to travel on paths and roads. The results of these studies demonstrate how bodily experiences with artifacts partly constrains not only how specific conceptual metaphors emerge, but how different metaphorical understandings are applied in talk about abstract entities and events.

Keywords: Metaphor; Embodied simulation; Psycholinguistics; Corpus linguistics.

1. Introduction

How do our bodily experiences motivate metaphorical meaning? Read the words *path* and *road* when they are used in the two different metaphorical contexts below, and consider whether they convey the same meaning.

---

* Acknowledgement: The study was made when one of the authors, Marlene Johansson Falck, was a postdoctoral fellow in the Department of Psychology at the University of California, Santa Cruz (UCSC), and funded by the Swedish Research Council. Send correspondences to: Raymond W. Gibbs, Jr. Dept. of Psychology University of California Santa Cruz, Santa Cruz, CA 95064, USA. Email ⟨gibbs@ucsc.edu⟩.

(1) The Spaniard lost 10–8 6–3 2–6 8–6 to Charlie Pasarell in 1967. And even if Agassi survives his first test, his **path** to a second successive final is strewn with trip wire, with former champions Boris Becker and Michael Stich top seed Pete Sampras and powerful ninth seeded Dutchman Richard Krajicek all in his half of the draw. [emphasis ours]

(2) The learner who is well on the **road** to being a competent reader does bring a number of things to the task, a set of skills and attributes many of which are still developing. He or she brings good sight and the beginnings of visual discrimination. [emphasis ours]

The meaning of *path* may be appropriate in (1) because of the uneven nature of Agassi's journey toward winning the tennis match, while *road* seems apt in (2) because the journey toward becoming a competent reader is well-established, and metaphorically well-travelled. The question explored in this article is whether people's experiences with different real-world paths and roads are predictable of how speakers use these two terms in talking about metaphorical journeys. We report the results of two studies, one a survey examining people's mental imagery about their embodied experiences with paths and roads and another a corpus analysis of the ways *path* and *road* are metaphorically used in discourse. Our hypothesis is that both people's mental imagery for *path* and *road*, and speakers' use of these words in metaphorical contexts are strongly guided by their embodied understandings of real-world events related to travel on paths and roads.

Previous corpus linguistic studies show that metaphorical uses of *path*, *road*, as well as *way*, are not only structured according to primary/conceptual metaphors such as ACTION IS MOTION, LIFE/A PURPOSEFUL ACTIVITY IS A JOURNEY, and PURPOSES ARE DESTINATIONS, but also appear to be influenced by people's embodied experiences with the specific concepts that these terms refer to in their non-metaphorical uses (Johansson Falck 2010, in press a). Thus, both similarities and differences between real world paths, roads and ways are reflected by how metaphorical paths, roads and ways are described both by the kinds and frequencies of obstacles that people face on these journeys, and the kinds of actions people engage in, on, or near metaphorical paths, roads or ways. These findings highlight the possibility that both similarities and differences between people's experiences of paths and roads in everyday life should influence the specific discourse functions of *path* and *road* as metaphor vehicles.

But there is still the need, in our view, to better establish a motivating link between people's real-world experiences of paths and roads and specific patterns of how *path* and *road* are used metaphorically in discourse. We more closely examined this possible connection by first collecting people's intuitions about their embodied experiences of paths and roads, and then using these nonlinguistic data to make predictions about extensive patterns of metaphorical *path* and *road* in the *British National Corpus (BNC)*. This strategy of studying people's folk ideas about some bodily or real-world experience and then using that data to predict people's metaphorical language use has been productively exploited in several previous psycholinguistic studies (Gibbs 1992; Gibbs et al. 1994). Yet the present studies extend previous work in psycholinguistics by applying the results from a psychological survey to corpus data, particularly in regard to the way journeys are perceived in path and road events, which provides a better reflection of ordinary metaphorical language use than that typically studied in psycholinguistic experiments.

At the same time, the present studies were motivated by emerging ideas in both cognitive linguistics and psychology that people's use and understanding of both metaphorical and non-metaphorical language is guided by processes of embodied simulation (Bergen 2007; Gibbs 2006a, 2006b; Gibbs & Matlock 2008). Most generally, an embodied simulation is understood as the "reenactment of perceptual, motor, and introspective states acquired during interactions with world, body, and mind" (Barsalou 2008: 618). Much behavioral and neuroscience research demonstrates how conceptual processing involves sensorimotor simulations (Gibbs 2006a). These experimental studies indicate that people's recurring embodied experiences often play a role in how people tacitly make sense of many metaphoric words and expressions.

For example, people's mental imagery for metaphorical phrases, such as *tear apart the argument*, exhibit significant embodied qualities of the actions referred to by these phrases (e.g., people conceive of the "argument" as a physical object that when torn apart no longer persists) (Gibbs et al. 2006). Wilson and Gibbs (2007) showed that people's speeded comprehension of metaphorical phrases like *grasp the concept* are facilitated when they first make, or imagine making, in this case, a grasping movement. Bodily processes appear to enhance the construction of simulation activities to speed up metaphor processing, an idea that is completely contrary to the traditional notion that bodily processes and physical meanings are to be ignored or rejected in understanding verbal metaphors (cf. Gibbs 1994). Furthermore, hearing fictive motion expressions implying metaphorical motion, such as *The road goes through the desert*, influences people's subsequent eye-movement patterns while looking at a scene of the sentence depicted (Richardson & Matlock 2007). This suggests that the simulation used to understand the sentence, in this case involving a particular motion movement of what the roads do, interacts with people's eye movements.

Experimental findings like these emphasize that people may be creating partial, but not necessarily complete, sensorimotor simulations of speakers' metaphorical messages that involve moment-by-moment "what must it be like" processes, such as grasping, that make use of ongoing tactile-kinesthetic experiences (Gibbs 2006b). These simulation processes operate even when people encounter language that is abstract, or refers to actions that are physically impossible to perform, such as "grasping a concept" because people can metaphorically conceive of a "concept" as an object that can be grasped. One implication of this work is that people do not just access passively encode conceptual metaphors from long-term memory during online metaphor understanding, but perform online simulations of what these actions may be like to create detailed understandings of speakers' metaphorical messages (Gibbs 2006b). We maintain that these simulation processes are also prominent in people's use and understanding of expressions like *his path to a second successive final is strewn with trip wire* in reference to Agassi' metaphorical journey to a tennis tournament championship as seen in (1). Thus, people's embodied simulation in regard to their imaginative understandings of traveling along different paths and roads provides an important constraint on what gets mapped in various metaphorical instances of *path* and *road*.

Another motivation for the work presented here concerns the most appropriate level of generality in explaining patterns of metaphorical language use, in this case the use of *path* and *road* as metaphorical vehicles in discourse. For example, a traditional view of conceptual metaphor theory might presume that people's use of *path* and *road* in metaphorical ways depends on the recruitment of entrenched conceptual metaphors, such as, again, ACTION IS MOTION, LIFE/A PURPOSEFUL ACTIVITY IS A JOURNEY, and PURPOSES ARE DESTINATIONS. Conceptual, and/or primary metaphors, may offer an important set of general constraints on people's thinking of and talking about metaphorical journeys, but these conceptual entities do not explain exactly why *path* and *road* are used in specific, and different metaphorical ways in discourse (Johansson Falck 2010).

For example, the idea that LIFE IS A JOURNEY, and its entailment that physical progress along some path/road is progress toward some metaphorical destination, does not explain why *path* seems appropriate in (1), with *road* being most appropriate in (2) above. But viewing conceptual metaphors as embodied simulations, guided by the specific words used by speakers and writers, provides far more details about the motion along the path/road, and the types of obstacles likely encountered along the way, inferences that seem present in people's different metaphorical uses of *path* and *road*. In this way, our preferred hypothesis on embodied simulations offers a more detailed constraint on metaphorical language use that is still quite general, but operates in a more nuanced manner depending on whether the simulations involve people's imaginative understandings of real-world paths or roads, and not just journeys more generally.

A complementary theoretical perspective with our own embraces the idea that varied metaphorical patterns of vehicle pairs, such as the German terms *Weg* (i.e., *path*) and *Bahn* (i.e., *course*), and many other uses of metaphor, are best explained in terms of the local interactions between the discourse participants, and not at the level of pre-existing conceptual analogies or metaphors (Zinken 2007). More specifically, this view maintains,

"the common ground for the negotiation of a figurative interpretation is the stereotypical encyclopaedic knowledge accessed by conventional lexical concepts associated with the vehicle. We should therefore expect that extended meanings are motivated by the particular conventions associated with a lexical item. The assumption that discourse metaphors are form-specific leads to the prediction that different lexical items with similar or overlapping conventional usages, which belong to the same superordinate category function differently as metaphor vehicles." (Zinken 2007: 451).

Evidence in favor of this alternative perspective comes from a corpus study in German that examined the metaphorical function of different vehicle pairs, including *Weg* (i.e., *path*), and *Bahn* (i.e., *course*). Most generally, people use these two terms differently in metaphorical contexts, with *Weg* primarily referring to the effort used to attain goals, and *Bahn* referring to a pre-determined trajectory followed to reach some metaphorical destination. Zinken suggests from these findings, and from the analysis of other vehicle pairs, that closely similar words often have quite different metaphorical functions, which do not arise from habitual analogies or conceptual metaphors per se, but emerge as specific form-meanings pairings between speakers (i.e., "conceptual pacts") in different conversational interactions.

We agree that people's conversational interactions are important in the ways words are used, metaphorically or otherwise, with participants sometimes clearly negotiating the way a word is to be used and understood in specific situations (Clark 1996; Gibbs 1999). But Zinken's (2007) work did not actually explore people's real conversational interactions or how various "conceptual pacts" were established for *path* and *course* or any other vehicle pairs studied. Zinken also limited his analysis to only so-called "active metaphors" that required "meta-lexical awareness" as when "the author made use of an interference between lexical concepts" by including a "tuning device" such as "so to speak," or inverted commas (Zinken 2007: 452). In this way, Zinken did not explore the full range of how any of the vehicle terms he studied were more completely used in discourse. Coherences between patterns at the level of lexical metaphor were not discussed and systematic correspondences at other levels of organization were dismissed as "post-hoc artefact[s] of sorting utterances on the part of researcher[s]" (Zinken 2007: 461) or as an additional layer of analogical schemas that may not be psychologically real.

For these reasons, we suggest that Zinken's theoretical emphasis on conceptual pacts downplays a key, intermediate level of analysis between abstract conceptual metaphors and local discourse interactions. Our studies explicitly sought evidence for an intermediate level of constraint on metaphor in terms of people's understandings of real-world artifacts (i.e., paths and roads) as shaped by embodied simulation processes.

2. Study 1: People's imagery for paths and roads

We first explored people's embodied understandings of paths and roads by asking them to imagine themselves "being on a path" or "being on a road" and then giving their ratings to several statements about their mental imagery for these experiences. Our general expectations were that people would give different responses to some of these questions about paths and roads, especially in regard to the types of actions they could make, and what types of properties they typically associated with paths and roads.

2.1. Methods

2.1.1. *Participants.* Twenty-four undergraduate students in Psychology at the University of California, Santa Cruz participated for course credit.

2.1.2. *Materials and procedure.* Participants were given a booklet that first asked them to create a mental image of "being on a path" and then, on the next page, to form a mental image of "being on a road." Following this, the participants turned the page and saw a series of questions, each of which could be answered by circling either the word *path* or *road*. These questions, shown in Table 1, were designed to elicit people's intuitions about their bodily experiences with paths and roads. The entire task took people only about 5 to 10 minutes to complete.

Table 1. *Proportion of responses to mental image questions in Study 1*

	Path	Road
Which is more likely to have obstacles along the way?	.58	.42
Which is more likely to be straight?	.16	.84
Which is more likely to go up and down?	.71	.29
Which is more likely to be wide?	.04	.96
Which is more likely to be paved?	.04	.96
Which is more likely to go through problematic terrain?	.87	.13
Which is more likely to take you to a specific destination?	.21	.79
Which is more likely to make you move fast?	.13	.87
Which is more likely to move you along in an aimless way?	.79	.21
Which is more likely for you to enjoy traveling?	.83	.17
Which is more likely for you to stop every now and then?	.83	.17
Which is more likely for you to be driving on?	.00	1.00
Which is more likely for you to be biking on?	.54	.46
Which is more likely for you to be moving along on foot?	1.00	.00

2.2. Results and discussion

Table 1 presents the proportion of times participants selected either *path* or *road* as answers to the 14 different questions. Chi-square statistical analyses on these data revealed that people thought of roads as being straighter than paths, $\chi^2 (1) = 10.67, p < .001$; paths as being more up and down than roads, $\chi^2 (1) = 4.17, p < .05$; roads as being much wider than paths, $\chi^2 (1) = 20.17, p < .001$; roads as being more paved than paths, $\chi^2 (1) = 20.17, p < .001$; paths as having more problematic terrains than roads, $\chi^2 (1) = 15.08, p < .001$; roads as leading to specific destinations more than paths, $\chi^2 (1) = 8.17, p < .01$; roads as being able to move fast on more so than paths, $\chi^2 (1) = 13.5, p < .001$; paths as being more aimless in their direction than roads, $\chi^2 (1) = 8.17, p < .001$; paths being more enjoyable to travel on than roads, $\chi^2 (1) = 10.67, p < .001$; paths as something one stops on more often than roads, $\chi^2 (1) = 10.67, p < .001$; roads as being something you drive on more than paths, $\chi^2 (1) = 24.0, p < .001$; and paths as being something you travel on foot more so than roads, $\chi^2 (1) = 24.0, p < .001$. The differences in people's choices of path and road for the obstacles and biking on questions were not statistically significant.

These results offer a compelling picture of the differences in people's embodied understandings of the artifacts paths and roads. Most generally, people think of paths as being more problematic to travel on, more up and down, more aimless in their direction, something that you stop on more often, and something you travel on foot significantly more often than is the case for roads. On the other hand, roads are viewed as straighter, wider, paved, leading to a specific destination, and something you drive along far more than is the case for paths.

One way of characterizing these findings is in terms of what paths and roads afford in terms on their possible, relevant bodily actions (Gibson 1979). Under this view, people do not perceive paths and roads apart from the actions they could possibly perform with each of these artifacts. Our perceptual systems evolved to facilitate the interaction with a real, three-dimensional world, so that perception is not a purely visual experience, taking place in the brain, but an act of the entire organism through guided exploration of the environment. People's knowledge of paths and roads, therefore, is deeply intertwined with the possible embodied possibilities that each of these artifacts affords, called "affordances," and is not simply a static catalogue of perceptual features of paths and roads. Under this view, motion should be highly relevant for participants' experiences of both paths and roads, but driving and heading for a specific destination are more relevant to people's experiences of roads, while walking, being aimless, and traveling on difficult terrains are more relevant to their experiences of paths.

Overall, the results of Study 1 demonstrated that people's understandings of paths and roads focus on what appears to be on the more central rather than peripheral aspects of their bodily actions relevant to these real-world artifacts (e.g., on driving, but not walking, on roads, and on walking, but not driving, on paths etc.). Traveling along paths is clearly different in important ways from that of roads. There is, however, a simple alternative explanation for the findings of Study 1 that is worth some consideration. People's different intuitions about paths and roads may be due to their retrieval of the conventional, semantic meanings for the words *path* and *road* and not from their embodied experiences with paths and roads. Of course, there may be links between people's understanding of word meanings and their experiences of the real-world referents for these words. Speakers may actually build richer understandings for the concepts of path and road given their vast experiences with the words *path* and *road* in different contexts, both metaphorical and otherwise.

Cognitive linguistic research on metaphor has not generally focused sufficiently on the role of linguistic meaning in the creation and continued use of metaphorical concepts, because of its strong emphasis on the experiential grounding of linguistic structure and behavior (Gibbs & Tendahl in press). To some extent, Zinken's (2007) project correctly attempts to highlight the significance of linguistic interaction in how people come to metaphorical understandings of different words. Despite our concerns about the limitations of his study, we fully agree that language use is a critical constraint on the way people conceive of different real-world entities (cf. Clausner and Croft 1997), including the artifacts of paths and roads.

We evaluated the specific idea that people's intuitions about their experience with paths and roads comes exclusively from their understandings of the conventional meanings of the words *path* and *road*. Determining the contents of any word meaning in people's mental lexicon is quite challenging. Nonetheless, we can look at the ways communities of people define *path* and *road* by examining different dictionary entries for these words to see if they contain evidence of the very specific intuitions about path and road observed in Study 1.

We did this by examining the listed senses of *path* and *road* in five dictionaries of American English [e.g., *The American College Dictionary (ACD), The American Heritage Dictionary of the English Language (AHDEL), NTC's Thesaurus of Everyday American English: The Most Practical Resource for American English (TEAE), Webster's New Encyclopedic Dictionary New rev. ed. 1996 (WNED)*, and *Merriam-Webster online dictionary (MW)*]. All the dictionaries first list specific definitions that apply to actual paths and roads (e.g., a *path* is "a way beaten or trodden by feet of men or beasts" and a *road* is "a clearly marked, often paved, way from one place to another," or "a place less enclosed than a harbor where ships may ride at anchor"). But the dictionaries differ in terms of which sense they list first, and the generality of each definition. For instance, some dictionaries first listed meanings of *road* that referred to a constructed way for the passage of vehicles, while others first list those that refer to a roadstead. There was also variation with respect to which definitions were listed. Some dictionaries, but not all, listed definitions that are general enough to be applicable to both concrete and metaphorical uses of a word (e.g., "a route, course, or track in which something moves"), definitions that apply to a roadstead, a railroad/railway, a garden path, or a track, or to metaphorical senses (e.g., "a course of action, conduct or procedure"). Finally, the dictionaries differed with respect to the circularity of their definitions. For instance, one of the dictionaries (*AHDEL*) first defined *path* as a "[a] trodden track or way" and *road* as a "an open way, generally public, for the passage of vehicles, persons, and animals", but then stated that *path* is "[a]ny road, way or track" and *road* is "[a] course or path."

Despite these differences, we examined each of the five dictionaries' entries for *path* and *road* and noted instances where a particular sense was identical to any of the students' strong intuitions about their embodied images of paths and roads obtained in Study 1. Table 2 presents a tally of the cases of overlap between dictionary definitions and participants' responses to the different questions posed in Study 1. For example, Study 1 showed that people viewed roads as being significantly more likely to be straight than were paths (Question 2). Yet none of the dictionaries gave any indication that a *road* was defined as being straight. Similarly, participants in Study 1 viewed paths as being more likely to go up and down than roads, but none of the dictionaries made any mention of this as being a sense of the word *path*. On the other hand, all five dictionaries noted that paths are usually traveled along by foot (Question 4), while four dictionaries stated that people usually drive on roads (Question 12).

Table 2. *Comparison between dictionary definitions and participants' responses to the questions posed in Study 1*

	Study 1	Dictionaries				
		ACD	AHDEL	TEAE	WNED	MW
Question 2 (straight)	road					
Question 3 (up/down)	path					
Question 4 (wide)	road	X			X?	X?
Question 5 (paved)	road	X	X?	X		
Question 6 (probl.terrain)	path					
Question 7 (destination)	road			X		X
Question 8 (move fast)	road					
Question 9 (aimless way)	path					X
Question 10 (enjoy)	path					
Question 11 (stop)	path					
Question 12 (driving)	road	X	X		X	X
Question 14 (on foot)	path	X	X	X	X	X

There were some cases in which the listed definitions for *path* or *road* could lead one to infer some characteristic that was congruent to participants' responses in Study 1. For instance, according to (*MW* and *WNED*), *road*, but not *path*, is "an open way for vehicles, persons and animals" while paths are "trodden" *(MW)* or "formed by repeated footsteps" *(WNED)*. The fact that roads are connected with vehicles and paths formed by footsteps seems to suggest that roads are wider. None of these two dictionaries, however, explicitly say which artifact is wider. Nonetheless, we included the ambiguous cases of inferred understanding in our analysis, but marked these separately as X? to indicate the uncertainty over whether a dictionary really contained that sense and was related to some specific intuition observed in Study 1.

In general, an analysis of the proportion of times that the five dictionaries listed definitions that were congruent with participants' intuitions in Study 1 showed an overlap of 12 out of 60 possibilities (20%), when adopting a strict criterion (e.g., exact match between definition and embodied intuition), and an overlap of 17 out of 60 possibilities (28%), when the ambiguous cases were included. These data are inconsistent with any claim that participants' responses in Study 1 about their images of paths and roads are due simply to people's understanding of the conventional meanings of *path* and *road*. To the extent that dictionaries reflect something of people's conventional understandings of *path* and *road*, the standard meanings of these terms was not nearly rich or extensive enough to account for people's responses in Study 1. We hasten to add, though, that people's broad experiences with the words *path* and *road* may still shape aspects of their understandings of how paths and roads work in the real-world (cf. Johansson Falck in press b). This issue will be discussed later.

3. Study 2: Corpus analysis of path and road

Study 2 provides a detailed analysis of the metaphorical functions of *path* and *road* in discourse as seen in the *British National Corpus (BNC)*. Our general hypothesis, again, was that the metaphorical use of *path* and *road* should reflect people's embodied simulations for their actions related to traveling along paths and roads in the real world. Differences between imaginary paths and roads should result in differences between the metaphorical uses of these terms. We expected to find strong correspondences between people's intuitions of their experiences with paths and roads and their metaphorical uses of the words *path* and *road* in discourse. The participants in Study 1 were United States students, and the discourse examined in Study 2 was British English. Of course, American and British English differ in certain respects, with speakers of both possibly having different metaphorical understandings of *path* and *road*. Yet our basic claim is that the metaphorical uses of *path* and *road* are strongly constrained by specific bodily interactions with path and road artifacts, which do not significantly differ for the US and UK speakers. Thus, Study 2 provides a strong test of the idea that people's use and understandings of *path* and *road* as metaphorical vehicles should be relatively consistent with their embodied, imaginative understandings of the differences between travel along paths and roads.

3.1. *Methods*

We first extracted 1000 random instances of *path* and *road* from the *British National Corpus (the BNC),* along with the surrounding context of 3–5 lines for each of these items. Next, we identified the metaphorical uses of *path* and *road* using *MIP* or the *metaphor identification procedure* (Pragglejaz Group 2007), with the slight modification that we only consulted a 3–5 lines of context, rather than the entire text, in making our metaphorical judgments. If there was ambiguity about this judgment given the short text, we then consulted a larger segment of the text to figure out the contextual meaning of each *path*- or *road*-instance.

At the next stage, we determined the source and target domains associated with each metaphorical use of *path* and *road* by paying close attention to the surrounding context in which each term was employed. This part of the analysis focussed on identifying (a) which source domains and (b) which target domains are described by means of these specific terms.

Finally, we made a more detailed analysis of the *path* and *road* instances that were viewed as referring to the same target domain. In this part of the analysis we focused on comparing the usage patterns of the *path*- and *road*-instances that are used in talk about the same target domain, and on identifying possible qualitative differences between the uses.

3.2. *Results and discussion*

The *MIP* analysis revealed that there were 284 (out of 1000 total) metaphorical uses of *path* (28%). But 40 of these were subsequently removed from the data because they referred to a proper name (e.g., *True Path Party*) or book titles. This left us with a corpus of 244 metaphorical instances of *path* for further consideration. A similar analysis using *MIP* indicated that there were 49 (out of 1000) metaphorical uses of *road* (4.9%), with 7 of these removed from the data given their being employed as proper names or book titles, leaving a 42 metaphorical *road* items.

Our analysis of the source domains was relatively easy in that each metaphorical instance of *path* and *road* (100%) reflected some aspects of TRAVEL/ MOTION (e.g., X is travelling or moving along a path or road).

The identification of the target domains involved a more complicated process. Each instance of *path* or *road* that was used to talk about people's lives and activities was sorted into one category, thus giving rise to the general target domain of COURSE OF ACTION/WAY OF LIVING. But some of these instances more specifically mentioned some type of purpose on the part of the person travelling along the path/road. Instances that belonged in the latter group were analyzed as members of the target domain category PURPOSEFUL ACTIVITY/LIFE. Furthermore, instances that did not refer to a specific type of activity, but rather some kind of development or process were analyzed as belonging to the target domain category DEVELOPMENTS/PROCESSES. Although some of these developments and processes were quite general, many referred to the more specific domains POLITICAL/FINANCIAL DEVELOPMENTS/PROCESSES, and COMPUTER/ MATHEMATICS DEVELOPMENTS/PROCESSES. Instances that did not belong in any of the above groups were categorized as OTHER.

Of course, cognitive linguistic analyses, like this one, face the difficult challenge of articulating the right level of specificity when positing the existence of both target and source domains within conceptual metaphor (Gibbs & Ferriera in press; Kövecses 2010, see also Clausner and Croft 1997). But our analysis clearly acknowledges that the target domains referred to by *path* and *road* metaphors were not completely independent categories, and may best be seen as a hierarchy of domains that ranged from quite general ones, down to ones that referred to very specific activities and processes.

Table 3 presents the proportion of times the various *path*- and *road*-instances fit each of the different target domain categories. The appendix provides examples of the discourse contexts representing each of these categories for *path* and *road*. The contexts in which *path* and *road* were metaphorically used suggest differences in the ways these two terms function as metaphor vehicles. Thus, *path* is used metaphorically most often in reference to COURSES OF ACTION/ WAYS OF LIVING, while *road* is used metaphorically much more in regard to PURPOSEFUL ACTIVITY and POLITICAL/FINANCIAL matters. Statistical analyses showed that, indeed, people talk of *path* significantly more often in relation to a given COURSE OF ACTION/WAY OF LIVING than is the case for *road*, χ^2 (1) = 128.56, $p < .001$; and also speak of *path* more than road in reference to DEVELOPMENT, χ^2 (1) = 18.13, $p < .001$, as well as COMPUTER/MATHEMATICAL DEVELOPMENT

Table 3. *Results of corpus Study 2*

Target domain	Path	Road
Course of Action/Way of living	.58	.12
Purposeful activity	.18	.36
Development	.07	.00
Political/Financial	.06	.52
Computer/Mathematics	.08	.00
Other	.03	.00

more specifically, χ^2 (1) = 20.11, $p < .001$, than they do *road*. However, *road* is used far more in talk about someone's PURPOSEFUL ACTIVITY/LIFE than is *path*, χ^2 (1) = 15.18, $p < .001$, and people speak of *road* more often in reference to POLITICAL/FINANCIAL processes than they do *path*, χ^2 (1) = 13.76, $p < .001$.

A comparison between this corpus linguistic investigation and Study 1 clearly shows that there is a close connection between the metaphorical uses of *path* and *road* and people's mental imagery for paths and roads. First, the focus on travel along the artifacts is shared between the two types of data. Second, the differences between the metaphorical functions of *path* and *road* in the corpus linguistic data are largely coherent with the differences found in the survey. For instance, the tendency for metaphorical uses of *road* to describe people's PURPOSEFUL ACTIVITIES/LIVES (e.g., *the road to riches and power on the grand scale*) is clearly in line with people's imaginative understandings of the road as a more efficient means of transportation than path. To someone who is eager to quickly reach a given goal, travelling along an artifact that is more likely to be wide, straight and paved, and to move people along in a vehicle towards a specific destination, must be a better option than travelling along an artifact that is more closely connected with aimless motion on foot, stopping every now and then, enjoying travelling, and going up and down through problematic terrain. The tendency to use road in talk about complex POLITICAL/ FINANCIAL DEVELOPMENTS/PROCESSES involving many (e.g., *if we continue to move down the road to a residual, extremely selectivist welfare system*) seem to match people's travel in a vehicle on a road better than an individual's travel on foot on a path. Moreover, the tendency to think of paths as artifacts that on which we move along on foot makes *path* more apt for structuring people's experiences of COURSES OF ACTION/WAY OF LIVING than *road*. Our manner of motion on an imaginary path (i.e., we walk in a more haphazard fashion up or down, sometimes enjoying our walk, and sometimes struggling through difficult terrain, and stopping every now and then) is probably much closer to the way we typically move around in our real lives than is manner of motion on an imaginary road where fast and efficient motion towards a given goal is likely. Accordingly, the imaginary path seems to better match the step by step features of metaphorical paths in talk about COMPUTER/MATHEMATICS DEVELOPMENTS/ PROCESSES.

Finally, we compared how *path* and *road* were used in talk about the same target domain, describing COURSES OF ACTION/WAYS OF LIVING, PURPOSEFUL ACTIVITIES/LIVES and POLITICAL/FINANCIAL DEVELOPMENTS/PROCESSES. In this part of the analysis, we specifically examined to what extent *path* and *road* were differentially used in talking about more problematic travel and obstacles, the direction of travel, and the presumed destination of travel, following the main findings from Study 1.

First, we compared instances of *path* and *road* used in talk about COURSES OF ACTION/WAYS OF LIVING. Not surprisingly, *path* was frequently used to talk of more difficult, and varied, difficulties in travel in these contexts (23%), but roads were never used in this way. On the other hand, only 12% of the *path* examples, but 60% (based on only 3 of 5 instances) of the *road* instances included explicit mention about where the artifact leads (i.e., *to eternity, to ruin, to stardom*). Unlike the examples of *roads in* these contexts that tend to lead *to* something, the prepositional phrases in the *path* expressions clearly focus on providing information about a specific COURSE OF ACTION/WAY OF LIVING represented by the path. This is reflected through the use of the prepositions *along* (36%) and *of* (14%) in *path* examples (e.g., *Tanzania's later advance along a socialist path,* or *the path of drinks and drugs/class conflict/Soviet favour/green consumerism*), compared to the use of *to* (9%) which focuses on the end result of someone's ACTIVITY/LIFE (e.g., *He may be setting a youth off down a path to nowhere*). Again, the metaphorical *path* seems less efficient than the metaphorical *road*.

The less efficient quality of people's imaginary paths through their LIVES/ACTIVITIES is consistent with the fact that more than 40% of all *path* instances included implicit or explicit mention of more than one possible path as seen in the use of pronouns such as *this, that, what, which, one* and *many* (e.g., *had to follow this path, it may be difficult to say which path led to success, it was known on what path he would be returning, one path of enquiry leads to,* and *by many paths*), modifiers such as *preferred, alternative, different, favoured* and *wrong* (e.g., *considered the preferred path,* and *is not always the surest path*), and the indefinite article *a* used together with a modifier and path (e.g., *an easy path, a delicate path*).

Overall, then, people use both *path* and *road* when referring to most any sort of COURSE OF ACTION/WAY OF LIVING, but differ in many more specific ways which of these two metaphorical terms are employed in context. We contend that these differences are at least partly, but still significantly, motivated by people's ongoing bodily experiences of traveling along these specific artifacts in the real world. Similar to the results above, this part of the analysis suggests that motion along metaphorical paths referring to PEOPLE'S ACTIVITIES/LIVES involve more difficult terrain, more stopping, and slower progress than does motion along metaphorical roads.

The same differences are seen in the ways that *path* and *road* are used to describe the target domain of PURPOSEFUL ACTIVITIES/LIVES. Again, there were many more mentions of the difficulties associated with travel along *paths* (38%) than *roads* (13%). These difficulties may be related to obstacles in or on the path/road (e.g., *their path to a winning was obstructed by an excellent performance from India,* or *the constant traps and barriers laid by the forces that would block our path and drag us down*), or they correspond to a difficult area that someone or something is leaving or trying to leave e.g., (*[people] seek a path out of divisive ideological camps,* or *break though the barriers of error to seek the road to truth*). Moreover, some of the prepositions with *path*, but none of the prepositions with *road* suggest that there are obstacles on the artifact, or that the area that the path goes through is problematic (e.g., *in the path of, path out of,* and *path through*). For example, in (3) below, the obstacles on the path come in the form of measures that make seeking asylum in the UK difficult.

(3) "Instead of introducing procedures which can be relied upon to identify and protect all those at risk of human rights violations in their own country, Government has introduced a range of measures which create obstacles in the **path** of those seeking asylum in the UK."

Again, paths, but not roads, are connected with choices between alternative courses of action. 21% of the *path* instances with the function of describing PURPOSEFUL ACTIVITIES/LIVES, but none of the *road* cases included words or phrases suggesting that there may be more than one path to achieve a goal (e.g., *only, best, the same, typical, a different path to the same goal*).

The close connection between people's metaphorical uses of *path* and *road* and their embodied experiences with these different artifacts is also evident in the ways these are used in talk of POLITICAL/FINANCIAL DEVELOPMENTS. Study 1 showed that imaginary roads are more likely to be perceived as straight, paved and wide than imaginary paths. From this we may infer that a larger number of people can travel along roads than paths, and that their surfaces are likely to be easier to distinguish from that of the land that they go through than those of paths. In the same way, then, the corpus linguistic study showed that metaphorical roads in POLITICAL or FINANCIAL contexts tend to be travelled by fairly large groups of people as they move according to well-defined, often planned, courses of action, developments or outcomes (e.g., towards *power, communism, socialism, serfdom, ruin, an extremely selectivist welfare system,* or *a republican state*). The groups of people on the *road* are typically referred to in a metonymic way by means of a geographical name, the name of a state, a company or a team etc. (e.g., *Britain, North America, a republican/German state, a royal house,* and *regional governments*). Their taking to the *road* symbolizes the beginning of a given course of action or development (e.g., there are *roads of monopoly, of monetary union, of EMU,* and *of different regional governments having different tax rates*), and their collective character is reminiscent of a vehicle full of people travelling down a real road.

The travel along the *road* towards a given outcome is emphasized by prepositions (e.g., *to*) that suggest motion towards something. 54% of the *road*-instances, but only one of the *path*-instances include such a preposition. Sentence (4) below, for instance suggests that European nations will be taken *to* the monetary union, EMU.

(4) "But West Germany, always cautious about monetary union, has shrugged aside attempts by the Italians to bring forward by several months the start of the inter-governmental conference that will discuss the **road** to EMU."

Unlike imaginary roads, imaginary paths are seen as unpaved, and more difficult to travel on. The less delineated, more aimless, quality of these paths matches the uses of *path* to describe POLITICAL or FINANCIAL DEVELOPMENTS. All the vehicles in these target domain contexts are abstract concepts whose value can change over time (e.g., *currency, production, ratio, costs, planned savings* and *investments, rate of interest, economy, real wages,* and *French capital*). These paths typically move up or down (e.g., *upward* or *downward*, or they are *upside-down U-paths*, or *growth paths*) rather than directed towards something. Neither the paths nor the roads in this type of context are connected with obstacles.

The findings from the psychological survey and the corpus linguistic investigation suggest that people's embodied understandings of paths or roads are quite predictable. When imagining themselves in the context of a real path or road, or when thinking about what it must be like to be located in the context of a metaphorical path or road, people tend to focus on what appears to be central and expected features. For example, Study 1 demonstrated that people imagine that roads are more efficient artifacts to travel along than are paths; the surfaces of roads are less rough than are those of paths (e.g., roads are paved, but not so for paths) and roads are generally considered straighter, faster and wider than paths. Accordingly, the term *road* is more often used in talk about activities that people want to be efficient than paths (e.g., PURPOSEFUL ACTIVITY/LIFE and FINANCIAL/POLITICAL DEVELOPMENTS/PROCESSES), and *paths* are more often used to describe actions or developments that may have a more hesitant, aimless, or step by step, quality than *roads* (e.g., COURSES OF ACTION/WAYS OF LIVING, other types of DEVELOPMENT and paths in COMPUTER/MATHEMATICS DEVELOPMENTS/PROCESSES. *Path* is used in talk about processes and *road* in talk about ends of processes and result. Finally, *path* is more closely connected to choices between different courses of action, compared to the much more efficient and single goal-oriented *road*.

4. Conclusion

Both studies suggest that when thinking about paths or roads in imaginative ways, people are strongly influenced by their interactions with the world around them, and what different artifacts best afford for embodied action. Thus, the details of the travel connected with these artifacts correspond with differences between the patterns involving paths or roads in the two types of data, which involved American students in Study 1 and British English being analyzed in Study 2.

The link between people's embodied understandings of paths and roads and the metaphorical uses of *path* and *road* in discourse has several theoretical implications. First, people's mental imagery for paths and roads and their different metaphorical uses of these terms are both motivated to a significant extent by their embodied understandings of paths and roads as artifacts meant for travel through space and by the specific contexts for travel that these related, but still quite different, artifacts provide. People mentally simulate different kinds of actions in journeys along paths and roads and apply these experiences to shape their in-the-moment metaphorical understandings of abstract actions through the use of *path* and *road*.

Second, the consistent patterns of findings for the psychological survey and the corpus investigation suggest that metaphorical language including terms that refer to artifacts is to some significant extent predictable. The fact that Study 1 employed American English speakers and Study 2 examined discourse from British English speakers also offers greater generality to the predictions we verified. People's metaphorical uses of *path* and *road* do not seem to be motivated by just any experience that they might have of paths or roads, but precisely by those experiences that are related to the functions of these artifacts. If metaphorical uses of other terms that refer to other artifacts are equally influenced by people's perception of these artifacts, then the patterns involving these terms should also be partly predictable from people's embodied understandings of these artifacts, or in terms of what these artifacts afford.

Most importantly, our findings point to the interaction between experiences at various levels of organization in metaphorical thought and language. Traditionally, metaphor theories have tended to focus either on the level of language, or on the level of thought, but not on how patterns at these two levels of organization are integrated (cf. Müller 2008). Zinken's (2007) study investigated the metaphorical functions of related vehicle terms, and speculated that these differences may arise from the interactions between speakers in discourse. But he voiced skepticism about the possibility that metaphorical meanings may be partly motivated by higher level generalizations as part of thought and from embodied experience. As he stated, ". . . it cannot be decided on the grounds of verbal behavioral data whether such general mappings are a psychologically real additional level of analogical schemes, or whether they are a post-hoc artifact of sorting utterances on the part of the researcher" (Zinken 2007: 461).

But our combination of a psychological investigation of people's experiences of paths and roads with an extensive corpus analysis of metaphorical *path* and *road* shows that neither explanations in terms of mappings at the levels of primary or complex metaphor, nor in terms of negotiations between speakers, sufficiently account for the link between metaphorical meaning, mind and world. Converging evidence from the psychological and corpus linguistic surveys indicates that people's perceptions of paths or roads are influenced by their understandings of these artifacts through embodied experience.

On the one hand, the focus on travel through space gives metaphorical *path* and *road* expressions a structure that is coherent both with other metaphorical uses of these terms, and with conventional motion metaphors such as ACTION/CHANGE/TIME IS MOTION, PURPOSES ARE DESTINATIONS, and LIFE/LOVE/PURPOSEFUL ACTIVITIES ARE JOURNEYS. On the other hand, differences between the contexts for travel along these artifacts result in differences between the metaphorical uses of the terms. Without a close connection between the metaphorical functions of *path* and *road* and the anticipations for bodily interaction that paths and roads afford, we are left with no apparent reason for why, for example, *road* is much more frequent in language about PURPOSEFUL ACTIVITIES/LIVES than *path*, and why *path* is more often used in language about, for example, people's WAYS OF LIVING. These differences, therefore, are not simply motivated by common conceptual metaphors or discrete conceptual pacts between speakers, but are significantly rooted in people's embodied simulations of different real-world experiences with artifacts.

However, our empirical findings, and emphasis on embodied simulations, should not be seen as a rejection of other constraints on metaphoric thought and language. People's experiences with language, including different uses of *path* and *road*, may lead them to form metaphorical concepts similar to COURSE OF ACTION/WAY OF LIFE. For example, people hearing repeated instances of path in contexts like "we were prepared to smooth a path of transfer" could facilitate understanding of how *path* can be metaphorically used in thinking about abstract courses of action. Similarly, hearing instances of road such as "they will be well on the road to enjoying reading" may enhance understanding of a specific metaphorical meaning of *road* to refer to PURPOSEFUL ACTIVITY/LIFE. Moreover, similar to culture (cf. Yu 2008: 259), language may partly filter people's bodily experiences. Johansson Falck (in press b), shows that speakers' L1 may function like a lens that influences how they conceive of, and talk about ideas and events metaphorically in their L2.

Nonetheless, the motivation for why we employ path and road for specific metaphorical purposes cannot be explained through a simple induction process from the vast collection of linguistic tokens. The difficulty is that speakers began using path and road to express metaphorical meanings in the first place, and these uses, as we have shown, are not at all arbitrary or from very local speaker-listener negotiations. Instead, the motivations for metaphorical word meanings arise from systematic, bi-directional couplings between embodied experience, thought, and language that are continually shaping one another in the minds of contemporary speakers. It may be difficult to tease apart different types of motivations (e.g., embodied, cognitive, linguistic, pragmatic) for why various words are ultimately used in specific metaphorical ways. At the very least, though, bodily experience provides a major role in how conceptual metaphors emerge and places an ongoing constraint on the ways different metaphorical understandings are applied, in nuanced ways, in talk of varying abstract entities and experiences.

Received 25 February 2011 *Umeå University*
Accepted 20 November 2011 *University of California, Santa Cruz*

Appendix
Examples of *path* and *road* in different contexts

COURSE OF ACTION/WAY OF LIVING

path
and a minority of them proved exceptionally capable. Some of our misgivings proved unfounded. We expected that a number—perhaps an embarrassingly large number—of students would decide that they simply did not like our courses, and we were prepared to smooth the **path** of transfer. In the event, there were a few who wished to leave, and a few others who decided that other initial choices had been mistaken, and who wished to join. In terms of students staying with their decisions, and continuing their studies

road
His quest for glory has caused him to stretch his energies to the absolute limit. And he accepts that he set out on the lonely **road** to stardom too early in life. 'The biggest mistake I made was to start playing professional golf so early,' he explains. 'I turned professional when I was only 16. It was my decision, mainly because I had nothing else to do.

PURPOSEFUL ACTIVITY/LIFE

path
The European central bank cannot function in a political vacuum. If it were to do so, the very existence of the currency union would be placed in jeopardy. The above considerations imply that the **path** to the European currency union is unlikely to be smooth. Concluding remarks The decision to proceed to a currency union and accordingly revise the Rome Treaty was reached on political grounds, just as was the case with the signing of the original Treaty

road
They become readers in the sense of having positive expectations and motivation long before they go to school. They will need to develop skills and to

exercise skills to become competent, independent readers, but they will be well on the **road** to enjoying reading. We are, of course, presuming a great deal. We are thinking of the advantaged children. We are thinking about those children who, whatever their socio-economic background, have parents who have the time, or somehow make the time,

DEVELOPMENT

path
NETWORK GENERAL'S SNIFFER GETS EXPERT EXTENSIONS Network General Corp, Menlo Park, California has enhanced its Distributed Sniffer System, and added Expert Analysis capabilities as the first phase of the product's development **path**. The new Expert Analysis software, which includes automatic problem identification, is claimed to provide three types of diagnostic information: Symptoms, Diagnoses and Explanations. At the lowest level, symptoms to which network managers are alerted include such things as a file

road (no examples)

POLITICAL/FINANCIAL

path
Indeed, as the **path** of economic development over the eighteenth century moved the composition of retained imports away from manufactured goods towards raw materials, the possibility of increasing revenue without harming the productive side of the economy narrowed steadily.

road
in resisting this idea, have become noticeably more enthusiastic of late. But West Germany, always cautious about monetary union, has shrugged aside attempts by the Italians to bring forward by several months the start of the inter-governmental conference that will discuss the **road** to EMU. This week President Mitterrand renewed the call for an early conference. Mr Delors, for whom EMU is the next castle in his European crusade, wants to drive EMU forward too. He hopes to sweeten EMU for the Germans by mixing in

COMPUTER/MATHEMATICS

path
We shall soon see that some good search algorithms involve remembering many states. Thus, if one search **path** turns out to be wrong, the planner can recover and try a different path. A plan is a path in the simulation from its start to a goal.

road (no examples)

References

Barsalou, Lawrence. 2008. Grounded cognition. *Annual Review of Psychology* 71. 230–244.
Bergen, Benjamin. 2007. Experiential methods for simulation semantics. In Monica Gonzalez-Marquez, Irene Mittelberg, Seana Coulson, & Michael J. Spivey (eds.), *Methods in Cognitive Linguistics*. 277–302. Amsterdam: Benjamins.
Clark, Herbert H. 1996. *Using Language*. Cambridge: Cambridge University Press.
Clausner, Timothy & William Croft. 1997. Productivity and schematicity in metaphors. *Cognitive Science* 21(3). 247–282.
Gibbs, Raymond W., Jr. 1992. What do idioms really mean? *Journal of Memory and Language* 31. 485–506.
Gibbs, Raymond W., Jr. 1994. *Poetics of Mind: Figurative Thought, Language, and Understanding*. Cambridge: Cambridge University Press.
Gibbs, Raymond W., Jr. 1999. *Intentions in the Experience of Meaning*. Cambridge: Cambridge University Press.
Gibbs, Raymond W. Jr. 2006a. *Embodiment and Cognitive Science*. Cambridge: Cambridge University Press.
Gibbs, Raymond W. Jr. 2006b. Metaphor interpretation as embodied simulation. *Mind and Language* 21. 434–458.
Gibbs, Raymond W. Jr. & Teenie Matlock. 2008. Metaphor, imagination and simulation: Psycholinguistic evidence. In R. W. Gibbs Jr. (ed.), *The Cambridge Handbook of Metaphor and Thought*. 247–261. Cambridge: Cambridge University Press.
Gibbs, Raymond & Lucianne Ferriera. in press. Do people infer the entailments of conceptual metaphors during verbal metaphor understanding? In Mario Brdar and Milena Fuchs (eds.), *Converging and Diverging Tendencies in Cognitive Linguistics*. Amsterdam: John Benjamins.
Gibbs, Raymond & Markus Tendahl. in press. Coupling of metaphor thought and communication: A reply to Wilson. *Intercultural Pragmatics*.
Gibbs, Raymond, Dinara Beitel, David Harrington, & Paul Sanders. 1994. Taking a stand on the meanings of *stand*: Bodily experience as motivation for polysemy. *Journal of Semantics* 11. 231–251.
Gibbs, Raymond, Jessica Gould, and Michael Andric. 2006. Imagining metaphorical actions: Embodied simulations make the impossible plausible. *Imagination, Cognition, & Personality* 25. 221–238.
Gibson, James. 1979. *The Ecological Approach to Visual Perception*. Boston: Houton Mifflan.
Johansson Falck, Marlene. 2010. Are metaphorical paths and roads ever paved? Corpus analysis of real and imagined journeys. *Review of Cognitive Linguistics* 8. 93–122.
Johansson Falck, Marlene. in press-a. Narrow paths, difficult roads, and long ways: Travel through space and metaphorical Meaning. In Carita Paradis, Jean Hudson, & Ulf Magnuson (eds.), *The Construal of Spatial Meaning: Windows into Conceptual Space*. Oxford: Oxford University Press.
Johansson Falck, Marlene. in press-b. Metaphor variation across L1 and L2 speakers of English: Do differences at the level of linguistic metaphor matter? In Fiona MacArthur, José Luis Oncins Martínez, Manuel Sánchez García, & Ana María Piquer Piriz (eds.), *Metaphor in use: Culture, Context, and Communication*. Amsterdam: John Benjamins.
Kövecses, Zoltán. 2010. *Metaphor: A Practical Introduction* (2nd edition). New York: Oxford University Press.
Müller, Cornelia. 2008. *Metaphors Dead and Alive, Sleeping and Waking: A Dynamic View*. Chicago/London: University of Chicago Press.
Pragglejaz Group. 2007. MIP: A method for identifying metaphorically used words in discourse. *Metaphor and Symbol* 22. 1–39.

Richardson, Daniel & Teenie Matlock. 2007. The integration of figurative language and static depictions: An eye movement study of fictive motion. *Cognition* 102. 129–138.

Wilson, Nicole & Raymond W. Gibbs. 2007. Real and imagined body movement primes metaphor comprehension. *Cognitive Science* 31. 721–731.

Yu, Ning. 2008. Metaphor from body and culture. In R. W. Gibbs Jr. (ed.), *The Cambridge Handbook of Metaphor and Thought*. 247–261. Cambridge: Cambridge University Press.

Zinken, Jörg. 2007. Discourse metaphors: The link between figurative language and habitual analogies. *Cognitive Linguistics* 18. 445–466.

Corpus

The *British National Corpus (BNC), XML Edition* (2007)

Dictionaries with abbreviations

Barnhart, Clarence L (& JessStein?) (eds.). 1955. *The American College Dictionary (ACD)*. New York: Random House.

Bertram, Anne. (ed.). 1995. *NTC's Thesaurus of Everyday American English: The Most Practical Resource for American English (TEAE)*. Lincolnwood, IL: *The National Textbook Company*.

Brown, L. (ed.). 1993. *The Shorter Oxford English Dictionary on Historical Principles (SOEDHP)* (4th edition). Oxford: Clarendon Press.

Rundell, M. & Fox, G. (eds.). 2007. *Macmillan English Dictionary for Advanced Learners, Second Edition (MEDAL)*. Oxford: Macmillan Education.

Merriam-Webster free online dictionary (MW). [accessed 20 September 2011]

Morris, William. (ed.). 1969. *The American Heritage Dictionary of the English Language (AHDEL)*. New York, NY: American Heritage Publishing Company.

Webster's New Encyclopedic Dictionary New Revised Edition. 1996. New York: Black Dog & Leventhal Publishers Incorporated.

The acquisition of the active transitive construction in English: A detailed case study*

Anna L. Theakston, Robert Maslen, Elena V. M. Lieven and Michael Tomasello

Abstract

In this study, we test a number of predictions concerning children's knowledge of the transitive Subject-Verb-Object (SVO) construction between two and three years on one child (Thomas) for whom we have densely collected data. The data show that the earliest SVO utterances reflect earlier use of those same verbs, and that verbs acquired before 2;7 show an earlier move towards adult-like levels of use in the SVO construction and in object argument complexity than later acquired verbs. There is not a close relation with the input in the types of subject and object referents used, nor a close adherence to Preferred Argument Structure (PAS) before 2;7, but both early and late acquired verbs show a simultaneous move towards PAS patterns in selection of referent type at 2;9. The event semantics underpinning early transitive utterances do not straightforwardly fit prototype (high or inalienable) notions of transitivity, but rather may reflect sensitivity to animacy and intentionality in a way that mirrors the input. We conclude that children's knowledge of the transitive construction continues to undergo significant development between 2;0 and 3;0, reflecting the gradual abstraction and integration of the SVO and VO constructions, verb semantics, discourse pragmatics, and the interactions between these factors. These factors are considered in the context of a prototype for the transitive construction.

---

* Acknowledgements: we would like to thank Thomas and his family for taking part in the study, Jeannine Goh and the army of transcribers at the Max Planck Child Study Centre, Manchester for turning the recordings into analysable data, and the editorial team and anonymous reviewers for their helpful comments. This research was funded by the Max Planck Institute for Evolutionary Anthropology, Leipzig. Portions of this work were presented at the 12th International Congress for the Study of Child Language with funding from a British Academy travel grant, Ref no. oc100451. E-mail: ⟨anna.theakston@manchester.ac.uk⟩.

Keywords: *transitive construction, language acquisition, construction semantics, preferred argument structure, prototypes*

1. Introduction

Transitive relations are at the heart of most, if not all, of the world's languages, thus child language researchers face the challenging task of explaining how children acquire the various linguistic devices, such as word order, case marking and subject-verb agreement, and prosody that can express transitive relations. Acquiring the transitive construction[1] means learning not only its syntactic form, but also the range of event types it can be used to encode, with the English transitive subject encompassing a range of semantic roles including agents, instruments, experiencers, and goals, and the object role including patients and themes among others. A number of theorists have argued that transitivity is a matter of degree, and that transitivity relations serve the requirement in discourse to foreground certain information. For example, Hopper and Thompson (1980) attempted to establish parameters for prototypical transitivity and presented a continuum along which 'High' transitivity was demonstrated to correlate, across a wide range of languages, with high potency of an agent, a high level of affectedness of an object, and the extent to which an event can be characterised as an 'action', among other factors. The ability to use the transitive construction in an adult-like way therefore also depends on having knowledge of the broadly applicable pragmatic factors that govern the order of mention of participants in discourse (old information is realised before new, thus new information is more likely to be realised as the object, and given information as the subject, of a transitive SVO clause) and of the appropriate linguistic forms to refer to the various participants (such that new information is typically realised with a lexical noun, whereas given information can be realised pronominally or omitted altogether). DuBois (1987) referred to this pattern, observed in a diverse range of languages, as Preferred Argument Structure (PAS). In addition, it is widely observed cross-linguistically that the subjects of transitive clauses tend to be animate, and often human, whereas objects are much more likely to be inanimate themes and patients (Givón 1983; DuBois 1987; Dowty 1991; Langacker 1991). Thus, an understanding of how different kinds of semantic and pragmatic information map onto the subject and object roles of the transitive construction is necessary to support adult-like use.

---

1. Throughout this paper the term *transitive construction* is used to refer to the active transitive construction containing a single verb with its subject and object arguments, although of course 'transitive' can also refer to multi-verb utterances or those with passive argument structure.

1.1. What are children's early transitive representations like?

Slobin (1982, 1985, see also Pinker 1984) suggested that children approach the acquisition task with biases that privilege the acquisition of some syntactic forms over others—an accessibility hierarchy—favouring prototypical events, in particular agent-patient relations in which an animate agent causes some change of state to an inanimate patient (Slobin's 'manipulative activity scene'). Under this approach, knowledge of the semantic-syntactic correspondences for canonically transitive scenes results in their early acquisition. However, children's early transitive utterances do not always encode prototypical agent-patient relations (Bowerman 1990; Lieven et al. 1997; Ninio 1999) casting doubt on this suggestion, and Slobin has since revised his earlier position as "crosslinguistic diversity precludes a pre-established table of correspondences between grammatical forms and semantic meanings" (Slobin 1997: 282).

Usage-based accounts highlight the low-scope nature of children's early utterances, focusing on initial periods of lexically specific combination (e.g. Tomasello 2003). In this approach, abstract knowledge of structure emerges gradually from concrete representations which are initially specific to particular predicates, in terms of both their semantic and combinatorial characteristics. However, the process of abstraction is not straightforward given that the English transitive construction encompasses such semantically contrasting bedfellows as *Billy pushes the car* [AGENT VERB PATIENT] and *Billy got a book* [GOAL VERB THEME]. From a usage-based perspective, children are assumed to acquire knowledge of the constructions of their language directly from the input to which they are exposed. Thus, they would be expected to acquire a range of semantically varied forms of the transitive construction if these verbs are frequent in the input. However, the process by which they realise that these varied forms are related is not entirely clear, although analogy and structure mapping are thought to be involved. Certainly, children take some time to demonstrate productivity in their transitive usage. English-speaking children are around 3;0 before they are consistently able to use a novel verb learned in an intransitive construction transitively (Tomasello and Brooks 1998; Brooks and Tomasello 1999), and only towards 4;0 can children consistently correct utterances with transitive novel and known low frequency verbs in non-canonical word orders (Akhtar 1999; Matthews et al. 2005). This suggests that children take some time to fully understand how agent and patient roles relate to their respective positions in transitive utterances in production. Although Naigles et al.'s (2009) diary study of eight children shows that the children demonstrate some degree of flexibility in their first transitive verb uses around or before 24 months of age, it is unclear to what extent they were generalising over different verbs as opposed to reproducing patterns of variability in use in their input.

However, in comprehension a rather different story emerges that has led some researchers to conclude that children show very early abstraction. Early studies showed that sentences containing known reversible action verbs with animate agents and patients are comprehended just as accurately by two- and four-year-olds as those with a prototypical animate agent and inanimate patient (de Villiers 1980; Corrigan 1988). Moreover, although two-year-olds comprehend sentences exhibiting the reverse pattern of inanimate agent-animate patient less well, this effect holds only for 'prototypical' verbs: inanimate-animate sentences with verbs low in prototypicality are comprehended just as accurately as those with animate agents (Corrigan 1988). However, as these studies examine known verbs, they do not determine how abstract the children's knowledge is. More recently, novel verb studies using the intermodal preferential looking paradigm have shown that at around two years of age children link transitive sentences with causative rather than non-causative actions (Naigles 1990; Hirsh-Pasek and Golinkoff 1996; Yuan and Fisher 2009). Researchers argue that by attending to the number of noun phrases in a sentence, children can infer the nature of the event (e.g. Landau and Gleitman 1985; Naigles 1990; Fisher 1996, 2002; Lidz et al. 2003). Furthermore, Gertner et al. (2006) demonstrated that 21 month olds could correctly identify the agent and patient of novel reversible causative transitive actions. Although there is some debate over the role of the training phase included in this study in determining the results (see Dittmar et al. 2008a), some level of comprehension appears to precede production by a significant time period.

On the other hand, studies using pointing and act-out methodologies have systematically varied the cues such as animacy, case marking, and word order that co-occur or conflict to indicate the agent and patient of novel reversible transitive actions in English (Ibbotson et al. 2011), English and German (Dittmar et al. 2008b) and English, German and Cantonese (Chan et al. 2009). In these studies, children successfully comprehend reversible transitive sentences at around age 2;6 when all cues work together, but only comprehend in adult-like ways at much later ages when cues are in conflict. These studies suggest that although relatively young children have a grasp of the most common or prototypical forms of the transitive construction in comprehension, they are still piecing together the fully abstract adult-like construction, and this may occur at different rates for different languages (see Ibbotson and Tomasello 2009 for a discussion, and Abbot-Smith et al. 2008 for cross-linguistic differences in production).

To date, studies of children's acquisition of the transitive construction have been limited in a number of ways. Although a large number of experimental comprehension and production studies exist, these largely focus on causative verbs, yet the transitive construction encompasses a wide range of varied semantic event types. On the other hand, analyses of naturalistic corpus data showing that children produce a range of transitive event types from early on (Bowerman 1990; Tomasello 1992; Lieven et al. 1997; Ninio 1999) are limited by the relatively sparse samples available for analysis or, in the case of diary data (e.g. Tomasello 1992; Naigles et al. 2009), by a lack of detailed input data for the children involved. Moreover, none of these studies has systematically examined a single data set for the relation between transitive utterances, the child's previous uses and input for the same verbs as well as their transitive event semantics and patterns of PAS.

In the current study, we test a number of hypotheses regarding acquisition of the transitive construction by systematically examining its development in a densely collected corpus from a single child learning English (Lieven et al. 2009). Unlike previous corpus-based studies, a densely collected corpus has the advantage of significantly increasing the likelihood of sampling low frequency items and uncovering otherwise overlooked patterns of acquisition (Tomasello and Stahl 2004).

1.2. *Aims of the study*

There were three main aims:

1.2.1. *Prior use of related lexical items and constructions.* Our first aim was to test the hypothesis that full SVO transitive utterances will be based on previously produced SV or VO combinations by examining the specific lexical items used in subject and object position in the earliest full SVO utterances. We also consider how transitive verbs acquired during the second half of the third year (2;7 to 3;0) are assimilated by assessing whether early acquired knowledge of the combinatorial properties of transitive verbs (from 2;1 to 2;6) is transferred to newly acquired verbs.

Tomasello (1992) claimed that for one child between the ages of 16 and 24 months, the best predictor of her use of a given verb was her previous use of that same verb rather than her current use of other verbs. The suggestion was that children's complex utterances are built up from earlier uses of the same lexical items. Later studies have sought to investigate this suggestion further and to identify a point in development at which the child's verb use becomes increasingly independent of previous use. McClure et al. (2006) found that at MLU Stage 2, early acquired verbs were used in longer utterances with a greater number of arguments than newly acquired verbs. However, they also report that the first uses of later acquired verbs were longer and more complex than the first uses of early acquired verbs, showing evidence for some generalisation which they attribute to the use of low-scope constructions organised around other word types. Lieven and colleagues' traceback methodology compares a child's utterances to utterances produced previously to determine their degree of similarity. They have demonstrated that although children's early utterances at around 2;0 are relatively creative, much of this creativity can be accounted for in terms of fairly minor changes to previously produced utterances. Over development, children's constructions increase in abstractness (e.g. Lieven et al. 2003, 2009; Dąbrowska and Lieven 2005).

1.2.2. *Verb semantics.* Our second aim was to test whether early transitive utterances pattern according to either the 'high transitivity' event semantics posited for adult language by Hopper and Thompson, or the inalienable transitivity semantics posited by Ninio.

Goldberg (1995, 1999) found that many of children's earliest verb utterances tend to express basic scenes such as someone acting on something forming "the building blocks for much of human cognition" (Goldberg 1999: 203). This view bears some resemblance to Hopper and Thompson's (1980) characterisation of high transitivity and suggests that the earliest transitive utterances may be those that encode a highly volitional agent acting on a highly affected patient (see also Slobin 1985). Ninio (1999) presented a contrasting proposal based on her finding that early VO and SVO utterances with transitive verbs typically involved verbs of obtaining, creation, perception, and ingestion, which score relatively poorly for transitivity. She claimed that these verbs express inalienable transitivity, i.e. a very tight relation between a verb and its object, and assigned them a 'pathbreaking' role in the acquisition of transitivity. In another proposal, Budwig (1995) suggested that children's early concept of agentivity revolves around the notion of control (over others and the environment) as well as incorporating actions on physical objects. Thus, children's early transitive utterances might be organised around a broad notion of agentivity rather than any particular semantically delimited set of verbs. The apparent discrepancies between these accounts mean it is unclear exactly how verb semantics might operate in the child's abstraction of the transitive construction (e.g. see Theakston et al. 2004, Naigles et al. 2009). Interestingly, Brown (2008) offers another way of conceptualising the acquisition of the transitive construction. She argues that in languages such as Tzeltal, children's initial transitive verb vocabularies are dominated by 'heavy' verb forms that, due to their specificity in meaning, do not in any obvious sense correspond to the semantics of the transitive construction in general. However, in languages that allow a high degree of argument ellipsis, highly specific verbs with concrete meanings allow children to recover omitted arguments by restricting the range of possible referents. Thus, it is possible that (in some languages at least) children begin by learning verbs that are tightly tied to very specific object forms, and only gradually extract the more abstract relation between transitive verbs and their objects in general.

Few studies exist that examine the role of verb semantics in the abstraction of the transitive construction. Abbot-Smith et al. (2004) exposed children to transitive sentences containing verbs of caused motion and tested their ability to generalise to novel verbs of (sound and light) emission. Although children generalised at levels similar to those observed when both training and test verbs expressed caused motion (Childers and Tomasello 2001), Abbot-Smith and Tomasello (in press) point out that the emission verbs could have been interpreted as causative, thus verb semantics may play a role in abstraction. Taking a slightly different approach, Ninio (2005) examined the role of semantic similarity in generalisation by noting the different types of direct objects produced in Hebrew-speaking children's earliest transitive VO utterances. She reported that there was very little overlap in the semantic roles of the direct objects produced with each child's first six VO verb types, claiming that semantic similarity is not necessary for generalisation. However, the extent to which children differentiated objects according to the criteria used in the study, and the extent to which the semantics of the utterances overlapped in broader terms such as those posited by Hopper and Thompson (e.g. 'affectedness of the object') is unclear. Taken together, these studies illustrate the considerable difficulties in establishing exactly how children interpret transitive verb meanings and the basis for early generalisation.

1.2.3. *Pragmatic development.* Our third aim was to test whether the child's early transitive utterances reflect PAS in the choice of referent type for, and animacy of, the subject and object roles. We also ask whether, in production, prototypical animate-subject inanimate-object transitive utterances are produced earlier than less prototypical inanimate-subject animate-object transitive utterances.

In addition to acquiring an abstract syntactic transitive construction allowing children to manipulate the roles of subject and object, children must also learn how these arguments should be realised in different pragmatic contexts. A large body of research suggests that in naturalistic contexts children show relatively good sensitivity to PAS from around age 2;0 (e.g. Allen 2000, Guerriero et al. 2001, Clancy 2003), using lexical nouns to encode new information about typically inanimate entities in the object role, and encoding given information with reference to animate agents in the subject role using pronouns (or omitting reference altogether). Tightly controlled experiments, however, suggest that knowledge undergoes development with 2-year-olds showing relatively less sensitivity to the knowledge states of others than 3- and 4-year olds, in particular in their use of pronouns (e.g. Matthews et al. 2006). It is an empirical question how knowledge of syntactic constructions (that may initially be based around pronouns in subject and/or object position) becomes integrated with knowledge of the pragmatic principles governing reference realisation (where use of pronouns is only pragmatically appropriate in contexts where the referent is already known to the interlocutors) and knowledge of PAS (subjects are encoded pronominally and objects as full lexical nouns).

2. Method

2.1. Participants

The data for the study were taken from a dense corpus containing the speech of one child (Thomas) and his mother (Lieven et al. 2009), available from the CHILDES database (MacWhinney 2000). Both participants are monolingual English speakers. The dyad was recorded for an hour five times a week (four audio and one video recording) from age 2;0 until 3;2 and from then on for five hours within one week every month until age 5;0. The recordings were conducted by trained staff from the Max Planck Child Study Centre at the University of Manchester. Thomas's family live in the Manchester area and he is an only child. Thomas's mother is the primary caregiver. At 1;11.14 Thomas's score on the McArthur CDI (Fenson et al. 1994) was at approximately the 25th percentile.

2.2. Transcription

Research assistants transcribed all of the recordings using standard CHAT procedures (MacWhinney 2000). Transcription was subsequently checked twice by trained assistants. Each utterance was linked to the sound file by a second transcriber and any discrepancies resolved. Then each transcript was run through the MOR program and any further errors were corrected.

2.3. Child data

The data used in this study covers the period from 2;1 to 3;0. We first created a master list of all the verbs produced by Thomas from 2;1 to 3;0 that could potentially have been used transitively. We then searched the data from 2;1 to 3;0 using the CLAN programs (MacWhinney 2000) to establish which of these verbs Thomas used in a transitive VO or SVO construction and extracted every multiword utterance in the corpus containing these verbs. We excluded from the analysis all imitations, self-repetitions and utterances containing routines (e.g. nursery rhymes, songs), along with any partially intelligible utterances or those made ambiguous by missing information (e.g. neither a subject nor object was produced), and questions (which, during the early period, are not very productive—see Dąbrowska and Lieven 2005 for an analysis of Thomas's early questions). Complex utterances, produced in increasing numbers from 2;7, were also excluded to allow a more controlled comparison between the earlier and later data. Complex utterances were defined as utterances including full (rather than contracted) modals, relative, temporal and adverbial clauses and uses of the verbs as verbal complements or as matrix verbs[2]. Coding was carried out by the second author. Approximately 65% of the data from 2;7 to 3;0 was coded independently by the first author to calculate reliabilities on the exclusion criteria for complex utterances. Agreement was high (99.4%, Cohen's kappa = 0.982), and for the data included in the reliability check, 23% of utterances were excluded according to the criteria. Each remaining utterance was then categorised according to the construction in which the transitive verb occurred (namely V, SV, VO and SVO). SV utterances included erroneous transitives (e.g. *I want*), as well as correct uses of alternating verbs (e.g. *I'm eating [it]*, *I'm rolling the ball/the ball's rolling*). VO utterances included potentially imperative forms. Each utterance was also coded according to the word type (pronoun [pN], proper noun [PN], or noun phrase [NP]) in subject and/or object position.

For the purposes of analysis, the data were split into two six-month periods from 2;1 to 2;6 and 2;7 to 3;0. The data were aggregated into months, each accounting for around 20 hours of recordings (max 22, min 18), and referred to by age beginning at 2;1 for the data taken from 2;00.12 to 2;01.11, and from then on in monthly samples until 3;0. From 2;7 to 3;0, all verbs were categorised as Old (those verbs appearing in the 2;1 to 2;6 data) or New (those not recorded at all before 2;7).

2.4. *Input data*

For the analyses concerning Thomas's data from 2;1 to 2;6, a sample of the mother's transitive usage was taken from the recordings at 2;4. The input sample was restricted to only those transitive verbs produced by Thomas in the 2;4 data when he began to produce a much wider range of verb types. Matching the input sample to Thomas's sample at 2;4 controls the input down to the child in terms of verb vocabulary and is likely to capture the most frequently produced verbs while ensuring sufficient variation in verb types to provide an overall impression of verb use. Complex utterances were excluded from the input sample as above to allow a direct comparison between the child and input data. Coding was carried out by the second author and approximately 10% of the input sample at 2;4 was coded independently by the first author showing high levels of agreement on the application of the inclusion criteria (94.8%, Cohen's

---

2. Within the usage-based approach, these sentences are instantiations of more complex constructions that are expected to show their own developmental trajectory, although there is likely to be some benefit accrued from the earlier use of the simple transitive SVO construction (see Abbot-Smith and Behrens 2006 for discussion of these ideas).

kappa = 0.892). A similar sample of input was taken from the recordings at 2;10, matched to Thomas's 2;10 verb vocabulary. This allowed comparison with his data from 2;7 to 3;0 controlling for any possible changes in input over development and taking into account the increase in his transitive verb vocabulary during the latter half of his third year.

Each utterance with a transitive verb in the input data was coded according to construction (SV, VO, SVO), the nature of the arguments in subject and object position (pronoun, proper noun, or noun phrase) and, in SVO utterances, the subject and object were coded for animacy (see below for further details).

2.5. Semantic event structure coding (child data 2;1 to 2;6)

We carried out three analyses on the data. First, we coded the verb types (separately for the SVO and VO constructions), based on their first use, according to whether they (a) were associated with highly transitive actions according to the criteria outlined by Hopper and Thompson (H&T), (b) fit Ninio's classes of creation, ingestion, perception, and obtaining denoting inalienable transitivity, or (c) fit neither category (see Appendix A for coding criteria). Coding of the full data set was carried out by the first author and for purposes of checking reliability, by a second trained coder. For further details of the H&T coding scheme and reliabilities, see below. For the Ninio coding, when both coders assigned a verb to one of Ninio's categories, they always chose the same category. Reliabilities calculated on whether or not coders placed individual verbs in one of Ninio's four categories showed a high rate of agreement (SVO 94.1%, kappa = 0.87, VO 92.6%, kappa = 0.80). Note that it was possible for the coders to assign a verb both high transitivity according to H&Ts criteria, and membership of one of Ninio's classes. This happened for four verbs in SVO (*do, pick up, eat* and *drink*) and five verbs in VO (*eat, drink, collect, bring* and *build*).

In our second analysis, we considered early event semantics in more detail by examining the first three utterances produced with each verb type (or fewer if Thomas produced less than three SVO or VO utterances with that verb in total from 2;1 to 2;6). Many verbs can exhibit either high or low transitivity, depending on the nature of their arguments and the context. For example, the verb *hit*, often seen as highly transitive, nevertheless has a rather different meaning in the context *The falling tree hit the ground* in which the subject lacks agency or volition, and the ground may remain relatively unaffected by the action. We coded each utterance according to kinesis, punctuality, volitionality, and affectedness of the object[3]. Again, coding was carried out by the first

---

3. We initially attempted to also code each utterance according to agency and individuation of the object. However, it proved difficult to establish with any accuracy the agency of the sentence subject (due to ambiguities in the assignment of agent potency to inanimate objects

author and a second trained coder. A high rate of agreement was achieved for all categories for SVO (kinesis, 90.6%, kappa = 0.76; punctuality, 90.6%, kappa = 0.81; volitionality, 96.7%, kappa = 0.89; affectedness of object 89.1%, kappa = 0.76) and VO utterances (kinesis, 88.1%, kappa = 0.73; punctuality, 88.2%, kappa = 0.74; volitionality, 85.0%, kappa = 0.56; affectedness of object 87.6%, kappa = 0.75). We also calculated an overall transitivity rating (out of four) for each utterance, such that an utterance scoring highly on all four measures would score four, whereas one scoring low on all measures would score zero. Utterances scoring three or four were deemed to have high transitivity, those scoring two or below to have low transitivity (this measure was used to code high transitivity for the first analysis). Again, there was a high rate of agreement between coders when comparing the binary rating of high/low for each utterance based on these composite scores (SVO 86.9%, kappa = 0.74; VO 89.7%, kappa = 0.79).

For our third analysis, we coded the subject and object arguments of all of Thomas's SVO and VO utterances for animacy and calculated the proportion of animate subjects and objects at each age. To avoid ambiguity, a strict coding scheme was adopted in which animate entities were deemed to be humans or human-like creatures (for example, characters from children's television programmes) and animals, whereas inanimate entities were deemed to be 'things' (including objects such as trains or cars which appear as characters in children's television programmes and move of their own accord), and also included body parts, for example hands, heads, and feet, which, although in a sense are animate, do not move of their own accord. The data was coded by the second author and approximately 20% of the data was coded for reliability by the first author resulting in a 100% rate of agreement.

3. Results: 2;1 to 2;6

3.1. *The distribution of utterances containing potentially transitive verbs across constructions*

From 2;1 to 2;6, Thomas produced 112 verbs in a transitive construction resulting in 1230 utterances with these verbs in the SV, VO and SVO[4] constructions

---

acting as agents, for example cars, trains, soft toys), and the individuation of the object (due to uncertainties about other objects present in the perceptual scene and the late mastery of linguistic means of encoding the definite/indefinite distinction) so these coding categories were removed. Other aspects of H&T's transitivity criteria (aspect, affirmation, mode) were also not easily applied as many of Thomas's early verbs were only produced in stem form, few included negation, and his early utterances typically corresponded to the here-and-now.

4. Thomas produced 2307 tokens of these verbs overall including single word utterances. Thomas's use of SV and VO constructions does not necessarily imply omitted arguments,

Table 1. Verb tokens and types produced with transitive verbs in the SV, VO and SVO constructions from 2;1 to 2;6.

	No. hrs	Verb tokens				Verb types		
		SV (ungrammatical)	VO	SVO	% SVO	SV (ungrammatical)	VO	SVO
2;1	22	3	4	3	30.0	3	4	3
2;2	21	6	20	0	0.0	5	11	0
2;3	22	5 (3)	100	9	7.9	4 (2)	21	7
2;4	22	44 (8)	199	50	17.1	25 (7)	37	12
2;5	22	82 (32)	239	62	16.2	30 (5)	51	19
2;6	18	49 (10)	271	84	20.8	25 (6)	58	18
Total	127	189	833	208	16.9			
Input 2;4	22	211	240	1081	70.6	33	39	52

(see Table 1), accounting for 0.8% of utterances at 2;1, increasing to 7.7% at 2;6. A small number of questions were recorded from 2;3 onwards, but the rest of Thomas's transitive verb use consisted of bare stems (e.g. *bash*), negations without arguments (e.g. *no bash*) and locatives without subject or object arguments (e.g. *put in trailer*). There is a relatively low proportion of full SVO compared to VO utterances, both in terms of verb types and tokens. We can therefore be confident that these data captured the beginnings of the development of Thomas's SVO construction in production (see Figure 1).

3.2. Were Thomas's early SVO utterances built on previous SV or VO combinations?

To test whether Thomas's SVO utterances were closely related to earlier produced SV or VO constructions, we examined whether the first SVO utterance produced with each verb was preceded by simpler construction(s) with the same verb. We then examined the lexical items and types of arguments (pronoun [pN], proper noun [PN] or full noun phrase [NP]) used in subject and object roles with each verb to determine whether there was overlap between the SV and VO constructions and the more complex SVO construction.

Of the 33 verbs Thomas produced in the SVO construction from 2;1 to 2;6, 26 had previously occurred in either the SV (1), VO (18) or both constructions (7). For the eight verb types previously produced in the SV construction, six (75%) had the same subject type (pN, PN or NP), and three of these contained the same lexical subject as the earlier SV construction (38%). For the 25 verbs

---

since these figures include permissible uses of verbs which enter into transitivity alternations (in SV, found at 2;4, 2;5 and 2;6, $\underline{M}$ = 25.46%), as well as imperatives (VO).

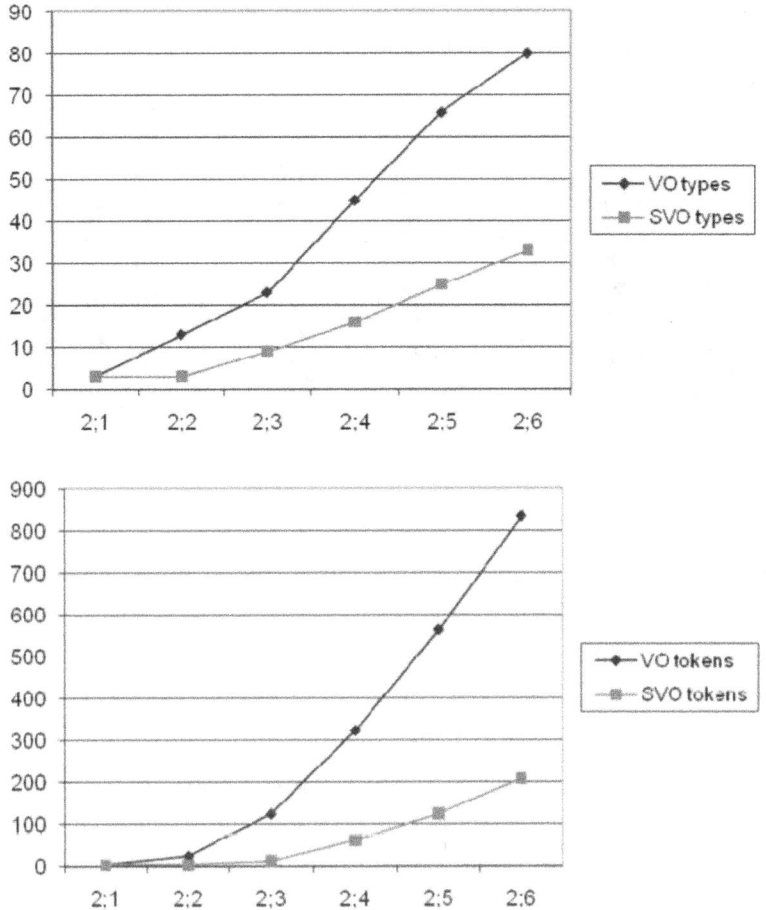

Figure 1. *Cumulative verb types and tokens produced in the VO and SVO constructions from 2;1 to 2;6.*

previously produced in the VO construction, 20 had the same object type (80%), and of these 14 shared the same lexical object as the earlier VO construction (56%). This suggests that, at least before 2;6, Thomas often relied on a particular word type that he had previously used as a subject or object with a specific verb, and on a specific lexical item previously produced as an object with that verb when he first employed it in the full SVO construction.

3.3. *Did Thomas's choice of subject and object referents conform to the input and/or PAS?*

We then examined whether Thomas showed a particular reliance on specific lexical items or broad classes of items in his early SVO utterances, and how

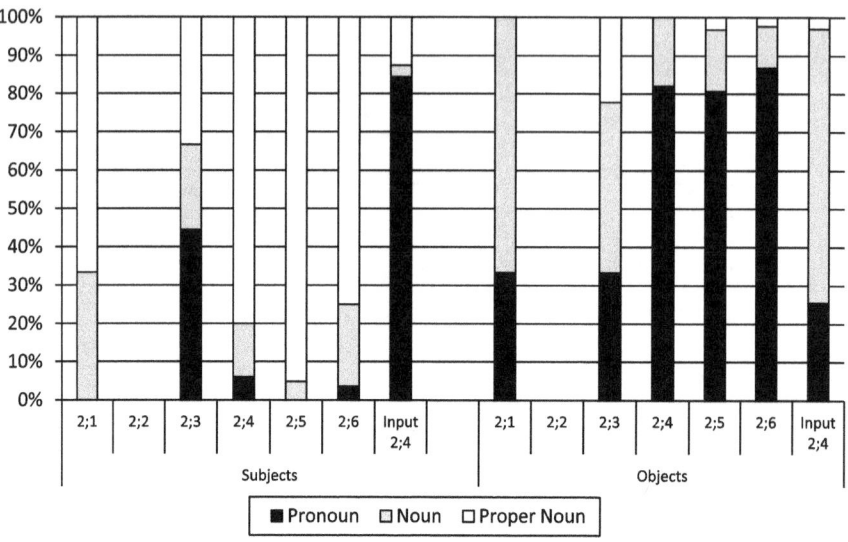

Figure 2. *Percentage of subjects and objects in the SVO construction that were pronouns, nouns and proper nouns between 2;1 to 2;6.*

this compared to use in the input. Of the very first occurrences of these 33 verbs in the SVO construction, 79% had either a proper noun (PN) subject (15), the pronominal object *it* (4), or both conforming to the construction *PN V it* (7). Of the seven verbs produced in the SVO construction that had no SV or VO precursors in our corpus, six conformed to the __ *V it* or *PN V* __ constructions, suggesting that there may be some early transfer between verbs in the SVO construction. The proportion of SVO subjects and objects across all of Thomas's SVO utterances (not just first uses) that were pronouns, noun phrases, or proper nouns at each age is shown in Figure 2. Again, especially from 2;4 to 2;6 when SVO use increased, there was a clear dominance of proper noun subjects and pronominal objects, with over 75% of objects realised as '*it*' (76%, 77% and 85% at 2;4, 2;5 and 2;6 respectively). This is in stark contrast to the patterns observed in Thomas's input where a much larger proportion of subjects in the SVO construction were pronouns and objects were nouns, in line with PAS. Thus, Thomas's early SVO utterances bore relatively little resemblance to the patterns observed in the input or those predicted on the basis of PAS with respect to the specific classes of lexical items instantiating the subject and object roles.

Of course, it is possible to argue that Thomas's VO utterances represented SVO utterances with omitted pronominal subjects as, in terms of information structure, pronouns tend to convey given information, and in many languages given information can often be omitted altogether (e.g. Clancy 2003). Thus,

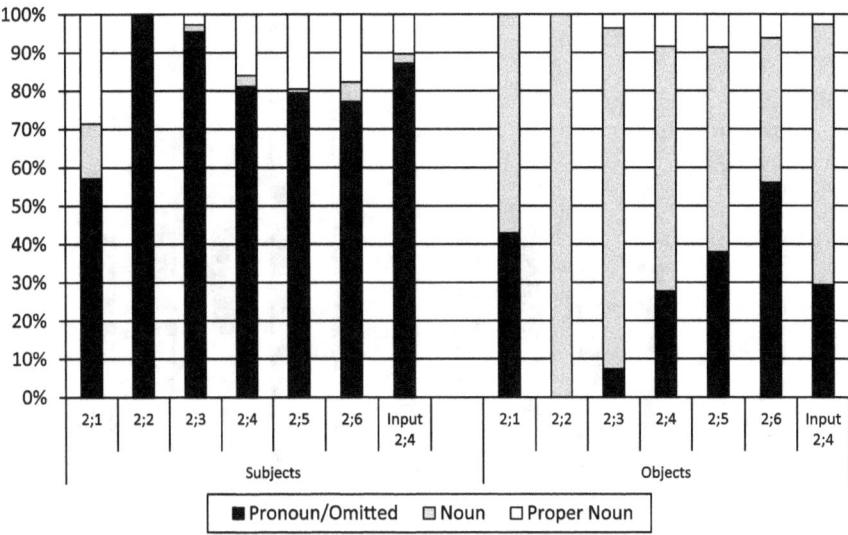

Figure 3. *Percentage of subjects and objects in the SVO and VO constructions that were pronouns (or omitted subjects), nouns and proper nouns between 2;1 to 2;6.*

collapsing across VO and SVO utterances by combining pronoun and omitted subjects may provide a fairer comparison of Thomas's data with the input (see Figure 3). When we compared the distribution of pronoun/omitted, noun, and proper noun subjects in Thomas's data in SVO and VO utterances combined at 2;6 with patterns in the input, a chi-squared test showed that the distribution was significantly different. Thomas produced more noun and proper noun subjects than his mother (χ^2 (2) = 22.47, p < 0.001, standardised residuals +2.19, +3.21 respectively) while his mother produced marginally more pronoun/omitted subjects (standardised residual = 1.84). Similarly, when we collapsed SVO and VO utterances and examined the distribution of objects, a chi-squared test revealed that at 2;6 Thomas produced a higher proportion of pronoun and proper noun objects and a lower proportion of noun objects than his mother (χ^2 (2) = 108.78, p < 0.001, standardised residuals +6.7, +2.86 and −5.72 respectively), reflecting in part the dominance of *it* in his SVO utterances. Despite the very high frequency of full SVO utterances containing the PAS pattern of pronominal subjects and noun objects in the input, Thomas started out producing SVO utterances with proper noun subjects and pronominal objects.

3.4. *What were the event semantics of Thomas's early transitive verb types?*

The verb types produced in the SVO and VO constructions were categorised as high transitivity (HT: on a fairly broad interpretation of H&T's criteria), inalienable transitivity (IT: belonging to one of Ninio's four classes, obtaining,

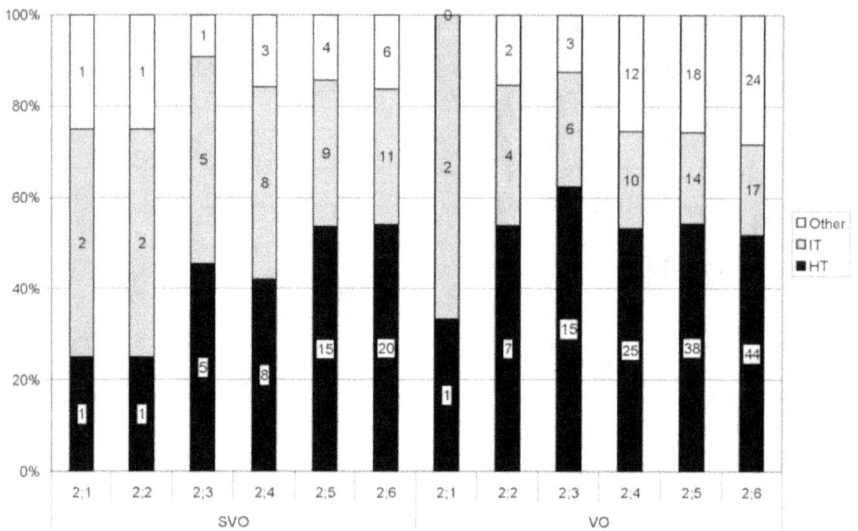

Figure 4. *Cumulative percentage of high transitivity (HT), inalienable transitivity (IT) and other verb types based on first verb use for the SVO and VO constructions.*
Nb: For SVO, at 2;1, 2;3, 2;4 and 2;6 one verb type appears in both the HT and IT groups (*do, pick[up], eat,* and *drink* respectively); for VO at 2;3, 2;4, and 2;6 one verb type appears in both HT and IT groups (*eat, drink,* and *build* respectively), and at 2;5 two verbs (*collect* and *bring*) appear in both HT and IT groups.

creation, perception, ingestion), or 'other' for those predicates which were not easily captured by either classification (e.g. *drop*, which scores low on the H&T criteria and is not among Ninio's subset of IT verbs), based on their first use. Figure 4 shows the cumulative frequencies of verb types across months, falling into the HT, IT, and 'other' categories for the SVO and VO constructions.

At 2;1 there appeared to be a small advantage for IT (2) over HT (1) verbs in the SVO and VO constructions, however any claim for early IT dominance is weakened by the fact that only three verb types were produced, one of the two IT verbs in SVO (*do*) was also coded as high in transitivity, and the third verb produced in the SVO construction fell into the 'other' category. For the SVO construction, there was again roughly equal use of HT and IT verbs at 2;3 and 2;4, and thereafter larger numbers of HT verbs were acquired, with IT and 'other' verbs acquired in lower but equal numbers from 2;5. In the VO construction, there was an earlier dominance of HT verbs (from 2;2), with verbs in the 'other' category also acquired at a similar or faster rate than IT verbs from 2;2.

The cumulative type frequencies of the verbs in each semantic group for the SVO and VO constructions show that both HT and IT verbs played an important role in early acquisition, and although 'other' verbs were less frequent, they appeared alongside the early HT and IT verbs. Although we are unlikely to have captured the very first verb uses, only three verb types were found in the SVO and VO constructions in the 22 hour sample at 2;1. Due to the increased density of our data over other naturalistic corpora we can be reasonably confident that we captured the early stages of acquisition. Thomas's data thus do not provide clear support for an early advantage for either notion (HT or IT) of transitive semantics.

3.5. *Do Thomas's early verbs have stable and adult-like event semantics?*

For this analysis, we looked in more detail at the extent to which Thomas's SVO and VO utterances scored highly on H&T's continuum of transitivity for those aspects that could sensibly be judged (kinesis, punctuality, volitionality, affectedness of the object). We asked how consistently Thomas's early utterances exhibited high transitivity, and which aspects of H&T's criteria were characteristic of his early utterances.

When we examined the verbs used at least twice in the SVO or VO constructions, we found that of the 20 used two or more times in the SVO construction, 18 (90%) received the same coding (10 HT, 8 show low transitivity LT), regardless of whether they were coded on the basis of the first utterance, or the first two/three utterances with that verb. For the VO construction, of the 61 verb types produced at least twice, 48 (78.7%; 26 HT, 22 LT) were categorised in the same way on the basis of both the first verb use and two/three utterances, whereas 13 verbs showed mixed coding, that is they were coded as high in some contexts and low in others. Thus, although overall around 81% of Thomas's verbs were used with stable event semantics, there is some evidence that even in early acquisition, some individual verbs are used more variably.

However, this kind of global analysis reveals little about the precise nature of early event semantics, as it is unclear exactly what properties of an utterance resulted in it exhibiting high or low transitivity. We therefore examined in detail which aspects of event semantics were central to Thomas's early SVO and VO constructions. Although overall 56% of Thomas's SVO and VO utterances exhibited high transitivity (a score of 3 or 4 on H&Ts criteria, see Table 2 for a breakdown of overall utterance categorisation according to the 4 criteria), utterances were not rated equally highly on the four aspects of transitivity coded for. A higher proportion of utterances received high transitivity ratings for kinesis (69.6%) and volition (78.1%) than for punctuality (41.6%) or affectedness of the object (46.6%). Recall that volition concerns the extent to which a subject/agent acts intentionally, and studies have shown that 18-month-old children discount accidental actions, imitating only intentional acts (e.g. Carpenter et al. 1998). There is reason to believe, therefore, that degree of intentionality is something children are likely to pay attention to when beginning to learn how events are expressed in their language. In contrast, Thomas seemed little

Table 2. *Aspects of utterance semantics relating to ratings of high transitivity*

	SVO	VO	Overall	
4	12.50	21.69	17.10	
3	43.75	34.39	39.07	
2	18.75	11.11	14.93	
1	20.31	19.58	19.94	
0	4.69	13.23	8.96	
	Kinesis	Punctuality	Volition	Affectedness of object
SVO				
% utterances HT	70.31	50.00	79.69	39.06
Total utterances	64	64	64	64
VO				
% utterances HT	68.95	33.16	76.44	54.21
Total utterances	190	190	191	190

Distribution of utterances according to ratings of high transitivity across the four semantic categories (0 = lowest in transitivity to 4 = highest in transitivity)

concerned with the extent to which the object of an action is affected. Without a detailed semantic coding of transitive utterances in the input, we cannot comment on whether Thomas's early transitive utterances display a different semantic pattern to those he hears. However, we can conclude that his early transitive utterances, although often exhibiting high transitivity, do so along only a limited range of semantic criteria in comparison with those suggested in the literature for adult speech.

To summarise, there is evidence that Thomas started out by producing both utterances that exhibited high transitivity and those that exhibited low transitivity, sometimes showing variation even within his uses of the same verb. However, a large proportion of his utterances scored highly with respect to kinesis and volition, suggesting that his early transitive constructions may have been organised around the extent to which an action was transferred from the agent to the patient, and the extent to which the agent acted intentionally.

3.6. *The role of animacy*

We first examined whether Thomas differentiated the subjects and objects of SVO utterances, and the objects of SVO and VO utterances, in terms of their animacy. The data showed that Thomas did indeed differentiate the subjects and objects of his SVO utterances, with an average of 97% of subjects being animate in comparison with just 11% of objects (see Table 3 for the proportion of animate subjects and objects at each age). In this respect then, Thomas's SVO utterances conform to PAS. Interestingly though, we also observed differences in the extent to which Thomas's objects in his SVO and VO utterances

Table 3. *Proportion of animate subjects and objects.*

Subjects	2;1	2;2	2;3	2;4	2;5	2;6	Input
SVO	1.00	–	1.00	0.92	1.00	0.95	0.95
Objects							
VO	0.00	0.15	0.09	0.16	0.13	0.13	
SVO	0.00	–	0.44	0.04	0.03	0.04	0.06

were animate. We compared the distribution of animate vs. inanimate objects in the VO and SVO constructions at 2;4, 2;5 and 2;6. Objects in VO utterances were significantly more likely to be animate than objects in SVO utterances (2;4 χ^2 [1] = 4.95, p = 0.026; 2;5 χ^2 [1] = 4.51, p = 0.034; 2;6 χ^2 [1] = 6.19, p = 0.013[5]), driven by the highly frequent use of the inanimate object referent *it* in SVO utterances. Thus, the differences observed in the kinds of lexical items used to express SVO and VO objects (with VO objects more likely to be NPs and SVO objects pNs) were mirrored in differences in the animacy of these two groups of objects.

Second, we looked at Thomas's SVO utterances as a whole to determine the semantic relations between the subject and object roles. The data revealed that 88.0% of Thomas's SVO utterances between 2;1 and 2;6 showed a pattern of contrasting animacy in subject and object positions, with subjects animate (and often human) and objects inanimate. A similar pattern was observed in the input with 88.9% of his mother's SVO utterances following this semantic pattern. Thus, although Thomas's SVO utterances differed from those he heard with respect to the particular lexical items he produced in subject and object position, with Thomas showing a greater reliance on proper noun subjects and pronominal objects while his mother used a higher proportion of pronominal subjects and noun objects, the semantics of his early SVO utterances matched those of his mother, at least when measured in terms of the animacy of the subject and object roles.

Thus, there is some evidence that Thomas's earliest representation of the SVO construction may reflect the prototypical semantic relationship between the subjects and objects of transitive clauses, but in terms of simple animacy and a high degree of intentionality on the part of the agent, rather than encompassing

---

5. Benjamini-Hochberg corrections were applied for multiple comparisons, these differences remained significant. In these analyses and others in this paper, we were interested in whether there was developmental change in a single child, and in comparing the child's language use to use in his input. Thus, the data points all come from the same speaker(s) and are, in this sense, not independent. We acknowledge that there is some debate over the appropriateness of the use of statistical tests that assume independence between data points, but apply these tests here (as has been done previously in the literature) to give a sense of the precise pattern of change over development.

the full range of H&Ts more sophisticated criteria. However, it is important to note that at 2;3 (following just three prototypical SVO utterances in our 2;1 sample) Thomas produced SVO utterances involving two animate entities (e.g. *I see you, Lala brush Molly*—6.1% of SVO input) and at 2;4 began to produce SVO utterances with inanimate subjects (e.g. *balloon bang head*—5.1% of SVO input). There were, however, no SVO utterances exhibiting the reverse inanimate-subject, animate-object pattern by 2;6. These data suggest that although the highly frequent animate-inanimate pattern is acquired early and could result in children having a better understanding of argument roles in utterances of this type, Thomas was also learning how to understand and produce reversible transitives and transitives with an inanimate subject from the beginnings of transitive verb use. Further evidence for this comes from his VO objects which contrasted with SVO objects in being more frequently animate entities, contributing to the acquisition of reversible transitives. Although the lack of inanimate-animate SVO utterances could suggest, in line with the results of comprehension studies (e.g. Corrigan 1988; Chan et al. 2009), that sentences where the prototypical role asymmetry is reversed pose particular problems in acquisition, inanimate-animate transitive sentences are also very infrequent in the input (0.19% of the input) and thus their absence from Thomas's data may reflect the relatively smaller size of his corpus in comparison with that of his mother.

3.7. *Summary of development from 2;1 to 2;6*

Between 2;1 and 2;6, Thomas produced an increasing number of transitive verb types, and produced these verbs in the SV, VO and the full SVO constructions. Initially, he produced only a handful of verb types in the SVO construction, and over three quarters of these verbs had previously appeared in the less complex SV or, more commonly, VO construction. Moreover, around three quarters of these verbs had previously appeared with the same type of subject or object, and around half with the same lexical item in the subject or object slot. An examination of the semantics associated with Thomas's early SVO and VO utterances suggested that he does not rely on a particular, semantically delimited set of verbs for his early transitive production, but rather is better characterised as producing, across semantic categories, utterances which conform to a dominant semantic pattern that favours animate (often human) subject referents perceived as having a high degree of intentionality in relation to inanimate objects.

By 2;6, Thomas's grasp of the SVO construction was still relatively non-adult-like in his nonconformity to preferred argument structure principles which favour pronominal subjects and lexical noun objects in accordance with the tendency for subjects to encode given and objects new information. Thomas relied instead on the pronominal form *it* in object position, and had a marked tendency to produce proper nouns in subject position. Even when Thomas's VO utterances were considered as examples of subject omission licensed by pragmatic factors similar to those that operate on pronominal reference, his transitive utterances still differed from those found in his mother's speech with respect to the way in which subjects and objects were realised.

We next examine how Thomas's knowledge of the transitive construction developed between 2;7 and 3;0, the age at which experimental production studies suggest that children begin to acquire productive use of the SVO construction (Tomasello 2003). We differentiate between Old verbs (those transitive verbs acquired prior to 2;7) and New verbs (those transitive verbs acquired between 2;7 and 3;0) to investigate whether these verb groups show different developmental trajectories towards adult-like usage. If acquisition proceeds gradually and on the basis of prior use, we might expect to see the earlier acquisition of the full SVO construction for Old verbs. To examine this issue, we conducted three analyses. First, we examined the proportional use of Old and New verbs in the SVO construction to determine whether Old verbs appeared in this construction earlier than New verbs. Second, as transitive objects are commonly realised in adult speech with lexical nouns, but can take a variety of forms from a simple pronoun (*it*) to much more complex noun phrases (NPs) (*The big yellow digger, the brown cow and the black horse*), we examined the complexity of the object arguments produced with Old and New verbs, in terms of their mean length of utterance (MLU) and the presence of determiners. If previous knowledge of the combinatorial properties of verbs contributes to the development of more abstract object slots, we might expect to see that the objects of Old verbs were longer and more likely to appear with determiners than those of New verbs. Finally, we examined the extent to which Thomas's SVO utterances conformed to preferred argument structure with respect to the types of subject and object referents he produced. Here we made no specific predictions regarding patterns of acquisition for Old and New verbs as it is not clear whether previous use of Old verbs with proper noun subjects and pronominal objects would be expected to promote the transition to PAS or, in contrast, hinder such a transition as the previous pattern of use may have been well entrenched.

4. Results: 2;7 to 3;0

4.1. *The distribution of utterances containing potentially transitive verbs across constructions*

Thomas produced 66 new transitive verb types from 2;7 to 3;0, 16 in the SVO construction, 24 in the VO construction, and 26 in both constructions. In the 2;1 to 2;6 data, Thomas used a much smaller proportion of his verb types and

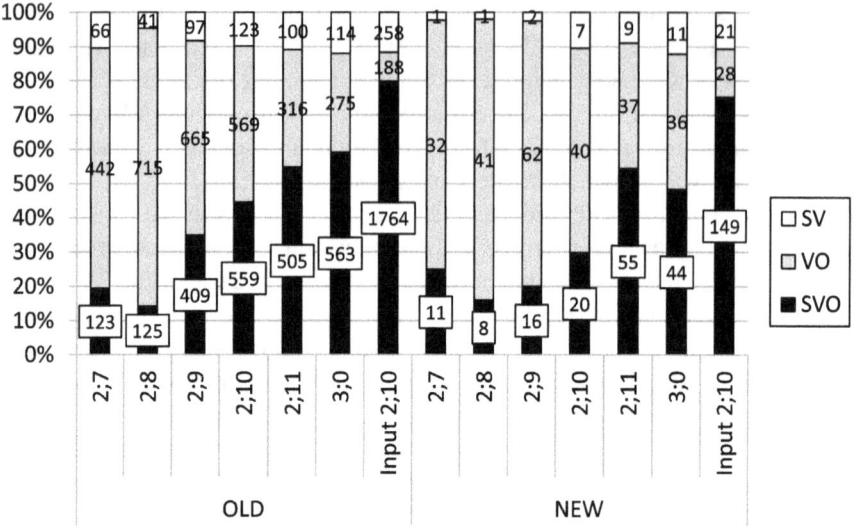

Figure 5. *Percentage of Old and New verb tokens produced in the SV, VO and SVO constructions from 2;7 to 3;0.*

tokens in the SVO construction, in comparison with his mother's verb use. We therefore examined the distribution of Old verb tokens (verbs first produced between 2;1 and 2;6) in the SVO construction relative to other constructions (VO & SV combined) in Thomas's 2;7 to 3;0 data and compared this with input data from the 2;10 sample to see whether he began to converge on adult patterns of verb use (see Figure 5). Firstly, there was a clear development toward the adult pattern with a steady increase in the proportional use of the SVO construction (chi-squared analyses revealed that there were significant differences between each consecutive month sample from 2;7 to 2.11 (χ^2 [1] values ranged from 7.54 to 112.32, p values < 0.01[6]), and a marginally significant increase from 2;11 to 3;0 (χ^2 [1] = 3.54, p = 0.06). However, even at 3;0, Thomas produced a significantly lower proportion of SVO utterances than his mother (χ^2 [1] = 146.43, p < 0.001). Secondly, at 2;9 Thomas showed a marked increase in the use of the SVO construction (standardised residual = +5.94). The interesting question, if we are looking for evidence of gradual abstraction of verb-general knowledge of the transitive construction, is whether this pattern was repeated for New verbs (see Figure 5).

The general trend for New verbs resembled the Old verb pattern, with a tendency for Thomas's distribution to be more like his mother's as he ap-

---

6. These findings are still significant when Benjamini-Hochberg corrections are applied, as are those for New verbs, and for the comparisons of Old and New verbs reported below.

proached 3;0. However, the most marked change in the proportion of New verb tokens produced in the SVO construction relative to other constructions (SV & VO combined) occurred somewhat later at 2;11 than for Old verbs (2;9), with the only significant increase in SVO use month by month occurring at 2;11, $\chi^2[1] = 9.87$, $p = 0.002$). The Old verbs reached 35% SVO use at 2;9, and 45% at 2;10, while New verb SVO utterances accounted for less than 30% of his verb uses until an increase to 54% at 2;11[7]. Thus, both Old and New verbs lagged significantly below the level of SVO use in the input even at 3;0. This difference reflects the higher proportion of VO utterances in Thomas's speech in comparison with the higher proportion of SVO utterances in the input (SV utterances account for 10–12% of the data for both Old and New verbs in Thomas's speech and the input).

To determine whether the apparent differences between Old and New verbs were statistically significant, chi-squared comparisons were carried out. First, it was necessary to establish whether Thomas's mother's proportional use of the SVO construction with Thomas's Old and New verbs was similar, as differences in the patterns of use in the input might account for differences in Thomas's use of these verbs. A chi-squared test showed that there was no difference in the proportional use of Old and New verbs in the SVO construction in the input (79.8% and 75.2% respectively, $\chi^2[1] = 2.32$, $p = 0.13$).

We then compared Thomas's use of the SVO construction with Old and New verbs at each age with a series of chi-squared tests. At 2;7 and 2;8, there were no differences in his use of the SVO construction (2;7, Old = 20%, New = 25%, $\chi^2[1] = 0.78$, $p = 0.38$; 2;8 Old = 14%, New = 16%, $\chi^2[1] = 0.13$, $p = 0.72$). At 2;9, however, Thomas produced his Old verbs in the full SVO construction significantly more often than his New verbs (Old = 35%, New = 20%, $\chi^2[1] = 7.44$, $p = 0.006$), and this was mirrored at 2;10 (Old = 45%, New = 30%, $\chi^2[1] = 5.68$, $p = 0.017$). Only at 2;11 did New verbs show the same proportional use in the SVO construction as Old verbs (Old = 55%, New = 54%, $\chi^2[1] = 0.01$, $p = 0.92$). Thus, Old verbs showed an earlier move towards adult-like use of the SVO construction than New verbs (which instead were produced in the VO construction).

4.2. Are Old verbs used with more complex object arguments than New verbs?

We calculated the MLU of object types (in morphemes) occurring with the SVO and VO constructions for Old and New verbs at 3;0, the latest data point

---

[7]. When we examined the number of verb types produced in the SVO construction each month, the same pattern emerged with Old verbs showing a marked increase in the number of verb

in this study, and then compared these values with Thomas's mother's object use with each group of verbs to determine whether the object arguments Thomas produced with Old verbs were closer to adult use than those he produced with New verbs. For the purposes of this analysis, we counted each utterance type only once to avoid, for example, multiple exact repetitions of utterances such as *Mummy do it* reducing the MLU of objects occurring in the SVO construction (thus *it* was counted only once if it occurred in multiple occurrences of *Mummy do it*, but was counted separately if it occurred in other utterances such as *Daddy do it* or *Mummy find it*). We combined VO and SVO utterances to allow a fair comparison (as Thomas omitted subjects more than his mother). Mann-Whitney tests showed that for Old verbs, Thomas's objects at 3;0 did not differ in length from those found in the input (Thomas $\underline{M}$ = 1.99, input $\underline{M}$ = 2.13, $\underline{U}$ = 521450.5, $\underline{N}$ = 2509, $\underline{p}$ = 0.10), whereas for New verbs, Thomas's objects at 3;0 were significantly shorter than those in the input (Thomas $\underline{M}$ = 1.38, input $\underline{M}$ = 1.85, $\underline{U}$ = 3667.5, $\underline{N}$ = 213, $\underline{p}$ = 0.001). This suggests that Thomas's use of Old verbs was more adult-like than his use of the more recently acquired New verbs, even at 3;0.

An examination of the object arguments Thomas produced with Old and New verbs revealed that he produced fewer determiners with his objects of New verbs than with his objects of Old verbs. To control for the fact that Thomas had a more limited vocabulary than his mother, we examined the use of 10 highly frequent determiners that were in Thomas's vocabulary (*a, another, any, his, my, some, that, the, this, your*). 47% of Thomas's Old verb objects occurred with one of these 10 determiners (this mirrored the pattern observed in the input where 43% of Old verb objects appeared with one of these high frequency determiners (a chi-squared test revealed that these distributions were not significantly different χ^2 [1] = 2.00, $\underline{p}$ = 0.16). However, only 20% of Thomas's New verb objects occurred with one of these highly frequent determiners in comparison with 37% of New verb objects in the input, a chi-squared test revealed this difference to be significant χ^2 [1] = 4.79, $\underline{p}$ = 0.029. This shows that although Thomas is able to employ a range of determiners with his Old verb objects, and these same determiners appear with equal frequency with both Old and New verbs in the input, Thomas fails to produce determiners with his New verb objects, resulting in the use of less complex NPs with these verbs. It is worth noting, however, that the MLU of objects with Old verbs remains slightly longer than with New verbs, even when the determiners are excluded from the calculation (Old verbs MLU = 1.46, New verbs MLU = 1.17). This suggests that the complexity associated with Old verb objects is not just

---

types produced in the SVO construction at 2;9, whereas New verbs showed an increase at 2;11.

restricted to the use of determiners, but is also likely to involve the greater use of adjectives, numerals, noun morphology and so on.

4.3. Did Thomas's choice of subject and object referents conform to PAS?

At 2;6, Thomas's use of both subjects and objects in the SVO construction differed from his mother's and contrasted with PAS. The distribution of subject and object types in SVO utterances for Old and New verbs from 2;7 to 3;0 is shown in Figure 6, and the same information is shown in Figure 7 when VO utterances were also included (in the category of pronoun/omitted subjects).

Before 2;9 Thomas relied heavily on proper noun subjects in SVO utterances with both Old and New verbs. From 2;9, however, there was a sharp increase in his use of pronominal subjects, although use was more varied for New than for Old verbs. From Figure 7, we can see that there was little difference in the proportional use of the combined category of pronominal and omitted subjects in SVO/VO between 2;8 and 2;9. This suggests that the increase in pronoun subjects in SVO at 2;9 reflected a concurrent decrease in the production of VO utterances in which the subject was omitted, and this occurred for both Old and New verbs. In particular, there was a sudden increase in the use of *I* which was produced in 308 SVO utterances (72%) at 2;9 across Old and New verbs (44 of 54 Old verb types and 5 of 8 New verb types in the SVO construction occurred with *I* as subject). However, there were 44 instances of *I* produced in SVO

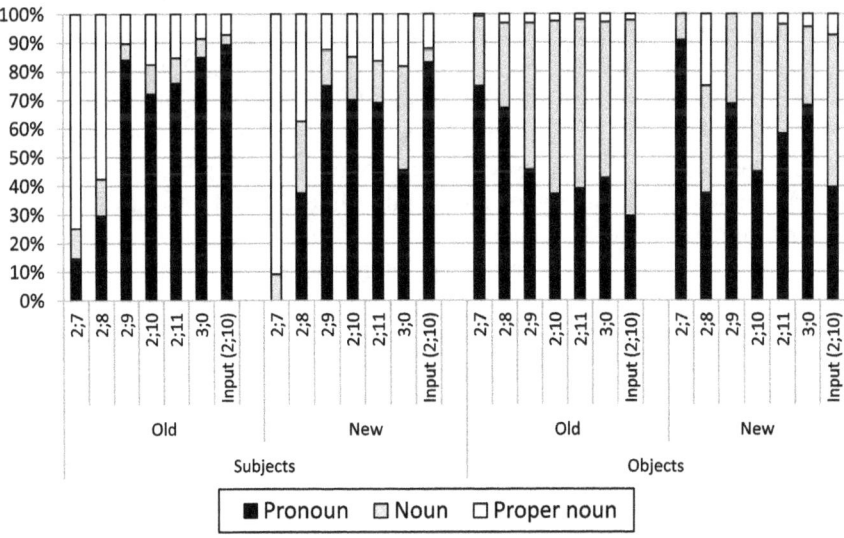

Figure 6. *Percentage of subjects and objects in the SVO construction that were pronouns, nouns, and proper nouns with Old and New verbs from 2;7 to 3;0.*

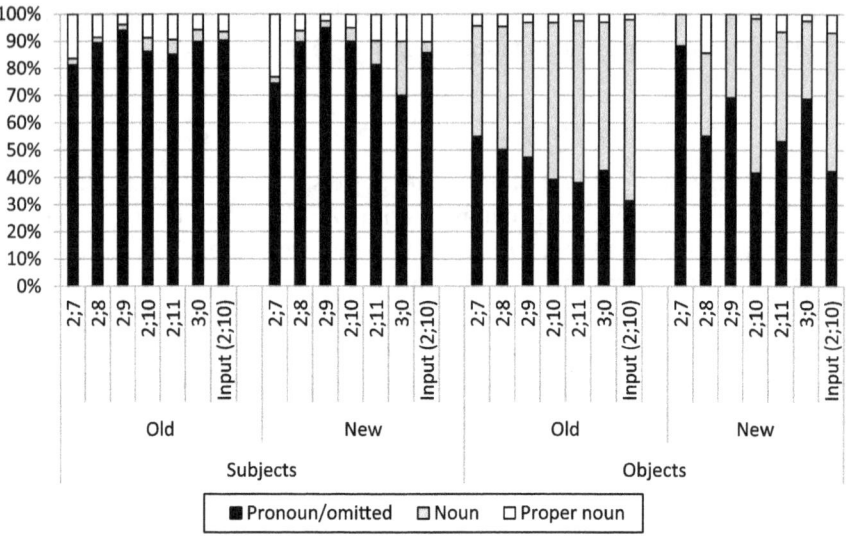

Figure 7. *Percentage of subjects and objects in the SVO and VO constructions that were pronouns (and omitted subjects), nouns, and proper nouns with Old and New verbs from 2;7 to 3;0.*

utterances prior to 2;9 illustrating that this was not a newly acquired lexical item. Indeed, extrapolating on the basis that our sample represents around 8% of the child's total output (Maratsos 2000), we can surmise that by 2;9, Thomas had produced something like 500 previous SVO utterances with *I* as subject. He also produced 14 other pronominal reference types at 2;9, ten of which were recorded prior to 2;9 although in small numbers. Thus, the underuse of pronouns in SVO utterances prior to 2;9 cannot be attributed to Thomas's lack of knowledge of the relevant lexical items, nor of how to combine them in SVO utterances. Rather, his ability to produce adult-like SVO utterances appeared to be undergoing gradual development.

With respect to object use in the SVO construction, at 2;7 and 2;8 Thomas used a high proportion of pronominal objects (although the pattern was less clear for New verbs due to the small number of utterances at 2;8). From 2;9 he began to move towards adult-like use with a greater tendency to produce noun objects, especially with Old verbs, mirroring the pattern in the input where only 30% of objects with Old verbs were pronominal compared to 40% of objects with New verbs. When VO utterances were also included the pattern was similar, although at 2;7 and 2;8 the proportion of noun objects with Old verbs increased, reflecting the earlier tendency for Thomas to produce noun objects in the VO construction and pronominal objects in the SVO construction.

To summarise, the data show that from 2;9 Thomas's use of the SVO construction came to much more closely resemble his mother's use, in particular in his production of transitive utterances containing pronominal subjects. However, Old verbs more reliably converged on the adult pattern for noun objects from 2;9, whereas New verbs continued to appear with higher levels of pronominal objects, even when compared against the higher level of pronominal object use in the input with New verbs.

4.4. *Summary of development from 2;7 to 3;0*

This series of analyses on Thomas's use of Old and New verbs between 2;7 to 3;0 revealed that even taking into account distributional differences in the input in the use of Old and New verbs, Thomas's use of Old verbs more rapidly converged on the adult pattern of use, whereas his use of New verbs lagged behind. More specifically, Old verbs in comparison with New verbs (1) showed an earlier move towards higher levels of use in the full SVO construction, (2) were produced with more complex object NPs, even at 3;0, and (3) appeared with lexical (rather than pronominal) objects earlier in development. All this evidence suggests that Thomas's greater experience of using his Old verbs confers an advantage on them in terms of development toward adult patterns of use. We therefore conclude that his knowledge of the transitive construction at 3;0 is still, in some important respects, fragmented and reliant on previous patterns of use. At same time, it is clear that knowledge of some aspects of the transitive construction, more specifically the use of pronominal subjects at 2;9, seems to generalise across verbs.

5. Discussion

In this study we set out to address a number of questions regarding the acquisition of the transitive SVO construction between two and three years of age. Specifically we asked whether early transitive utterances (1) were built on the previous use of simpler constructions, (2) reflected patterns in the input and/or PAS with respect to the kinds of lexical items used in subject and object positions, (3) showed evidence of either the event semantics associated with high transitivity or of inalienable transitivity, and (4) reflected patterns in the input and/or PAS with respect to the animacy of the subjects and objects. To address these questions, we carried out an exhaustive analysis of the simple transitive utterances produced in dense data from one child (Thomas) between two and three years of age.

First, we found evidence that Thomas's transitive verb use was closely related to his prior use of those same verbs. From 2;1 to 2;6 he showed little use of the full SVO construction, but those SVO utterances that he did produce tended to share the same subject and object type, and for objects the same lexical item as he had previously produced in either an SV or VO construction with that same verb. Broadly speaking, his early SVO utterances could be characterised by low level constructions organised around proper noun subjects and pronominal objects. During the latter half of Thomas's third year (2;7–3;0), we found that verbs acquired before 2;7 had accrued some advantage that was carried over into later use. These verbs were produced in the SVO construction earlier than verbs learned after 2;6, and the objects of Thomas's New verbs were less complex and appeared with fewer determiners than his objects of Old verbs. These data are consistent with earlier studies that suggested that knowledge of the transitive construction builds up gradually on the basis of prior use (Tomasello 1992; Lieven et al. 2003), and that frequent subjects and/or objects may play a particularly important role in the abstraction of a variable verb slot (Lieven et al. 1997; Pine et al. 1998; Jones et al. 2000; Childers and Tomasello 2001; Savage et al. 2003, 2006; Laakso and Smith 2007). On the other hand, both verb groups shifted towards greater pronominal subject use in the SVO construction at 2;9, suggesting some degree of generalisation across verbs. This asymmetry between subject and object use with Old and New verbs suggests that Thomas was sensitive to a critical distinction between the subjects and objects of transitive events. In the input subjects are often realised pronominally (and refer to a limited set of animates) and thus take a limited range of forms, whereas objects are often realised as full nouns and encompass a much wider variety of items. If we add to this the fact that many early acquired verbs exhibit particularly strong relations with their objects (Brown 2008), this might lead children to accept generalisations across the subject slot of the transitive construction, but to show less readiness to generalise across the object slot.

One question that arises from these data is whether Thomas's increase in pronominal subject use at 2;9 is restricted to the transitive construction. According to some theories, the subject of the transitive construction is represented separately from the subject of, say, the intransitive construction (e.g. Croft 2001), and on this kind of account, generalisation across constructions will take developmental time. On the other hand, previous research suggests that each construction does not develop in isolation, but rather can have a positive (or negative) impact on the acquisition of other constructions (e.g. Abbot-Smith and Behrens 2006). Although a detailed examination of construction networks is beyond the scope of the current paper, we briefly examined the kinds of subjects Thomas produced with his intransitive verbs between 2;7 and 3;0. The data show that at 2;9, the critical age when we observed an increase in pronominal subjects in transitive utterances, the proportion of pronoun subjects produced in the intransitive also increased (57% at 2;9 vs. 18% at 2;8). However, at 2;9 pronoun subject use in the intransitive (57%) was somewhat lower than in the transitive (84% for Old verbs, 75% for New verbs), the form 'I' accounted for only 22% of Thomas's intransitive subjects in comparison with 72% in the transitive. This is likely to reflect the fact that in adult (and child) language, the intransitive subject argument is associated with both a larger proportion of lexical nouns used to denote new entities in the discourse, and a larger number of inanimate referents than the subject of transitives (e.g. DuBois 1987; Clancy 2003), and lends further support to the suggestion that constructions develop, at least to some degree, independently. Of course, it is possible that stronger relations would be found between the simple transitive and other more complex transitive constructions that share similar discourse pragmatics, but this would require further detailed investigation.

Second, we found that Thomas's SVO utterances contrasted with patterns of use in the input and those of PAS in his choice of subject and object referents. However, Thomas's objects in his VO utterances were more likely to be full nouns, more closely resembling the input and PAS. Why did Thomas's SVO and VO utterances differ in this respect? One possibility is that this reflected sensitivity to discourse pragmatics, with the SVO construction used when the subject represented new information and the object was given, and the VO construction used when the object represented new information and the subject was given. On balance, however, this seems unlikely. The majority of Thomas's proper noun subjects referred to either himself, his mother, the family cat, or the research assistant, all of whom almost certainly represented given information in the context, and related analyses of Thomas's and other children's data show that between 2;1 and 2;7 they sometimes produced lexical subjects when the referent was fully accessible yet omitted subjects when the referent represented new information (Hughes and Allen 2009). This incomplete understanding of pragmatic principles suggests that discourse pragmatics are not the primary explanation for the contrast between the objects in Thomas's SVO and VO constructions. Another possibility is that this reflected a processing trade-off between the subject and object roles in production such that when Thomas produced a full noun object, he tended to omit the subject, whereas when he produced the subject he was only able to produce a less complex pronominal object (e.g. Bloom 1990). However, Freudenthal et al. (2007) demonstrated, using a computational model with an utterance-final bias, that the observed association between the length of the verb phrase and the presence/omission of a subject argument can be explained in terms of performance-limited learning. If children are limited in how much information they are able to learn at any one time, utterances including longer verb phrases are less likely to be fully learned than those with shorter verb phrases, thus sentences with pronominal objects are more likely to be learned with their subject arguments than are those with longer noun phrase objects. As learning within their model is dependent on frequency of exposure, this could also account for our finding that

Thomas's Old verbs appear with longer object NPs and show an earlier move to the full SVO construction than his New verbs. We conclude that in production at least, Thomas was unable to manipulate the subject and object roles in an adult-like way due to a reliance on input-based learning (albeit with variation in the lexical items used in subject and object positions) and relatively low levels of generalisation across verbs.

Thirdly, we found that the semantics of Thomas's early transitive utterances were varied, encompassing verbs exhibiting high transitivity (Hopper and Thompson 1980) and inalienable transitivity (Ninio 1999), as well as some verbs that corresponded to neither categorisation. These data share similarities with Brown's (2008) data on Tzeltal, and Naigles et al.'s (2009) data on American-English where children acquire both semantically general and very specific verbs from the earliest stages of verb acquisition. Detailed analysis revealed that Thomas's transitive utterances were best characterised as encoding intentional agents and the transfer of an action from agent to patient. It is important to note that the event semantics for some verbs differed from one instance to another, cautioning against categorising verb types in the absence of contextual information (see Naigles et al. 2009 for similar arguments with respect to the semantic flexibility with which children use their early verbs), and that some verbs appeared to match both the HT and IT coding criteria, questioning the extent to which these categories differ. Thus, although there is a fierce debate over the central nature of transitivity, as exemplified by the proposals for prototypical transitivity outlined by H&T and Ninio, among others (see Næss 2007 for a discussion of prototypicality and markedness in transitive constructions), it is not clear that these specific differences are relevant for the language-learning child.

Finally, we observed a close relation between Thomas's SVO utterances and those of his mother and of PAS in terms of the animacy of his subjects and objects, with a majority of utterances encoding an animate agent and an inanimate patient. Thus, although Thomas's utterances did not map onto those in his input or PAS in terms of the specific referent types in subject and object position, there was overlap in terms of his broad utterance semantics. One possibility is that his early transitive construction was organised at a very general level in terms of animate agents engaging in interaction with the world in ways which actively involve patients that may be, but are not necessarily, affected by the interaction. This is certainly consistent with Budwig's (1995) work on early notions of agentivity, although in Thomas's data we have not attempted to determine whether different pragmatic functions are associated with different forms of self reference. In recent work, we have evaluated another characterisation of the transitive prototype, namely an utterance in which there is maximal differentiation between the subject (agent) and object (patient), both physically and with respect to the semantic roles that they play in the event

(Næss 2007). Our data suggest that adults show a prototype effect (and mistakenly 'recall' prototypical transitive sentences that they have not heard before), showing that Næss's characterisation of the transitive has some psychological reality for adults. However, 5 year olds did not show this effect, more accurately retaining item-based memory for the exact exemplars they were exposed to in training (Ibbotson et al. in press). This suggests that although a large majority of children's early transitive utterances conform to the prototypical pattern of intentional animate-agent acting on inanimate-patient, this may not amount to the same thing as possessing the kind of tightly integrated network of transitive utterances organised around a semantic prototype proposed for the adult transitive construction.

There are a number of possible reasons for this, two of which we outline here. First, there is a wealth of evidence for individual verb effects in language processing both in children (e.g. Corrigan 1986, 1988; Naigles et al. 2009, Pyykkönen et al. in press) and adults (e.g. Trueswell and Tanenhaus 1994). These verb-specific effects show that even beyond determining whether a given verb can be used transitively (cf. see Naigles [2003] for arguments against indiscriminate verb generalisation), children must establish, at the lexical level, the precise types of objects that are appropriate for use with a given verb or semantic class of verbs to use language conventionally. Second, it is not clear that our intuitions regarding which subjects and objects are animate necessarily match those of the child. In the child's world, inanimate entities are frequently animated and act independently in television programmes and books, and children are prone to talk about what their toys are 'doing' even when the toys are manipulated by the child (especially in blame assignment for misdemeanours—*The car knocked my drink over!*). Thus, we are unable to tell with great accuracy to what extent early transitive utterances exhibit the PAS pattern of animate agents affecting inanimate patients, and thus to what extent they conform to an adult-like prototype.

In recent work building on the competition model (Bates and MacWhinney 1987), some researchers have argued for prototype effects of a slightly different kind in children's acquisition of the transitive construction. The argument goes that the prototype is an utterance in which multiple cues redundantly indicate participant roles, with deviations from the prototype resulting in lower levels of accuracy in children's ability to identify the agent of a transitive causative action (Dittmar et al. 2008b, Chan et al. 2009, Ibbotson et al. 2011). From this perspective, the prototype is not necessarily defined in terms of the semantic relation between the agent and patient (e.g. Næss 2007, Hopper and Thompson 1990), but rather in terms of a set of criteria associated with the agent and/or patient. Thus, the agent might typically be the first mentioned participant in an event, often animate, and represented by a nominative form. Although studies have only been carried out with causative action verbs, these criteria could equally well apply to non-causative scenes, provided that the 'agent' was animate, and thus constitute a broad schema for the interpretation of the transitive construction. These broad heuristics for sentence interpretation could operate much earlier in development than the more fine-grained semantic representations needed for a full understanding of the prototypicality of agent-patient relations. The current study shows that Thomas's input contained a large proportion of transitive sentences that exhibited the animate-agent inanimate-patient pattern, and only a very small proportion of utterances that showed the reverse animacy pattern. If this is representative of the input children are exposed to, it is perhaps not surprising that children have been shown to be sensitive to animacy in their identification of the agent of an action (Chan et al. 2009), but it is important to note that these kinds of animacy effects do not automatically entail that the animate agent acts entirely intentionally, or that the object of the action is highly affected. Further studies are needed to pinpoint exactly what aspects of animacy are relevant in children's early sentence interpretation strategies.

It is clear that Thomas's transitive construction was undergoing gradual development in production, yet comprehension studies show earlier generalisation in some children with highly causative verbs at least. What then, if anything, can these data say about the comprehension-production asymmetry? Thomas's SVO utterances showed a marked tendency to encode animate agents and inanimate patients, a pattern also mirrored in his input. At the same time, however, his VO utterances frequently contained animate patients thus, for Thomas at least, VO utterances were not simple parallels of SVO utterances, and agents and patients were not clearly differentiated in terms of their animacy. The animacy issue is further confounded by the fact that some inanimate entities may be perceived as animate by young children. If, like Thomas, children typically encounter a range of both agents and patients that exhibit animacy characteristics, this could explain why one of the first things English-speaking children show sensitivity to in their comprehension of the transitive construction is the order of mention of the agent and patient, allowing them to perform accurately in comprehension tests (e.g. Gertner et al. 2006, Ibbotson et al. 2011). Even before children begin to produce transitive utterances themselves they are exposed to very large numbers of utterances in which two participants who may be poorly differentiated in terms of their animacy are causally related, and we might assume therefore that they have developed an effective strategy for interpreting what they hear.

However, the task in production is rather different. Performance-limited, frequency-driven learning provides one explanation for why Thomas produced SVO utterances with pronominal objects and VO utterances with full noun objects, and for why Old verbs showed an advantage over New verbs. But Thomas's SVO and VO constructions also differed in their relation to PAS, suggesting that he had not yet integrated his knowledge of these partially overlapping constructions. Integration would require a proper understanding of how pragmatic principles influence choice of referring expression. Although even two-year-olds show some sensitivity to discourse pragmatic principles, in the absence of a full understanding, it is perhaps clearer why children are conservative in their use of novel verbs (Tomasello 2003). Knowledge of both the typical realisation of arguments in the input and of pragmatic principles works against the production of two full noun phrases as agent and patient of a novel verb. In addition, children learn a wide range of different semantic verb types from the beginning of acquisition, yet verbs are choosy in their selection of object referents. Children's sensitivity to this property of the input is likely to limit extensive generalisation of the SVO construction across verbs in production.

The data presented in this study suggest that although previous studies have shown children to have some degree of competence in their comprehension of reversible transitive sentences at around age 2;0, Thomas's understanding of how to produce the SVO construction continues to develop throughout his third year. Coming back to our three aims, our data suggest that previous verb use does indeed provide a foundation for later use (aim 1), and this may reflect frequency-driven learning from the input, with the statistical properties of the input driving generalisation when and where it occurs. In terms of aim 2, identifying the semantics of the early transitive construction, this is best captured by a broad range of verb semantics, held together by an intentional agent, and it remains an empirical question when Thomas might arrive at an adult-like prototype of the transitive, however that may be defined. Finally, early but partial knowledge of discourse pragmatic principles appears to interact with Thomas's developing knowledge of the SVO construction, adding a further layer of complexity to the acquisition of the SVO construction in production (aim 3).

Of course, the trade-off for analysing a particularly dense corpus allowing more accurate inferences to be drawn regarding the timing and pattern of acquisition is that this study included data from only one child. It is highly likely that different patterns of acquisition would be observed in other children learning English (e.g. Naigles et al. 2009), and in other languages. On the other hand, nor is the child in this study likely to be unique in his pattern of acquisition. As such, the data presented in this paper require explanation within an integrated theory of how children acquire grammatical constructions, allowing for individual differences in the patterns of acquisition observed. We would predict that with adequate language samples, it should be possible to trace the gradual pattern of acquisition and pinpoint in more detail exactly how knowledge of the transitive construction develops over time, and the relation between comprehension and production. Our hypothesis that children start out with constructions that are partially related, and at the same time underspecified with regard to their appropriate use, requires further investigation.

Received 28 May 2010
Accepted 10 July 2011

University of Manchester
Max Planck Child Study Centre
Max Planck Institute for Evolutionary Anthropology

Appendix A: Semantic coding criteria

<u>Ninio's coding categories:</u>
Obtaining verbs:	e.g. *get, give, bring, find, want, take*
Perception verbs:	e.g. *see, hear*
Ingestion/consumption verbs:	e.g. *eat, drink*
Creation verbs:	e.g. *make, do, prepare, build, draw*

These verbs are examples—there are likely to be others that seem to fit these criteria and should be coded as such. The above categories contrast with what Ninio calls 'typical highly transitive verbs such as *kill, break, burn, cut, freeze, roll, clean* and so on, which involve a highly active subject who changes the state of an object by the act' (Ninio, 1999: 642).

<u>Hopper & Thompson's (1980) High transitivity</u>:
A hypothetical utterance exhibiting very high transitivity would express affirmatively, and in realis mode, a highly kinetic and punctual telic action, with two or more participants. The agent would be highly potent and act entirely deliberately, and the highly individuated object would be totally affected by the action. The following definitions were used (taken from Hopper & Thompson 1980: 252–253):

KINESIS: Actions can be transferred from one participant to another; states cannot. Thus something happens to Sally in *I hugged Sally*, but not in *I like Sally*.

PUNCTUALITY: Actions carried out with no obvious transitional phase between inception and completion have a more marked effect on their patients than actions which are inherently on-going; contrast *kick* (punctual) with *carry* (non-punctual).

VOLITIONALITY: The effect on the patient is typically more apparent when the agent/subject is presented as acting purposefully; contrast *I wrote your name* (volitional) with *I forgot your name* (non-volitional).

AFFECTEDNESS OF OBJECT/PATIENT: The degree to which an action is transferred to a patient is a function of how completely that patient is

AFFECTED; it is done more effectively in *I drank up the milk* than in *I drank some of the milk*

References

Abbot-Smith, Kirsten, & Heike Behrens. 2006. How known constructions influence the acquisition of other constructions: The German passive and future constructions. *Cognitive Science* 30 (3). 995–1026.
Abbot-Smith, Kirsten, Elena V. M. Lieven, & Mike Tomasello. 2004. Training 2;6-year-olds to produce the transitive construction: The role of frequency, semantic similarity and shared syntactic distribution. *Developmental Science* 7. 48–55.
Abbot-Smith, Kirsten, Elena V. M. Lieven, & Mike Tomasello. 2008. Graded representations in the acquisition of English and German transitive constructions. *Cognitive Development* 23. 48–66.
Abbot-Smith, Kirsten & Mike Tomasello. in press. The influence of frequency and semantic similarity on how children learn grammar. *First Language*.
Akhtar, Nameera. 1999. Acquiring basic word order: Evidence for data-driven learning of syntactic structure. *Journal of Child Language* 26. 339–356.
Allen, Shanley E. M. 2000. A discourse-pragmatic explanation for argument representation in child Inuktitut. *Linguistics* 38 (3). 483–521.
Bates, Elizabeth, & Brian MacWhinney. 1987. Competition, variation, and language learning. In Brian MacWhinney (ed.), Mechanisms of language acquisition (pp. 157–193). Hillsdale, NJ: Erlbaum.
Bloom, Paul. 1990. Subjectless sentences in child language. *Linguistic Inquiry* 21 (4). 491–504.
Bowerman, Melissa. 1990. Mapping thematic roles onto syntactic functions: Are children helped by innate linking rules?. *Linguistics* 28 (6). 1253–1289.
Brooks, Patricia, & Mike Tomasello. 1999. How children constrain their argument structures. *Language* 75. 720–738.
Brown, Penelope. 2008. Verb specificity and argument realization in Tzeltal child language. In Melissa Bowerman & Penelope Brown (eds.), Crosslinguistic perspectives on argument structure. Implications for learnability. Hillsdale, NJ: Erlbaum.
Budwig, Nancy. 1995. *A Developmental–functionalist Approach to Child Language*. Mahwah, NJ: Erlbaum.
Carpenter, Malinda, Nameera Akhtar & Mike Tomasello. 1998. Sixteen-month-old infants differentially imitate intentional and accidental actions. *Infant Behavior and Development* 21. 315–330.
Chan, Angel, Elena V. M. Lieven, & Mike Tomasello. 2009. Children's understanding of the agent-patient relations in the transitive construction: Cross-linguistic comparisons between Cantonese, German and English. *Cognitive Linguistics* 20 (2). 267–300.
Childers, Jane & Mike Tomasello. 2001. The role of pronouns in young children's acquisition of the English transitive construction. *Developmental Psychology* 37. 730–748.
Clancy, Patricia. M. 2003. The lexicon in interaction. Developmental origins of preferred argument structure in Korean. In John. W. Du Bois, Lorraine E. Kumpf & William J. Ashby (eds.), *Preferred Argument Structure. Grammar as Architecture for Function*. Amsterdam, Philadelphia: John Benjamins.
Corrigan, Roberta. 1986. The internal structure of English transitive sentence. *Memory & Cognition* 14 (5). 420–431.
Corrigan, Roberta. 1988. Children's identification of actors and patients in prototypical and nonprototypical sentence types. *Cognitive Development* 3. 285–297.

Croft, William. 2001. *Radical Construction Grammar: Syntactic Theory in Typological Perspective*. Oxford: Oxford University Press.
Dąbrowska, Ewa & Elena V. M. Lieven. 2005. Towards a lexically specific grammar of children's question constructions. *Cognitive Linguistics* 16 (3). 437–474.
de Villiers, Jill. 1980. The process of rule learning; a new look. In Keith Nelson (ed.), *Children's Language (Vol. 2)*. New York: Gardner Press.
Dittmar, Miriam, Kirsten Abbot-Smith, Elena V. M. Lieven, & Mike Tomasello. 2008a. Young German children's early syntactic competence: a preferential looking study. *Developmental Science* 11 (4). 575–582.
Dittmar, Miriam, Kirsten Abbot-Smith, Elena V. M. Lieven, & Mike Tomasello. 2008b. German children's comprehension of word order and case marking in causative sentences. *Child Development* 79 (4). 1152–1167.
Dowty, David. 1991. Thematic proto-roles and argument selection. *Language* 67 (3). 547–619.
DuBois, John. W. 1987. The discourse basis of ergativity. *Language* 63. 805–855.
Fenson, Larry, Philip Dale, J. Reznick, Elizabeth Bates, Donna Thal, & S. Pethick. 1994. *Variability in Early Communicative Development*. Chicago, IL: University of Chicago Press.
Fisher, Cynthia. 1996. Structural limits on verb mapping: The role of analogy in children's interpretations of sentences. *Cognitive Psychology* 31. 41–81.
Fisher, Cynthia. 2002. Structural limits on verb mapping: the role of abstract structure in 2.5-year-olds' interpretations of novel verbs. *Developmental Science* 5 (1). 55–64.
Freudenthal, Daniel, Julian M. Pine, & Fernand Gobet. 2007. Understanding the developmental dynamics of subject omission: the role of processing limitations in learning. *Journal of Child Language* 34. 83–110.
Gertner, Yael, Cynthia Fisher, J. & Eisengart. 2006. Learning words and rules: Abstract knowledge of word order in early sentence comprehension. *Psychological Science* 17. 684–691.
Givón, Talmy. 1983. *Topic Continuity in Discourse: A Quantitative Cross Language Study. Typological Studies in Language*, Vol. 3. Amsterdam: John Benjamins.
Goldberg, Adele. 1995. *Constructions: A Construction Grammar Approach to Argument Structure*. Chicago: University of Chicago Press.
Goldberg, Adele. 1999. The emergence of the semantics of argument structure constructions. In Brian. MacWhinney (ed.), *The Emergence of Language*. Mahwah, NJ: Erlbaum.
Guerriero, A. M. Sonia., A. Cooper, Yuriko Oshima-Takane, & Yoko Kuriyama. 2001. A discourse-pragmatic explanation for argument realization and omission in English and Japanese Children's speech. In Anna H.-J. Do, Laura Domínguez & Aimee Johansen (ed.), *BUCLD 25 Proceedings*. Somerville, MA: Cascadilla Press.
Hirsh-Pasek, Kathy., & Roberta M. Golinkoff. 1996. *The Origins of Grammar: Evidence from Early Language Comprehension*. Cambridge, MA: MIT Press.
Hopper, Paul. J., & Sandra A. Thompson. 1980. Transitivity in grammar and discourse. *Language* 56. 251–299.
Hughes, Mary E. & Shanley Allen. 2009. Child-directed speech and the development of referential choice in child English. Paper presented at the biennial conference of the *Society for Research in Child Development, Denver, April 2009*.
Ibbotson, Paul. Anna L. Theakston, Elena V. M. Lieven, & Mike Tomasello. 2011. Acquiring the transitive construction in English: the role of pronoun frames. *Language Learning and Development* 7. 1–16.
Ibbotson, Paul. Anna L. Theakston, Elena V. M. Lieven, & Mike Tomasello. In press. Semantics of the Transitive Construction: prototype Effects and Developmental Comparisons. *Cognitive Science*.
Ibbotson, Paul & Mike Tomasello. 2009. Prototype Constructions in Early Language Acquisition. *Language and Cognition* 1(1). 59–85.

Jones, Gary, Fernand Gobet, & Julian M. Pine. 2000. A process model of children's early verb use. In Lila. R. Gleitman & Aravind K. Joshi (eds.), *Proceedings of the 22nd Annual Meeting of the Cognitive Science Society*. Mahwah, NJ: Erlbaum.

Laakso, Aarre. & Linda B. Smith. 2007. Pronouns and verbs in adult speech to children: A corpus analysis. *Journal of Child Language* 34 (4). 725–763.

Landau, Barbara & Lila Gleitman. 1985. *Language and experience: Evidence from the Blind Child*. Cambridge, MA: Cambridge University Press.

Langacker, Ronald. 1991. *Foundations of Cognitive Grammar (Vol. 2)*. Stanford: Stanford University Press.

Lidz, Jeffery, Henry Gleitman & Lila Gleitman. 2003. Understanding how input matters: verb learning and the footprint of universal grammar. *Cognition* 87. 151–178.

Lieven, Elena V. M., Julian M. Pine, & Gillian Baldwin. 1997. Lexically-based learning and early grammatical development. *Journal of Child Language* 24 (1). 187–220.

Lieven, Elena V. M., Heike Behrens, Jennifer Speares, & Mike Tomasello. 2003. Early syntactic creativity: A usage-based approach. *Journal of Child Language* 30 (2). 333–367.

Lieven, Elena V. M., Dorothe Salomo, & Mike Tomasello. 2009. Two-year-old children's production of multiword utterances: a usage-based analysis. *Cognitive Linguistics* 20 (3). 481–509.

MacWhinney, Brian. 2000. *The CHILDES Project: Tools for Analysing Talk*. Mahwah, NJ: Erlbaum.

Maratsos, Michael. 2000. More overregularizations after all. *Journal of Child Language* 28. 32–54.

Matthews, Danielle, Elena V. M. Lieven, Anna L. Theakston & Mike Tomasello. 2005. The role of frequency in the acquisition of English word order. *Cognitive Development* 20. 121–136.

Matthews, Danielle, Elena V. M. Lieven, Anna L. Theakston & Mike Tomasello. 2006. The effect of perceptual availability and prior discourse on young children's use of referring expressions. *Applied Psycholinguistics* 27. 403–422.

McClure, Kathy, Julian. M. Pine & Elena. V. M. Lieven. 2006. Investigating the abstractness of children's early knowledge of argument structure. *Journal of Child Language* 33. 693–720.

Næss, Åshild. 2007. *Prototypical Transitivity*. Typological Studies in Language, 72. John Benjamins Publishing Company. Amsterdam/Philadelphia.

Naigles, Letitia R. 1990. Children use syntax to learn verb meaning. *Journal of Child Language* 17. 357–374.

Naigles, Letitia R. 2003. Paradox lost? No, paradox found! Reply to Tomasello & Akhtar 2003. *Cognition* 88. 325–329.

Naigles, Letitia, R., Erica Hoff, & Donna Vear. 2009. Flexibility in early verb use: Evidence from a multiple-n diary study. *Monographs of the Society for Research in Child Development* 74 (2). 1–143.

Ninio, Anat. 1999. Pathbreaking verbs in syntactic development and the question of prototypical transitivity. *Journal of Child Language* 26. 619–653.

Ninio, Anat. 2005. Testing the role of semantic similarity in syntactic development. *Journal of Child Language* 32. 35–61.

Pine, Julian M., Elena V. M. Lieven & Caroline F. Rowland. 1998. Comparing Models of the Development of the English Verb Category. *Linguistics* 36 (4). 807–830.

Pinker, Steven. 1984. *Language Learnability and Language Development*. Cambridge, MA: Harvard University Press.

Pyykkönen, Pirita, Danielle Matthews & Juhani Järvikivi. in press. Three-year-olds are sensitive to semantic prominence during online language comprehension: A visual world study of pronoun resolution. *Language and Cognitive Processes*.

Savage, Ceri, Elena V. M. Lieven, Anna L. Theakston & Mike Tomasello. 2003. Testing the abstractness of young children's linguistic representations: Lexical and structural priming of syntactic constructions? *Developmental Science* 6(4). 557–567.

Savage, Ceri, Elena V. M. Lieven, Anna L. Theakston & Mike Tomasello. 2006. Structural Priming as Implicit Learning in Language Acquisition: The Persistence of Lexical and Structural Priming in 4-year-olds. *Language Learning and Development* 2 (1). 27–49.

Slobin, Dan. I. 1982. Universal and particular in the acquisition of language. In Lila. R. Gleitman & Eric. Wanner (eds.), *Language Acquisition: The State of the Art*. Cambridge, UK: Cambridge University Press.

Slobin, Dan. I. 1985. Crosslinguistic evidence for the Language-Making Capacity. In Dan I. Slobin (ed.), *The Crosslinguistic Study of Language Acquisition. Vol. 2: Theoretical Issues*. Hillsdale, NJ: Erlbaum.

Slobin, Dan. I. 1997. The origins of grammaticalizable notions: Beyond the individual mind. In Dan I. Slobin (ed.), *The Crosslinguistic Study of Language Acquisition Vol. 5: Expanding the Contexts*. Hillsdale, NJ: Erlbaum.

Theakston, Anna. L., Elena. V. M. Lieven, Julian. M. Pine & Caroline. F. Rowland. 2004. Semantic generality, input frequency and the acquisition of syntax. *Journal of Child Language* 31. 61–99.

Tomasello, Mike. 1992. *First Verbs: A Case Study of Early Grammatical Development*. Cambridge: Cambridge University Press.

Tomasello, Mike. 2003. *Constructing a Language: A Usage-based Theory of Language Acquisition*. Cambridge, MA: Harvard University Press.

Tomasello, Mike & Patricia Brooks. 1998. Young children's earliest transitive and intransitive constructions. *Cognitive Linguistics* 9. 379–395.

Tomasello, Mike & Daniel Stahl. 2004. Sampling children's spontaneous speech: How much is enough? *Journal of Child Language* 31. 101–121.

Trueswell, John. C. & Mike K. Tanenhaus. 1994. Toward a lexicalist framework for constraint-based syntactic ambiguity resolution. In Charles Clifton, Lyn Frazier, & Keith Rayner (eds.), *Perspectives in Sentence Processing*. Hillsdale, NJ: Erlbaum.

Yuan, Sylvia. & Cynthia Fisher. 2009. "Really? She blicked the baby?". Two-year-olds learn combinatorial facts about verbs by listening. *Psychological Science*, 20 (5), 619–626.

Discovering constructions by means of collostruction analysis: The English Denominative Construction*

Beate Hampe

Abstract

Complex-transitive argument structures have received a large amount of attention from syntacticians of both formalist and cognitive-functional orientations. To account for expressions with causative resultative meanings, construction grammar has postulated a family of argument-structure constructions whose core is constituted by the Caused-Motion Construction and the Resultative Construction, exhibiting a locative complement and a predicative complement in the form of an AjP, respectively. Argument structures with NP complements, however, have been largely neglected. The present study investigates these patterns in the International Corpus of English *(ICE-GB)* by means "collostruction analysis". It shows that the formal distinction between AjP and NP complements corresponds to a constructional distinction hitherto unrevealed, viz. that between the Resultative Construction and another argument-structure construction, here called the "Denominative Construction". Apart from improving existing descriptions of the network of complex-transitive argument-structure constructions, this study demonstrates that collostruction analysis can be employed in an exploratory way to discover constructions.

Keywords: Usage-based model; construction grammar; argument-structure construction; the English Denominative Construction; the English Resultative Construction; collostruction analysis.

---

* This article originates in a talk given at CSDL 8. I wish to thank my anonymous reviewers as well as Holger Diessel and the editor of this journal for their very helpful comments on earlier drafts. Moreover, I am very grateful to Stefan Th. Gries for kindly providing a list of the verb-lemma frequencies in the ICE-GB as well as the software *Coll.Analysis 2.0.1* in R, which was used for carrying out all collostruction analyses. All remaining errors are my own. Email: Beate Hampe <beate.hampe@uni-erfurt.de>

1. Introduction

For more than two decades, argument structures labelled "complex-transitive" (henceforth "cxtr.") by major reference grammars (e.g. Huddleston and Pullum 2002: 251–266; Quirk et al. 1985: 1195–1202) have attracted considerable interest both from formalist/generative schools (e.g. Aarts 1992, 1995; Carrier and Randall 1992; Hoekstra 1988; Levin and Rappaport 1991, 1995; Rapoport 1990, 1999; Rothstein 2006) and from linguists working within a construction-based framework (e.g. Boas 2003; Broccias 2003, 2007; Goldberg 1995; Goldberg and Jackendoff 2004). In both research traditions, expressions with a locative complement mostly realised as a prepositional phrase (see [1]) or a predicative complement in the form of an adjectival phrase (see [2]) have received the bulk of attention.[1] Scholars generally agree that the PP or AjP in (1) and (2) relate to the post-verbal NP in a way that can be expressed by a copular clause (hence the term "secondary predication"), and furthermore that both are semantically "resultative", i.e. specify the result of a change of location or state which is caused by the subject-NP referent and undergone by the object-NP referent (hence the term "resultative phrase"). Though the same can be said about example (3), expressions with a NP complement have been almost entirely excluded from consideration.[2]

(1) *The warm air rising up pushes other air [$_{PP}$ out of the way].* <W2B-025>[3]
(2) *If you have fresh maggots, riddle them [$_{AjP}$ clean] with a riddle tray.* <W2D-017>
(3) *Keith Joseph had appointed me [$_{NP}$ a part time Special Adviser].* <W2B-012>

The strong focus on expressions with resultative meanings in most generative and cognitive-functional work has nearly eclipsed a fact that is well-documented in major reference grammars, viz. that the cxtr. patterns also code for a range of non-resultative meanings. These are usually brought together under the labels of *depictive* or *current* (e.g. Aarts 1995; Biber et al. 1999: 151; Halliday 1967; Huddleston and Pullum 2002: 251), because the predicative complement does not denote a resultant property, but "gives a property of the predicand argument at the time of the situation under consideration" (Huddleston and

---

1. Huddleston and Pullum's (2002: 257–260) terms *locative* and *predicative complement* are identical to what Quirk et al. (1985: 56) call *obligatory object-related adverbial* and *object complement*, respectively. The latter is sometimes also called *object predicative* (Biber et al. 1999: 130).
2. Cf. however Aarts (1995: 79): "Secondary predicates . . . can be NPs, APs or PPs."
3. Illustrative corpus examples are taken from the ICE-GB or the BNC, World Edition; all ID-codes of the source files are given in angled brackets. Corpus examples may have been shortened, but not lexically altered.

Pullum 2002: 251).[4] As the distinction between resultative and depictive meanings is a subtle one in some cases and as the group of cxtr. expressions with non-resultative meanings is rather heterogeneous at that, the subsequent paragraphs will briefly survey the verb classes listed by standard reference grammars as capable of appearing in the cxtr. patterns (cf. Huddleston and Pullum 2002: 264–266; Givon 1993: 125; Quirk et al. 1985: 1196–1200).

Resultative meanings are firstly expressed by the dynamic "resulting" verbs, i.e. generic lexical causatives like *make, render* or *turn*, whose cxtr. uses with predicative complements are firmly lexicalized (see [4a]). Secondly, a large and open class of activity or accomplishment verbs like *hammer, knock, paint, brush*, etc., can optionally take a predicative complement (see [2], [4b]). Of these, the class of declarative speech-act verbs like *appoint, proclaim* or *declare* (see [4c]) constitutes a special case of particular relevance to the present concerns.

(4)   a.   *They wanted us to* make *them [$_{NP}$ the private owners of the huge nearby common]*. <S2B-025>
       b.   *Two people were* shot *[$_{AjP}$ dead]*. (+ passive) <W2C-019>
       c.   *Israel* proclaimed *the committees [$_{AjP}$ illegal]*. <BNC-APD>

When stative "current" verbs like *keep, hold*, and *leave* occur with a locative or predicative complement, the non-resultative meanings expressed are closely related to resultative ones, because the scenes denoted incur the forceful maintenance of a location or state, i.e. the prevention—rather than causation—of a change of location or state (see [5]).

(5)   a.   *And do you* keep *it [$_{PP}$ in a garage]*. <S1B-074>
       b.   *I know that I did I did not want to* leave *it [$_{AjP}$ open] over night.* <S1B-069>

It is far less clear, however, in which way the remaining verb classes with non-resultative meanings are related to those with resultative ones. According to Quirk and colleagues, object-related predicative complements are also found with factual speech-act verbs, i.e. verbs of saying and calling (see [6]), verbs of intellectual activity (see [7]) as well as, more marginally, volitional verbs (see [8]).

(6)   a.   *And if the orientation is at right angles to the stimulus, it is* termed *[$_{AjP}$ diatropic]*. (+ passive) <W2A-025 >
       b.   *We have* called *this investigation [$_{NP}$ Operation Still]*. <W2C-011>
(7)   a.   *Diagnosis is not* considered *[$_{AjP}$ important]*. (+ passive) <W1A-007>

---

4.   Halliday (1967: 62) notes that secondary predicates can occur with action clauses ("resultative") as well as clauses of being and ascription ("depictive").

b. *We* think *that [$_{NP}$ the most effective approach to supporting people]*. <S1B-057>

(8) *I* want *him [$_{AjP}$ dead, dead, DEAD]*. <BNC example, cited in Gonzálvez-García 2009>

The present study works towards closing one of the research gaps identified by taking a closer look at the neglected pattern with NP complement, both in isolation and as a part of the network of the cxtr. argument structures comprising also expressions with PP and AjP complements. To this end, it investigates all three patterns in the British part of the *International Corpus of English* (ICE-GB).

The analysis offered presupposes a sign-based approach to language, in which syntactic generalizations are seen as resulting from frequency-driven processes of schematization over actual usage events that are meaningful to their participants (e.g. Bybee 2006; Bybee and Thompson 2000; Diessel 2007). In such a framework, the emergent linguistic system is expected to consist of partially redundant, interlinked schematizations, including low-level generalizations (e.g. Croft 2003; Dąbrowska 2009, submitted; Diessel 2004: 23–37; Goldberg 2006: 12; Langacker 2000: 3).[5] The theoretical assumptions underlying this paper are thus in line with those made by various usage-based construction grammars (e.g. Goldberg 2006; Langacker 1988, 2000; Taylor 2002), which view the language system as an array of symbolic units that vary in terms of their respective degrees of schematicity, internal complexity and productivity, and which treat *all* conventional composite structures, irrespective of the presence of any unpredictable properties, as form-meaning pairings, i.e. *constructions* (e.g. Goldberg 2006: 5; Langacker 2000: 2). Towards the syntactic pole of the "constructicon" (Jurafsky 1992; Goldberg 1995: 5), units are characterized by high degrees of complexity and schematizity, ranging from a very large and highly varied class of "formal idioms" (e.g. Fillmore et al. 1988) to fully schematic as well as highly productive phrasal and clausal structures. Of the latter, argument-structure constructions as complex and fully schematic symbolic units denoting generic event frames (Goldberg 1995: 5; 1998a: 205; Langacker 1991: 293–304) have been a major point of interest from early on.

The crucial role attributed to linguistic performance in usage-based models (cf. Barlow and Kemmer 2000) has initiated what can by now be called an empirical turn in construction grammar. Pioneered by empirical research on the acquisition of syntactic constructions (e.g. Dąbrowska 2000; Tomasello

---

5. This is in line with independent corpus-linguistic findings on the collocational restrictions limiting "open" syntactic choices and on the role of prefabricated chunks in language use (e.g., Dąbrowska 2004: 18–25; Pawley and Syder 1983; Sinclair 1992: 110–115; Schönefeld 1999, 2002: 247–301; Wray 2002).

2000; 2003; Diessel 2004; Dąbrowska and Lieven 2005; Casenhiser and Goldberg 2005; Goldberg et al. 2004, 2005), the use of a growing range of methods from quantitative corpus linguistics has come to be one of its hallmarks (e.g. Diessel 2008; Gries 2005; Gries and Stefanowitsch 2006; Hilpert 2008; Stefanowitsch 2008; Szmrecsanyi 2005; Wiechmann 2008; Wulff 2003, 2009). Corpus-based research on the lexical realisations of syntactic constructions in general—and of argument-structure constructions in particular—has profited from the application of various methods from the family of "collostruction analysis" developed by Stefan Th. Gries and Anatol Stefanowitsch. To date, collostruction analysis has successfully been employed to investigate the precise functional load of syntactic constructions both synchronically and diachronically, and to spell out the subtle functional differences between related constructions participating in what has traditionally been treated as syntactic alternations (cf. Stefanowitsch and Gries 2003, 2005; Gries and Stefanowitsch 2004a, 2004b; Gries et al. 2005; Hilpert 2008; Gries and Hilpert 2008). This paper adds to this list by showing that collostructional analysis can also be used to discover syntactic constructions. It is demonstrated that, in order to account for the presence of major non-resultative verb classes, the standard inventory of the cxtr. argument-structure constructions needs to be revised and extended in a way that relates straightforwardly to the formal difference between the patterns with AjP and NP complements.

In order to contextualize the present investigation, section 2 will survey the most relevant aspects of the preceding formalist as well as cognitive-functional research on the cxtr. argument structures.

2. Complex-transitive argument structures

2.1. *Resultatives*

When speaking of resultative constructions, scholars from the generative/ formalist and construction-based traditions refer to slightly different, though overlapping, sets of expressions. The former focus more narrowly on a syntactic alternation that verbs from various aspectual classes can undergo in order to acquire a causative resultative interpretation and cxtr. argument frame which they do not exhibit outside that construction (e.g. Aarts 1995; Rappaport and Levin 2001, Rapoport 1990, 1999; Rothstein 2006; Wanner 1999: 147–159, examples in [9] taken from these sources). Expressions containing transitive or intransitive (non-telic) activity verbs (see [9a–9c]) and especially verbs with non-subcategorized ("fake") objects (see [9b–9d]) are well-known cases in point. With the deletion of the resultative phrase, the resultative interpretation disappears in all of these examples, and the respective expressions only remain grammatical if no fake objects are involved (see [9a]).

(9) a. *Boaz* hammered *the metal [AjP smooth]*.
   b. *My son always* runs *his trainers [AjP threadbare]*. vs. **My son always* runs *his trainers*.
   c. *Lucille* laughed *herself [AjP sick]*. vs. **Lucile* laughed *herself*.
   d. *John* sang *the baby [AjP asleep]*. vs. **John* sang *the baby*.

Expressions with accomplishment verbs are sometimes viewed as "false" resultatives (e.g. Rapoport 1999), due to the fact that the resultative phrases only specify an aspect already inherent in the telic verbal meanings (see [10a–10b]). Expressions with lexical causatives, finally, are of no interest at all, because here the predicative complement is an element of the verbal subcategorization frame. Its deletion is thus never tolerated and incurs either the loss of grammaticality (see [11a]) or a change in the meaning of the verb phrase, which may or may not lead to unacceptability (see [11b]).

(10) a. *An attempt to* entice *puffins [PP back to Ailsa Craig] is to be made next month.* <W2C-015>
   b. *Add the meat . . . , but not* chopped *[AjP too fine]*. (+ passive, + non-finite clause) <W2D-020>
(11) a. *Blizzards could* render *them [AjP half blind]*. <S2B-024> vs. **Blizzards could render them*.
   b. *something that's* made *the Range Rover [AjP so good]* <S2A-055> vs. *something that's made the Range Rover*

Much formalist work on AjP complements serving as resultative phrases has stressed that these are an integral part of the verb phrase and must be distinguished from optional adjective phrases that are depictive adjuncts (e.g. Aarts 1995: 78–80; Rapoport 1999: 653–654; Rothstein 2006; see [12], [13] adapted from these sources). The latter generally specify temporary attributes of the NP they relate to, thus resembling adverbials of duration that can also take on conditional overtones (see [12b]). As adjuncts, they can in principle also pre-modify the NP under scope, though this incurs the loss of the conditional implications (see [12c]). While usually modifying the post-verbal NP, depictive adjuncts can also relate to a pre-verbal one (see [13a]), which may give rise to scope ambiguities if the contextual constraints do not rule out either of the two possibilities for adjunct scope (see [13b]).

(12) a. *Bill cuts the bread hot.* ('while the bread is hot')
   b. *Bill eats the carrots raw.* ('while/if the carrots are raw')
   c. *Bill cuts the hot bread. Bill eats the raw carrots.*
(13) a. *Bill sliced the meat drunk.* ('while Bill was drunk')
   b. *The artist painted the woman naked.* ('while the artist/the woman was naked')

In contrast, resultative phrases can only be predicated of the post-verbal NP (see [14a]).[6] They cannot undergo the modifier alternation without losing their resultative interpretation or acceptability (see [14b]–[14c]), taken from Levin and Rappaport 1991, Boas 2003). They thus behave like arguments, though they are also highly peculiar in providing a secondary predicate as well as in being lexically highly dependent on the verb (e.g. Aarts 1995: 93–96, Goldberg and Jackendoff 2004: 558–563).

(14) a. They stripped me *[$_{AjP}$ completely naked]*. <S2A-050>
 b. He wiped *the slate clean.* vs. *He wiped the clean slate.*
 c. *They drank the pub dry.* vs. **They drank the dry pub.*

Construction-based approaches have rendered the distinction between real and false resultatives largely irrelevant (e.g. Goldberg 1995: 50–59, 184–185; Goldberg and Jackendoff 2004; Goldberg 2006: 42–43). A network of closely related constructions, the core of which is constituted by the "Caused-Motion Construction" (henceforth CMC, see [1]) and the "Resultative Construction" (henceforth RC, see [2]), respectively, has been postulated in order to account for all expressions with causative resultative meanings (cf. Goldberg 1995: 152–227, 180–198). The realisations of the resultative phrases as either locative complements or adjectival predicatives reflect the fact that the event frames denoted incur the causation of a (literal or metaphorical) change of location ([X MAKE [Y MOVE Z]]) or of state ([X MAKE [Y BECOME Z]]).[7]

As argument-structure constructions are symbolic units, the focus of interest has shifted from the syntactic properties of the aspectual classes partaking in a syntactic alternation to the lexical meanings that are compatible with a given constructional meaning (Goldberg 1997, 1998a, 1998b). If there is a mismatch between the verb's argument roles and meaning and those of the construction, their respective specifications are "fused". The construction "coerces" the verbal meaning into a causative resultative interpretation, licensing the resultative phrase and sometimes also a fake object (cf. Goldberg 1995: 50–59; Goldberg and Jackendoff 2004: 547–552; Michaelis 2003a: 176–184, 2003b).[8]

---

6. Constructions with subject host (*They ran into the woods. They followed the scout into the woods.*) are resultative, but not causative (Goldberg and Jackendoff 2004; Boas 2003: 7). To capture this, Levin and Rappaport (1995: 34) formulated the "direct-object restriction". For a survey of formalist positions on object vs. subject hosts in resultatives, see Rothstein (2006: 226–228).
7. While the distinction between the CMC and the RC has been recently de-emphasized (e.g. Boas 2003: 6; Broccias 2003, 2007; Goldberg and Jackendoff 2004), there are also arguments supporting the distinction (cf. Hampe 2011).
8. Due to the regularity of these processes across argument-structure constructions, much construction-based work has revolved around issues of constructional polysemy (e.g. Goldberg 1992; Goldberg 1995: 31–43; Goldberg 1997: 386, 1998b: 45–49, 2006: 34; Taylor 1998).

From the construction-grammar perspective, the combination with a generic lexical causative (see [11]) presents the most straightforward case in the CMC or RC, viz. a simple instantiation, because the verb shares its meaning and argument slots with those of the respective construction (cf. Goldberg 1997: 386, 1998b: 46). Otherwise, lexically more specific accomplishment or activity verbs in the CMC or RC may elaborate the constructional meaning by spelling out details of the action causing the change (see [15a]–[15b]). Motivated by conceptual metonymy, these can also relate to the means or instruments employed (see [16a]–[16b]) (cf. Goldberg 1997: 389–390, 1998b: 46).

(15) a. *The ice will shear off* dragging *you [$_{PP}$ down into the open chasm beneath you]*. <S2B-024>
b. *The next morning Benjamin* shook *me [$_{AjP}$ awake]*. <BNC example, taken from Boas 2003: 4>
(16) a. *When a defender has once been* forced *[$_{PP}$ into a position like this in a match]* . . . (+ passive) <W2D-015>
b. *Several boats will* ferry *the Warfarin [$_{AvP}$ across]*. <W2C-015>

Speech-act verbs like *call* or *invite* (see [17a]–[17b]) may take on resultative meanings in the CMC because successful speech acts, which bring about the intended change in their perlocutions, present a social means of causation (cf. Goldberg 1995: 167). In the RC, this is paralleled by the previously mentioned group of declarative speech-act verbs, which are resultative because the speech acts denoted cause a very precisely defined change in the social domain (see [4c], [18a]–[18b]) that relates to a selected (social) property of the object-NP referent. Despite their initial characterisation as verbs with optional predicative complements, their cxtr. uses really constitute highly specific lexical causatives, because their respective speech-act meanings depend on and are firmly lexicalised in the pattern with AjP complement.

(17) a. *I* called *him [$_{PP}$ into my office]*. <BNC-F9Y>
b. *I will be ringing you personally to* invite *you [$_{PP}$ into my office]*. <W1B-016>
(18) a. *He could be released after being* declared *[$_{AjP}$ insolvent]*. (+ passive) (+ non-finite clause) <W2B-006>
b. *This is an appeal . . . that Mr Leonard Jerome Daniel be* adjudged *[$_{AjP}$ bankrupt]*. (+ passive) <S2A-069>

2.2. Depictives

Though most of the literature on secondary predication has focussed on the distinction between resultative complements and depictive adjuncts (e.g. Rothstein 2006: 213; Rapoport 1990: 35, 1999: 653–654), several authors have noted that some non-resultative secondary predicates are like complements (cf.

Aarts 1995: 81; Gonzálvez-García 2009: 666). The distinction between depictive complements and adjuncts is a particularly subtle one, as the former characterize concomitant properties of the object-NP referent, i.e. properties that are temporally co-extensive with (rather than resulting from) the processes expressed by the lexical meanings of the verbs. Syntactically, however, depictive complements behave like resultative phrases: Unless they profile an aspect of the meaning of the verbal base (see [19a]), their deletion may cause a change in the meaning of the verb phrase or the loss of acceptability (see [19b]–[19c]). The modifier alternation yields similar results (see [19d]–[19e]). And, finally, fake objects are also found with depictive complements (see [19c], [19e]).

(19) a. *She* labelled *some experimental items [_{AjP} unsuitable].*
b. *She* calls/considers *the applicant [_{NP} a genius].* vs. *She calls/considers the applicant.*
c. *He* calls/thinks *himself [_{NP} a genius].* vs. **He calls/thinks himself.*
d. *She* called/believed *the scientist [_{AjP} crazy].* vs. *She called/believed the crazy scientist.*
e. *They* call/deem *the novel [_{AjP} debatable].* vs. **They call/deem the debatable novel.*

Block (19) demonstrates that cognition verbs and factual speech-act verbs clearly take depictive complements. Verbs of volition, preference, liking, desire or need, on the other hand, provide the most conspicuous illustration of the difficulties involved in distinguishing depictive adjuncts from complements. The depictive AjP in (20), for instance, can be argued to constitute complements of the respective verbs of volition and preference. Those in (21), on the other hand, invite an adjunct interpretation, because they are all deletable and can be paraphrased by means of a durational adverbial or undergo the modifier alternation. In addition, with some verbs, the object-related AjP can receive a complement or adjunct interpretation (see [22]). Because of these problems, the present study leaves these verb groups to further research.

(20) a. *I* want *him [_{AjP} dead, dead, DEAD].* <BNC example, cited in Gonzálvez-García 2009> ('I want him to be dead.')
b. *There are times ... that I* wish *myself not [_{NP} a prince], but [_{NP} a simple fellow].* <BNC example, cited in Gonzálvez-García 2009> ('I wish I were a simple fellow.')
c. *He* prefers *his coffee hot.* ('He prefers his coffee to be hot.')
(21) a. *He* needs *the veggies fresh.* ('He needs the veggies while they are fresh', 'He needs the fresh veggies')
b. *He* likes *his steaks raw.* ('He likes his steaks while they are raw.', 'He likes his raw steaks'.)

(22) *He* wants *his enemy alive*. ('He wants his enemy to be/stay alive.' or 'He wants his enemy while he is alive.')

Expressions with depictive complements raise a number of issues concerning the constructional inventory required for an adequate characterisation of the cxtr. argument structures, because they make it plain that the mapping from form to function in these patterns is not unique. Nevertheless, construction grammarians have until recently been hesitating to extend their investigations to expressions with depictive complements. The remainder of this section will provide a brief survey of the existing construction-based work on each of the non-resultative verb classes.

To start with the least problematic case, it was indicated previously that the cxtr. uses of current verbs refer to the forceful maintenance of a current location or state of the object-NP referent, i.e. to the prevention of a change (see [5a]–[5b]).[9] These "forced location/state" uses do not require the introduction of new constructional distinctions, because the difference between them is not reliably marked by morpho-syntactic means, but largely achieved by the main verb as the primary predicator (cf. Hampe 2011).[10] Moreover, the scenarios of causation and prevention are force-dynamically related. An inclusion of these uses into the current descriptions of the semantics of the CMC and the RC, yielding (X MAKE [Y MOVE/STAY Z]] and [X MAKE [Y BECOME/REMAIN Z]), respectively, is thus perfectly in line with previous observations that verbs in the CMC can refer to a range of force-dynamically related scenarios in which a change of location is not caused, but enabled, permitted, supported or blocked (cf. Goldberg 1997: 393–394).[11]

Of the remaining non-resultative verb classes, cognition verbs and factual speech-act verbs (see [6]–[7]) have been observed to be of central importance to the two cxtr. patterns with predicative complements (Hampe and Schönefeld 2006; Gonzálvez-García 2009). Both studies agree that expressions with cognition verbs refer to subjective assessments, i.e. scenarios in which the subject-NP referent ascribes to the referent of the object-NP an attribute (see [7a]) or categorization (see [7b]) with a relatively high degree of certainty. Expressions

---

9. Goldberg et al. (2005) include cases of what they call "caused location" in their corpus analysis of the acquisition of the CMC.
10. Even in the CMC, the preposition or adverb serving as the secondary predicator does not always code the distinction between location and direction. In the ICE-GB, the verb *put*, for example, is more strongly associated with *on* and *in* than with the path-prepositions *onto* and *into*.
11. The 'blockage' use (e.g. *They were not allowed [PP out of the room] until they had an answer*... [+ passive] <BNC-A0T>) construes a static scene dynamically and is thus not identical with the "forced location" use of the CMC, exhibiting a "current" verb and requiring a static interpretation.

with factual speech-act verbs refer to scenarios in which such an ascription is verbalized, i.e. where either the object-NP referent as a whole (see [6b]) or one of its attributes/properties (see [6a]) are named. In order to distinguish these uses of the cxtr. patterns from their resultative ones, Hampe and Schönefeld (2006) refer to them as "attributive" ([X THINK [Y BE Z]]) and "denominative" ([X SAY [Y BE Z]]), respectively. As these terms provide an opportunity to extend the existing terminology for depictive complements in analogy to what is common practice with respect to resultative ones, I will in the following adhere to them.

While Hampe and Schönefeld (2006) merely raise the issue that some additional generalizations, at least at a verb-class based level, are needed in order to capture the distinction between resultative, denominative and attributive expressions, Gonzálvez-García (2009: 669–670, 676–681) actually postulates two argument-structure constructions, the "Evaluative Subjective Transitive Construction" and the "Declarative Subjective Transitive Construction", as major sub-constructions of an overarching "Subjective Transitive Construction".[12] Based on an in-depth qualitative analysis of a large number of corpus occurrences in the British National Corpus, cross-checked for native-speaker acceptance, Gonzálvez-García (2009) provides the verbs in (23) and (24) as attested in the two constructions.[13]

(23) *account, acknowledge, adjudge, adjudicate, assume, believe, conceive, conclude, consider, count, deem, discover, dream, envisage, esteem, estimate, expect, fancy, feel, fear, figure, find, guarantee, hail, hold, imagine, judge, know, mark?, mistake for, picture, presume, rank, rate, reckon, recognize, regard, remember, repute, reveal, see, suppose, show, take, take for, think, value, visualize, warrant, watch, vote*

(24) *acclaim, anoint, brand, call, certify, code-name, confess, confirm, declare, decree, diagnose, dub, label, mean?, misname, name, nickname, pass, proclaim, profess, pronounce, rename, report, rule, say, state, style, tag, term, title, understand?*

Most relevant to the present concerns, neither Hampe and Schönefeld (2006), nor Gonzálvez-García (2009) clarify whether the difference between resultative, attributive and denominative uses of the cxtr. patterns is bound to the syntactic difference between the two kinds of predicative complements. On the contrary, it is precisely the capacity to occur as either AjP or NP that is

---

12. Though there are also postulations for expressions with volitional and related verbs, given as the "Manipulative" and "Generic" Subjective Transitive Construction (Gonzálvez-García 2009: 670), these are not considered here because of the difficulties expounded.
13. The question marks are not contained in the original, but were inserted here to indicate items whose membership in the class is doubtful.

currently assumed to constitute the hallmark of predicative complements (cf. Gonzálvez-García 2009; Goldberg 2006: 21; note 2).

Following a basic tenet in functional linguistics which assumes differences in syntactic form to reflect semantico-pragmatic differences, the present paper argues that the formal versatility observable with predicative complements should matter to a sign-based approach to argument structures, in particular since the prototypical conceptualizations referred to by nouns differ *in kind* from those denoted by adjectives (cf. Langacker 1987: 183–222; Givon 1984: 51–56, Lehmann 1991). The former denote relatively autonomous entities in some cognitive domain which are characterized by bundles of properties and, though non-referential in predicative function, serve the purpose of reference in other argument positions. The latter, in contrast, designate single attributes and function as modifiers of the former. Though the relations they denote are atemporal in Langacker's sense, adjectives are positioned between nouns and verbs on a scale of time-stability. It is thus very unlikely that the formal difference between AjP and NP complements does not also incur considerable functional differences that a constructional analysis should reflect.

2.3. *The complex-transitive pattern with NP complement*

As indicated previously, the cxtr. pattern with NP-complement has not been systematically investigated at all in either tradition, with some surveys of secondary predication not even citing examples (e.g. Rapoport 1990, 1999; Rothstein 2006). Resultative examples with an NP complement are problematic for generative accounts, because such a complement cannot get its thematic role and case marking from a verb that has already licensed these for the direct object. They should thus be restricted to expressions with lexical causatives or false resultatives (see [25a]–[25b]). Example (25c), however, exhibits a fake object and would thus have to count as a "real" resultative in any approach.

(25) a. *This* makes *Bonfire Night [NP the enemy of advertising]*. <W2E-003>
 b. *Keith Joseph had* appointed *me [NP a part time Special Adviser]*. <W2B-012>
 c. *... a resolution* declaring *Yiddish [NP the national Jewish language]*. (+ non-finite relative clause) <S2B-042>

The following collection of some of the rare examples with NP complement cited in the literature on secondary predication (see [26]–[28] taken from Aarts 1995, Rothstein 2006) illustrates that the pattern is by no means restricted to resultative meanings.

(26) a. *They* elected *me [NP senior treasurer]*. ('They made me senior treasurer by electing me.')

      b. *The people* crowned *him [NP King]*. ('The people made him King by crowning him.')
      c. *The committee* appointed *her [NP senior lecturer]*. ('They made her senior lecturer by appointing her.')
(27) a. *They* baptised *him [NP Jim]*. (*'They made him [NP Jim] by baptizing him').
      b. *We* named *her [NP Catherine]*.
(28) *John* considers *Mary [NP a genius]*.

In analogy to what was said previously about expressions with constitutive speech-act verbs in the AjP pattern, the examples in (26) are resultatives proper as they refer to the causation of a social change (hence the possibility of a paraphrase with *make*). Semantically, expressions with NP complement differ from those with AjP complement in that they refer to the creation of a new social role or identity of the object-NP referent, which is defined by a whole cluster of attributes, not a single one. Whether the expressions in (27) are resultative as well, however, is less certain. Both the paraphrase with *call* and the fact that the NP complement can also be realised by a proper noun may be taken to suggest that the expressions in (27) are denominative, i.e. refer to mere naming scenarios—although expressions with declarative speech-act verbs that refer to ritualised naming events (see [27a]) certainly border on resultative uses proper. No matter which position is taken on this issue, the common denominator between (26) and (27) is without doubt constituted by the denominative, not the resultative element. A plausible hypothesis to pursue is therefore that the pattern with NP complement typically expresses naming events rather than causation scenarios per se.

The question then is whether occurrences of generic lexical causatives like *make* or *render* or of attributive verbs like *consider* or *think* would necessarily constitute counter-evidence to this hypothesis. I suggest that this is not the case, as occurrences of verbs from both classes in this pattern are well motivated. A brief reflection on the relations between resultative, denominative and attributive meanings, which may have been veiled by the resultative-depictive dichotomy, will suffice to clarify the claim that the three meanings form a continuum and are clearly distinct only in the respective prototypical instances.

As regards the relation between resultative and denominative meanings, the previous discussion has expounded that the class of declarative speech-act verbs constitutes an intermediate case by being resultative and denominative simultaneously. Generic lexical causatives are thus hyperonyms to (i.e. semantically included by) these verbs. With respect to the relation between attributive and denominative meanings, it is helpful to consider another cxtr. argument-structure construction of English, the so-called *as*-predicative, which predominantly expresses attributive and denominative meanings, but strictly excludes resultative ones (cf. Gries et al. 2005, 2010).

(29) a. *Say uhm our language tends to be* known *[as [$_{AjP}$ rich and specific]].* (+ passive) <S1B-003>
 b. *And that is how it originally was* named *[as [$_{NP}$ Duck Street]].* (+ passive) <S1A-028>
(30) a. *The stages involved can be* categorized *[as [$_{NP}$ stimulus reception]].* (+ passive) <W2A-025>
 b. *Some sections of the crowd* denounced *President Bush John Major and Neil Kinnock [as [$_{NP}$ killers]].* <S2B-004>
(31) *Even a religious leader who said this would nowadays be* branded *[$_{NP}$ a fundamentalist].* (+ passive) <S2B-029>

Besides its large central attributive verb class, which comprises such cognition verbs as *regard*, *see*$_{cog}$, *know*, *view*, *recognize*, etc. (see [29a]), and its much smaller denominative verb group, containing verbs like *name*, *cite* or *refer to* (see [29b]), the *as*-predicative also typically occurs with a number of verbs that are vague with respect to the attributive-denominative distinction: Firstly, a range of verbs like *categorize*, *define*, *class*, etc. exhibit both a speech-act and a cognition sense, because they express categorical judgements which can easily become overt in acts of naming (see [30a]). Secondly, and vice versa, some verbs of calling (e.g. *denounce*, *portray*, *depict*) refer to acts of naming that clearly externalize a categorical judgement that is highly evaluative (see [30b]). The latter case does occur in the NP pattern as well (see [31]).

From these considerations, it can be concluded that acts of naming take up a mid-position on a cline between attributive meanings on the one hand and denominative ones on the other.

3. Corpus study

3.1. Methodology

As indicated previously, the corpus study aims at an empirical assessment of the constructional inventory so far suggested for the English cxtr. patterns. It asks which form-meaning pairings are validated or must even be postulated on the basis of quantitative corpus evidence, and will ascertain whether the difference between AjP and NP complements incurs a functional difference that is related to the distinction between resultative, denominative and attributive meanings.

The balanced corpus used for the quantitative part of this investigation is the British part of the INTERNATIONAL CORPUS OF ENGLISH (ICE-GB, 1 million words), which is word-class tagged as well as parsed for syntactic function.

The formal and functional distinctions offered by the corpus parse largely follow those made by Quirk et al. (1985). In order to maximize *recall* (i.e. the retrieval of relevant target structures from the data base) within the limits of feasibility, a relatively unspecific query was employed, utilizing only the VP-feature "complex-transitive". In order to maximize *precision* (i.e. the percentage of true hits in the final data set), the entire output delivered by the concordance software ICE-CUP was manually coded and sorted into separate concordances according to whether the verb co-occurred with a locative complement *[Subj V Obj$_{Dir}$ Compl$_{Loc}$]* or with a predicative one of either adjectival or nominal form: *[Subj V Obj$_{Dir}$ Compl$_{Pred}$(AjP)]* and *[Subj V Obj$_{Dir}$ Compl$_{Pred}$(NP)]*. In accordance with the previous discussion, an expression was counted as an instance of a cxtr. pattern, if the complement was (i) non-deletable altogether (e.g. *render, deem*); (ii) not deletable without a change in the semantics of the VP (e.g. *keep, make, find$_{cog}$, consider, call*); or (iii) deletable, but coding for a kind of information already inherent in the verb's semantic profile (e.g. *appoint, name, label*).

Each token was coded for the lemma of the verb appearing as main predicator as well as the overall corpus frequency of this lemma. In the patterns with locative and AjP complements, each token was additionally coded for the lemma of the lexical head of the complement. In a second step of the manual coding, all instances of verbal ellipsis were recovered from the data set. In a second frequency count, the number of verb tokens was adjusted in all cases where multiple complements occurred with only one verbal predicate (see [32]).[14]

(32) It is better *called* [$_{AjP}$ usual], [$_{AjP}$ believable], [$_{AjP}$ unsurprising]. <W2E-004>

The resulting frequency lists then provided the input to several collostruction analyses. Simple collexeme analyses (Stefanowitsch and Gries 2003) were applied to evaluate the verb lemma frequencies in the cxtr. patterns, because previous collexeme analyses of English argument-structure constructions had shown that the semantic potential of a given syntactic pattern is precisely reflected by its strongest "collexemes", i.e. the lexical items most strongly "attracted" to it (Stefanowitsch and Gries 2003). In addition, experimental work on the English *as*-predicative had demonstrated that the degree of attraction determined by a collexeme analysis outperforms both unevaluated frequency data and other statistical measures proposed in the literature (such as "faith" or

---

14. In the data set without correction for verbal ellipsis, examples with more than one verb but only one RP were coded for each verb separately, while examples with several RPs but only one verb were coded as only one instance of the verb in the construction.

Table 1. *Input data for a simple collexeme analysis.*

	Construction Y	¬ Construction Y	Row totals
Verb X	A: frequency of X in Y	B: frequency of X in other constructions	corpus frequency of X
¬ Verb X	C: frequency of Y with other verbs	D: number of other verbs in other constructions	all verbs other than X
Column totals	corpus frequency of Y	all constructions other than Y	all verb constructions

"conditional probability") as a predictor of actual behaviour in both language production and comprehension (cf. Gries et al. 2005, in press).[15]

Apart from the lemma frequency, i.e. the number of the observed tokens of a verbal lexeme X in the constructional slot investigated (Table 1: cell A), a simple collexeme analysis makes use of the following further data: all occurrences of verb X in argument structures other than Y (Table 1: cell B), all occurrences of argument structure Y with verbs other than X (Table 1: cell C) as well as the frequency of all verbal argument structures that are not Y and do not contain X (Table 1: cell D). To avoid an overestimation of the degree of attraction between a given verb and the construction, the verb frequencies appearing as A in the simple collexeme analyses were not corrected for verbal ellipsis.

In order to assess whether the token frequency of any given verb in the construction is significantly above or below the frequency expected at chance level, the frequency distribution in this cross-tabulation is evaluated by a standard significance test. Due to the nature of linguistic data, this is normally the Fisher/Yates Exact Test, as it also works with exhaustive data sets that contain large amounts of low-frequency items. The output of this analysis is a precise *p*-value for each collexeme observed, which is referred to as its "collostruction strength" (henceforth also "coll. str.").[16] For convenience, the *p*-value is usually given log-transformed to the basis 10: In terms of the traditional thresholds of significance, this means that a collostruction strength larger than 3 corresponds to a *p*-value smaller than 0.001; a collostruction strength larger than 2 corresponds to a *p*-value smaller than 0.01; and a collostruction strength larger than 1.301 corresponds to a *p*-value still smaller than 0.05. As the term "collostruction strength" implies, this *p*-value is interpreted as a measure of the strength of the association between a construction and its collexemes, so that the latter can be ranked according to their respective degrees of "attraction" to or "repulsion" by the construction. Attraction occurs when the observed num-

---

15. Gries et al. (2005, 2010) employed a sentence-completion experiment and a non-accumulative self-paced reading paradigm.
16. This *p*-value incorporates the effect size (cf. Gries and Stefanowitsch 2004b: 124, note 2).

Table 2. *Input data for a distinctive collexeme analysis.*

	Construction Y	Construction Z	Row totals
Verb X	**A:** frequency of X in Y	**B:** frequency of X in Z	frequency of X in Y and Z
¬ not Verb X	**C:** frequency of other verbs in Y	**D:** frequency of other verbs in Z	frequency of verbs other than X in Y and Z
Column totals	frequency of Y	frequency of Z	corpus frequency of Y and Z

ber of lexical tokens is significantly higher than chance, repulsion when it is significantly lower.[17]

In addition to the simple collexeme analyses, two (pairwise) "distinctive collexeme analyses" (cf. Gries and Stefanowitsch 2004b) were employed to compare the lexical realisations of the three cxtr. patterns. The method is able to detect areas of lexical divergence between constructions, i.e. can pin down which of the lexemes occurring in two constructions are most distinctive for either of them. As it thereby blends out overlaps, it provides a kind of information very different from that gained by a simple collexeme analysis. In view of the assumed functional significance of the formal difference between AjP and NP complements, this method presents a very valuable additional tool. As a distinctive collexeme analysis does not make use of any frequency data of verb uses outside the constructions investigated (cf. Table 2), all input frequencies were corrected for verbal ellipsis.

In order to amend the preceding two kinds of "coarse-grained" analysis (Gries 2006), which only consider the constructions' main verb slot, with a slightly more fine-grained one, I also carried out "co-varying collexeme analyses" (Gries and Stefanowitsch 2004a; Stefanowitsch and Gries 2005) of the data from the patterns with locative and adjectival complements. For each pattern, these determine which combinations of the lexical verbs as main predicators with the heads of their complements as secondary predicators occur significantly above chance level and thus can be said to systematically co-select one another. The verb frequencies used were again corrected for verbal ellipsis (cf. Table 3).

As the facilitating and even "path-breaking" role of single, high-frequency exemplars in the acquisition of argument structures has been emphasized in

---

17. A given verb's rank in the collexeme list may diverge dramatically from that in the respective raw-frequency list: The resultative verb *make*, for instance, occurs 24 times in the pattern with locative complement, occupying rank 13 in its frequency list, but does not constitute a significantly attracted collexeme of the CMC (coll. str. = 0.52062), due to the fact that it occurs 1,927 times in other constructions in the corpus.

Table 3. *Input data for a co-varying collexeme analysis.*

	Word Y as head of complement	¬ Word Y as head of complement	Row totals
Verb X	**A:** all combinations of X with Y	**B:** all combinations of X with words other than Y	frequency of the construction with X
¬ verb X	**C:** all combinations of other verbs with Y	**D:** all occurrences of the construction containing neither X or Y	frequency of the construction with verbs other than X
Column totals	frequency of the construction with word Y as head of complement	frequency of the construction with words other than Y as head of complement	frequency of the construction investigated

much previous construction-based work (cf. Goldberg 1998a, 1999, 2006: 75–92; Goldberg et al. 2004; Casenhiser and Goldberg 2005), selected results from a child-language study based on the Manchester corpus of the CHILDES database are additionally reported in the discussion section in order to support some of the generalizations drawn from the quantitative analysis of the adult data from the ICE-GB.[18]

3.2. *Hypotheses*

In accordance with the preceding discussion, it is hypothesized that the two cxtr. patterns with predicative complements exhibit functional differences. Concerning the AjP pattern, it is expected that existing postulations on the RC will be largely confirmed—and amended with respect to the central status of the forced-state uses with current verbs. (I.a)–(I.d) present the precise corollaries of this hypothesis in collostructional terms, i.e. in terms of attracted and distinctive verb classes:

(I.a) A class of generic lexical causatives like *make* and *render* will be most strongly attracted to the argument structure as well as distinctive for it in all comparisons. If this group contains caused-motion verbs, their motion meaning will have bleached (e.g. *get*, *set*) and they will be distinctive only in the comparison with the NP pattern.

(I.b) The top collexemes will also include current verbs denoting forced-state scenarios. Due to the forced location uses of the same verbs in the

---

18. The Manchester sub-corpus of the British part of the CHILDES data base contains 12 parallel data sets with the transcripts of the audio recordings of 34 interviews and free-play sessions conducted in regular intervals with six boys and six girls between 2 to 3 years of age, all first-born, monolingual, and home-raised (cf. Lieven et al. 2004).

pattern with locative complement, these will be distinctive only in the comparison with the NP pattern.

(I.c) A group with a high type frequency containing verbs coding for the way, means or instrument of the action causing the change—including declarative speech-act verbs—will be significantly attracted to the construction, though less so than the former two groups.

(I.d) If generic denominative verbs like *call* or *name* appear among the construction's attracted collexemes, they will not be distinctive in the comparison with the NP pattern.

The NP pattern, on the other hand, is hypothesized to be characterized by denominative expressions. A confirmation of the assumptions given in (II.a)–(II.c) would justify the postulation of a new argument-structure construction pairing the NP pattern with the denominative semantics (x SAY [Y BE z]).

(II.a) A large class of denominative collexemes with a high type frequency will be strongly attracted to and distinctive for the NP pattern only.

(II.b) Generic verbs of naming will be more strongly attracted than verbs referring to more specific ones denoting the way, means or instrument of the action accomplishing the naming. Of the latter, declarative speech-act verbs will constitute an important subgroup.

(II.c) Generic lexical causatives like *make* are expected to be attracted to the pattern, but will not be distinctive for it in the comparison with the AjP pattern.

The status of attributive expressions in the two patterns with predicative complements is difficult to predict on the basis of existing research, although it follows from the preceding discussion that generic attributive verbs must play at least a minor role in the NP pattern.

3.3. *Results*

The ICE-GB search for all verb phrases parsed as "complex-transitive" returned 4,019 sentences, which contained 3,513 true hits. Of these, 1,576 exhibit a predicative complement in the form of an AjP or NP. Corrected for verbal ellipsis, this frequency rises to 1,624. Instances of the pattern with locative complement, i.e. the CMC, are by far the most numerous ones, constituting 55.14 per cent of all true hits (cf. Table 4). However, this section will only report those aspects of the results for this pattern which support the functional characterization of the two patterns with predicative complement (for the full results, see Appendix, Tables I and IV).

Tables I to III in the Appendix display the results of the simple collexeme analyses for the three cxtr. patterns. Most strikingly, each of these attracts with

160   B. Hampe

Table 4.   *Complex-transitive argument structures in the ICE-GB.*

	Verb tokens	Verb tokens corrected for verbal ellipsis
Pattern with locative complement	1,937	2,083
Pattern with AjP complement	908	951
Pattern with NP complement	668	673
Total number	3,513	3,707

infinite collostruction strength (i.e. an infinitely small *p*-value) exactly one semantically generic high-frequency verb. Perfectly coinciding with existing postulations about the core meanings of the CMC and RC, these are the caused-motion verb *put* and the lexical causative *make* in the patterns with locative and AjP complement, respectively. A first confirmation of the hypotheses given in (II.a)–(II.b) about the denominative character of the pattern with NP complement is provided by the fact that the speech-act verb *call* presents its leading collexeme. The three top collexemes *put*, *make* and *call* are also the items most distinctive for their respective patterns in the two comparisons (cf. Appendix, Tables IV, V). Completing this picture, the results of the studies of the English *as*-predicative in the ICE-GB by Gries and colleagues (2005, 2010) show the attributive verb *regard* to be its strongest collexeme. The top collexemes of each of the four cxtr. argument structures of English—*put*, *make*, *call* and *regard*—thus provide highly plausible core meanings for these four patterns: caused-motion, resultative, denominative and attributive. In the following, all results relevant to hypotheses I and II will be reported in detail, starting with the results of the simple collexeme analysis of the pattern with AjP complement (cf. Appendix, Table II).

Hypotheses (I.a) and (I.b) are confirmed in as far as the central collexeme group contains a number of generic lexical causatives, including the bleached caused-motion verbs *get* and *set* as well as the forced-state verbs *keep* and *leave* (cf. [33a]). In accordance with (I.c), the group with the highest type frequency occupying most of the subsequent positions in the collexeme ranking down to a significance level of 0.05 is constituted by verbs denoting the way, means or instrument of the action causing the change (see [33b]). Among these, there are also two declarative speech-act verbs (see [33c]). As hypothesized in (I.d), finally, the generic factual speech-act verb *call* is likewise attracted, though by far not as strongly as any of the top generic causatives. It appears at rank 15 and remains isolated.

(33)   Collexemes in the AjP pattern:
  a.   collexemes denoting the causation/prevention of change (rank):
       make (1), *keep* (3), *leave* (4), *render* (5), *get* (7), *set* (10)

b. collexemes denoting the manner/means/instrument of the action causing the change (rank): *prise* (11), *strip* (12), *shoot* (14), *comb* (17), *jerk* (18), *riddle* (18), *tickle* (18), *wrench* (18), *clamp* (19), *stuff* (19), *cut* (20)
c. collexemes verbs denoting declarative speech acts (rank): *declare* (9), *adjudge* (16)

In further confirmation of (I.a)–(I.b), the two distinctive collexeme analyses corroborate the results of the simple one (cf. Appendix Table IV, V). The top lexical causatives *make* and *render*—but not the bleached caused-motion verbs *get*, *set* and *drive*—are among the collexemes that are most distinctive for the AjP pattern in the direct comparison with the pattern with locative complement. In addition, all of these as well as the forced-state verbs *keep*, *leave* and *have* are distinctive in the comparison with the NP-pattern, marking out the AjP pattern as resultative.[19] Confirming (I.d), finally, the factual speech-act verb *call* is distinctive only in the comparison with the pattern with locative complements, but not in the comparison with the NP-pattern.

Concerning the NP pattern (cf. Appendix, Table III), the results clearly confirm (II.a), which predicts generic denominative verbs in the majority of the top ranks of the collexeme list (see [34a]). In accordance with (II.b), the next group in the ranking is constituted by a range of more specific verbs denoting the way, means or instrument of the action accomplishing the naming (see [34b]). This class also contains a group of declarative speech-act verbs with a higher type frequency than that of the corresponding class in AjP pattern (see [34c]). As predicted by II.c, finally, the generic lexical causatives *make* and *render* are also among the strongly attracted collexemes, occupying ranks 2 and 15, respectively, but being non-distinctive in the comparison with the AjP pattern.

(34) Collexemes in the NP pattern:
a. generic denominative collexemes: *call* (1), *term* (4), *name* (5)
b. verbs denoting manner/means/instrument of the action accomplishing the naming: *date* (3), *entitle* (7), *label* (8), *nickname* (9), *mark* (10), *dub* (11), *code-name* (12), *re-name* (16), *brand* (17), *rank* (20), *paint* (21)
c. verbs denoting declarative speech acts: *proclaim* (14), *elect* (18), *appoint* (19), *declare* (22), *designate* (23).

These results are impressively strengthened by the results of the distinctive collexeme analysis comparing the two patterns with predicative complements

---

19. Contrary to expectations, but without consequences for the functional characterization of the AjP pattern, *keep* and *leave* express "forced state" more often than "forced location" and are distinctive even in the comparison with the pattern with locative complements.

(cf. Appendix, Table V). In full confirmation of (II.a) and (II.b), the list of distinctive collexemes for the NP pattern exclusively contains denominative verbs, both generic ones in rank 1, 3 and 4 (*call, name, term*) and more specific ones in ranks 2, 4, 6 and 7 (*date, entitle, mark, label*).

Taken together, the results provide a striking demonstration of the central importance of denominative meanings in the NP pattern. As the confirmation of (II.a)–(II.c) was said to require the postulation of an new argument-structure construction, section 4.1 will introduce the properties of the English "Denominative Construction" and bring in further data from both adult and child language to support its postulation.

What was not predicted at all, however, is the way in which attributive collexemes are associated with the patterns with predicative complements. While the collexeme list of the NP pattern only exhibits one strongly attracted, but isolated and non-distinctive attributive collexeme, viz. *consider* in rank 6 (cf. Appendix, Table III), a very strongly attracted group of attributive verbs appears among the most central collexemes of the AjP pattern. Its leading collexeme, *find* in rank 2, is accompanied by *consider* and *deem* in ranks 6 and 8. That *find* is used as a verb of intellectual activity here is proved by the adjectives occurring as its co-varying collexemes: *difficult, hard, useful* and *guilty*, all of which denote abstract properties (cf. Appendix, Table II). Moreover, in the comparison with the pattern with locative complement, a group of highly distinctive collexemes consisting of $find_{cog}$, *think* and *consider* in ranks 2 to 4 follows only resultative *make* itself and even precedes a range of resultative verbs in the subsequent ranks (cf. Appendix, Table IV). Similarly, the collexemes $find_{cog}$, *think* and see_{cog} are also distinctive in the comparison with the NP-pattern, marking out attributive expressions (with the exception of *consider*) as a specialty of the AjP pattern (cf. Appendix, Table V). Although the class of attributive collexemes in this pattern is smaller than the corresponding class in the *as*-predicative, it includes at least $find_{cog}$, *consider, deem* and most likely also *think*, as the latter's absence from the collexeme list of the AjP pattern must be regarded as an artefact of the corpus methodology: it was not feasible to correct the very high corpus frequency of *think* (required for cell B of the input data for the collexeme analysis) for its appearance in the parenthetical comment clause *I (/we) think*.

4. Discussion

4.1. *The English Denominative Construction*

The results of the collexeme analyses contrast with basic assumptions of preceding approaches to the argument structures with predicative complements, which have viewed their capacity to appear as either AjP or NP as a hallmark

Syntax:	Subject	Verb	Object$_{Dir}$	Compl$_{Pred}$ (NP)
Roles:	X: AGENT	Predicator	Y: THEME	Z: DENOMINATION
Semantics:	[X SAY [Y BE Z]]			
Correlation:	very strong correlation with the passive voice			

Figure 1. *The English Denominative Construction (DC).*

of that syntactic function. Instead, they suggest that the pattern with NP complement is an argument-structure construction in its own right, as a large and varied class of denominative collexemes, represented by the factual speech-act verb *call*, is very strongly attracted to as well as distinctive for it in the direct comparison with the AjP pattern, i.e. the RC. I thus postulate the English "Denominative Construction" (DC) as a further cxtr. argument-structure construction of English, which refers to naming scenarios, i.e. to instances of linguistic categorization, in accordance with what was said previously about the entity construal expressed by a NP. Figure 1 summarizes the main features of the DC. Its postulation presents a revision of Gonzálvez-Garcia's (2009) "Declarative Transitive Construction", whose semantic specifications are identical to those of the DC, but whose formal specifications are not.

One highly conspicuous formal feature of the DC, viz. its strong association with the passive-voice, was not predicted, though reference grammars mention the tendency of some speech-act and cognition verbs to prefer the passive voice when appearing in this pattern (e.g. Quirk et al. 1985: 1199). With hindsight, however, it appears well motivated that expressions with denominative meanings tend to demote the agent by combining with the passive construction: With the exception of externalized evaluative judgements, acts of naming are typically no idiosyncratic, private acts, but present the conventions of a speech community. This will often make the specification of an individual agent responsible for the naming either impossible or irrelevant. It is worth discussing the relevant findings in more detail, as they strengthen the claim that the NP-pattern presents an argument structure in its own right, the DC, with semantic and syntactic properties distinct from those of the RC.

Of all transitive verb phrases in the ICE-GB, 18.99 per cent (i.e. 14,257 out of 75,169 tokens) are parsed as passives.[20] With these general proportions in

---

20. The retrieval of all transitive VPs was not based on the ICE-parse feature *transitive*, as this would have excluded all VPs parsed as *mono-*, *di-*, or *complex-transitive*. Instead, all VPs parsed as *intransitive* (32,989 tokens) or *copular* (30,374 tokens) were subtracted from the overall number of VPs (138,532 tokens) yielding 75,169 transitive tokens. As 14,275 VPs in

Table 5. *Association of the cxtr. patterns with the* be-*passive construction in the ICE-GB.*

	Tokens	Passivized Tokens observed	Passivized Tokens expected	Significance test
DC	668	386 (57.78%)	126.85 (18.99%)	Chi-squared = 654.92, df = 1, p < 2.2e-16
RC	908	133 (14,65%)	172.43 (18.99%)	Chi-squared = 11.02, df = 1, p = 9.01e-04
as-predicative	687	384 (55.89%)	130.46 (18.99%)	Chi-squared = 609.58, df = 1, p < 2.2e-16
Attrib./denom. collexemes in the AjP-pattern	68	37 (54.41%)	54.41 (18.99%)	Chi-squared = 55.59, df = 1, p = 8.94e-14
Resultative collexemes in the NP-pattern	84	8 (9.52%)	15.88 (18.99%)	Chi-squared = 4.87, df = 1, p = 0.0273

the corpus providing the baseline, no more than 126.85 of the 668 instances of the NP pattern would be expected to occur in the passive voice at a chance basis. However, the observed number of passives is significantly higher, amounting to 57.78 per cent. A similar feature has been observed to hold for the English *as*-predicative, the argument-structure construction semantically most closely related to the DC (Gries et al. 2005). In stark contrast, this tendency towards the passive voice cannot be observed for the AjP pattern, i.e. the RC (cf. Table 5). Expressions in that argument structure generally tend to occur in the active voice significantly more often than would be expected on a chance basis—despite the presence of a strong attributive-denominative collexeme class containing *find, consider, deem, think, declare, call* and *adjudge*. When inspected in isolation, this class behaves like the *as*-predicative and the DC in that it shows a strong association with the passive construction. It is thus not surprising either that the group of attracted resultative collexemes in the NP pattern, which consists of the generic resultative collexemes *make* and *render* as well as the declarative speech-act verbs *appoint, proclaim, declare, elect* and *designate*, also goes significantly against the overall trend of the DC towards the passive and instead behaves more like verbs in the RC (cf. Table 5).

The generalizations made about the adult data so far are strongly supported by acquisitional data from the Manchester corpus of CHILDES, which show the NP pattern to occur with denominative verbs from the very beginning.[21]

---

the ICE-GB are parsed as <passives>, the remaining 60,894 transitive VPs are assumed to be in the active voice.
21. The query in the Manchester corpus was lexically determined and checked the occurrence of the leading adult collexemes in child language. These were: (i) in the pattern with locative

Table 6. Realisation of the predicative complement with resultative and denominative verbs in the Manchester corpus.

	AjP pattern	NP pattern
Denominative verbs (*call, name*)	5 (with colour adjectives)	148
Resultative verbs (*make, get, put, set*)	188	4 (only with *make*)

Table 7. Association of the denominative and resultative verbs with the be-*passive* construction in the Manchester-corpus.

	active	passive
Denominative verbs (*call, name*)	11	142
Resultative verbs (*make, get, put, set*)	192	0

Make, the leading adult resultative collexeme in this argument structure, is the only resultative collexeme that is also used by the children (though only very rarely so); while attributive verbs do not appear at all in the entire corpus. Though the earliest child uses of these patterns are entirely item-based, i.e. present "verb islands" (Tomasello 2000) around the two verbal types *call* and *name*, the tendency of the children's patterns with AjP and NP complements towards the expression of resultative and denominative meanings, respectively, is even clearer than in the adult data (cf. Table 6; $p_{\text{Fisher exact}} < 2.2\text{e-}16$, odds ratio = 1211.449).[22]

Moreover, the tendency of expressions with resultative and denominative meanings towards the active and passive voice, respectively, is strongest in the children's data, too (cf. Table 7; $p_{\text{Fisher exact}} < 2.2\text{e-}16$, odds ratio: inf). This is all the more astonishing in view of the fact that children below 36 months of age do not normally make much use of the passive voice at all.

4.2. Low-level constructions

This investigation has established the cxtr. pattern with NP complement as an argument-structure construction in its own right, the English Denominative Construction. At the same time the results for the AjP pattern have turned out to be rather mixed: On the one hand, they confirm expectations arising from

---

complement: *put, place, bring, get/have got, take, turn*; (ii) in the AjP pattern: *make, find, keep, leave, render, consider, deem, declare, set*; (iii) in the NP pattern: *call, date, term, (nick-)name, entitle, label, mark*.

22. The only AjP complements with denominative verbs are colour adjectives. As these do not differ in form from the corresponding colour nouns, it cannot be excluded that even these do in fact present NP-complements.

existing work on the RC that expressions denoting both the causation and prevention of change are of central importance to this pattern. On the other hand, they also make it clear that, at least in adult use, this pattern also centrally codes for attributive meanings. Though a discussion of the strong attributive verb class in the AjP pattern is beyond the confines of this paper, its presence cannot pass entirely uncommented, as it clearly differs qualitatively from the appearance of the isolated collexeme *call* in this argument structure or from the appearance of the collexemes *make* and *render*—or indeed *consider*—in the NP pattern. On the basis of data about other argument-structure constructions in the cxtr. network and about the appearance and use of the various cxtr. patterns in child language, Hampe (2011) argues that these findings about a central attributive verb group in the AjP pattern do not invalidate its description as the RC, despite the fact that resultative and attributive verb groups cannot easily be connected via one of the standard polysemy links. Most relevant to this issue is the fact that cxtr. expressions with attributive meanings—including those of the *as*-predicative—occur extremely late in acquisition.[23] Child-language data indicate that the attributive verb group remains lexically defined and is hooked, as it were, onto a pre-existing constructional network which consists initially of the CMC only, but is soon extended by the appearance of the RC and, even before the end of the third year of life, also the (lexically defined) core of the DC.

Taking up the more general issue of the role of low-level generalizations here, the results about the presence of a few generic resultative and attributive collexemes in the NP pattern—or of an isolated denominative collexeme in the AP pattern—invite the following line of reasoning: While it was stressed previously that the entity construal invited by the NP complement is in accordance with naming scenarios, this provides a default only (see [6a] and [6b]). Though there is a strong tendency for entities to be named more often than their attributes, the latter is of course possible and not even marginal, which is underlined by the occurrence of *call* as a strong collexeme of the adult AjP pattern. Similarly, the manipulation of object-properties may be more common than the creation of entirely new entities, but the latter also occurs with notable frequency, as is not only shown by the presence of *make* as the second collexeme of the NP pattern, but also by its very strong class of declarative speech-act verbs. By analogy, the presence of a strongly attracted attributive group in the AjP pattern (vis-á-vis the isolated collexeme *consider* in the NP pattern) indicates that judgements about object properties are more typical than categorical judgements. While none of this is in any way surprising by itself, the corpus

---

23. Gries et al. (in press) report that there is not a single instance of the *as*-predicative in the child speech recorded in the entire British and American files of CHILDES.

results about attributive, denominative and resultative verb groups in the two patterns with predicative complements suggest how this is handled by the grammar: Only the leading generic resultative, denominative and attributive collexemes occur in both patterns with a frequency significantly above chance. It can thus be assumed that construals which diverge from the respective default are captured by low-level generalizations, i.e. by item-based constructions which are bound to the leading collexemes of the default pattern (see [35] and [36]). In a usage-based model, these lexically determined constructions are plausibly assumed to exist in addition to and below the generalizations presented by the RC and the DC as the fully schematic argument-structure constructions.

(35) (X [NP: AGENT] *call* Y [NP: THEME] Z [NP/AjP: DENOMINATION]) + strong correlation with the passive voice[24]

(36) (X [NP: AGENT] *make/render* Y [NP: THEME] Z [AjP/NP: RESULTANT ATTRIBUTE/ENTITY]) + strong correlation with the active voice[25]

This amounts to saying that the syntactic flexibility between an adjectival and a nominal realisation, previously viewed as one of the hallmarks of predicative complements, is *not* relevant at the highest, fully schematic level, but should be seen as a property of a number of verb- or verb-class based generalizations (Croft 2003). Without a recognition of these low-level schemas, the functional range of the cxtr. patterns cannot be fully captured, because they are so deeply entrenched that they can act as model constructions after which expressions with other verbs from the same classes which are not themselves attracted to the syntactic pattern can be coined in an analogous way (see [37]).

(37) a. But Iraqi propaganda *painted* it [NP a glorious victory for Saddam]. <W2E-002>
b. By that reckoning I can certainly *count* myself [NP a real climber]. <BNC example, cited in Gonzálvez-García 2009>

5. Concluding remarks

To return to the initial discussion of the empirical turn in Cognitive Linguistics, it is doubtlessly the most notable result of this study that, without the systematic

---

24. 294 of 450 occurrences (= 65.33%) of *call* in the NP pattern occur in the passive (exp.: 85.45; chi-squared 629.47, df = 1, p < 2.2e-16). 5 of 10 instances (= 50%) of *call* in the AjP pattern also occur in the passive.
25. Only 37 of the 380 occurrences (= 9.74%) of *make* in the AjP pattern are in the passive (exp.: 72.16; chi-squared 21.06, df = 1, p = 4.45e-06). Likewise, only 4 of the 73 occurrences (= 5.48%) of *make* in the NP pattern are in the passive (exp.: 13.86, chi-squared 8.64, df = 1, p = 0.00329), while the 2 occurrences of *render* in the same argument structure are both in the active.

investigation of the relevant kinds of empirical data, our accounts of the linguistic regularities may remain partial and not fully deserve the label *usage-based*. Most conspicuously, the systematic quantitative analysis of a large data set has led to the discovery and precise description of a new argument-structure construction, postulated as the English Denominative Construction (DC). This discovery would not have been possible on the basis of a qualitative analysis of even considerable amounts of authentic cxtr. expressions with attributive and denominative meanings. The generalizations presented here thus diverge considerably from those given by Gonzálvez-García (2009) for the two major "Subjective-Transitive Constructions".

While this study has confirmed the causative resultatives, i.e. the CMC and RC, as the core of the network of the cxtr. argument structures, it has also shown that this network cannot be adequately portrayed without a careful consideration of expressions with denominative and even attributive meanings. Of particular interest to a cognitively inspired construction-based approach should be the finding that the leading collexemes of the four cxtr. argument-structure constructions, i.e. *put*, *make*, *call* and *regard*, refer to four basic experiential scenarios, specified here as "caused-motion", "resultative", "denominative" and "attributive". It has been demonstrated that these scenarios are clearly distinct only in the prototypical cases and that, perhaps rather unexpectedly, acts of naming occupy the middle ground in a continuum of tightly interlinked and mutually motivating meanings ranging from the actual manipulation of entities to subjective judgements.

While the results of the present study account for cxtr. expressions with denominative meanings, a lot more research on the basis of sufficiently dense corpus data from late childhood is required to arrive at firm statements about the precise constructional status of cognition verbs in the AjP pattern. Overall, the findings imply that, below the level of the lexically fully schematic argument-structure constructions, i.e. the CMC, RC and DC, there is a largely unexplored amount of generalizations about the syntactic behaviour of single verbs or verb classes, which do not only play a more important role than assumed in preceding descriptions of the complex-transitive network, but possibly also a different one. And while the results reported so far have provided a colourful illustration of the complex web of interrelations that have long been regarded as typical of constructional networks (e.g. Fillmore et al. 1988), they also invite more work on the precise nature of the motivating links holding these together.

Received 13 December 2009 *University of Erfurt*
Revision received 14 October 2010

Appendix

Table I. *Top 20 collexemes and strongest co-varying collexemes in the cxtr. pattern with locative complement.*

	Collexeme (obs/exp freq)	Coll. str.	Co-varying collexemes, in the order of decreasing collostruction strength
1	put (369/10.84)	INFINITE	on, in
2	keep (115/5.76)	111.8233	in, within, up, together, under
3	place (66/1.66)	88.7889	upon, before, above, on, on top of, between, beside
4	bring (78/6.45)	57.8145	to, home, under, clear, up
5	get (175/45.81)	50.2560	from, out, in front of, (Det.) way round, out of, here
6	set (35/2.80)	26.8457	away, back, apart
7	leave (50/8.16)	23.2400	behind, at, in, underneath
8	take (81/23.12)	21.0073	away from, to, from, aside
9	turn (37/4.73)	20.9701	into, upside down
10	find (54/13.16)	17.0952	in, nearby, throughout
11	bear (20/2.13)	13.2036	in
12	send (26/4.84)	11.1460	to, onto
13	push (15/1.38)	10.9807	beyond, the other way, out of, underneath, over
14	hold (23/4.32)	9.8637	together, in, by
15	shove (6/0.11)	9.6920	none significantly associated
16	force (13/1.3)	9.1583	into, off, apart
17	base (15/1.99)	8.7220	upon, on, at
18	lay (13/1.54)	8.2443	before, on
19	tuck (6/0.18)	7.9307	inside, away
20	locate (8/0.48)	7.7215	in

Table II. *Top 20 collexemes and strongest co-varying collexemes in the cxtr. pattern with AjP-complement.*

	Collexeme (obs/exp freq)	Coll. Str.	Co-varying collexemes, in the order of decreasing collostruction strength
1	make (395/12.79)	INFINITE	sure, clear, good, easy, aware, plain, redundant, different, possible
2	find (135/6.17)	133.1381	difficult, hard, useful, guilty
3	keep (87/2.70)	101.6946	informed, happy, secret, high, safe, open, clean, closed, constant, cool, moist, separate, warm
4	leave (43/3.82)	30.3022	alone, open, isolated
5	render (13/0.12)	24.5001	acceptable, answerable, half-blind, persuasive, stone-dead, superfluous, uncongenial, useless, unfit, vulnerable
6	consider (17/1.74)	11.4199	horrible, demeaning, funny, indissoluble, manlike, normal, unseemly, unwieldy, valid, worthy, adequate, conscious
7	get (56/21.47)	9.7603	right, wrong, straight, together, involved, interested, ready

Table II (*Continued*)

	Collexeme (obs/exp freq)	Coll. Str.	Co-varying collexemes, in the order of decreasing collostruction strength
8	*deem* (5/0.06)	8.8303	cured, reasonable, unfounded, adequate, appropriate
9	*declare* (7/0.35)	7.1611	insolvent, unsafe, inappropriate, fit
10	*set* (11/2.12)	4.9192	alight, free, straight, adrift, aflame, circulating
11	*prise* (2/0.01)	4.3670	free, open
12	*strip* (3/0.10)	3.9188	ballock-naked, naked, bare
13	*drive* (5/0.85)	2.7574	crazy, mad, potty
14	*shoot* (3/0.38)	2.1783	dead
15	*call* (10/4.26)	1.9306	believable, dismaying, predictable, trophic, unsurprising, usual, accountable, proper, sophisticated, boring, independent
16	*adjudge* (1/0.01)	1.8837	bankrupt
17	*comb* (1/0.01)	1.8837	tidy
18	*jerk* (1/0.02)	1.7090	awake
	riddle (1/0.02)		clean
	tickle (1/0.02)		pink
	wrench (1/0.02)		free
19	*clamp* (1/0.03)	1.5855	shut
	stuff (1/0.03)	1.5855	full
20	*cut* (4/1.14)	1.5482	free, short

Table III. *All significantly attracted collexemes in the cxtr. pattern with NP-complement.*

No	Collexeme (obs./exp. freqency)	Coll. str.	No	Collexeme (obs./exp. frequency)	Coll. str.
1	*call* (450/3.14)	INFINITE	13	*be-born* (4/0.35)	3.3480
2	*make* (73/9.41)	40.4180	14	*proclaim* (2/0.03)	3.3186
3	*date* (22/0.31)	34.1153	15	*render* (2/0.09)	2.4714
4	*term* (15/0.10)	30.0944	16	*re-name* (1/0.00)	2.3166
5	*name* (16/0.20)	26.1788	17	*brand* (1/0.01)	2.0166
6	*consider* (20/1.28)	17.1717	18	*elect* (2/0.16)	1.9292
7	*entitle* (10/0.28)	12.4891	19	*appoint* (2/0.17)	1.9050
8	*label* (6/0.07)	10.4460	20	*rank* (1/0.01)	1.8416
9	*nickname* (3/0.01)	6.9517	21	*paint* (2/0.25)	1.5803
10	*mark* (6/0.26)	6.6320	22	*declare* (2/0.26)	1.5500
11	*dub* (2/0.0096)	4.6338	23	*designate* (1/0.03)	1.4778
12	*code-name* (2/0.014)	4.1581			

Table IV. *Top 10 distinctive collexemes in the comparison of the patterns with locative complement and AjP-complement.*

No	Pattern with loc. complement		Pattern with AjP complement	
	Collexeme (obs./exp.)	Coll. str.	Collexeme (obs./exp.)	Coll. str.
1	*put* (384/269)	55.474	*make* (394/131)	192.326
2	*bring* (87/60)	14.447	*find* (141/62)	31.742
3	*place* (68/47)	11.248	*think* (20/7)	8.972
4	*take* (95/69)	10.331	*consider* (17/5)	8.613
5	*turn* (38/27)	5.132	*render* (13/4)	6.579
6	*send* (28/19)	4.594	*keep* (93/67)	4.053
7	*have* (107/89)	3.599	*declare* (7/2)	3.536
8	*bear* (20/14)	3.276	*call* (12/5)	3.395
9	*get* (196/174)	3.095	*leave* (46/30)	3.263
10	*play* (27/20)	2.754	*deem* (6/2)	3.030

Table V. *Top 10 distinctive collexemes in the comparison of the patterns with AjP-complement and NP-complement.*

No	Pattern with AjP complement		Pattern with NP complement	
	Collexeme (obs./exp.)	Coll. str.	Collexeme (obs./exp.)	Coll. str.
1	*make* (394/274)	42.821	*call* (452/192)	209.590
2	*find* (141/87)	25.782	*date* (22/9)	8.499
3	*keep* (93/56)	19.539	*name* (16/7)	6.163
4	*get* (57/33)	13.570	*term* (15/7)	4.781
5	*leave* (46/27)	10.901	*entitle* (10/4)	3.840
6	*have* (23/13)	5.398	*mark* (6/2)	2.299
7	*set* (11/6)	2.569	*label* (6/3)	1.644
8	*think* (20/13)	2.484		
9	*see* (9/5)	2.100		
10	*render* (13/9)	1.690		

References

Aarts, Bas. 1992. *Small clauses in English, the nonverbal types*. Berlin/New York: Mouton de Gruyter.

Aarts, Bas. 1995. Secondary predicates in English. In Bas Aarts & Charles F. Meyer (eds.), *The verb in contemporary English: Theory and description*, 75–101. Cambridge: Cambridge University Press.

Barlow, Michael & Suzanne Kemmer (eds.). 2000. *Usage-based models of language*. Standford, CA: CSLI Publications.

Biber, Douglas, Stig Johansson, Geoffrey Leech, Susan Conrad & Edward Finegan. 1999. *Longman grammar of spoken and written English*. Harlow: Longman.

Boas, Hans C. 2003. *A constructional approach to resultatives*. Stanford, CA: CSLI-Publications.

Broccias, Cristiano. 2003. *The English 'change complex'*. Berlin/New York: Mouton de Gruyter.

Broccias, Cristiano. 2007. Unsubcategorised objects in English resultative constructions. Nicole Delbecque & Bert Corneille (eds.), *On interpreting construction schemas: From action and motion to transitivity and causality*, 103–124. Berlin/New York: Mouton de Gruyter.
Bybee, Joan. 2006. From usage to grammar: The mind's response to repetition. *Language* 82. 711–733.
Bybee, Joan & Sandra Thompson. 2000. Three frequency effects in syntax. *Berkeley Linguistics Society* 23. 65–85.
Carrier, Jill & Janet H. Randall. 1992. The argument structure and syntactic structure of resultatives. *Linguistic Inquiry* 23, 173–234.
Casenhiser, Devin M., & Adele E. Goldberg. 2005. Fast mapping between a phrasal form and meaning. *Developmental Science* 8–6, 500–508.
Croft, William. 2003. Lexical rules vs. constructions: A false dichotomy. In Hubert Cuyckens, Thomas Berg, Rene Dirven & Klaus-Uwe Panther (eds.), *Motivation in language*, 49–68. Amsterdam/Philadelphia: John Benjamins.
Dąbrowska, Ewa. Submitted. The mean lean grammar machine meets the human mind: Empirical investigations of the mental status of linguistic rules.
Dąbrowska, Ewa. 2009. Words as constructions. In Vyvyan Evans & Stéphanie Pourcel (eds.), *New directions in Cognitive Linguistics*. Amsterdam/Philadelphia: John Benjamins, 201–223.
Dąbrowska, Ewa. 2000. From formula to schema: The acquisition of English questions. *Cognitive Linguistics* 11, 83–102.
Dąbrowska, Ewa. 2004. *Language, mind and brain: Some psychological and neurological constraints on theories of grammar*. Washington, D.C.: Georgetown University Press.
Dąbrowska, Ewa & Elena Lieven. 2005. Towards a lexically specific grammar of children's question constructions. *Cognitive Linguistics* 16, 437–474.
Diessel, Holger. 2004. *The acquisition of complex sentences*. Cambridge: Cambridge University Press.
Diessel, Holger. 2007. Frequency effects in language acquisition, language use, and diachronic change. *New Ideas in Psychology* 25, 108–127.
Diessel, Holger. 2008. Iconicity of sequence: A corpus-based analysis of the positioning of temporal adverbial clauses in English. *Cognitive Linguistics* 19, 465–490.
Fillmore, Charles, Paul Kay & M. C. O'Connor. 1988. Regularity and idiomaticity in grammatical constructions: The case of 'let alone'. *Language* 64, 501–538.
Givon, Talmy. 1984. *Syntax: A functional-typological introduction. Volume 1*. Amsterdam/Philadelphia: John Benjamins.
Givon, Talmy. 1993. *English grammar: A function-based introduction. Volume 1*. Amsterdam/Philadelphia: John Benjamins.
Goldberg, Adele. E. 1992. The inherent semantics of argument structure: The case of the English ditransitive construction. *Cognitive Linguistics* 3, 37–74.
Goldberg, Adele. E. 1995. *Constructions: A construction-grammar approach to argument structure*. Chicago: The University of Chicago Press.
Goldberg, Adele. E. 1997. The relationship between verbs and constructions. In Marjolijn Verspoor, Kee-Dong Lee & Eve Sweetser (eds.), *Lexical and syntactical constructions and the construction of meaning*. Amsterdam/Philadelphia: John Benjamins, 383–398.
Goldberg, Adele. E. 1998a. Patterns of experience in patterns of language. In Tomasello (ed.), 203–219.
Goldberg, Adele. E. 1998b. Semantic principles of predication. In Jean-Pierre Koenig (ed.), *Discourse and cognition: Bridging the gap*, 41–54. Stanford, CA: CSLI Publications.
Goldberg, Adele. E. 1999. The emergence of argument structure semantics. In Brian MacWhinney (ed.), *The emergence of language*, 197–212. Hillsdale, NJ: Lawrence Erlbaum.
Goldberg, Adele. E. 2006. *Constructions at work*. Oxford: Oxford University Press.

Goldberg, Adele E. & Ray Jackendoff. 2004. The English resultative: A family of constructions. *Language* 80, 532–568.
Goldberg, Adele E., Devin M. Casenhiser & Nitya Sethuraman. 2004. Learning argument-structure generalizations. *Cognitive Linguistics* 15, 289–316.
Goldberg, Adele E., Devin M. Casenhiser & Nitya Sethuraman. 2005. The role of prediction in construction learning. *Journal of Child Language* 32, 407–426.
Gonzálvez-García, Francisco. 2009. The family of object-related depictives in English and Spanish. Towards a usage-based constructionist analysis. *Language Sciences* 31, 663–723.
Gries, Stefan Th. 2005. Syntactic priming: A Corpus-based approach. *Journal of Psycholinguistic Research* 34, 365–399.
Gries, Stefan Th. 2006. Introduction. Gries, Stefan Th. & Anatol Stefanowitsch (eds.), 1–17.
Gries, Stefan Th. & Martin Hilpert. 2008. The identification of stages in diachronic corpora: Variability-based neighbour clustering. *Corpora* 3, 59–81.
Gries, Stefan Th. & Anatol Stefanowitsch. 2004a. Covarying collexemes in the *into*-causative. In Michel Achard & Suzanne Kemmer (eds.), *Language, culture and mind*, 225–236. Stanford: CSLI Publications.
Gries, Stefan Th. & Anatol Stefanowitsch. 2004b. Extending collostructional analysis. *International Journal of Corpus Linguistics* 9, 97–129.
Gries, Stefan Th. & Anatol Stefanowitsch (eds.). 2006. *Corpora in Cognitive Linguistics: Corpus-based approaches to syntax and lexicon*. Berlin/New York: Mouton de Gruyter.
Gries, Stefan Th., Beate Hampe & Doris Schönefeld. 2005. Converging evidence. Bringing together experimental and corpus data on the association of verbs and constructions. *Cognitive Linguistics* 16, 635–676.
Gries, Stefan Th., Beate Hampe & Doris Schönefeld. 2010. Converging evidence II: More on the association of verbs and constructions. In Sally Rice & John Newman (eds.), *Empirical and Experimental Evidence in Cognitive Functional Research*, 59–72. Stanford: CSLI Publications.
Halliday, M. A. K. 1967. Notes on transitivity and theme in English: Part 1. *Journal of Linguistics* 3, 37–81.
Hampe, Beate. 2011. Metaphor, constructional ambiguity and the causative resultatives. In Sandra Handl & Hans-Jörg Schmid (eds.) *Windows to the mind*, 185–215. Berlin/New York: Mouton de Gruyter.
Hampe, Beate & Doris Schönefeld. 2006. Syntactic leaps or lexical variation? More on creative syntax. Stefan Th. Gries & Anatol Stefanowitsch (eds.) *Corpora in Cognitive Linguistics: Corpus-based approaches to syntax and lexicon*, 127–158. Berlin/New York: Mouton de Gruyter.
Hilpert, Martin. 2008. *Germanic future constructions*. Amsterdam/Philadelphia: John Benjamins.
Hoekstra, T. 1988. Small clause results. *Lingua* 74, 101–139.
Huddleston, Rodney & Geoffrey K. Pullum. 2002. *The Cambridge grammar of the English language*. Cambridge: Cambridge University Press.
Jurafski, Daniel. 1992. An on-line computational model of human sentence interpretation: A theory of the representation and use of linguistic knowledge. Unpublished doctoral dissertation, University of California at Berkeley (available as UC Berkeley Computer Science Division Technical Report #92/676).
Langacker, Ronald W. 1987. *Foundations of cognitive grammar*. Volume 1. Stanford, CA: Stanford University Press.
Langacker, Ronald W. 1988. A usage-based model. In Brygida Rudzka-Ostyn (ed.) *Topics in Cognitive Linguistics*, 127–161. Amsterdam/Philadelphia: John Benjamins.
Langacker, Ronald W. 1991. *Foundations of cognitive grammar*. Volume 2. Stanford, CA: Stanford University Press.

Langacker, Ronald W. 2000. A dynamic usage-based model. In Michael Barlow & Suzanne Kemmer (eds.) *Usage-based models of language*, 1–64. Stanford, CA: CSLI Publications.
Lehmann, Christian. 1991. Predicate classes and participation. In Hansjakob Seiler & Waldfried Premper (eds.) *Partizipation: Das sprachliche erfassen von sachverhalten*, 183–239. Tübingen: Narr.
Levin, Beth & Malka Rappaport (Hovav). 1991. Wiping the slate clean: A lexical-semantic exploration. *Cognition* 41, 123–151.
Levin, Beth & Malka Rappaport (Hovav). 1995. *Unaccusativity: At the syntax-semantics interface*. Cambridge, MA: The M. I. T. Press.
Lieven, Elena, Julian Pine, Caroline Rowland & Anna Theakston. 2004. Manchester corpus of the child language date exchange system (CHILDES), document 1-59642-044-8
Michaelis, Laura. 2003a. Word meaning, sentence meaning, and syntactic meaning. In Hubert Cuyckens, René Dirven & John Taylor (eds.) *Cognitive approaches to lexical semantics*, 163–209. Berlin/New York: Mouton de Gruyter.
Michaelis, Laura. 2003b. Headless constructions and coercion by construction. Elaine J. Francis & Laura A. Michaelis (eds.) *Mismatch, form-function incongruity and the architecture of grammar*, 259–310. Stanford, CA: CSLI Publications.
Pawley, Andrew & Frances H. Syder. 1983. Two puzzles for linguistic theory, Native-like selection and native-like fluency. Jack Richards & Richard Schmidt (eds.), *Language and Communication*. London: Longman, 191–226.
Quirk, Randolph, Sidney Greenbaum, Geoffrey Leech & Jan Svartvik. 1985. *A comprehensive grammar of the English language*. London/New York: Longman.
Rappaport Hovav, M. & Beth Levin. 2001. An event-structure account of English resultatives. *Language* 77, 766–797.
Rapoport, Tova R. 1990. Secondary predication and the lexical representation of verbs. *Machine translation* 5, 31–55.
Rapoport, Tova R. 1999. Structure, aspect and the predicate. *Language* 75, 653–677.
Rothstein, Susan. 2006. Secondary predication. In Martin Everaert & Hen van Riemsdijk (eds.) *The Blackwell companion to syntax*. Oxford: Blackwell Publishing, 209–233.
Schönefeld, Doris. 1999. Corpus linguistics and cognitivism. *International Journal of Corpus Linguistics* 4, 131–171.
Schönefeld, Doris. 2002. *Where lexicon and syntax meet*. Berlin/New York: Mouton de Gruyter.
Sinclair, John. 1992. *Corpus. Concordance. Collocation*. Oxford: Oxford University Press.
Stefanowitsch, Anatol. 2008. Negative entrenchment: A usage-based approach to negative evidence. *Cognitive Linguistics* 19, 513–531.
Stefanowitsch, Anatol & Stefan Th Gries. 2003. Collostructions: Investigating the interaction between words and constructions. *International Journal of Corpus Linguistics* 8, 209–243.
Stefanowitsch, Anatol & Stefan Th Gries. 2005. Covarying Collexemes. *Corpus Linguistics and Linguistic Theory* 1, 1–43.
Szmrecsanyi, Benedikt. 2005. Language users as creatures of habit: A corpus-based analysis of persistence in spoken English. *Corpus Linguistics and Linguistic Theory* 1, 113–149.
Taylor, John R. 1998. Syntactic constructions as prototype categories. In Michael Tomasello (ed.) 177–202.
Taylor, John R. 2002. *Cognitive grammar*. Oxford: Oxford University Press.
Tomasello, Michael. 2000. First steps towards a usage-based theory of language acquisition. *Cognitive Linguistics* 11, 61–82.
Tomasello, Michael. 2003. *Constructing a language: A usage-based theory of language acquisition*. Cambridge, MA/London: Harvard University Press.
Tomasello, Michael (ed.). 1998. *The new psychology of language*. Volume 1. Hillsdale, NJ: Lawrence Erlbaum.

Wanner, Anja. 1999. *Verbklassifizierung und aspektuelle alternationen im Englischen*. Tübingen: Max Niemeyer.
Wiechmann, Daniel. 2008. Initial parsing decisions and lexical bias: Corpus evidence from local NP/S ambiguities. *Cognitive Linguistics* 19, 447–464.
Wray, Alison. 2002. *Formulaic language and the lexicon*. Cambridge: Cambridge University Press.
Wulff, Stephanie. 2003. A multifactorial corpus analysis of adjective order in English. *International Journal of Corpus Linguistics* 8, 245–282.
Wulff, Stephanie. 2009. *Rethinking idiomaticity*. London: Continuum.

Phonological similarity in multi-word units*

Stefan Th. Gries

Abstract

In this paper, I investigate the phonological similarity of different elements of the phonological pole of multi-word units. I discuss two case studies on slightly different levels of abstractness. The first case study investigates lexically fully-specified V-NP$_{DirObj}$ idioms such as kick the bucket *and* lose one's cool; *the idioms investigated are taken from the Collins Cobuild Dictionary of Idioms (2002). The second case study investigates the lexically less specified way-construction, which is exemplified by* He fought his way through the crowd *(cf. Goldberg 1995: Ch. 9), on the basis of data from the British National Corpus 1.0.*

I show that both patterns exhibit a strong phonological within-pole relation, namely a strong preference for having their slots filled with phonologically similar elements, where phonological similarity is manifested in alliteration patterns. These preferences are statistically significant when compared to chance-level expectations derived both from the corpora and from the CELEX database (Baayen et al. 1995) and are explained on the basis of Langacker's concept of syntactic and phonological constituents as well as current exemplar-/usage-based approaches.

Keywords: Semantic and phonological constituents, semantic and phonological poles, alliteration, corpus data, CELEX.

---

* I thank audiences at CSDL 2006 and 2010 (in particular Luca Onnis) as well as the anonymous reviewers and the editors for their comments. The usual disclaimers apply. Email address for correspondence: <stgries@linguistics.ucsb.edu>.

1. Introduction

A central notion within many frameworks that can be subsumed under the heading of Cognitive Linguistics is that of a unit. In Langacker's Cognitive Grammar, for example, a unit is defined as

a structure that a speaker has mastered quite thoroughly, to the extent that he can employ it in largely automatic fashion, without having to focus his attention specifically on its individual parts for their arrangement [. . .] he has no need to reflect on how to put it together. (Langacker 1987: 57)

In Cognitive Grammar, the linguistic system is argued to consist of symbolic units, i.e., units that are conventionalized associations of a phonological pole (i.e., a phonological structure) and a semantic/conceptual pole (i.e., a semantic/conceptual structure). The notion of a symbolic unit is not restricted to morphemes or words, but also comprises more abstract grammatical patterns. More specifically, symbolic units as defined above can exhibit different degrees of complexity: they can range from morphemes or monomorphemic words to polymorphemic words, fully-fixed multi-word expressions, partially-filled multi-word expressions, up to lexically completely unspecified syntactic and/or argument structure constructions. The more often a speaker/hearer encounters a symbolic unit, the more entrenched this unit becomes in his linguistic system and the more automatically the unit is accessed. Thus, unit status correlates positively with a speaker/hearer not analyzing the internal structure of a unit.

The relations between the parts of a unit can be explored in two different ways. First, the relation between the phonological pole(s) and the semantic pole(s), which I refer to as *between-pole relation*, is usually not motivated such that the conceptual content of a unit is not predictable from the phonological unit with which it forms a symbolic unit; this is of course the arbitrariness of the sign as already discussed by de Saussure. However, between-pole relations and the notions that are relevant in their discussion—arbitrariness, iconicity, and motivation (cf. Van Langendonck 2007 for a recent overview)—are *not* my concern here (but cf. below, in particular n. 12). This paper is about what I will call *within-pole relations*. In Cognitive Linguistics, there has been a lot of work on relationships holding between the different parts of a unit's semantic pole, but there has been little work that specifically addresses phonological within-pole relations. Sometimes, however, such relations surface in surprisingly clear ways. In Gries (2006a), I studied the verb *to run* on the basis of corpus data and noted that most of the idiomatic expressions that *to run* participated in involved alliterations: *to run rampant, to run riot, to run roughshod, to run the risk, to run into rapture*. This unexpected phenomenon stimulated the exploration reported on in this paper. More specifically, I explore to what degree this is an isolated instance or whether this is actually a more widespread phenomenon in need of an explanation. In this paper, I therefore investigate this specific kind of phonological within-pole relations, namely the relation of phonological similarity of different elements of the phonological pole of symbolic units. I discuss two case studies on slightly different levels of abstractness. The first case study in Section 2 investigates lexically fully-specified V-NP$_{DirObj}$ idioms such as *kick the bucket* and *lose one's cool*; the idioms investigated are from the *Collins Cobuild Dictionary of Idioms*. The second case study in Section 3 investigates the *way*-construction exemplified by *He fought his way through the crowd*, which is lexically only partially specified: the direct object must be *way*, but many different verbs can be inserted into the verb slot. This construction will be investigated on the basis of data from the British National Corpus 1.0. As I will show below, both case studies show a strong and statistically highly significant alliteration effect: verbs and DO head nouns in V-NP$_{DirObj}$ idioms are much more often alliterative than expected by chance, and verbs in the *way*-construction are much more likely to begin with [w] than expected by chance; in both case studies, chance is computed in four different ways. In addition, the verb and the head nouns in alliterative V-NP$_{DirObj}$ idioms exhibit markedly larger degrees of collocational attraction to each other than in non-alliterative idioms; similarly, the verb of the *way*-construction is much more strongly attracted to the *way*-construction if it begins with [w]. Section 4 will discuss motivations for, and implications of, these findings and draw conclusions.

2. Lexically-specified V-NP$_{DirObj}$ idioms

2.1. *Data and methods*

The kind of idioms to be investigated in this section are lexically-specified V-NP$_{DirObj}$ idioms. The 211 lexically-specified V-NP$_{DirObj}$ idioms to be investigated here can be characterized as follows:

- they feature a full lexical verb;
- they feature an NP as a direct object of said verb;
- the V usually takes no further complements or adjuncts;
- the idiom is reasonably frequent, which is operationalized such that it occurs at least 105 times in the 211 m word corpus on which the Collins Cobuild Dictionary of Idioms is based.[1]

---

1. This frequency threshold is based on the dictionary's ordinal frequency labeling of idioms: idioms with a frequency of once per 2 million words or higher were marked with three diamonds and included. This yields 211 idioms with a frequency of 105 or more. Thanks to Stefanie Wulff for making this list available to me.

Some representative examples are listed in (1).

(1) a. spill the beans
    b. gain some ground
    c. get the boot
    d. lend a hand
    e. bite the bullet

These idioms were explored according to the following four methodological steps:

(i) measuring the amount of alliteration effects for the idioms; and for comparison;
(ii) computing baseline amounts of alliteration that are based on the word-initial phonemes and their frequencies; these baseline computations can be and were done in three different ways;
(iii) computing a baseline amount of alliteration based on a control group of non-idiomatic V-NP$_{DirObj}$ sequences;
(iv) computing collocational statistics for the verbs and nouns in the idioms and control structures.

As for step (i), for each of these idioms, I noted the initial segment of the verb and the initial segment of the head noun of the NP$_{DirObj}$. In the case of *bite the bullet*, this means noting [b] and [b]; for *lose face*, it means [l] and [f]; etc. If the NP$_{DirObj}$ also involved additional content words as part of the idiom, the initial segments of these were also noted.[2] Thus, for *fight a losing battle*, the three pairs [f] [l], [f] [b], and [l] [b] were noted; similarly, for *keep a straight face*, I noted [k] [s], [k] [f], and [s] [f]. All pronunciations of words were straightforward to code and automatically extracted from the phonological data available in the CELEX database (cf. below) and I then counted the observed number of alliterations, i.e., the number of instances where one content word in the V-NP$_{DirObj}$ idiom begins with the same sound as another content word.

As for step (ii), it is clear that the observed percentage of alliterations must be compared to some kind of baseline to determine whether it is greater or less than chance would lead one to expect. However, there are at least three different ways in which this expected baseline frequency can be computed:

– without regard to any frequencies;
– with regard to type frequencies;
– with regard to token frequencies.

---

2. The notion of *content word* is used here merely as a convenient traditional cover term for nouns, verbs, adjectives, and adverbs.

In what follows, each of these methods will be characterized briefly.[3] The logic of the first method is this: each word in the phonological part of the CELEX database (<EPW.CD>) begins with one out of 47 different phonemes; these run the whole gamut from highly frequent consonant phonemes to much less frequent diphthongs. Thus, there are 47 · 47 different possible combinations of word-initial segments of two words. Of these 47 · 47 different possible combinations of word-initial segments of two words, 47 will involve the same segment at the beginnings of both words; thus, the expected baseline percentage is 1 ÷ 47.

While this method is simple and straightforward, it also comes with one big problem: it does not take into consideration the frequencies with which each of the 47 phonemes occurs word-initially in differently frequent words. Thus, the high likelihood of two s's at the beginning of words—because [s] is a highly frequent segment—is severely downplayed. This may therefore strongly decrease the expected baseline percentage and, thus, lead us to believe in an effect that a more careful operationalization would not identify. The second method therefore takes frequencies of *types* into account. There are 87,263 different word types in the CELEX database, each beginning with one of 47 different phonemes. Thus, one can use each phoneme's probability to occur *type*-initially in the computation of the expected baseline percentage such that

– the probability p that both words of a V-NP$_{DirObj}$ idiom begin with [s] is the squared percentage of word types starting with [s], or more formally:
$p_{type}([s...]...[s...]) = p_{type}[s...] \cdot p_{type}[s...]$;
– $p_{type}([s...]...[t...]) = p_{type}[s...] \cdot p_{type}[t...]$;
– $p_{type}([s...]...[\text{ɪə}...]) = p_{type}[s...] \cdot p_{type}[\text{ɪə}...]$; etc.

Of course, the first two examples are rather likely whereas the third one is not. In this method, the expected baseline percentage is therefore the sum of all probabilities of all pairs with identical segments.

The third method is very similar to the second, but differs in one crucial respect. In the previous method, the probabilities p were based on the frequencies of word types with initial phonemes in the CELEX database. This, however, disregards the frequencies with which these types occur. The third method, therefore, goes yet another step further and also includes the *token* frequencies of the relevant words. There are 18,580,121 word tokens in the CELEX database, again each beginning with one out of 47 different phonemes. Thus, one can use each phoneme's probability to occur *token*-initially in the computation of the expected baseline percentage such that

---

3. All the data extraction, computations, and graphs were performed/created with R for Windows 2.11.1 patched (cf. R Development Core Team 2010).

- the probability p that both words of a V-NP$_{DirObj}$ idiom begin with [s] is the squared percentage of word tokens starting with [s], or more formally:
  $p_{token}([s...]...[s...]) = p_{token}[s...] \cdot p_{token}[s...]$;
- $p_{token}([s...]...[t...]) = p_{token}[s...] \cdot p_{token}[t...]$;
- $p_{token}([s...]...[\text{ɪə}...]) = p_{token}[s...] \cdot p_{token}[\text{ɪə}...]$; etc.

with the only difference to the above being that now the percentage is based on token—not type—frequencies. Again, the expected baseline percentage is therefore the sum of all probabilities of all pairs with identical segments.[4]

As for step (iii), I randomly sampled two transitive clauses from each of the 170 spoken data files whose names began with S1A or S2A in the fully parsed British Component of the International Corpus of English (ICE-GB) and counted alliterations in this control group of V-NP$_{DirObj}$ structures as above for the idioms (i.e., including adjectival modifiers etc.).

Finally as for step (iv), I explored whether the idioms—both with and without alliterations—exhibited higher collocational attractions between the verb and the noun. To that end and as an approximation, I retrieved the frequency in the British National Corpus World edition of each verb and noun lemma from the idioms and the control verbs as well as the number of times they co-occurred in the same sentence. These frequencies were then used to compute two measures of collocational strength, Mutual Information (*MI*) and the *t*-score, since these are known to exhibit very different statistical behavior and, thus, cover different possible outcomes. These measures of collocational strength were then used as dependent variables, while the independent variables were V-NP$_{DirObj}$ group (idiom vs. control) as well as Alliteration (yes vs. no).

2.2. Results and interim conclusion

The V-NP$_{DirObj}$ idioms contained 35 alliterations out of 310 content word pairs (211 lexically specified idioms many of which had additional content words that were added to the overall number of content word pairs as explained above). Consequently, the observed percentage of alliterations is $35 \div 310 = 0.1129$ and some random examples are listed in (2).

---

4. There are actually analogous ways to compute baseline percentages which are not based on the (type or token) frequencies of word-initial segments, but which are based on the (type or token) frequencies of segments *anywhere in the word*. However, this would introduce strong biases into the computation. Since this study is concerned with alliteration effects which by definition occur word-initially, it is less than desirable to deal with co-occurrence frequencies of [s] / [z] and [ŋ], which are strongly inflated due to the role these phonemes play in plural or progressive-*ing* suffixes (especially the latter would be particularly problematic since [ŋ] does not even occur word-initially in English.

(2) a. bite the bullet
    b. burn bridges
    c. gain ground
    d. make a mark
    e. turn the tables

Alliterations with *s* (7) and *b* (6) were most common, but let us now look at the results of the three baseline computation approaches of step (ii), which involved the phonemes and their frequencies. As for the first method, in the CELEX database, the number of different phonemes is 47 so that, according to method 1, the expected baseline percentage is $1 \div 47 = 0.0213$. As for the second method, I generated a symmetric 47×47 co-occurrence matrix that contained all 47 phonemes in the rows and in the columns and the probability of co-occurrence in the word-initial slots for each of the $47 \cdot 47 = 2{,}209$ possible combinations of two phonemes in the cells. For example, $p([s\ldots])$ is 0.1186 so the cell for [s] / [s] contains $p([s\ldots]) \ldots [s\ldots])$, which amounts to approximately $0.1186 \cdot 0.1186 = 0.0141$ etc. Summing up the main diagonal, which contains the positions where the first and second phoneme are identical, results in the expected baseline percentage, which turns out to be 0.0595. This figure is higher than $1 \div 47$ since it now includes the information that some phoneme repetitions are rather likely, given the high word-initial frequencies of phonemes such as [s], [t], etc. As for the third method, the logic is exactly the same, and the sum of the main diagonal of the 47×47 co-occurrence matrix yields an expected baseline percentage of 0.0473.

Step (iii), the analysis of control V-NP$_{DirObj}$ structures from the ICE-GB spoken data yielded altogether 32 alliterations out of 667 content word pairs, i.e., a proportion of 0.04798.

These results are represented in Figure 1 and can be summarized very straightforwardly.

The observed tendency for alliterations in the analyzed lexically-specified V-NP$_{DirObj}$ idioms is indicated by the solid horizontal line. It is between 1.9 and 5.3 times as strong as expected, and all differences between the observed baseline and the three baseline percentages (the three bars from the left) as well as the non-idiomatic V-NP$_{DirObj}$ structures are highly significant according to exact binomial tests (all p's < 0.001).[5]

---

5. An exact binomial test is a test that can be used to determine the probability to get n or more white balls out of an urn when one draws d balls (with replacement) and the urn contains x white and y red balls. For example, if an urn contains $x = 10$ red and $y = 10$ white balls, the probability to draw a red ball (with replacement) is always 0.5. To now compute how likely it is that you get $n = 3$ or $n = 4$ red balls when you draw $d = 4$ balls (with replacement) from that urn, you can enter the following sum(dbinom(n, d, $x/(x+y) = p$(red ball))) into R: sum(dbinom(3:4, 4, 0.5)), which would return that this probability is 0.3125. Thus, the

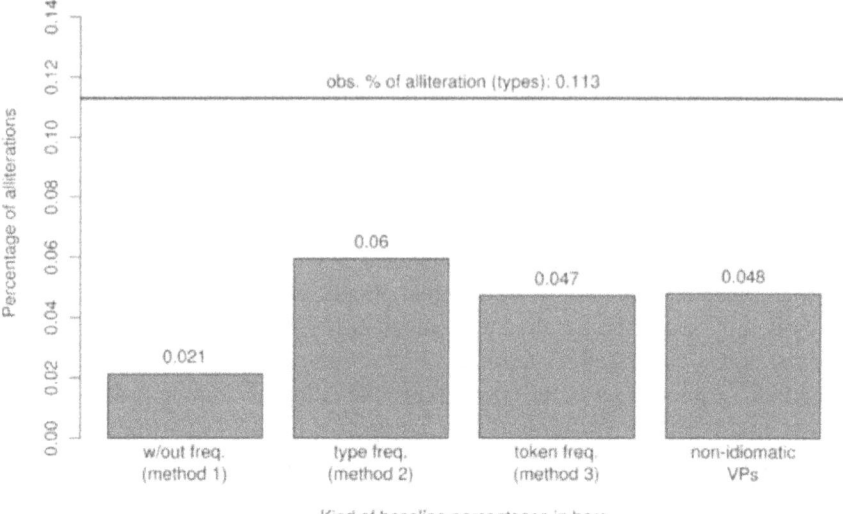

Figure 1. *Observed and expected percentages of alliterations in V-NP$_{DirObj}$ idioms*

Now, what about step (iv), the collocational attraction of verbs and nouns in the four groups? These data are somewhat difficult to evaluate with the usual statistical tools since they involve (i) very different sample sizes and (ii) very heterogeneous data. This is because (i) there are many more non-alliterating idioms than alliterating ones and many more control V-NP$_{DirObj}$ structures than idioms, and (ii) collocation strengths can be extremely variable across all groups, which makes their variances so large as to not allow ANOVAs or similar procedures. (The ANOVAs I ran were in fact characterized by many violations of distributional assumptions.) The problem is exacerbated by the fact that the tested hypothesis only affects, and hence constrains, the collocation strengths of the lowest-frequency sets of items—alliterative idioms—whereas the collocation strengths of the other sets will run the whole gamut from very high to very low. Put differently, the data require that one test a small high-variance sample to a partially-overlapping even higher-variance sample. I am therefore using a descriptive approach and summarize the results with medians in Figure 2.

---

exact binomial test is the better (since exact) counterpart of a chi-square goodness-of-fit test applied to a binary variable. In this case, chisq.test(c(3, 1), p=c(0.5, 0.5)) would return the very similar *p*-value of 0.3173; cf. Sheskin (2007) or Gries (2009) for details. The exact binomial tests were therefore computed as follows:

- method 1: sum(dbinom(35:310, 310, 1/47)) = 2.011489e-15;
- method 2: sum(dbinom(35:310, 310, 0.05950193)) = 0.0002375707;
- method 3: sum(dbinom(35:310, 310, 0.04727673)) = 2.228605e-06.

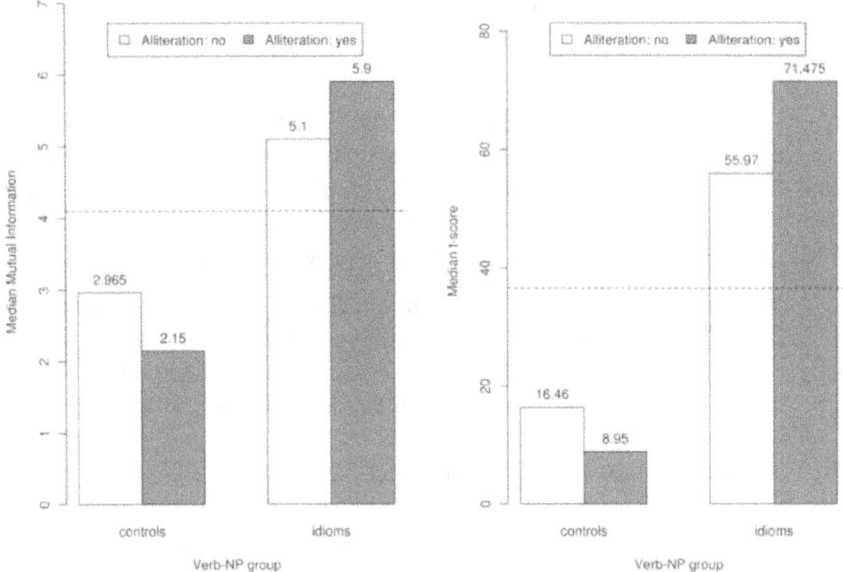

Figure 2. *Collocational attractions in V-NP$_{DirObj}$ idioms as a function of V-NP structure type and alliterations (left panel: MI, right panel: t)*

Both measures yield very similar results: Unsurprisingly, the idioms exhibit higher collocational strengths than the control V-NP$_{DirObj}$ structures. More interesting, however, is the suggestive interaction: Idioms exhibit a higher median collocational strength than controls, but in idioms the alliterative expressions have a higher collocational strength than the non-alliterative ones, whereas in controls this effect is reversed. In other words, the components of V-NP$_{DirObj}$ idioms exhibit the highest collocational attraction if they also alliterate.

3. The *way*-construction

3.1. *Data and methods*

The construction to be investigated in this section is the lexically partially specified *way* construction (cf., among others, Goldberg 1995: Ch. 9). The *way*-construction has the formal characteristics listed in (3a) and is exemplified in (3b) and (3c); cf. Stefanowitsch and Gries (2005) for comprehensive corpus data.

(3)   a.   SUBJ$_{theme}$ V$_{move}$ POSS *way* [$_{PP}$ P NP/S]$_{path}$
      b.   ... as the British Task Force made its way across the Atlantic. (BNC: FNX)

c. ... some expanse of water found its way into the picture. (BNC: C9W)

The semantics of the construction can be characterized as follows: the referent of the subject moves along, or creates, the path denoted by the PP, and the movement of the referent of the subject usually does not come easily in the sense that it involves laboriously circumventing or forcefully overcoming some obstacles on the way or creating the path in the first place. As with the V-NP$_{DirObj}$ idioms, several methodological steps are necessary:

(i) measuring the amount of alliteration effects for the *way*-constructions (once with verb types, once with verb tokens); and for comparison;
(ii) computing baseline amounts of alliteration that are based on the word-initial phonemes and their frequencies; these baseline computations were done in three different ways;
(iii) computing a baseline amount of alliteration based on a control group of transitive VPs with *way* as the direct object;
(iv) computing the collostructional attractions of the verbs to the *way*-construction.

As for step (i), the data set used in the present analysis is based on a concordance of any verb followed by any possessive pronoun (tag: DPS) followed by *way* in the British National Corpus 1.0 (British National Corpus Consortium 1994), which was subsequently cleaned manually; this procedure yielded 5,831 instances of the *way*-construction.[6] For each of these constructions, I noted the initial segment of the verb in the verb slot. In the case of *banged her way*, this means noting [b]; for *wound your way*, it means [w] etc. Again, all pronunciations of words were obvious and automatically extracted from the CELEX database. The observed percentage of alliterations was then computed in two ways, one for types and one for tokens. For types, I counted the number of verb types beginning with [w] and divided this number by the number of all verb types. For tokens, I counted the number of verb tokens beginning with [w] and divided this number by the number of all verb tokens.

As for step (ii) and as before, one needs expected baseline percentages against which we can compare the observed percentages; again as before, there are three different ways to arrive at such baseline percentages: without frequency information, with type-based frequency information, and with token-based frequency information. As for the first method, all verbs in the phonological part of the CELEX database start with one out of 39 different phonemes, which is why the expected baseline percentage will be $1 \div 39$. For the same reasons as above, however, we will also want to compute expected baseline

---

6. This data set is the one used in Stefanowitsch and Gries (2005).

percentages on the basis of the frequencies of the verbs in the CELEX database. Thus and as for the second method, there are 8,504 different verb *types* in the CELEX database. Of these 8,504 different verb types, x will begin with [w], so the expected baseline percentage will be $x \div 8,504$. As for the third method, there are 3,310,984 different verb *tokens* in the CELEX database. Of these, x will begin with [w], so the expected baseline percentage will be $x \div 3,310,984$.[7]

As for step (iii) and to be able to compare the *way*-constructions to cases where *way* is a direct object but not part of the *way*-construction, I also retrieved all instances of *way* used as a direct object in a transitive VP from the ICE-GB and annotated those that were not *way*-constructions for whether the first segment of the verb was a [w] or not.

Finally for step (iv), I computed a collexeme analysis for the *way*-construction using the data from Stefanowitsch and Gries (2005). That is, for each verb attested in the *way*-construction, I computed how much it 'likes' to occur in the *way*-construction given its overall frequency of occurrence. Again, to cover different measures of association, I used a bi-directional measure ($-\log_{10} p_{\text{Fisher-Yates exact}}$ as used by, say, Stefanowitsch and Gries 2003 or Gries et al. 2005) and a uni-directional measure, namely ΔP (cf. Ellis and Ferreira-Junior 2009). Then I computed the median degrees of attraction for alliterative and non-alliterative *way*-constructions.

3.2. Results and interim conclusion

The *way*-construction data from the BNC contained 32 alliteration types out of 492 types, i.e., an observed alliteration percentage of $32 \div 492 = 0.065$. For the tokens, I found 764 alliteration cases out of 5,831, i.e., an observed alliteration percentage of $764 \div 5,831 = 0.131$.

Let us again now look at the results of step (ii), the three methods to compute the baseline percentages. As for the first method, in the CELEX database, there are 39 different phonemes that verbs begin with; thus, the expected baseline percentage is $1 \div 39 = 0.0256$. As for the second method, $x = 226$, i.e., there are 226 verb types beginning with [w] in the CELEX database so the expected baseline percentage is $226 \div 8,504 = 0.0266$. As for the third method, $x = 167,254$, i.e., there are 167,254 verb tokens beginning with [w]

---

7. The frequencies for this comparison were also based on CELEX as opposed to the BNC because (i) that makes sure that the source of the type and token frequencies used for computing the baselines is the same in both case studies and (ii) it is virtually impossible to use the BNC for this in the first place: contrary to the CELEX database the more than 900,000 word types of the BNC are not phonologically annotated so that no (semi-)automatic extraction of their pronunciation is possible.

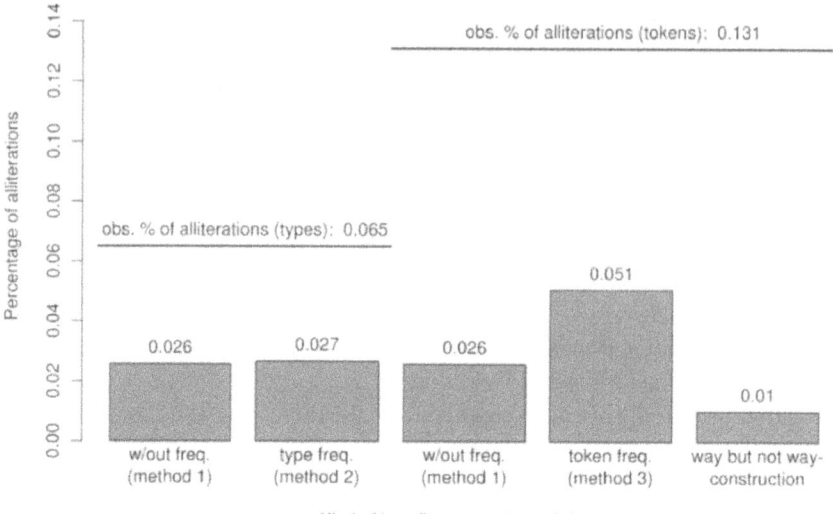

Figure 3. *Observed and expected percentages of alliterations in* way-*constructions*

in the CELEX database so the expected baseline percentage is 167,254 ÷ 3,310,984 = 0.0505.

As for step (iii), the search of *way* used as a direct object in a transitive VP yielded 99 instances that were not *way*-constructions, of which only one featured an alliteration; this baseline is therefore 1 ÷ 99 = 0.01.[8]

As in the case of V-NP$_{DirObj}$ idioms, these results can be summarized very straightforwardly; cf. Figure 3, the type alliteration data are represented on the left, the token data on the right. The observed tendency for alliterations in the partially lexically-specified *way*-construction for types and tokens are again indicated by the solid horizontal lines. For types, the percentage of alliterations is 2.54 times as high as the baseline percentage computed without regard to frequencies and 2.44 times as high as the baseline percentage computed with regard to type frequencies; both of these differences are highly significant according to exact binomial tests.[9] For tokens, the percentage of alliterations is 5.1 times as high as the baseline percentage computed without regard to frequencies, 2.59 times as high as the baseline percentage computed with regard to token frequencies, and 13 times as high as in the non-*way*-constructions;

---

8. For these uses of *way*, no type counts were made because it is not clear how much in common these uses would have to have to constitute different types.
9. The exact binomial tests for the type-based tests were computed as follows:
   - method 1: sum(dbinom(32:492, 492, 1/39)) = 2.323575e-06;
   - method 2: sum(dbinom(32:492, 492, 226/8504)) = 4.797799e-06.

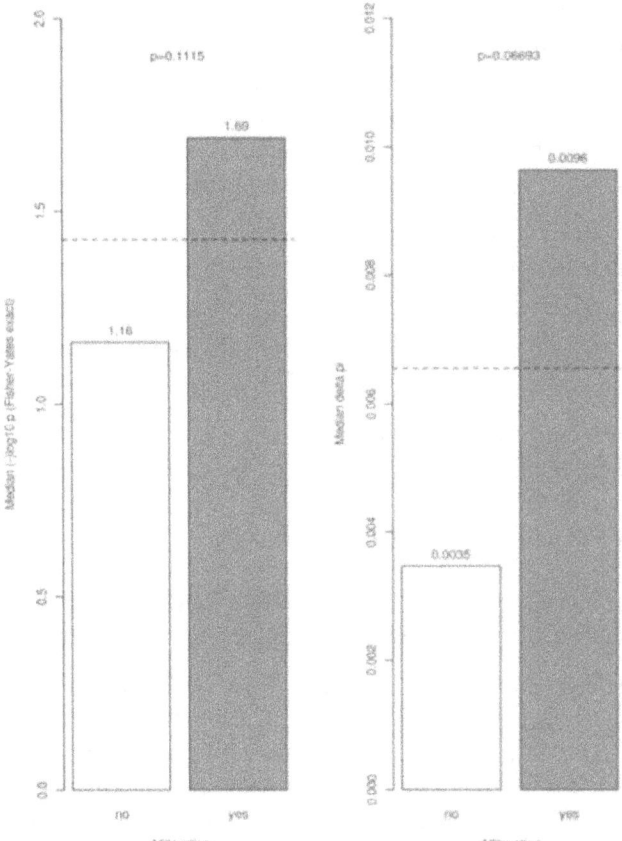

Figure 4. *Median association strengths for alliterative as well as non-alliterative way-constructions (left panel: $-\log_{10} p_{Fisher\text{-}Yates\ exact}$; right panel: ΔP)*

all of these differences are highly significant according to exact binomial tests.[10]

With regard to step (iv), the median collostruction strengths are represented in Figure 4. Again, the data exhibit a large amount of heterogeneity and the values of interest are from the lowest-frequency set of items: alliterative *way*-constructions. As before, the results are suggestive. While they do not reach standard levels of significance, the median collostruction values are higher for

---

10. The exact binomial tests for the token-based tests were computed as follows:
    - method 1: sum(dbinom(764:5831, 5831, 1/39)) = 8.516058e-292;
    - method 3: sum(dbinom(764:5831, 5831, 167254/3310984)) = 1.302444e-123;
    - non-*way*-constructions: sum(dbinom(764:5831, 5831, 1/99)) = 0.

the alliterative *way*-constructions: for ΔP, the alliterative *way*-constructions' median is nearly three times as high as for the non-alliterative ones. For the other measure, the difference is not as pronounced, but it may be interesting to point out that the median of the alliterative *way*-constructions is above the collostruction strength value that represents significant attraction (namely 1.301, as $-\log_{10}$ of $0.05 = 1.301$) whereas the other one is below that.

4. Conclusions and outlook

For two kinds of symbolic units differing in schematicity, fully lexically-specified V-NP$_{DirObj}$ idioms and partially lexically-specified *way*-constructions, the results are unambiguous:

- there are strong alliteration effects;
- these differ significantly from baselines regardless of how expected and/or observed frequencies are computed;
- these differ significantly from non-conventionalized but otherwise parallel structures;
- these are weakly but suggestively correlated with measures of collocational/collostructional attraction, which they appear to reinforce.

These findings raise several questions. First, does this phenomenon serve some function? Second, if so, which function is that? Third, why is this effect observable in the form of alliterations? I do not have definitive answers to all these questions, but some speculations are possible, and the speculations regarding the questions are interrelated and compatible with an exemplar-/usage-based approach. I believe this phenomenon is not just an aberration or an accident and also not just due to subconscious priming effects. The lexically-specified idioms may at least in part be due to alliteration effects in the sense that the alliteration facilitated the lexicalization of some of the idioms. The *way*-construction, by contrast, is of course not due to lexicalized wordplay—since the filler of the verb slot may vary—but the frequencies of some verbs may be boosted by the alliteration effect.

For both kinds of construction, one may speculate that, at some point in time, people created an expression, and because of the alliteration effect, the creation was both fun to produce and easy to memorize (if only unintentionally) and continued to be used until it became entrenched enough to be part of the language system, a process not unlike that undergone by, for example, new subtractive word-formations such as blends and complex clippings such as *chunnel, foolosopher*, etc. This account would fit in well with two different notions or strands of research in usage-based cognitive linguistics.

First, the present findings fit in with the growing recognition of the relevance of analogy and similarity for language learning and processing as well as the role of chunking (particularly for prefabs) in contemporary exemplar-/usage-based approaches. (I am following Gentner and Markman's [1997: 48] definitions.) For instance, it is well-known that (i) similarity of novel utterances to conventionalized utterances is correlated with the novel utterances' acceptability (Bybee 2010: 59), that (ii) a structure *S* at some point in time in a text/discourse primes a itself again at a later point more if the structures as well as how its slots are filled exhibit similarity (cf. Gries 2005, Szmrecsanyi 2005, Snider 2009), and that (iii) similarity on various levels (graphemic, segmental, phonemic, syllabic) facilitates the emergence and perseverance of newly-coined subtractive word-formation processes (cf. Gries 2004, 2006b).

However, while these types of similarity are at work over larger time periods—from priming effects within one text/discourse to the larger time periods time involving language acquisition and change—the present data add to our inventory of similarity effects an interesting much more *local*, within-VP phenomenon. But how can this be explained—what is the mechanism giving rise to this? I propose that this finding can be accounted for elegantly on the basis of the second notion, namely Langacker's (from my point of view under-appreciated) approach towards constituency. Cognitive Grammar does not view constituency as it is seen in, say, generative approaches to grammar. Rather, it distinguishes semantic/conceptual constituents and phonological constituents. Semantic/conceptual constituents are considered to be based on links that combine corresponding elements such that one element fulfills a valence requirement and elaborates an element of another element. One of the other semantic/conceptual groupings mentioned by Langacker (1997) is actually the kind of V-NP$_{DirObj}$ idiom investigated here; it is worth quoting a passage here at length:

Another kind of conceptual group is the semantic pole of a complex lexical item such as *make headway* or *the cat is out of the bag*. It is well known that idioms are often phonologically discontinuous [. . .], hence not symbolized by a classical phonological constituent. This is unproblematic in cognitive grammar, which regards such symbolization as a minor and dispensable part of an idiom's characterization. An idiom resides primarily in a complex of semantic correspondences and symbolic links involving individual elements [. . .] (Langacker 1997: 15)[11]

With regard to phonological constituents, Langacker argues for the existence of several kinds of phonological groupings, of which temporal contiguity

---

11. It is intriguing to notice that the two expressions Langacker refers to here also exhibit phonological similarity even though not in the form of alliterations: in *make headway*, both words feature a continuant followed by the same vowel ([**meɪk hedweɪ**]), and in *the cat is out of the bag*, the two content words are both monosyllabic plosive$_{bilabial}$-æ-plosive ([ðə **kæt** ɪz aʊtə ðə **bæg**]).

is of course the most basic. Others include rhythmic cohesiveness, "stress, pitch level, and even *similarity in segmental content* (e.g., Spanish *la gata blanca* 'the white female cat')" (Langacker 1997: 22; my emphasis, STG). One example he discusses is that in.

(4) Any linguist is capable of making theoretical proposals, but only an *MIT* linguist is capable of making *interesting* theoretical proposals.

The semantic/conceptual constituent in question here is the focus indicated by the italicized words. Thus, the constituent is not held together by valence links, he argues, but by the abstract similarity of "degree of interest or informativeness." However, the focus is symbolized phonologically "by a phonological grouping based on unreduced stress."[12] This approach is in turn very much related to the facilitatory effects of similarity in exemplar-based approaches towards grammaticalization, onstructionalization, or conventionalization of prefabs as discussed by Bybee. For example, this is how Bybee (2010: 62–63) characterizes the workings of exemplar-based models: "entries sharing phonetic and semantic features are *highly connected* depending upon the degree of similarity" (my emphasis, STG).

Given all of the above, my hypothesis is that the recognition of the semantic constituent of the idioms/*way*-constructions is facilitated by the recognition of the phonological similarity based on the alliterations that the constructions studied here exhibit; recall the emphasized part of the Langacker quote regarding segmental similarity above. And in fact it is well-known by now that phonological information facilitates learning of higher-level sequences. Saffran et al. (1996) is perhaps the most-cited study to have shown that infants and young children can identify probabilistic tendencies that facilitate word segmentation in a stream of syllables. Even more pertinently, Onnis et al. (2005), for example, have shown that artificial language learners can identify words with non-

---

12. Reviewers of this paper were convinced that the discussion of the within-pole phonological relation of alliteration should involve the notion of iconicity. While I disagree with that assessment, it is possible to see a relation between Langacker's phonological constituency on the one hand and diagrammatic iconicity on the other hand, where I follow Van Langendonck's (2007: 398) definition:

   a diagram is a systematic arrangement of signs that do not necessarily resemble their referents but whose mutual relations reflect the relations between their referents. More specifically, the constellation of the object and of its diagram is similar, but the individual referents and the individual signs themselves need not resemble each other.

   From that perspective, one could argue that the observed alliteration effects constitute a case of diagrammatic iconicity: the *s-s*, *b-b*, etc. alliterations are not similar to their referents, but the relation of similarity that they exhibit reflects that together they make up a unit. However, Langacker does not appear to consider this connection necessary himself, and I concur.

adjacent syllable dependencies when the two non-adjacent syllables exhibit phonological similarity, where phonological similarity was operationalized on the basis of the first segment of the syllable, which fits nicely with the present case where content words in constructions exhibit phonological similarity, also in the form of alliterations.

Thus, the recognition of the phonological similarity of the elements studied here results in a higher degree of connectivity of the idioms' discontinuous constituents, which in turn facilitates and feeds back into (i) their perception as component parts of a greater whole and (ii) their undergoing the processes of chunking and subsequent constructionalization (cf. Bybee 2010: Section 3.2), but also their greater perseverance and internal collocational/collostructional coherence.

But if there is something to the above hypothesis, the question remains, why alliterations (rather than rhymes or, as in Langacker's example, other characteristics of words)? Currently, it is not clear which characteristic will be most likely to exhibit such similarity effects, but this is an empirical question and, thus, a problem shared by many researchers; for example Bybee (2010: 62) faces a similar explanatory problem for her treatment of *strung* verbs. The present study focused on word-initial alliteration effects, and Onnis et al.'s (2005) artificial language learning data exhibited a similar alliterative effect. And while Bybee (2010: 62) states that "the *final* consonants of the *strung* verbs are more important than the *initial* ones," (my emphasis, STG) six pages later she also does point out that some verbs that have been added to the class of *strung* verbs "also begin with a sibilant or sibilant cluster, increasing the phonetic similarity of the words as wholes." For yet another phenomenon that is connected to the present one theoretically (in terms of having recently been studied from a cognitive usage-based perspective) as well as empirically (in terms of exhibiting statistically significantly overrepresented word-initial phonological similarities), consider phonaesthemes (cf. Bergen 2004). Phonaesthemes, i.e., "frequently recurring sound-meaning pairings that are not clearly contrastive morphemes" (Bergen 2004: 290), are often observed from many examples of words sharing a particular sub-morphemic onset (such as *sl-*, *sn-*, or *gl-*, to name but the most widely-cited examples). Finally, previous studies have shown that *x* segments of the beginning of a word increase its chance of being recognized more than the same number of segments of its end (cf. Noteboom 1981).

In sum, the present study's observation that word beginnings are important and that the perception of phonological similarity may aid the identification of semantic/conceptual constituents/poles and their constructionalization is not as isolated or arbitrary an observation as it may seem. If (some part of) the function of these alliteration effects was to support the recognition of semantic/conceptual constituents by providing support for the recognition of a phonological constituent, then word beginnings would be a good place for this kind of support. This does of course not mean that word beginnings are always or mostly the most important determinant of language processing and change. For example, I fully accept Bybee's analysis that *strung* verbs are more revealingly analyzed on the basis of their rhymes. All of the above merely goes to show that different parts of words can be (more) relevant to different phenomena, and I have already pointed to cases where, say, the phonological similarity of words may be more distributed across the word (e.g., recall note 11 and the above allusion at blends). Thus, ultimately a broader and multiply granular view of similarity may be required for further study, and I will return to this now.

In this connection, there are several possible ways to follow up on the results of this study. The most obvious of these is to enlarge the database to see whether the same results will be obtained. This can mean increasing the numbers of V-NP$_{DirObj}$ and related idioms and *way*-constructions. For example, a few examples I randomly overheard or noticed in writing are suggestive: *going great guns, give the devil his due, cut corners, pull the plug, do the trick,* and *gimme a break.* Similarly, Bybee's (2010: 60) mention of three prefabs includes *black and blue* and *bread and butter.* Another possible extension would of course be to investigate more and more different multi-word symbolic units, i.e., other constructions. On the one hand, just studying more constructions and/or idioms could be interesting. On the other hand, it could be worthwhile to find out how schematic, or lexically-filled, the constructions in focus have to be. This study looked at fully-filled and partially-filled structures but what about even more rigid constructions (e.g., proverbs) or, on the other side of the continuum, what about constructions with two schematic slots? Preliminary analysis of the *into*-causative (e.g., *he tricked her into buying that thing*) suggest an absence of alliteration effects; it seems that such similarity effects are not just a function of conventionalization but also of degree of schematicity. This would be a computationally and data-intensive task, but it could also open up interesting perspectives for our understanding of, say, the syntax-phonology interface, especially since it is already well-known that, for example, rhythmic alternation patterns influence both morphological and syntactic variation phenomena (cf. Schlüter 2003 and Gries 2007 respectively for examples).

More interestingly, one could extend and/or refine the notion of phonological similarity that is used. This can on the one hand mean looking for similarities in places other than word beginnings (although we have seen above why word beginnings may be a particularly salient point to begin with): in studies on blends and complex clippings, Gries (2004, 2006b) discusses a variety of other ways in which phonological similarity can be observed on the level of words and word combinations, and some or even many of these, such as string-edit distances, may be applicable here, too. For example, even if one restricts one's attention to word beginnings, the present analysis can be refined by widening the scope to (i) encompass not just initial segments, but complete onsets or even complete words and/or (ii) along the lines of note 11, include phonological similarity below the segmental level: *do the trick* and *gimme a break* do not involve segmental identity, but in *do the trick*, both the verb and the noun feature alveolar plosives, and in *gimme a break*, both the verb and the noun involve voiced plosives. In that regard: if features do play a role, which kinds of features are relevant: manner? place? voicing? These extensions and others can provide interesting insights regarding (i) the role that phonological constituency plays in multi-word units, (ii) the overall characterization of the forms in which phonological constituency can be manifested, as well as (iii) providing additional evidence for the multitude of similarity-, and thus categorization-based, processes in language that are at the heart of current theories involving exemplar-/usage-based models.

Received 10 August 2008 *University of California,*
Revision received 24 September 2010 *Santa Barbara*

References

Baayen, R Harald, Richard Piepenbrock, & Leon Gulikers (ed.). 1995. *The CELEX Lexical Database (CD-ROM)*. Linguistic Data Consortium, University of Pennsylvania, Philadelphia, PA.

Bergen, Benjamin J. 2004. On the psychological reality of phonaesthemes. *Language* 80 (2). 290–311.

British National Corpus Consortium. 1994. *The British National Corpus 1.0.*

Bybee, Joan. 2010. *Language, usage, and cognition*. Cambridge: Cambridge University Press.

Collins *Cobuild Dictionary of Idioms*. 2002. 2nd edition. London: Harper Collins.

Ellis, Nick C. & Fernando Ferreira-Junior. 2009. Constructions and their acquisition: Islands and the distinctiveness of their occupancy. *Annual Review of Cognitive Linguistics* 7. 187–220.

Gentner, Dedre & Arthur B. Markman. 1997. Structure mapping: a theoretical framework for analogy. *Cognitive Science* 7 (2). 155–170.

Goldberg, Adele E. 1995. *Constructions: A Construction Grammar approach to argument structure*. Chicago, IL: The University of Chicago Press.

Gries, Stefan Th. 2004. Isn't that fantabulous? How similarity motivates intentional morphological blends in English. In Michel Achard & Suzanne Kemmer (eds.), *Language, culture, and mind*, 415–428. Stanford, CA: CSLI.

Gries, Stefan Th. 2005. Syntactic priming: A corpus-based approach. *Journal of Psycholinguistic Research* 34 (4). 365–399.

Gries, Stefan Th. 2006a. Corpus-based methods and cognitive semantics: The many meanings of *to run*. In Stefan Th. Gries & Anatol Stefanowitsch (eds.), *Corpora in cognitive linguistics: Corpus-based approaches to syntax and lexis*, 57–99. Berlin, New York: Mouton de Gruyter.

Gries, Stefan Th. 2006b. Cognitive determinants of subtractive word-formation processes: A corpus-based perspective. *Cognitive Linguistics* 17 (4). 535–558.

Gries, Stefan Th. 2007. New perspectives on old alternations. In Jonathan E. Cihlar, Amy L. Franklin, & David W. Kaiser (eds.), *Papers from the 39th regional meeting of the Chicago Linguistics Society: Vol. II. The Panels*, 274–292. Chicago, IL: Chicago Linguistics Society.

Gries, Stefan Th. 2009. *Statistics for linguistics with R: a practical introduction*. Berlin & New York: Mouton de Gruyter.
Gries, Stefan Th., Beate Hampe, & Doris Schönefeld. 2005. Converging evidence: Bringing together experimental and corpus data on the association of verbs and constructions. *Cognitive Linguistics* 16 (4). 635–676.
Langacker, Ronald W. 1987. *Foundations of Cognitive Grammar Vol. I: Theoretical prerequisites*. Stanford, CA: Stanford University Press.
Langacker, Ronald W. 1997. Constituency, dependency, and conceptual grouping. *Cognitive Linguistics* 8 (1). 1–32.
Noteboom, Sieb G. 1981. Lexical retrieval from fragments of spoken words: Beginnings vs. endings. *Journal of Phonetics* 9 (4). 407–224.
Onnis, Luca, Padraic Monaghan, Korin Richmond, & Nick Chater. 2005. Phonology impacts segmentation in online processing. *Journal of Memory and Language* 53 (2). 225–237.
R Development Core Team. 2010. *R: A language and environment for statistical computing*. R Foundation for Statistical. Computing, Vienna, Austria. ISBN 3-900051-07-0, URL http://www.R-project.org.
Saffran, Jenny R., Richard N. Aslin, & Elissa L. Newport. 1996. Statistical learning by 8-month-old infants. *Science* 274 (5294). 1928–1928.
Schlüter, Julia. 2003. Phonological determinants of grammatical variation in English: Chomsky's worst possible case. In Günter Rohdenburg & Britta Mondorf (eds.), *Determinants of grammatical variation in English*, 69–118. Berlin, New York: Mouton de Gruyter.
Sheskin, David J. 2007. *Handbook of parametric and nonparametric statistical procedures*. 4th edition. Boca Raton, FL: Chapman & Hall/CRC.
Snider, Neal. 2009. Similarity and structural priming. In Niels A. Taatgen & Hedderik van Rijn (eds.), *Proceedings of the 31th Annual Conference of the Cognitive Science Society*, 815–820. Austin, TX: Cognitive Science Society.
Stefanowitsch, Anatol & Stefan Th. Gries. 2003. Collostructions: Investigating the interaction between words and constructions. *International Journal of Corpus Linguistics* 8 (2). 209–243.
Stefanowitsch, Anatol & Stefan Th. Gries. 2005. Covarying collexemes. *Corpus Linguistics and Linguistic Theory* 1 (1). 1–43.
Szmrecsanyi, Benedikt. 2005. Language users as creatures of habit: a corpus-based analysis of persistence in spoken English. *Corpus Linguistics and Linguistic Theory* 1 (1). 113–150.
Van Langendonck, Willy. 2007. Iconicity. In Dirk Geeraerts & Hubert Cuyckens (eds.), *The Oxford Handbook of Cognitive Linguistics*, 394–418. Oxford & New York: Oxford University Press.

The acquisition of questions with longdistance dependencies

*Ewa Dąbrowska, Caroline Rowland and Anna Theakston**

Abstract

A number of researchers have claimed that questions and other constructions with long distance dependencies (LDDs) are acquired relatively early, by age 4 or even earlier, in spite of their complexity. Analysis of LDD questions in the input available to children suggests that they are extremely stereotypical, raising the possibility that children learn lexically specific templates such as WH *do you think* S-GAP? *rather than general rules of the kind postulated in traditional linguistic accounts of this construction. We describe three elicited imitation experiments with children aged from 4;6 to 6;9 and adult controls. Participants were asked to repeat prototypical questions (i.e., questions which match the hypothesised template), unprototypical questions (which depart from it in several respects) and declarative counterparts of both types of interrogative sentences. The children performed significantly better on the prototypical variants of both constructions, even when both variants contained exactly the same lexical material, while adults showed prototypicality effects for LDD questions only. These results suggest that a general declarative complementation construction emerges quite late in development (after age 6), and that even adults rely on lexically specific templates for LDD questions.*

---

* Correspondence addresses: Ewa Dąbrowska, School of English Literature, Language and Linguistics, University of Sheffield, Sheffield, S10 2TN, UK, e-mail: ⟨e.dabrowska@shef.ac.uk⟩; Caroline Rowland, School of Psychology, University of Liverpool, Liverpool, L69 7ZA, UK, e-mail: ⟨crowland@liverpool.ac.uk⟩; Anna Theakston, School of Psychological Sciences, University of Manchester, M13 9PL, UK, ⟨anna.theakston@manchester.ac.uk⟩. The research described here was supported by grant number AH/F001924/1 from the Arts and Humanities Research Council awarded to the first author. Acknowledgements: We would like to thank Claire Anderson, Hayley Lee, and Sarah Street for help with the data collection and coding, and Devin Casenhiser for his comments on an earlier version of this paper.

Keywords: language acquisition; long-distance dependencies; questions; complementation; usage-based approaches.

1. Introduction

Questions and other constructions with long-distance dependencies (henceforth LDDs) have been the object of a considerable amount of research in the generative tradition (see for example, Cheng and Corver 2006; Chomsky 1977 and the references in (1) below). More recently, they have also attracted the attention of cognitive linguists (see e.g., Ambridge and Goldberg 2008; Dąbrowska 2004, 2008, in prep.; Goldberg 2006; Verhagen 2005, 2006). An interesting property of these constructions is that they contain a dependency between a WH word in the main clause and a gap in a subordinate clause, as shown in the examples in (1). In principle, there can be any number of clauses intervening between the WH word and the gap, so such dependencies are often referred to as 'unbounded'.

(1) (a) What$_1$ will John claim that you did ____$_1$? (Culicover 1997: 184)
    (b) Which problem$_1$ does John know (that) Mary solved ____$_1$? (Ouhalla 1994: 72)
    (c) Who$_1$ did Mary hope that Tom would tell Bill that he should visit ____$_1$? (Chomsky 1977: 74)
    (d) Which problem$_1$ do you think (that) Jane believes (that) Bill claims (that) Mary solved ____$_1$1? (Ouhalla 1994: 71)

In contrast to these constructed examples, spontaneously produced LDD questions virtually never contain more than one finite subordinate clause (Dąbrowska in prep., for example, did not find a single instance of a dependency over more than one clause boundary in her sample of 423 LDD questions with finite complement clauses extracted from the spoken part of the British National Corpus). They are also extremely stereotypical (much more so than the corresponding declaratives[1]): the main clause subject is usually *you*, the verb *say* or *think*, and the auxiliary nearly always *do*; moreover, the main clause rarely contains any additional elements (Dąbrowska 2004, in prep.; Verhagen 2005). In the spo-

---

1. Declaratives with verb complement clauses are also quite stereotypical, but much less so. In the BNC data analysed by Dąbrowska (in prep.), the two most frequent declarative formulas, *I think S* and *I mean S*, accounted for only 35 percent of all utterances; and there was considerably more type variation in every syntactic position in the main clause. Verhagen (2005) reports very similar results for Dutch.

ken BNC data analysed by Dąbrowska, 67 percent of the LDD questions had the form *WH do you think S-GAP?* or *WH did you say S-GAP?*, where S-GAP is a subordinate clause with a missing constituent. Most of the remaining questions were minimal variations on these patterns: that is to say, they contained a different matrix subject *or* a different verb *or* a different auxiliary *or* an additional element like an adverbial or complementizer; only 4 percent departed from the prototype in more than one respect. The extreme stereotypicality of spontaneously produced LDD questions has led some researchers (e.g., Dąbrowska 2008; Verhagen 2005) to hypothesise that while English speakers have a general complementation construction for declaratives, their knowledge about LDD questions may be most appropriately captured by means of two lexically specific templates, *WH do you think S-GAP?* and *WH did you say S-GAP?*, rather than by an abstract schema.

Researchers working within the generative tradition, in contrast, maintain that our knowledge about such constructions is expressed in terms of very general principles which apply not just to LDD questions but also to other related constructions such as indirect questions and relatives, and that, in spite of their complexity, the relevant principles are acquired by age four or even earlier (de Villiers 1995; de Villiers et al. 1990; Philip and de Villiers 1993; Thornton and Crain 1994). Thornton and Crain (1994, Experiment 1) elicited long-distance WH questions from children aged from 3;0 to 4;8, and found that seven out of the fifteen children in the study (all aged 3;11 or above) were able to produce adjunct questions (e.g., *What way do you think the Smurf went to the donut store?*), and nine out of the fifteen (all aged 3;8 or above) produced argument questions (e.g., *What do you think is in the box?*). Interestingly, children sometimes produced questions like (2) and (3), with a WH word at the beginning of both the main clause *and* the subordinate clause.

(2) What do you think what is in the box?
(3) What way do you think how he put out the fire?

Thornton and Crain regard such 'medial WH' questions as evidence for the cyclic application of movement (and hence appear to have included them in their count of productive uses of the construction, although this is not entirely clear from their description of the experiment). Note, however, that such utterances could also be produced by simply juxtaposing two independent questions (*what do you think? + what is in the box?*) or an independent question and an indirect question (*what way do you think? + how he put out the fire?*).

Thornton and Crain (1994) also tested children's comprehension of questions with long distance dependencies. The experiment involved playing a guessing game with Kermit the Frog. The child was asked to hide one of two objects in a particular location, and Kermit had to guess which object the child hid. Kermit always guessed incorrectly, and the experimenter then asked questions about what Kermit had said and about the true identity of the hidden object. An example of the protocol used in the experiment is given in (4).

(4) (i) Kermit: I think you probably hid the baby under there.
(ii) Experimenter: What did he say's under there?
(iii) Child The baby!
(iv) Experimenter: What is under there?
(v) Child: A bear!
(Thornton and Crain 1994: 243)

The children (aged from 3;0 to 4;1) did not make any errors, which led Thornton and Crain to conclude that they understand questions with LDDs, and hence have the relevant grammatical knowledge, by age 3;0. The fact that they were not able to produce them until 8–11 months later, the researchers argue, is attributable to performance factors.

This conclusion, however, is premature. In order to give the correct response to the experimenter's first question, the child needs to process only the main clause in the prompt (*What did he say?*). The pragmatically most appropriate answer is *the baby*, since this is the only item of new information in (4i): all the other elements in the sentence express information that is shared by the discourse participants. Therefore, the fact that the children responded appropriately does not tell us very much about their knowledge of constructions with long distance dependencies. Similar criticisms can also be made of the other comprehension studies mentioned earlier (de Villiers 1995; de Villiers et al. 1990; Philip and de Villiers 1993): the fact that children sometimes interpret LDD questions as questions about the subordinate clause doesn't necessarily mean that they have the complex syntactic representations attributed to them by generative linguists.

However, the elicitation study does suggest that children can produce LDD questions from about 3;8 to 3;11. This is corroborated by analyses of children's spontaneous speech (Dąbrowska 2004; Thornton 2008). It should be pointed out, however, that children's LDD questions are even more stereotypical than adults, which raises the possibility that they are produced using lexically specific templates. Consider the first twelve LDD questions from the Abe corpus (Kuczaj 1976) in the CHILDES database:

(5) (a) which snake did he say was in the United States? (3;8)
(b) what do you think's under here? (3;10)

(c) what do you think's under here? (3;10)
(d) he's hopping to dinosaur+land what do you think the kangaroo's gon (t)a think? (3;11)
(e) I didn't know I saw him and he said ⟨hi # Abe⟩ ["] and he hitted me on the back Mommy # what do you think this is? (3;11)
(f) I know what put this here why do you think this doesn't work? (3;11)
(g) look at all those dinosaurs where do you think they're going? (3;11)
(h) no I don't # because this is gon (t)a be a dinosaur thing Mommy # look what I found where do you think the other one is? (3;11)
(j) well # how long do you think it would have to take to that crane? (3;11)
(k) what # why do you think his sword is pointing that way? (3;11)
(l) when do you think we're going to fix it? (3;11)
(m) where do you think the other army man can be? (3;11)

The Abe transcripts contain a total of 44 questions with a dependency between a WH word in the main clause and a gap in a finite subordinate clause, all recorded between the ages of 3;8 and 4;9[2]. Forty-two of these have the form *WH do you think S-GAP?* and one (interestingly, the very first LDD question in the corpus) has the form *WH did NP say S-GAP?* The remaining question (*what do you think that I was singing?*, produced at age 4;0) is a minimal variation on the *WH do you think S-GAP?* template.

To summarise, Thornton and Crain (1994) have demonstrated that four-year-olds can produce questions of the form *WH do you think S-GAP?* This, however, does not necessarily mean that they have mastered the LDD question construction, let alone other constructions involving 'movement': it is also possible that they are simply using a lexically specific template. We know that lexically specific formulas or templates play an important role in early language acquisition (Dąbrowska 2004; Lieven et al. 1997; Tomasello 2003). But do children hear enough LDD questions in order to learn such templates?

---

2. In addition, at age 2;10 Abe imitated an adult LDD question (*know what do you think it was?*)

Questions with long-distance dependencies are a relatively infrequent construction: in the spoken part of the British National Corpus, for example, they occur with a frequency of about 42 per million words (Dąbrowska in prep.). More relevant for our purposes, however, is their frequency in language addressed to children. Since child-directed speech contains a relatively high proportion of questions, it is possible that LDD questions are also more frequent in this type of discourse.

To determine how often children hear LDD questions, we used CLAN software (MacWhinney 1995) to extract all instances of the construction from the Manchester corpus (Theakston et al. 2001), which consists of transcriptions of 402 hours of spontaneous interaction between 12 two-year-old children and their families. We found 325 tokens, all produced by adults. Since the corpus contains 1 450 000 adult words in total, the normalised frequency of LDD questions in the input is 225 per million words—about five times higher than in adult discourse[3].

This means that children hear an LDD question approximately once every 70 minutes on average—about as often as they hear words like *bus, old*, and *able*. LDD questions in the input are also extremely stereotypical. In 99 percent of the instances we analysed, the auxiliary in the main clause was some form of *do;* in 91 percent, the main clause subject was *you*; in 96 percent, the main verb was *think* or *say;* and only 2 percent of the main clauses contained additional elements such as complementizers or a direct object[4]. In fact, 85 percent of the questions fit the lexically specific template *WH do you think S-GAP?*; the second most frequent template, *WH did NP say S-GAP?* accounted for a further 9 percent. Most of the remaining questions involve minimal modifications of these templates (e.g., they contained a different subject *or* a different auxiliary *or* an overt complementizer).

Thus, it does not seem unreasonable to suppose that the children in the Thornton and Crain (1994) studies could have been relying on lexically specific templates. To test this hypothesis, we compared children's performance on prototypical questions (i.e., those which match one of the two high-frequency templates found in the input) and unprototypical questions (those which depart from the template in several respects). In the experiments described below we used a simpler task than Thornton and Crain (sentence repetition rather than production) and tested older chil-

---

3. Note that the figures given in the text are for LDD questions involving a dependency between a WH word in the main clause and a gap in the finite subordinate clause.
4. Some of the questions also contained utterance-initial elements such as *and, so, um*, and *well*. These were not counted as optional elements in the main clause.

dren (aged from 4 to 6). Our prediction was that children will perform more accurately on prototypical questions than on unprototypical questions.

We used sentence repetition rather than elicited production because this method is thought to provide a more direct reflection of children's underlying competence while also allowing more control over what they say (Lust et al. 1998). To be able to repeat a complex sentence correctly, a child must be able to reconstruct its grammatical structure; and the errors that children make on the task often provide useful clues about their interpretation of the sentence (Slobin and Welsh 1973; Santelmann et al. 2002).

2. Study 1

In this experiment, we tested children's ability to repeat three types of questions: prototypical, unprototypical, and deeply embedded questions with long distance dependencies. Prototypical questions instantiated the *WH do you think S-GAP?* template. Unprototypical and deeply embedded questions departed from the template in various ways: the former had different lexical content in the main clause, and the latter contained a dependency spanning two clause boundaries (see Table 1 for examples). Such questions also depart from the LDD question prototype, though in a different way from the 'unprototypical' questions: they contain an additional element (the extra complement clause) between the main clause and the clause containing the gap.

According to generativist accounts of question formation, WH movement applies cyclically, so in principle, once children have learned to form simple questions and sentences with complement clauses, they ought to be able to produce LDD questions with any number of clauses intervening between the filler and the gap. However, questions with very long dependencies (spanning two or more clause boundaries) are difficult to process (Frazier and Clifton 1989; Hawkins 1999; Kluender and Kutas

Table 1. *Examples of sentences used in Study 1*

Condition	Example
Prototypical LDD questions	*What do you think the boys will really like?*
Unprototypical LDD questions	*What does the man really hope they will like?*
Deeply embedded LDD questions	*What do you think he said they will like?*
Prototypical declarative	*I think the boys will really like their shoes.*
Unprototypical declarative	*The man really hopes they will like their shoes.*
Deeply embedded declarative	*I think he said they will like their shoes.*

1993), and therefore one might expect poorer performance on such sentences. Generativist accounts, therefore, predict equally good performance on prototypical and unprototypical questions (since they are equally complex syntactically), and possibly some difficulties with deeply embedded questions. On the other hand, accounts which assume that children rely on lexically specific templates like *WH do you think S-GAP?* predict that children will do well on questions that match the templates but have problems with both unprototypical and deeply embedded questions.

2.1. *Method*

2.1.1. *Participants.* Thirty-four monolingual English-speaking children aged from 4;6 to 5;3 (mean 4;10) participated in the experiment. There were 14 boys and 20 girls. The children were recruited from a primary school in the North-West of England. Three additional children (all boys) were tested but not included in the final sample either because they failed to complete the task (2 children) or because of experimenter error (1 child).

2.1.2. *Design.* The experiment employed a 3 × 2 within-subjects design with two independent variables: prototypicality (with three levels: prototypical, unprototypical , and deeply embedded sentences) and construction type (with two levels: declaratives and questions). The dependent measures were, for each child, the number of correctly repeated sentences.

2.1.3. *Materials.* Prototypical LDD questions consisted of a WH word (*what, who,* or *where*) followed by *do you think* followed by a subordinate clause containing a lexical subject and an adverb (see Table 1). Unprototypical questions consisted of a WH word followed by the auxiliary *does,* a lexical NP, an adverb, a different matrix verb (*hope, expect,* or *believe*), and a subordinate clause with a pronominal subject. Deeply embedded questions consisted of a WH word followed by *do you think* followed by two complement clauses, the first consisting of the pronoun *he* or *she* and the verb *said,* and the second containing a pronominal subject, a verb, and another word. Since these sentences differ in lexical content, we used declarative sentences as controls. The declaratives contained the same lexical material as the interrogatives, except that they lacked an auxiliary and the WH word was replaced with a noun phrase or prepositional phrase as appropriate. A full list of the test sentences is given in Appendix 1.

All the test sentences were nine words long. There were three sentences in each condition, giving a total of 18 test sentences, nine interrogatives and nine declaratives. In addition, there were eight simpler practice sentences (four interrogatives and four declaratives).

Associated with each sentence was a picture depicting the people and objects mentioned in it. The picture was shown to the children before they heard the test sentence, in order to maintain their interest and help them remember the sentences.

The child's interlocutor during the experiment was Dobbin-the-magic-pony, a stuffed toy with a loudspeaker hidden inside. After the child attempted to imitate a sentence, the experimenter used a remote control to play a pre-recorded comment, so that Dobbin appeared to be responding appropriately to the child's utterances.

2.1.4. *Procedure.* The children were tested individually in a quiet room in their school by a female experimenter. The testing sessions typically lasted about ten minutes, and were audio-recorded for later checking. At the beginning of the session the experimenter introduced Dobbin-the-magic-pony, and explained to the child that they were going to play a game:

We are going to play a copying game, OK? I will ask a question about a picture, and you have to ask Dobbin exactly the same question. It's very important that you say exactly the same thing. Can you do this?

When the child agreed to play the game, the experimenter produced the first practice question, showed the child the corresponding picture, and asked him/her to repeat it. If the child imitated the question correctly, the experimenter used the remote control to play a pre-recorded answer using the loudspeaker hidden inside Dobbin; if not, the experimenter repeated the question until the child was able to imitate correctly.

Experimenter:	*What is the boy doing?*
Child:	*What is the boy doing?*
Dobbin:	*He's trying to scare his sister.*

After four practice questions, the experimenter proceeded with the test items. During the test, Dobbin responded after the child produced a complete sentence, whether or not it was the same as the model. If the child was unable to repeat the entire sentence after a single presentation, the experimenter repeated it a second time.

The declaratives were tested using a similar method. First, the experimenter explained the rules of the game:

In this game, I will say something about the picture, and you have to repeat exactly the same thing. Do you want to try? Remember, you have to repeat exactly the same thing.

Again, the instructions were followed by four practice items and the test items themselves. The procedure was exactly the same, except that this time Dobbin commented on the statement the child repeated:

Experimenter: The girl is pushing the boy.
Child: The girl is pushing the boy.
Dobbin: That's naughty!

The order of the two 'games' was counterbalanced across children. Within each block, the sentences were presented in a different random order for each child.

2.1.5. *Scoring.* The dependent variable was the number of correctly repeated sentences. Responses containing false starts (as in 6) and self-corrections (7) were coded as correct if there were no other errors.

(6) ⟨what does the man⟩ [/] what does the man really hope they will like?
(7) what do you think they [//] the boys will really like?

2.2. Results

Information about the mean number of correctly repeated sentences in each condition (out of a maximum score of 3) is given in Table 2. To determine whether the children performed differently across sentence types a 2 (construction type) × 3 (prototypicality) ANOVA was carried out. The results showed significant main effects of construction, $F(1,33) = 5.63$, $p = 0.024$, $\eta_p^2 = 0.15$ and prototypicality, $F(2,66) = 66.04$, $p < 0.001$, $\eta_p^2 = 0.67$. The interaction between construction and prototypicality approached significance: $F(2,66) = 2.99$, $p = 0.057$, $\eta_p^2 = 0.08$.

Table 2. *Mean number (standard deviation) of correctly repeated sentences*

Condition	Questions mean (SD)		Declaratives mean (SD)	
Prototypical	1.74	(1.11)	2.21	(0.91)
Unprototypical	0.82	(0.90)	1.03	(1.00)
Deeply embedded	0.44	(0.75)	0.38	(0.70)

The results show that the children were significantly more accurate at repeating declaratives than questions. Planned repeated t-tests were performed to investigate the significant effect of prototypicality. As predicted by the lexically specific template hypothesis, performance on prototypical questions was significantly better than on unprototypical or deeply embedded questions (prototypical question v. unprototypical question: $t(33) = 5.34$, $p < 0.001$; prototypical question v. deeply embedded question, $t(33) = 6.77$, $p < 0.001$). There was also a difference between unprototypical and deeply embedded questions, $t(33) = 2.13$, $p = 0.04$; note, however, that this difference is no longer significant after the Bonferroni correction for multiple comparisons.

However, a similar pattern of results was found for declarative sentences. The children imitated prototypical declaratives better than both unprototypical declaratives and deeply embedded declaratives (prototypical declarative v. unprototypical declarative, $t(33) = 7.59$, $p < 0.001$; prototypical declarative v. deeply embedded declarative: $t(33) = 9.79$, $p < 0.001$), and unprototypical declaratives better than deeply embedded declaratives ($t(33) = 3.85$, $p = 0.001$).

There was also a marginally significant interaction so planned t-tests were performed to investigate this further. Children were significantly more accurate at imitating prototypical declaratives than prototypical questions; $t(33) = 2.69$, $p = 0.01$. However, there were no significant differences in their accuracy at imitating the two unprototypical constructions, $t(33) = 1.49$, $p = 0.15$, or between the two deeply embedded constructions, $t(33) = 0.42$, $p = 0.68$.

2.3. Discussion

Study 1 showed that children find prototypical declaratives the easiest construction type to imitate. Prototypical questions were significantly harder for the children to imitate. However, both were significantly easier than unprototypical declaratives and questions, both of which children found difficult (on average they imitated only 1 out of 3 correctly). Multiple embedded constructions were the most difficult, with very few correct imitations.

The experiment thus revealed a strong prototypicality effect for *both* interrogatives and declaratives. There are two possible explanations for these results. First, it is possible that children use lexically specific templates to produce both declaratives and questions at this age. This interpretation is supported by work that suggests that declaratives with verb complement clauses produced spontaneously by young children are quite formulaic (Bloom et al. 1989; Diessel 2004); and an experimental study by Kidd et al. (2006) which found that children aged from 2;10 to 5;8 repeated complex declaratives more accurately when the matrix clause contained a verb which frequently occurs with sentential complements rather than in other syntactic constructions. Thus, it is possible that children have lexically specific templates for both constructions.

An equally plausible alternative interpretation is simply that the children found it easier to repeat sentences with high frequency verbs, possibly because they are more familiar. Study 2 was designed to discriminate between these two possibilities.

3. Study 2

Study 2, like study 1, was designed to compare children's performance on prototypical and unprototypical questions with long distance dependencies and their declarative counterparts. In contrast to study 1, however, the prototypical and unprototypical variants of both constructions contained exactly the same lexical material. If the prototypicality effects observed in study 1 were due merely to the lexical properties of the test sentences, they should disappear once these are controlled for. If, on the other hand, children have lexically specific templates for both constructions, we should find prototypicality effects for questions and for declaratives.

A second issue investigated was the age at which children develop verb-general knowledge about the two constructions. According to the constructivist view of language acquisition, development proceeds from lexically specific formulas to more abstract patterns, and is not necessarily synchronous: that is to say, abstract patterns may emerge at different times for different constructions. We know that verb-general knowledge about basic argument-structure constructions emerges in the third year of life or even earlier (Tomasello 2003; Goldberg 2006). The results of study 1 and the Kidd et al. study suggest that even as late as 5, children's knowledge about complementation may still be expressed in terms of verb-specific patterns such as *NP think S, NP say S*. Since abstraction is thought to be largely driven by high type frequency (Bybee 2001; Tomasello 2003), and since LDD questions are much more stereotypical than declaratives with verb complement clauses (Verhagen 2005; Dąbrowska in prep.), a fully general LDD construction should emerge even later, or not at all: it is possible that even adults rely on lexically specific patterns for this complex structure (cf. Verhagen 2005; Dąbrowska 2008). Thus, we expect to find an interaction between prototypicality, construction and age: specifically, prototypicality effects for declaratives, but not for questions, should disappear, or at least diminish, in older children.

3.1. Method

3.1.1. Participants.
Thirty-seven monolingual English-speaking children participated in the study, 18 five-year-olds (aged 4;8-5;9, mean 5;3, 10 girls and 8 boys) and 19 six-year-olds (aged 6;0-6;9, mean 6;5, 6 girls and 13 boys).

The children were recruited from a primary school in the North-West of England. One five-year-old did not attempt to repeat any of the sentences and was excluded from the analysis.

3.1.2. Design.
The experiment employed a $2 \times 2 \times 2$ mixed-subjects design with two within-subject independent variables: prototypicality (with two levels: prototypical and unprototypical) and construction type (declaratives and questions) and one between subjects independent variable of age (five-year-olds and six-year-olds). The dependent measures were, for each child, the number of correctly repeated sentences.

3.1.3. Materials.
Four types of sentences were used in the experiment: prototypical and unprototypical LDD questions, and their declarative counterparts. Prototypical questions had the hypothesised LDD question formula (*what do you think* or *what did you say*) in the main clause and a subordinate clause consisting of a heavy NP (4 words), an adverb and a verb which can take sentential complements (either *hope* or *expect*). The unprototypical questions contained exactly the same lexical material, but the content words which appeared in the main clause in the prototypical variant now appeared in the subordinate clause, and vice versa (see Table 3).

In the declarative counterparts of LDD questions, the WH word was replaced with a pro-form (*so* or *it*). To keep the number of words the same in both constructions, the auxiliary *will* was added to the subordinate clause. There were four items in each condition, giving a total of 16 sentences (plus six fillers and three sentences used for warm-ups). A full list of the test sentences is given in Appendix 2.

Table 3. *Examples of sentences used in Study 2*

Condition	Example
Prototypical question	What do you think the funny old man really hopes?
Unprototypical question	What does the funny old man really hope you think?
Prototypical declarative	I think the funny old man will really hope so.
Unprototypical declarative	The funny old man really hopes I will think so.

3.1.4. *Procedure* Examination of the recordings for Study 1 revealed that the experimenter tended to articulate the non-prototypical LDD questions more slowly and more clearly than the prototypical variants, and we were concerned that this might influence the results. Therefore, the model sentences used in Study 2 were pre-recorded by a research assistant who was unaware of the purpose of the study and who was instructed to take great care to use the same speed and prosody throughout. During the experiment, the recorded sentences were played (in random order) using a loudspeaker hidden inside Dobbin. Each model sentence was followed by a beep, and the child was asked to repeat the sentence after the beep. Once the child had imitated the sentence, the experimenter provided an appropriate response (an answer to the question or a comment, as in Study 1). The reason for the beep was to introduce a short delay, and thus make the task slightly more difficult, since we were testing older children.

Apart from these two changes, the procedure was the same as in Study 1.

3.2. *Results*

3.2.1. *Target responses.* Table 4 shows the mean number of correctly repeated sentences (out of a maximum of four correct responses). These data were analysed using a $2 \times 2 \times 2$ ANOVA with the within participants factors of construction (declarative, question) and prototypicality (prototypical, unprototypical) and the between-participants factor of age (5-year-olds, 6-year-olds). The analysis revealed no significant main effects and no interactions. The main effect of prototypicality neared significance ($F(1, 34) = 3.50$, $p = 0.070$, $\eta_p^2 = 0.09$), with more correct responses for prototypical than unprototypical sentences. No other effects neared significance.

As is evident from these figures, the children found the task extremely difficult. In fact, 14 out of 17 five-year-olds and 13 out of 19 six-year-olds did not repeat a single sentence correctly: thus the differences reported

Table 4. *Mean number (standard deviation) of correctly repeated sentences (study 2, strict scoring)*

Condition	5-year-olds (*SD*)		6-year-olds (*SD*)	
Prototypical question	0.53	(1.18)	0.21	0.535
Unprototypical question	0.41	(1.18)	0.16	0.375
Prototypical declarative	0.29	(0.69)	0.47	1.020
Unprototypical declarative	0.24	(0.56)	0.11	0.459

above are attributable entirely to data from the remaining 9 children. The difficulty could be to the delay or the greater complexity of the experimental sentences. It is also possible that imitating a "disembodied" computer-produced voice (rather than simply imitating the person sitting next to them) requires greater concentration. It should also be pointed out that many of the errors that the children produced—for instance, omission of the adverb or one of the adjectives—are clearly uninformative with regard to their knowledge about question formation and complementation. We therefore reanalysed the data using a more focussed scoring method in which the child was given credit for a sentence if the only error(s) involved (a) omission or placement of the adverb, or substitution of a different adverb and/or (b) omission of the determiner or the adjective(s) inside the heavy NP, or substitution of a different adjective. Thus, under the new scoring system, all the responses given in (8) were coded as correct imitations of the target sentence *What does the pretty little girl really expect you said?*

(8) (a) What does the pretty little girl expect you said? [omission of adverb]
(b) What does the little girl expect you said? [omission of adverb and adjective]
(c) What does the really pretty girl expect you said? [misplacement of adverb and omission of adjective]
(d) What does the small little girl probably expect you said? [substitution of adverb and substitution of adjective]

The number of correct responses using this scoring method are given in Table 5. An ANOVA on these figures revealed a significant main effect of construction, $F(1,34) = 6.47$, $p = 0.016$, $\eta_p^2 = 0.16$, with the children correctly imitating more question than declaratives, and a significant main effect of prototypicality, $F(1, 34) = 5.82$, $p = 0.021$, $\eta_p^2 = 0.15$, with performance better on prototypical than unprototypical sentences, as predicted by the lexically specific template hypothesis. The main effect of age was not significant. However, there was a significant interaction

Table 5. *Mean number (standard deviation) of correctly repeated sentences (study 2, focused scoring)*

Condition	5-year-olds (SD)		6-year-olds (SD)	
Prototypical question	1.35	(1.46)	1.47	(1.22)
Unprototypical question	1.24	(1.25)	1.00	(0.94)
Prototypical declarative	0.71	(1.05)	1.53	(1.17)
Unprototypical declarative	0.47	(0.87)	1.00	(1.20)

between construction and age, $F(1, 34) = 7.51$, $p = 0.010$, $\eta_p^2 = 0.18$. The five-year-olds performed better on questions than on declaratives (prototypical declarative v. prototypical question: $t(16) = 32.67$, $p = 0.02$; unprototypical declarative v. unprototypical question: $t(16) = 2.89$, $p = 0.01$). However, by six years, the children's accurate imitation of declaratives had improved and the children were equally good on both constructions (prototypical declarative v. prototypical question: $t(18) = 0.21$, *ns*; unprototypical declaratives v. unprototypical question: $t(18) = 0.00$, *ns*).[5]

The younger children's better performance on interrogative utterances is surprising, since questions are less frequent than declaratives and commonly regarded as more complex syntactically: in a generative framework, for example, WH questions require WH movement and T to C movement (subject-auxiliary inversion). Further research will be necessary to determine whether this is a genuine developmental effect, and, if so, to explore the reasons for it. It is possible that the difference is attributable to our test materials. As explained in the Method section, the subordinate clause in the declaratives, but not in interrogatives, contained the auxiliary *will*, and the children sometimes omitted it, placed it in the main clause, or substituted a different auxiliary in its place. Such errors were relatively infrequent, with a mean frequency in the five-year-old group of 0.35 instances per child for both prototypical and unprototypical declaratives,[6] so they cannot fully account for the interrogative advantage in this age group. However, it is possible that the fact the subordinate clause in the declarative sentences always referred to an event which occurred at a different time than the event described in the main clause was an additional source of difficulty and thus contributed to errors elsewhere in the sentence. (Note that in Study 1, where all sentences had *will* in the subordinate clause, we observed the opposite pattern: children performed better on declaratives than on interrogatives.) Whatever the reason for the differences in performance on the two constructions in the five-year-

---

5. To ensure that the results reported in the preceding section were not simply an artefact of the scoring method we also recoded the data from Study 1 using the new method and conducted a second ANOVA on these figures. The results were similar to those reported in the main text, except that the main effects are slightly larger (for construction, $F(1, 33) = 11.49$, $p = 0.002$, $\eta_p^2 = 0.26$; for prototypicality, $F(2, 66) = 82.15$, $p < 0.001$, $\eta_p^2 = 0.71$), and the construction x prototypicality interaction is now significant ($F(2, 66) = 4.28$, $p = 0.018$, $\eta_p^2 = 0.12$).
6. This is the number of responses in which children omitted, misplaced, or replaced *will* and made no other errors (apart from those allowed in the focused scoring system). In other words, the scores for declaratives given in Table 5 would increase by 0.35 if children were given credit for these responses.

old group, it is important to stress that they do not affect our findings about prototypicality, since the critical comparisons were between prototypical and unprototypical interrogatives (neither of which contained *will*) and prototypical and unprototypical declaratives (which both contained *will*).

3.2.2. *Errors.* The children made a variety of errors, mostly omissions or substitutions of lexical material. Most of the errors were quite unsystematic; three types of incorrect response, however, recurred in a number of children and provide some additional clues about the source of their difficulties with the constructions under investigation. We discuss these in more detail in this section.

Monoclausal responses. The children sometimes produced a simple clause instead of a complex one. These errors can be divided into three types:

- main clause only (e.g., *What does the tall woman expect?* for *What does the tall young woman probably expect you think?*)
- subordinate clause only (e.g., *What does the little boy hope?* for *What did you say the scared little boy probably hopes?*)
- amalgam of main and subordinate clause (e.g., *What does the funny old man think?* for *What does the funny old man really hope you think?*)

The frequencies of these three types of errors in each condition, collapsing the data across children, are given in Table 6.

Table 6. *Frequency of monoclausal responses in Study 2*

	Prototypical questions	Unprototypical questions	Prototypical declaratives	Unprototypical declaratives
Main clause only	0	7	0	8
Subordinate clause only	39	0	35	0
Amalgam of main and sub. cl.	1	8	0	3

Subordinate clause only responses were the most common, accounting for 74 percent of all monoclausal responses, and show a striking pattern: they occur only with the prototypical variant of each construction. This makes sense: the main clause in the prototypical question and prototypical declarative condition contains a light verb functioning as an epistemic marker (Thompson 2002; Verhagen 2005); thus, in imitating the subordinate clause only, the child repeats the gist of the stimulus sentence, showing that s/he has understood it. Main clause only responses, in contrast, occurred only with unprototypical variants. Such responses are more difficult to interpret. In this case, it is the main clause that contains the semantically 'heavier' verb, so one could argue that the main clause contains the main thrust of the question. However, such responses could also arise if the child simply repeated the first (and hence most salient) clause in the stimulus sentence, without processing the subordinate clause at all. Finally, amalgams of the main and subordinate clause clearly involve a change in meaning, and thus indicate that the child had not understood the stimulus sentence. Such errors occur overwhelmingly (over 90 percent of the time) in unprototypical variants, especially unprototypical questions. In short, while monoclausal responses are considerably more frequent with prototypical variants of both constructions, the distribution of errors strongly suggests that it is the unprototypical variants which the children find more difficult to understand.

Medial WH questions. Like the children tested by Thornton and Crain (1994), the children in this study sometimes inserted an additional WH word at the beginning of the subordinate clause: for instance, one child produced (10) in response to the prompt in (9):

(9) *what does the tall young woman probably expect you think?*
(10) *what does the tall young woman probably expect what you think?*

There were nine errors of this kind, made by six children. Interestingly, all of them occurred in the unprototypical question condition. Since this is clearly an immature form, the fact that such errors occurred only in unprototypical questions suggests that they were causing the children more difficulty than the prototypical variant.

Lexical substitution errors involving verbs. Another common error involved replacing the verb in the main or subordinate clause with another verb, usually another complement-taking verb used in the experiment. In the unprototypical variants replacing the main clause verb with *think* or *say* makes the sentence more similar to the prototype. In the prototypical variant, on the other hand, the main clause verb is *think* or *say*, so replacing it with another verb makes the sentence less prototypical. Thus, reliance on lexically specific templates would make children prone to make the first type of error but not the second one. There were 14 verb substitutions in the main clauses of unprototypical questions, 11 of which involved replacing the main clause verb with *think* or *say*, and only 4 in prototypical questions, two of which involved replacing one template verb (*say*) with another (*think*). In declaratives, there were 17 main clause verb substitution errors in unprototypical variants, 12 of which involved

Table 7. *Frequency of lexical substitution errors in Study 2*

Type of error	Prototypical questions	Unprototypical questions	Prototypical declaratives	Unprototypical declaratives
Simple substitution in main clause	4*	14	9**	17
Simple substitution in subordinate clause	2	6	7	5
Reversal of main and subordinate verb	0	3	0	12

*2 of these are *think* for *say* substitutions
**5 of these are *think* for *say* substitutions

replacing the main clause verb with *think* or *say*, and 9 in prototypical variants, 5 of which were *think* for *say* substitutions. Thus, only six main clause verb substitution errors (out of a total of 44) involved replacing the verb in the hypothesised template with another verb.[7] Although there were not enough errors for statistical analysis, the trend suggests that children had a tendency to choose prototypical verbs in the place of non-prototypical ones, which would be consistent with the lexically specific template hypothesis.

Note, however, that there is a confound: *think* and *say* are also the most frequent complement taking verbs, and have more general meanings than *hope* and *expect*, so the observed pattern of errors could be a result of the child simply substituting a more basic verb for a less basic one. If this were the case, we would expect to find the opposite pattern in the subordinate clause, where the verb is *hope* or *expect* in the prototypical variants and *think* or *say* in the unprototypical variants: that is to say, substitution errors in the subordinate clause should be more frequent in the prototypical variants. This is clearly not the case (see Table 7): verb substitutions in the subordinate clause are, if anything, more frequent in unprototypical sentences.

A third type of substitution error involved reversing the two verbs, i.e., putting the main clause verb in the subordinate clause and the

---

7. In three of these, the child replaced the main clause verb with the verb that was used in the subordinate clause, thus using the same verb in both clauses (e.g., *I hope the funny old man will hope so* for *I think the funny old man will really hope so*). In the remaining three, the child used the main clause verb from the immediately preceding sentence. Thus, such responses are best regarded as anticipation and perseveration errors respectively.

subordinate verb in the main clause. (Note that reversal errors were excluded from the counts of simple substitution errors.) Reversal errors in prototypical sentences would make them less prototypical. Reversal errors in unprototypical sentences would make them more prototypical. As shown in Table 7, there were 14 reversal errors in our data all in non-prototypical utterances (3 in questions, 11 in declaratives). Again, the trend is to replace a non-prototypical verb with a prototypical one. Thus, the pattern of lexical substitution errors also supports the hypothesis that the prototypical variants of both constructions are more basic.

4. Study 3

Study 2 revealed prototypicality effects for both questions and declaratives. These effects cannot be attributed simply to the lexical properties of the stimuli, since the prototypical and unprototypical variants of the experimental sentences contained exactly the same lexical material. However, the predicted interaction with age did not occur: both five- and six-year-olds performed better on prototypical variants of both constructions, suggesting that both groups rely on lexically specific templates for declaratives as well as for interrogatives.

It is possible, of course, that complementation constructions continue to develop after age 6. To investigate this possibility, we administered a version of the repetition task to adults. If adults rely on lexically specific templates to produce and understand LDD questions but have a more general complementation pattern for declaratives, we would expect to find an interaction between construction type and prototypicality: specifically, adults should perform better on prototypical than unprototypical LDD questions, while there should be no corresponding difference, or a much smaller difference, in performance on declaratives. Study 3 was designed to test this prediction.

4.1. *Method*

4.1.1. *Participants* Nine adults (3 males and 6 females) aged between 30 and 50 participated in the experiment. All spoke English as their first language and were employed by a university in the north of England, either as lecturers or as administrative staff.

4.1.2. *Design.* The experiment employed a 2 × 2 within-subjects design with two within-subject independent variables: prototypicality (with two levels: prototypical, unprototypical) and construction (declaratives and questions). The dependent measures were, for each participant, the number of correctly repeated sentences.

Table 8. *Mean number (standard deviation) of correctly repeated sentences (Study 3)*

Condition	No. correct	(SD)
Prototypical question	3.22	(0.83)
Unprototypical question	2.22	(1.48)
Prototypical declarative	2.56	(0.73)
Unprototypical declarative	2.67	(1.12)

4.1.3. *Materials and procedure.* The materials and procedure were identical to those for study 2 with one difference. Since a pilot study showed that the task used in Study 2 was too easy for adults, the participants were asked to count backwards from 10 to 1 before attempting to repeat each sentence. This introduced a delay of about 10 seconds and prevented them from rehearsing the test sentence during the delay. Also, we did not use the toy interlocutor: the participants were simply asked to repeat each test sentence. The 'strict' scoring method was used when coding the results: that is to say, any omission or change to the stimulus sentence was coded as incorrect.

4.2. *Results and discussion*

Table 8 shows the number of correctly repeated sentences in each condition. These results were analysed using a 2 (construction) × 2 (prototypicality) ANOVA. The main effects of construction and prototypicality were not significant. However, as predicted, there was a significant interaction between construction type and prototypicality, $F(1,8) = 8.16$, $p = 0.021$, $\eta_p^2 = 0.51$: prototypical questions were repeated correctly significantly more often than unprototypical questions ($t(8) = 2.68$, $p = 0.028$), while there was no difference in performance on declaratives ($t(8) = 0.26$, *ns*). This suggests that even adults make use of lexically specific templates for LDD questions, but not declaratives, with finite complement clauses.

5. General discussion

The differences in performance on prototypical and unprototypical variants described above are fully compatible with a lexical template account. However, it should be noted that there is yet another explanation which may be able to account for our results. The prototypical and unprototypical sentences in our experiments were not in fact identical in form, in that the adverb modified the subordinate clause verb in the former and the main clause verb in the latter. Thus, the observed differences could conceivably be attributed to form frequency, **if** the prototypical structures (i.e., WH Aux NP V [NP Adv V] and NP V [NP (Aux) Adv VP]) turned out to be more frequent than the 'unprototypical' variants (WH Aux NP Adv V [NP V] and NP Adv V [NP (Aux) Adv VP]).

One problem with this alternative explanation is that such structures are exceedingly rare. None of the 325 LDD questions in child-directed speech that we extracted from the Manchester corpus contained an adverb premodifying either the main or the subordinate verb; there are also no instances of an adverb premodifying either the main or the subordinate verb in a declarative sentence with a finite verb complement clause. A somewhat larger sample of 423 instances of LDD questions extracted from Spoken BNC contained one question in which the main clause verb was premodified by an adverb and four in which there was an adverb premodifying the subordinate verb. The sample is too small to determine if the difference is statistically significant; however, even if it was, it is highly unlikely that speakers are sensitive to such tiny differences in frequency. Spoken BNC contains about 10 million words, which means that the normalised frequencies of the sequences WH Aux NP Adv V [NP V] and WH Aux NP V [NP Adv V] are 0.1 and 0.4 per million words respectively.

A second problem with the account is that it cannot explain the interaction between prototypicality and construction type found in the adults. As we saw in the preceding section, adults were significantly better at repeating prototypical than unprototypical LDD questions, but showed no corresponding differences for declarative sentences. However, the BNC data indicate that declarative sentences with finite verb complement clauses are similar to LDD questions in that they are about four times more likely to contain an adverb premodifying the subordinate verb than the main verb. (A matched sample of 423 declaratives with finite verb complement clauses from Spoken BNC contained 22 instances of the former and only 5 of the latter.) We conclude that form frequency cannot account for the observed pattern of results.

6. Conclusion

Our results indicate that children continue to rely on lexically specific templates for both LDD questions and declaratives with finite verb complement clauses as late as age 6. Study 1 revealed that four-year-old children imitate prototypical variants of both constructions more accurately than unprototypical variants (which had the same grammatical structure but differed in lexical content) as well as deeply embedded sentences (which had a more complex syntactic structure). Study 2 replicated this result with older children in a design which, importantly, controlled for the possibility that the prototypical sentences are easier to repeat because they contain higher-frequency verbs. Study 3 demonstrated that even adults show the prototypicality effect for questions, but not for declaratives.

These results are consistent with the predictions of the usage-based approach, according to which children's knowledge about complementation constructions is best captured in terms of lexically specific templates acquired by generalizing over attested instances of the relevant constructions. They are difficult to accommodate in the generative framework, which assumes that children have abstract syntactic representations and general operations such as WH movement. Generative accounts predict that children should perform equally well on prototypical and unprototypical variants of both constructions, since these were matched for syntactic complexity. Syntactic complexity may play a role in performance: in Study 1, the children performed slightly more accurately on 'unprototypical' questions and declaratives than on 'deeply embedded' sentences. Such effects, however, are relatively small in comparison to the purely lexical effects, and they can also be accommodated in a usage based framework: as pointed out earlier, deeply embedded sentences are also less prototypical instances of the relevant constructions.

More strikingly, our results suggest that even adults rely on lexically specific templates for questions with long distance dependencies. This accords well with previous research on LDD questions in the usage-based framework, which has shown that (i) LDD questions in adult speech and writing are also very stereotypical (Verhagen 2005; Dąbrowska in prep.); (ii) prototypical LDD questions, i.e., questions of the form *WH do you think S-GAP?* and *WH did you say S-GAP?*, are produced more fluently than non-prototypical questions (Dąbrowska in prep.); and (iii) prototypical LDD questions are judged to be more acceptable than non-prototypical questions—and LDD questions which depart from the prototype in several respects are judged as bad as some clearly ungrammatical sentences (Dąbrowska 2008).

The fact that speakers use lexically specific templates does not of course preclude the possibility that they have more abstract constructions as well. However, our results, and the research cited earlier in this paper, show the lexically specific variants have a privileged status, in that they are ontogenetically earlier, apparently easier to access, and preferred by speakers.

Received 28 January 2008　　　　　　　　　　*University of Sheffield*
Revision received 14 July 2008　　　　　　　*University of Liverpool*
　　　　　　　　　　　　　　　　　　　　　　University of Manchester

Appendix 1: Sentences used in Study 1

Prototypical LDD questions What do you think the boys will really like? Where do you think the girls will actually go? Who do you think really likes these smelly socks?	*Prototypical declaratives* I think the boys will really like their shoes. I think the girls will actually go to school. I think my neighbour really likes these smelly socks.
Unprototypical LDD questions What does the man really hope they will like? Where does the girl actually expect they will go? Who does the boy really believe likes smelly socks?	*Unprototypical declaratives* The man really hopes they will like their shoes. The girl actually expects they will go to school. The boy really believes my neighbour likes smelly socks.
Deeply embedded LDD questions What do you think he said they will like? Where do you think she said they will go? Who do you think he said likes smelly socks?	*Deeply embedded declaratives* I think he said they will like their shoes. I think she said they will go to school. I think he said his neighbour likes smelly socks.

Appendix 2: Sentences used in Studies 2 and 3

Prototypical LDD questions What do you think the funny old man really hopes? What do you think the tall young woman probably expects? What did you say the pretty little girl really expects? What did you say the scared little boy probably hopes?	*Prototypical declaratives* I think the funny old man will really hope so. I think the tall young woman will probably expect it. I said the pretty little girl will really expect it. I said the scared little boy will probably hope so.
Unprototypical LDD questions What does the funny old man really hope you think?	*Unprototypical declaratives* The funny old man really hopes I will think so.

What does the tall young woman probably expect you think?	The tall young woman probably expects I will think so.
What does the pretty little girl really expect you said?	The pretty little girl really expects I will say it.
What does the scared little boy probably hope you said?	The scared little boy probably hopes I will say it.

References

Ambridge, Ben and Adele E. Goldberg
    2008   The island status of clausal complements: Evidence in favor of an information structure explanation. *Cognitive Linguistics* 19(3), 357–389.

Bloom, Lois, M. Rispoli, B. Gartner and J. Hafitz
    1989   Acquisition of complementation. *Journal of Child Language* 16,101–120.

Bybee, Joan
    2001   *Phonology and Language Use.* Cambridge: Cambridge University Press.

Cheng, Lisa Lai-Shen, and Norbert Corver (eds.)
    2006   *Wh Movement: Moving On.* Cambridge, MA: MIT Press.

Chomsky, Noam
    1977   On *wh*-movement. In Culicover, Peter W., Thomas Wasow, and Adrian Akmajian (eds.), *Formal Syntax.* Academic Press, New York, 71–132.

Culicover, Peter W.
    1997   *Principles and Parameters: An Introduction to Syntactic Theory.* Oxford. Oxford University Press.

Dąbrowska, Ewa
    2004   *Language, Mind and Brain. Some Psychological and Neurological Constraints on Theories of Grammar.* Edinburgh: Edinburgh University Press.

Dąbrowska, Ewa
    in prep.   Prototype effects in questions with unbounded dependencies.

Dąbrowska, Ewa
    2008   Questions with unbounded dependencies: A usage-based perspective. *Cognitive Linguistics* 19, 391–425.

de Villiers, Jill
    1995   Empty categories and complex sentences: The case of wh-questions. In Fletcher, Paul and Brian MacWhinney (eds.), *The Handbook of Child Language.* Oxford: Blackwell, 508–540.

de Villiers, Jill, Thomas Roeper, and Anne Vainikka
    1990   The acquisition of long-distance rules. In Frazier, Lyn and Jill de Villiers (eds.), *Language Processing and Language Acquisition.* Dordrecht: Kluwer, 257–297.

Diessel, Holger
    2004   *The Acquisition of Complex Sentences.* Cambridge: Cambridge University Press.

Frazier, Lyn and Charles Clifton, Jr.
    1989   Successive cyclicity in the grammar and the parser. *Language and Cognitive Processes* 4, 93–126.

Goldberg, Adele E.
  2006 *Constructions at Work. The Nature of Generalization in Language.* Oxford: Oxford University Press.
Hawkins, John A.
  1999 Processing complexity and filler-gap dependencies across grammars. *Language* 75, 244–285.
Kidd, Evan, Elena Lieven and Michael Tomasello
  2006 Examining the role of lexical frequency in the acquisition and processing of sentential complements. *Cognitive Development* 21, 93–107.
Kluender, Robert and Marta Kutas
  1993 Subjacency as a processing phenomenon. *Language and Cognitive Processes* 8, 573–633.
Kuczaj, Stan A.
  1976 *-ing, -s* and *-ed:* A study of the acquisition of certain verb inflections. Doctoral dissertation, University of Minnesota.
Lieven, Elena V., Julian M. Pine and Gillian Baldwin
  1997 Lexically-based learning and early grammatical development. *Journal of Child Language* 24, 187–219.
Lust, Barbara, Suzanne Flynn and Claire Foley
  1998 What children know about what they say: Elicited imitation as a research method for assessing children's syntax. In McDaniel, Dana, Cecile McKee and Helen Smith Cairns (eds.), *Methods for Assessing Children's Syntax.* Cambridge, MA: MIT Press, 55–76.
MacWhinney, Brian
  1995 *The CHILDES Project: Tools for Analyzing Talk.* Hillsdale, NJ: Lawrence Erlbaum.
Ouhalla, Jamal
  1994 *Introducing Transformational Grammar: From Rules to Principles and Parameters.* London: Edward Arnold.
Philip, William and Jill de Villiers
  1993 Monotonicity and the acquisition of weak Wh-islands. In Clark, Eve V. (ed.), *Proceedings of the Twenty-fourth Annual Child Language Research Forum.* Stanford: CSLI, 99–111.
Santelmann, Lynn, Stephanie Berk, Jennifer Austin, Shamitha Somashekar and Barbara Lust
  2002 Continuity and development in the acquisition of inversion in yes/no questions: dissociating movement and inflection. *Journal of Child Language* 29, 813–840.
Slobin, Dan I. and Charles A. Welsh
  1973 Elicited imitations as a research tool in developmental psycholinguistics. In Ferguson, C. and D. Slobin (eds.), *Studies of Child Language Development.* New York: Wiley.
Theakston, Anna, Elena Lieven, Julian Pine and Caroline Rowland
  2001 The role of performance limitations in the acquisition of verb-argument structure. *Journal of Child Language* 28, 127–152.
Thompson, Sandra
  2002 "Object complements" and conversation. Towards a realistic account. *Studies in Language* 26, 125–164.
Thornton, Rosalind
  2008 Why continuity? *Natural Language and Linguistic Theory* 26, 107–146.

Thornton, Rosalind and Stephen Crain
    1994   Successful cyclic movement. In Hoekstra, Teun and Bonnie D. Schwartz (eds.), *Language Acquisition Studies in Generative Grammar*. Amsterdam: John Benjamins, 215–252.

Tomasello, Michael
    2003   *Constructing a Language: A Usage-Based Theory of Child Language Acquisition*. Cambridge, MA: Harvard University Press.

Verhagen, Arie
    2005   *Constructions of Intersubjectivity: Discourse, Syntax and Cognition*. Oxford: Oxford University Press.

Verhagen, Arie
    2006   On subjectivity and 'long distance *Wh*-movement'. In Athanasiadou, Angeliki, Costas Canakis, and Bert Cornillie (eds.), *Various Paths to Subjectivity*, 323–346. Berlin: Mouton de Gruyter.

Iconicity of sequence: A corpus-based analysis of the positioning of temporal adverbial clauses in English

*Holger Diessel**

Abstract

Recent work in functional and cognitive linguistics has argued and presented evidence that the positioning of adverbial clauses is motivated by competing pressures from syntactic parsing, discourse pragmatics, and semantics. Continuing this line of research, the current paper investigates the effect of the iconicity principle on the positioning of temporal adverbial clauses. The iconicity principle predicts that the linear ordering of main and subordinate clauses mirrors the sequential ordering of the events they describe. Drawing on corpus data from spoken and written English, the paper shows that, although temporal clauses exhibit a general tendency to follow the main clause, there is a clear correlation between clause order and iconicity: temporal clauses denoting a prior event precede the main clause more often than temporal clauses of posteriority. In addition to the iconicity principle, there are other factors such as length, complexity, and pragmatic import that may affect the positioning of temporal adverbial clauses. Using logistic regression analysis, the paper investigates the effects of the various factors on the linear structuring of complex sentences.

Keywords: iconicity; temporal adverbial clauses; constituent order; competing motivations; logistic regression.

---

* I would like to thank Karsten Schmidtke, Daniel Wiechmann, and especially Beate Hampe for many helpful comments and suggestions. All remaining errors are, of course, mine. Contact address: University of Jena, Institut für Anglistik/Amerikanistik, Ernst-Abbe-Platz 8, 07743 Jena, Germany. Author's email address: holger.diessel@uni-jena.de.

1. Introduction

Adverbial clauses are subordinate clauses that are combined with a main clause in complex sentences. As can be seen in examples (1) to (4), in English the adverbial clause may precede or follow the associated main clause. This raises the interesting question of what motivates the sequential ordering of main and subordinate clauses. When does the adverbial clause precede the main clause and when does it follow it?

(1) *If* it's a really nice day, we could walk.
(2) I'd quite like to go to Richmond Park *because* I was reading about it in this novel.
(3) *When* you get a tax rebate, you get the money back after about a year, don't you?
(4) Weigh up all these factors carefully *before* you commit yourself to the manoeuvre.

1.1. *Competing motivations for the positioning of adverbial clauses*

In a recent paper, Diessel (2005) argued that the ordering of main and adverbial clauses is motivated by functional and cognitive pressures from three sources: (1) syntactic parsing, (2) discourse pragmatics, and (3) semantics. Drawing on Hawkins' (1994, 2004) processing theory of constituent order and complexity, he shows that adverbial clauses are easier to process, and thus more highly preferred, if they follow the main clause. According to Hawkins, the human processor prefers linear structures that allow for fast and easy access to the recognition domain. The recognition domain is defined as the string of linguistic elements that must be processed and kept in working memory until the parser has accessed all immediate constituents of a phrase once the mother node of the phrase has been recognized.

Complex sentences consist of two clauses functioning as the immediate constituents of a bi-clausal structure, which is organized by the subordinate conjunction creating the mother node $S_{complex}$ that dominates the complex sentence construction (cf. Hawkins 1994: 360). If the adverbial clause follows the main clause, the subordinate conjunction establishes the $S_{complex}$-node right after the main clauses has been processed and before the adverbial clause is accessed, which means that the two immediate constituents of the complex sentence can be attached to their mother node (i.e., $S_{complex}$) as soon as this node is constructed. In contrast, if the adverbial clause precedes the main clause, the subordinate conjunction establishes the $S_{complex}$-node right at the beginning of the bi-clausal structure, which means that the human parser first has to process the adverbial clause before the second immediate constituent, i.e., the main clause, can be attached to S$_{complex}$. Complex sentences with an initial adverbial clause thus have a longer recognition domain (5a) than complex sentences with final adverbial clauses (cf. 5b and cf. Diessel 2005). If the human processor prefers complex sentences with final adverbial clauses, one has to ask what motivates the occurrence of initial adverbial clauses. Why do speakers prepose adverbial clauses if complex sentences with final adverbial clauses are easier to parse?

(5) a. [When ....]$_{SUB}$ [............]$_{Main}$ recognition domain

b. [.............]$_{Main}$ [when ......]$_{SUB}$ recognition domain

One factor that motivates the preposing of adverbial clauses is their pragmatic function. A number of studies have argued and presented evidence that the discourse function of an adverbial clause varies with its position relative to the main clause (cf. Chafe 1984; Diessel 2005; Ford 1993; Givón 1990: 846–847; Ramsay 1987; Thompson and Longacre 1985; Thompson 1985, 1987; Verstraete 2004). If the adverbial clause follows the main clause it tends to provide new information, or else functions as an afterthought; but if the adverbial clause precedes the main clause, it serves to organize the information flow in the ongoing discourse. As Chafe (1984), Givón (1990: 846–847), and others have argued, initial adverbial clauses provide a guidepost for the interpretation of subsequent clauses; they are often used at the beginning of a new paragraph or a new turn to organize the transition between discourse topics. In other words, the occurrence of initial adverbial clauses is motivated by particular discourse-pragmatic functions. Complex sentences containing initial adverbial clauses can be seen as particular constructions that speakers use to stage information, i.e., to lay a thematic foundation for the following discourse (cf. Ford 1993: Ch 3; Givón 1990: 846–847; Thompson 1987; Verstraete 2004).

However, this general orientation function of initial adverbial clauses does not explain why certain semantic types of adverbial clauses occur in initial position more readily than others. In addition to syntactic parsing and discourse pragmatics, we thus have to consider the meaning of complex sentences to account for the sequential ordering of main and subordinate clauses. In the literature, the following major semantic types of adverbial clauses are usually distinguished: temporal clauses, indicating a temporal relationship between two events; conditional clauses, expressing a condition or prerequisite for the realisation of the main clause event;

causal clauses, providing a cause or reason for the proposition expressed in the main clause; result clauses, referring to the result or consequence of the main clause event; and purpose clauses, denoting the goal or purpose of the activity expressed in the main clause (see Quirk et al. 1985: Ch 12 for a detailed discussion of the various semantic types of adverbial clauses).

Using corpus data from both spoken and written genres, a number of studies have demonstrated that temporal, conditional, causal, result, and purpose clauses tend to occur in different positions relative to the main clause (cf. Altenberg 1984; Biber et al. 1999: 820–825; Diessel 1996, 2005; Ford 1993; Quirk et al. 1985: Ch 12; Ramsay 1987). To simplify, conditional clauses usually precede the main clause, temporal clauses are commonly used both before and after the main clause, and causal, result, and purpose clauses predominantly follow the associated main clause.

Interestingly, the same positional patterns have also been observed in many other languages across the world. Investigating the distribution of adverbial clauses in a representative sample of the world's languages, Diessel (2001) identified two common cross-linguistic patterns. There are languages in which all adverbial clauses precede the main clause, unless they are extraposed (e.g., Japanese), and there are languages in which the positioning of adverbial clauses varies with their meaning (e.g., Punjabi). In the latter language type, conditional clauses usually precede the main clause, temporal clauses exhibit a mixed pattern of pre- and postposing, and causal, result, and purpose clauses commonly follow the associated clause (see also Hetterle 2007).

1.2. Iconicity of sequence

Another factor that seems to influence clause order is iconicity. The notion of iconicity comprises two basic types, diagrammatic iconicity, which is concerned with structural (or relational) similarities between the sign and the referent, and imagic iconicity, which is concerned with substantial similarities between the sign and the referent (e.g., sound symbolism). The notion of diagrammatic iconicity has been used in various functional and cognitive explanation of linguistic structure (cf. Croft 2003: Ch 4.2; Dressler 1995; Fenk-Oczlon 1991; Givón 1985, 1991; Haiman 1980, 1983, 1985, 1994, 2006; Haspelmath forthc.; Itkonen 2004; Jakobson 1965[1971]; Plank 1979; Tabakowska et al. 2007; Taylor 2002: 45–48). The general idea "behind [diagrammatic] iconicity is that the structure of language reflects in some way the structure of experience" (Croft 2003: 102); but this general notion of iconicity subsumes a wide variety of different meanings.¹ In this paper, I concentrate on a particular subtype of diagrammatic iconicity, iconicity of sequence, which refers to the sequential ordering of linguistic elements in discourse and complex sentences. Note that this kind of iconic motivation cannot be explained by frequency of occurrence (cf. Haspelmath 2008) or effort reduction (cf. Haiman 2006) as other types of iconicity.

There are a number of studies suggesting that clause order in complex sentences is usually iconic. For instance, Lehmann (1974) and Haiman (1978, 1983) argued that conditional clauses tend to precede the main clause because conditional clauses refer to an event that is conceptually prior to the one expressed in the main clause; Greenberg (1963 [1966]) proposed that purpose clauses follow the main clause because they denote the intended endpoint or result of the activity expressed in the associated clause (cf. Schmidtke in press); and Clark (1971) argued that *after*-clauses precede the main clause more often than *before*-clauses, because *after*-clauses refer to an event that occurs prior to the one in the main clause, whereas *before*-clauses refer to a posterior event (cf. Diessel 2005).

While all of these studies suggest that iconicity of sequence is an important determinant of the linear structuring of complex sentences, it must be emphasized that the distributional properties of certain semantic types of adverbial clauses are not consistent with the iconicity principle. In particular, the positioning of causal clauses violates the iconicity of sequence. Although causes and reasons are conceptually prior to the effect expressed in the main clause, causal clauses tend to occur sentence-finally (cf. Altenberg 1984; Diessel 2001, 2005; Ford 1993: Chs 3–4; Hetterle 2007). Across languages, causes and reasons are commonly expressed in constructions that follow the semantically associated clause, suggesting that iconicity of sequence is not relevant for the positioning of causal clauses. Diessel (2006) argues that the tendency of causal clauses to follow the main clause is motivated by the fact that causal clauses are primarily

---

1. In a recent review of the literature, Haspelmath (2008) identified eight different subtypes of (diagrammatic) iconicity: (1) iconicity of quantity (greater quantities are expressed by more linguistic structure), (2) iconicity of complexity (more complex meanings are expressed by more complex forms), (3) iconicity of cohesion (semantic cohesion is reflected in structural cohesion), (4) iconicity of paradigmatic isomorphism (one meaning, one form in the system), (5) iconicity of syntagmatic isomorphism (one form, one meaning in the clause), (6) iconicity of sequence (sequences of form match sequences of experiences), (7) iconicity of contiguity (semantically associated elements occur adjacent to each other), and (8) iconicity of repetition (repetition in linguistic form reflects repeated experiences).

used to back up a previous statement that the hearer may not accept or may not find convincing.

Moreover, while the positioning of conditional clauses is consistent with the iconicity of sequence, there is an alternative explanation for their distribution. Conditional clauses precede the main clause because they denote a hypothetical situation, providing a conceptual framework (or mental space) for the interpretation of subsequent clauses (cf. Dancygier 1998; Dancygier and Sweetser 2000; Lehmann 1974). If the conditional clause follows the main clause, the hearer may at first misinterpret the preceding main clause as a factual statement. Since the revision of a previous utterance increases the processing load, there is a strong motivation to place conditional clauses before the main clause (cf. Diessel 2005). Thus, it seems that the iconicity principle is not immediately relevant for the positioning of causal and conditional clauses.

Moreover, one might hypothesize that iconicity of sequence, which denotes the temporal dimension of experience, primarily concerns the ordering of temporally related clauses. Previous studies suggest that temporal clauses denoting a prior event precede the main clause more often than temporal clauses of posteriority (cf. Clark 1971; Diessel 2005). But although iconicity of sequence has been widely discussed in the literature, it has never been systematically investigated. It is the purpose of this study to fill this gap. Using corpus data from spoken and written English, the paper presents the first quantitative analysis of the positioning of temporal adverbial clauses to systematically investigate the effect of the iconicity principle on clause order.

2. Analysis

The analysis concentrates on five types of temporal clauses marked by the subordinating conjunctions *when, after, before, once*, and *until*. The five conjunctions have been chosen for two reasons: first, they are among the most frequent temporal conjunctions in English, and second, they are semantically especially interesting for the purpose of this study.

When-clauses are interesting because *when* is the only temporal conjunction in English that does not specify the temporal sequence between main and adverbial clauses. As can be seen in examples (6) to (8), *when*-clauses denote situations that can occur prior, posterior, or simultaneously to the one expressed in the main clause.

(6) We shall make up our mind *when* the IMF has reported. [prior]
(7) They had already made breaches in the defensive wall of sand [...] *when* the order came. [posterior]
(8) I did cook occasionally, *when* they were out. [simultaneous]

The four other conjunctions are interesting because they form semantic pairs: *after* and *before* describe a temporal sequence of two events from reverse perspectives (cf. 9–10). *After*-clauses refer to an event that precedes the one expressed in the main clause, whereas *before*-clauses refer to a posterior event. The iconicity principle would thus predict that *after*-clauses precede the main clause more frequently than *before*-clauses.

(9) a. *After* her father died, of course, Isabel's trust fund included quite a substantial holding in the company. [prior]
   b. I put Emily back in her own bed, *after* she'd fallen asleep. [prior]
(10) a. *Before* the debt crisis set in, Brazil was enjoying growth rates of 7 percent per year. [posterior]
   b. The heat [...] from the sun is retained by the earth for a while, *before* it's radiated away. [posterior]

Quirk et al. (1985: 1082) point out that *after*- and *before*-clauses are not generally converses of one another. Both clause types have special uses in which the two constructions have different meanings. For instance, a complex sentence with a *before*-clause referring to a non-factual (or counterfactual) situation does not have the same meaning as the corresponding complex sentence with an *after*-clause (cf. 11–12); but constructions of this type are rare (examples 11–12 are the only counterfactual *before*-clauses in the entire database).

(11) a. An Asian man [...] triggered the alarm *before* I could stop him.
   ≠ I could stop an Asian man, *after* he triggered the alarm.
(12) a. *Before* he could move in for the tackle, Hughes had driven the ball high past Grobbelaar from 25 yards.
   ≠ He could move in for the tackle, *after* Hughes had driven the ball high past Grobbelaar from 25 yards.

Once and *until* parallel *after* and *before*: an adverbial clause introduced by *once* refers to a prior event, whereas an adverbial clause marked by *until* denotes a posterior situation. However, *once* and *until* differ from *after* and *before* in that they introduce adverbial clauses that are telic: *once* indicates a designated starting point of the situation expressed in the main clause and *until* marks its endpoint (cf. 13–14).

(13) a. *Once* the problem became clear, policy was tightened. [prior]
   b. We'll be pretty busy *once* our course gets back into full swing. [prior]
(14) a. *Until* I'd spoken to William Davis I'd no idea that the monarchy was the only bright spot on our horizon. [posterior]

b. There should be no further cuts in interest rates, *until* the underlying rate of inflation begins to tumble. [posterior]

Note that all five conjunctions can have non-temporal meanings (cf. Quirk et al. 1985: 1078–1086). *When*-clauses may have a conditional interpretation, *after*-clauses are sometimes interpreted with a causal connotation, *before*-clauses can express a purpose or goal, *once*-clauses are often conditional, and *until*-clauses may express a combination of time, purpose, and result. However, these non-temporal semantic features are not or only weakly grammaticalized; they usually emerge as conversational implicatures from the interpretation of temporal clauses in the discourse context.[2]

2.1. *Study 1*

2.1.1. *Methods.* The analysis is based on data from the British Component of the International Corpus of English (ICE-GB). The ICE-GB corpus consists of 1 million words compiled from a wide variety of spoken and written genres. The corpus is tagged and includes detailed information about syntactic structure. For this study, I randomly selected 200 *when*-clauses, 200 *after*- and *before*-clauses (100 *after* and 100 *before*), and 200 *once*- and *until*-clauses (100 *once* and 100 *until*). Half of the data come from spoken discourse, the other half come from written genres. The study is restricted to finite adverbial clauses and disregards participle constructions and gerunds. After the initial search, I excluded all adverbial clauses that were not relevant for the purpose of the current investigation. Specifically, I excluded adverbial clauses that are inserted into the main clause (cf. 15) and adverbial clauses that do not occur with an associated main clause (cf. 16).

(15) And the reason for that before you ask me was that uhm everybody was confusing my brain.
(16) Uhm half an hour after I leave probably.

Moreover, I excluded adverbial clauses that are related to the main clause at the speech act level (cf. Hengeveld 1989). There were, for instance, several *before*-clauses that speakers used as independent speech acts to coordinate the interaction between the speech participants (cf. 17–18).

---

2. In some uses, the non-temporal meanings have been conventionalized as in *I would vote for Kennedy before I vote for Bush*; but constructions of this type are rare.

Table 1. *Raw frequencies*

	Spoken	Written	Total
when	94	95	189
after	47	50	97
before	41	46	87
once	48	50	98
until	49	50	99
Total	279	291	570

(17) Now before you ... uhm ... break into groups and look at the results of the two analyses and try and see what's going on ... any sort of questions?

(18) Uhm well before we get into the detailed discussion of all of this have you got something else Mary?

Since adverbial clauses of this type do not describe a sequence of two related events, they were disregarded. Table 1 shows the frequency of the five conjunctions after the irrelevant items were excluded.

All sentences were manually coded for two features: (1) the position of the adverbial clause relative to the main clause (initial ADV-clause vs. final ADV-clause), and (2) the conceptual order of main and adverbial clauses (prior ADV-clause vs. posterior ADV-clause vs. simultaneous ADV-clause). The data were separately coded by the author and a student assistant; intercoder reliability was very high, with almost 100 percent.

2.1.2. *Results.* The majority of temporal clauses follow the main clause. Overall, there are 166 initial and 404 final adverbial clauses in the data, i.e., 70.9 percent of the temporal clauses follow the main clause and only 29.1 percent precede it. Figure 1 shows the proportions of initial and final adverbial clauses expressing a prior, posterior, or simultaneously occurring event. As can be seen in the graph, 53.9 percent (N = 119) of the prior adverbial clauses precede the main clause, 22.2 percent (N = 36) of the simultaneous adverbial clauses are preposed, and only 5.9 percent (N = 11) of the posterior temporal clauses are placed before the associated main clause. There is thus a clear correlation between conceptual order and linear structure: temporal clauses denoting a prior event precede the main clause more often than temporal clauses denoting a simultaneously occurring event, which in turn are more frequently preposed to the main clause than temporal clauses of posteriority. A 2×3 χ^2-analysis

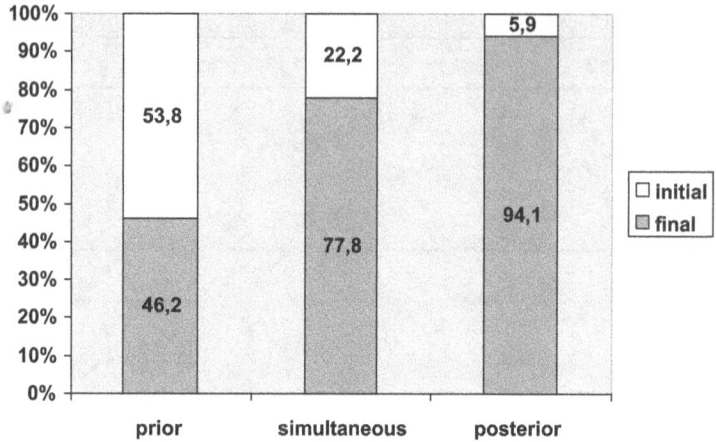

Figure 1. *Conceptual order and linear structure*

revealed that the association between conceptual order and linear structure is significant ($\chi^2 = 185.13$, $df = 2$, $p < 0.001$).

While there is a preference for an iconic clause order, it must be emphasized that a significant number of complex sentences violate the iconicity of sequence. If we disregard adverbial clauses referring to a simultaneously occurring event, there are 295 complex sentences with iconic and 113 complex sentences with non-iconic clause orders, i.e., 27.7 percent of the temporal clauses examined in this study violate the iconicity principle. Interestingly, complex sentences containing initial adverbial clauses are more consistent with the iconicity principle than complex sentences containing final adverbial clauses. As can be seen in Figure 2, if the adverbial clause precedes the main clause, 91.5 percent (N = 119) of all sentences are iconic, but if the adverbial clause follows the main clause, only 63.3 percent (N = 176) exhibit an iconic ordering ($\chi^2 = 35.25$, $df = 1$, $p < 0.001$).

Since the positioning of temporal adverbial clauses varies with the subordinate conjunction, I also examined the positional patterns of individual types of temporal clauses. As can be seen in Table 2, *when*-clauses tend to follow the main clause: 51 *when*-clauses precede the main clause and 138 *when*-clauses occur after it. The majority of the *when*-clauses denote a situation that occurs simultaneously to the one expressed in the main clause. As can be seen in this table, there are 26 prior *when*-clauses, 162 simultaneous *when*-clauses, and only 1 posterior *when*-clause.

The positioning of the *when*-clause correlates with the conceptual order: 57.7 percent of the prior *when*-clauses precede the main clause, but

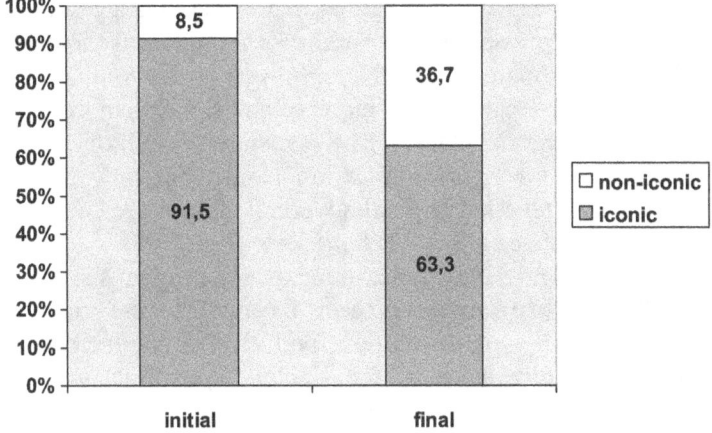

Figure 2. *Clause order and iconicity*

Table 2. When-*clauses—conceptual order and linear structure*

Linear order	Prior	Simultaneous	Posterior	Total
Initial	15	36	0	51
Final	11	126	1	138
Total	26	162	1	189

Table 3. After- *and* before-*clauses—conceptual order and linear structure*

Linear order	after	before	Total
initial	27	6	33
final	70	81	151
Total	97	87	184

only 22.3 percent of the simultaneously occurring *when*-clauses are preposed. Leaving aside the one posterior *when*-clause, a 2×2 χ^2-analysis revealed a significant association between linear structure and conceptual order ($\chi^2 = 14.26$, $df = 1$, $p < 0.001$), confirming the hypothesis that clause order is iconic.

Like *when*-clauses, *after*- and *before*-clauses tend to occur at the end of a complex sentence. As can be seen in Table 3, there are 151 final and only 33 initial *after*- and *before*-clauses in the data. Of the initial subordinate clauses, 27 are introduced by *after* and only 6 are introduced by *before*. A 2×2 χ^2-analysis revealed a significant association between clause order and clause type ($\chi^2 = 13.66$, $df = 1$, $p < 0.001$), suggesting that the conceptual order expressed by *after* and *before* influences the ordering of main and the subordinate clauses. Note, however, that complex sentences with initial adverbial clauses are more often iconic than complex sentences with final adverbial clauses: 81.8 percent ($N = 27$) of the sentences with initial *after*- and *before*-clauses are iconic, but only 53.6 percent ($N = 81$) of the sentences with final adverbial clauses are consistent with the iconicity of sequence ($\chi^2 = 8.868$, $df = 1$, $p < 0.003$).

Interestingly, *before*-clauses functioning as independent speech acts (see examples 18–19 above) always precede the main clause: there are five *before*-clauses of this type in the data and all five clauses occur before the main clause. However, even if we include speech act *before*-clauses into the analysis, adverbial clauses marked by *after* precede the main clause significantly more often than adverbial clauses marked by *before* ($\chi^2 = 7.411$, $df = 1$, $p < 0.006$).

Finally, *once* and *until* parallel *after* and *before* in that they indicate a temporal sequence between two situations: *once*-clauses are conceptually prior to the event in the main clause, while *until*-clauses denote a posterior situation. However, the distributional contrast between *once* and *until* is much more pronounced than the distributional contrast between *after* and *before*. As can be seen in Table 4, 77 *once*-clauses precede the main clause but only 5 *until*-clauses are preposed. A 2×2 χ^2-analysis revealed that the distributional difference between *once* and *until* is highly significant ($\chi^2 = 109.56$, $df = 1$, $p < 0.001$). Once again, the iconicity principle is more consistent with complex sentences containing initial adverbial clauses than with complex sentences containing final adverbial clauses: 93.9 percent ($N = 77$) of the initial adverbial clauses occur in complex sentences that are iconic, but only 81.7 percent ($N = 94$) of the final adverbial clauses are embedded in an iconically structured sentence ($\chi^2 = 6.182$, $df = 1$, $p < 0.013$).

To summarize, we have seen that the positioning of temporal adverbial clauses varies with conceptual order: temporal clauses denoting a prior event precede the main clause significantly more often than temporal clauses denoting a simultaneous event, which in turn are more frequently

Table 4. *Once- and* until-*clauses—conceptual order and linear structure*

Linear order	once	until	Total
initial	77	5	82
final	21	94	115
Total	98	99	197

preposed to the main clause than temporal clauses of posteriority. The analysis suggests that iconicity of sequence has a significant effect on the positioning of temporal adverbial clauses in English. However, the data also reveal that the iconicity principle cannot be the sole determinant of the sequential structuring of complex sentences because 27.3 percent of the sentences examined in this study do not have an iconic clause order; that is, more than a quarter of all sentences violate the iconicity of sequence. Moreover, the iconicity principle does not explain why complex sentences with initial adverbial clauses are more often iconic than complex sentences with final adverbial clauses (cf. Figure 2), and why the positioning of the temporal adverbial clause varies with the subordinate conjunction. For instance, although both *after* and *once* introduce prior adverbial clauses, *once*-clauses precede the main clause more often than *after*-clauses (cf. Tables 2 and 3). In order to account for these findings, we have to include additional factors into the analysis. The second study was designed to investigate the combined effect of the iconicity principle and other factors influencing clause order in English.

2.2. *Study 2*

Based on the previous research (see Section 1.1.), we may hypothesize that in addition to iconicity of sequence the following factors are relevant for the positioning of temporal adverbial clauses:

1. The semantic relationship between main and adverbial clauses. Complex sentences containing temporal adverbial clauses often imply a conditional, causal, or purposive relationship (see above). Since conditional clauses tend to precede the main clause, while causal and purpose clauses usually follow it, it is a plausible hypothesis that the positioning of temporal adverbial clauses is affected by their implicit meanings. This may account for the distributional differences between *once*-clauses, which are often conditional, and *after*-clauses, which can be causal.
2. The length of the adverbial clause. It is well-known that heavy constituents tend to occur sentence-finally (Behaghel 1932). There are two explanations for this: information structure and syntactic parsing (see Wasow 2002 for a review of the literature). In the discourse-pragmatic literature it is commonly assumed that given information tends to precede new information because new information needs to be grounded in information that is already known to the hearer. Since new information needs more explicit coding than given information, long constituents tend to occur at the end of a sentence (cf. Dik 1989: 351). Alternatively, Hawkins (2004: 104–108) argued that

right-branching languages like English tend to place long constituents at the end of the sentence because the order short-before-long is easier to parse than the reverse ordering (see above). Since adverbial clauses are heavy constituents it is a plausible hypothesis that the predominance of final temporal clauses results from the weight of these constructions. Moreover, we may assume that temporal clauses preceding the main clause tend to be shorter than temporal clauses that follow it (cf. Diessel 2005).

3. The complexity of adverbial clauses. Hawkins (1994, 2004) argued that constituent order is crucially affected by the structural complexity of linguistic elements. Specifically, he claimed that in right-branching languages like English, syntactically complex structures tend to occur sentence-finally because in final position they are easier to parse. Since adverbial clauses can vary in terms of their complexity, we may assume that initial temporal clauses are structurally less complex than final adverbial clauses.

2.2.1. *Methods.* In order to test these hypotheses, I conducted a binary logistic regression analysis, in which all of the above mentioned factors are taken into account. Logistic regression analysis is an extension of ordinary regression analysis, in which the dependent variable is categorical (rather than continuous as in ordinary regression analysis) (cf. Tabachnik and Fidell 2004: Ch 12; Backhaus et al. 2006: Ch 7). The goal of binary logistic regression analysis is to predict the value of the dichotomous dependent variable from one or more predictor variables that can be continuous, discrete, dichotomous, or a mix of them (cf. Tabachnik and Fidell 2004: 517; Backhaus et al. 2006: 428).[3] In the current study, logistic re-

---

3. Logistic regression analysis involves the same formula as ordinary regression analysis except that the dependent variable is expressed by the natural logarithm of the odds, i.e., $\ln(p/1-p) = a + bx$. The odds provide a probability measure that is defined as the ratio of the probability that an event A will occur and the probability that the event A will not occur, i.e., odds $= P(A)/1 - P(A)$. The odds must be distinguished from simple probabilities. For instance, in a corpus of a 100 complex sentences with 40 initial adverbial clauses and 60 final adverbial clauses, the odds of randomly selecting an initial adverbial clause are $40/60 = 0.666$, and the odds of randomly selecting a final adverbial clause are $60/40 = 1.5$. By contrast, the probability of selecting an initial adverbial clause is 0.4 and the probability of selecting a final adverbial clause is 0.6. Probability values increase linearly, but the odds increase exponentially (cf. $10/90 = 0.11$, $20/80 = 0.25$, $30/70 = 0.43$, $40/60 = 0.66$, $50/50 = 1$, $60/40 = 1.5$, $70/30 = 2.3$, $80/20 = 4$, $90/10 = 9$, $95/5 = 19$, $99/1 = 99$). The natural logarithm of the odds transfers the exponential curve into a symmetrical S-curve which defines the two outcomes of a binary logistic regression analysis (cf. Tabachnik and Fidell 2004: Ch 7; Backhaus et al. 2006: Ch 7).

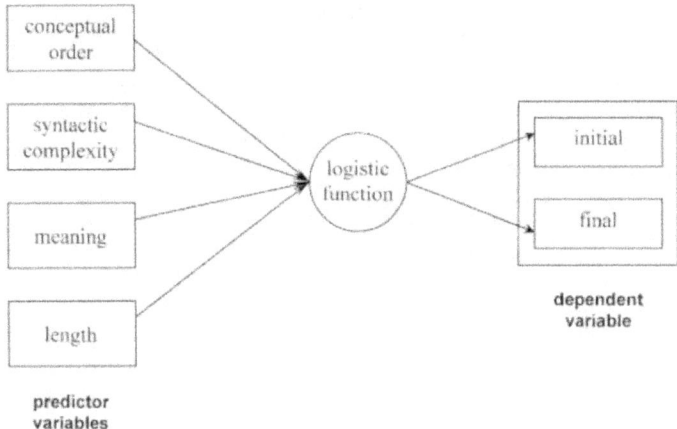

Figure 3. *Research design*

gression analysis was used to predict the position of the adverbial clause (i.e., initial or final) from the following set of predictors: conceptual order (i.e., iconicity), meaning, length, and syntactic complexity. Figure 3 shows the research design.

Conceptual order and syntactic complexity were coded as dichotomous variables: adverbial clauses denoting a prior event were distinguished from adverbial clauses denoting a posterior or simultaneously occurring event, and simple adverbial clauses consisting of a single clause were distinguished from complex adverbial clauses containing another subordinate clause. Meaning was coded as a discrete variable with three levels: (i) purely temporal, (ii) temporal with an implicit conditional meaning, and (iii) temporal with an implicit causal or purposive meaning. Finally, length was coded as a continuous variable, measured by dividing the number of words in the adverbial clause by the total number of words in the complex sentence.[4] For all features, intercoder reliability was at least 95 percent.

2.2.2. *Results.* Table 5 shows the raw frequencies of the categorical predictors, i.e., conceptual order, complexity, and meaning, and Figure 4 shows the histograms of the continuous predictor, relative length (i.e., the ratio of adverbial clause/complex sentence), for final and initial temporal clauses.

---

4. For instance, if the adverbial clause consists of 6 words and the complex sentence of 13 words, the relative length of the adverbial clause is $6/13 = 0.4615384$, i.e., 46.15 percent.

Table 5. *Frequencies of the categorical predictor variables*

VARIABLE	LEVEL	INITIAL	FINAL	TOTAL
Conceptual order	1. posterior/simultaneous	47	302	349
	2. prior	119	102	221
Complexity	1. simple	138	309	447
	2. complex	28	95	123
Meaning	1. purely temporal	89	299	388
	2. conditional	76	52	128
	3. causal/purposive	1	53	54

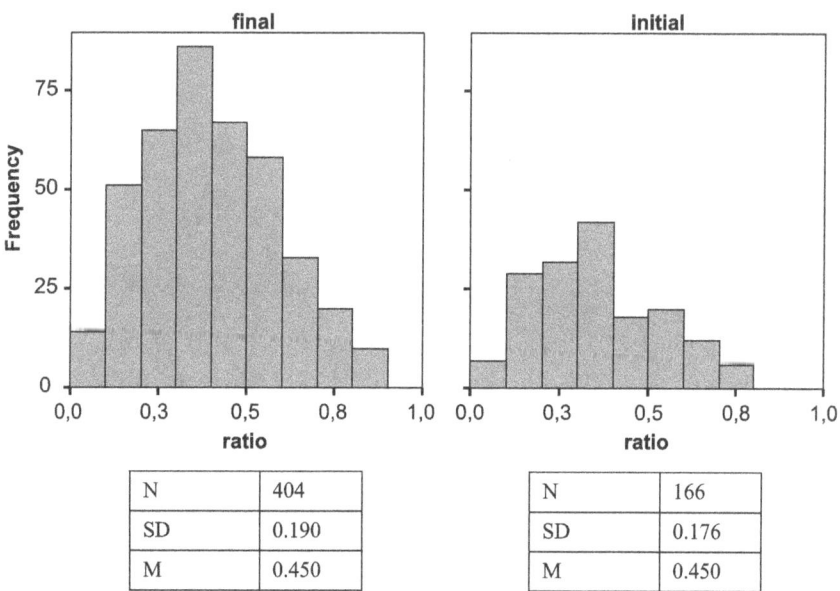

Figure 4. *Frequency of the relative length of initial and final temporal clauses*

Note that the frequency distributions are consistent with the proposed hypotheses: prior temporal clauses precede the main clause on average more often than posterior and simultaneous temporal clauses. In addition, Table 5 shows that simple adverbial clauses are more often preposed to the main clause than complex adverbial clauses (i.e., adverbial clauses including another subordinate clause), and that temporal clauses with an implicit conditional meaning tend to precede the main clause, whereas temporal clauses with an implicit causal or purposive meaning almost always follow it. The histograms show that the average relative length of final temporal clauses is greater than the average relative length of initial adverbial clauses, but the difference is small: if the adverbial clause follows the main clause the mean relative length of the adverbial clause is 45 percent, and if the adverbial clause precedes the main clause the mean relative length of the adverbial clause is 40.5 percent of the entire sentence. In order to test if and to what extent these asymmetries are relevant for the positioning of temporal adverbial clauses, I conducted a stepwise logistic regression analysis starting with the maximal model in which all predictor variables and their interactions are included in the regression. This model is compared to the null (or empty) model in which none of the predictor variables is included (cf. Tabachnik and Fidell 2004: Ch 12; Backhaus et al. 2006: Ch 7). In the current study, the maximal model was significantly different from the null model, indicating that the predictors as a group reliably distinguish between initial and final position. However, since the interactions between the various predictor variables were not significant, they were excluded from the model (cf. Crawley 2005: 104). In the next step, I computed a regression model including only the predictor variables without their interactions. In this model, three of the predictor variables turned out to be significantly related to the dependent variable, i.e., conceptual order, meaning, and length. Since syntactic complexity was not significantly related to clause order, it was removed from the regression model. The resulting minimally adequate model fit the data significantly better than the null model ($\chi^2 = 174.69$, df = 4, p < 0.001) and had almost the same explanatory power (Nagelkerke's $R^2 = 0.38$) as the maximal model (Nagelkerke's $R^2 = 0.39$). The overall prediction accuracy increased from 70.9 percent in the null model to 80 percent in the minimally adequate model, which is a reasonable improvement given that prediction accuracy can only increase if the model correctly predicts some of the initial adverbial clauses (which account for only 29.1 percent of the data).

As in ordinary multiple regression analysis, regression coefficients indicate the effect of the individual predictor variables on the outcome; but since the regression coefficients of logistic regression analysis are difficult to interpret, they are commonly transformed into odds ratios, which is a measure of effect size that indicates the likelihood of a particular outcome to occur.[5] Table 6 provides a summary of the analysis of the predictor variables in the minimally adequate model.

---

5. Odds ratios are calculated by dividing the odds of an event occurring by the odds of another event occurring. For instance, if 65 percent of the days during one year are sunny and 35 percent are rainy, the odds of a sunny day are 1.86 and the odds of a rainy day are 0.54 and the odds ratio (sunny/rainy) is 3.43, which means that a sunny day is 3.43 times more likely to occur than a rainy day.

Table 6. *Results of the logistic regression analysis*

Factor	reg. coef. B	Wald χ^2	df	p	odds ratio	lower CI	upper CI
Conceptual order	1.902	73.69	1	0.001	6.70	4.34	10.35
Meaning		41.07	2	0.001			
a. causal/purpose	−2.775	7.27	1	0.007	0.06	0.01	0.469
b. conditional	1.364	31.20	1	0.001	3.91	2.42	6.31
Length	−1.343	7.39	1	0.001	0.19	0.06	0.63

The regression coefficients indicate the direction of change induced by a particular predictor: positive values (which correspond to odds ratios larger than 1.0) indicate that the predictor variable increases the likelihood of the adverbial clause to precede the main clause; negative values (which correspond to odds ratios smaller than 1.0) indicate that the predictor variable decreases the likelihood of the adverbial clause to precede the main clause. The Wald χ^2-values and the associated levels of significance indicate that the predictor variables (conceptual order, meaning, and length) are significant. The odds ratios show the change in odds for an adverbial clause to be placed in initial position. For instance, the odds ratio for conceptual order indicates that for adverbial clauses denoting a prior event the odds of preceding the main clause are 6.7 times larger than the odds for adverbial clauses denoting a posterior or simultaneous event. The two final columns show the lower and upper boundaries of the confidence intervals for the odds ratios (cf. Backhaus et al. 2005: 475–476).

Note that conceptual order and conditional meaning increase the likelihood of the adverbial clause to precede the main clause (compared to posterior/simultaneous temporal clauses with purely temporal meaning), whereas a causal/purposive meaning and an increase in length decrease the likelihood of the adverbial clause to precede the main clause (compared to purely temporal clauses that are shorter). Note also that conceptual order, i.e., the encoding of a prior event, is the strongest predictor for the initial occurrence of a temporal adverbial clause.

Since the positioning of temporal adverbial clauses varies with the subordinate conjunction (see above), I also computed regression models for individual types of temporal clauses. Specifically, I developed three separate logistic regression models for *when*-clauses, *after*- and *before*-clauses, and *once*- and *until*-clauses using the same stepwise procedure as in the model described above (Table 7 in the Appendix provides a summary of the frequency data). Interestingly, while conceptual order had a significant effect on the positioning of all temporal clauses (*when*: $\chi^2 = 12.149$,

$df = 1$, $p < 0.001$; *after/before*: $\chi^2 = 14.504$, $df = 1$, $p < 0.001$; *once/until*: $\chi^2 = 32.285$, $df = 1$; $p < 0.001$), meaning and length were only significant for certain types of temporal clauses, suggesting that the effect of conceptual order is more consistent across clause types than the effect of the other predictor variables. Meaning was significant for the positioning of conditional *once-* and *until-*clauses ($\chi^2 = 6.491$, $df = 1$; $p < 0.011$) and marginally significant for the positioning of causal/purposive *after-* and *before-*clauses ($\chi^2 = 3.601$, $df = 1$; $p < 0.061$); but although *when-*clauses were often used with an implicit conditional meaning, conditionality did not affect their position ($\chi^2 = 9.546$, $df = 1$; $p < 0.010$). Length was only significant for *once-* and *until-*clauses ($\chi^2 = 6.491$, $df = 1$; $p < 0.011$), but not for *when-*, *after-*, and *before-*clauses (*when*: $\chi^2 = 2.000$, $df = 1$, $p > 0.157$; *after/before*: $\chi^2 = 0.398$, $df = 1$, $p > 0.528$).

3. Discussion

The analysis suggests that iconicity of sequence has a strong and consistent effect on the linear structuring of complex sentences with temporal adverbial clauses. Temporal clauses referring to a prior event precede the main clause more often than temporal clauses expressing a simultaneously occurring event, which in turn precede the main clause more often than temporal clauses of posteriority. The iconicity of sequence is in accordance with both complex sentences in which the conceptual order of main and adverbial clauses is encoded by the subordinate conjunction (i.e., *after-*, *before-*, *once-*, and *until-*clauses) and complex sentences in which the conceptual order is inferred from the meaning of the whole sentence because the conjunction itself does not express a particular order (i.e., *when-*clauses). In both types of sentences, clause order correlates with conceptual structure: *after-* and *once-*clauses, referring to a prior event, precede the main clause significantly more often than *before-* and *until-*clauses, denoting a posterior situation, and *when-*clauses referring to a prior event are more frequently preposed to the main clause than *when-*clauses denoting a posterior or simultaneously occurring event. The analysis also revealed that complex sentences including initial adverbial clauses are more consistent with the iconicity principle than complex sentences including final adverbial clauses: while complex sentences with initial adverbial clauses are almost always iconic, more than one third of all complex sentences with final adverbial clauses violate the iconicity of sequence.

Another factor that correlates with the positioning of temporal adverbial clauses is their implicit meaning. About one third of all adverbial clauses examined in this study imply a conditional, causal, or purposive relationship between the events expressed by main and subordinate clauses. Like ordinary conditional clauses, temporal clauses with an implicit conditional meaning tend to precede the main clauses, and like ordinary causal and purposive clauses, temporal clauses with an implicit causal or purposive meaning almost always follow it. This may explain why *once*- and *after*-clauses differ in their distribution: although both types of adverbial clauses denote a prior event, *once*-clauses, which are often conditional, precede the main clause more often than *after*-clauses, which are frequently used with an implicit causal meaning. Note that in the logistic regression analysis the meaning of the adverbial clause had less predictive power than iconicity of sequence. Moreover, the analysis showed that while the iconicity principle influenced all temporal clauses, the implicit meaning was only relevant for certain types of temporal clauses.

Apart from conceptual order and implicit meaning, the length ratio of main and adverbial clauses was a significant predictor of clause order. The analysis revealed that initial temporal clauses account for a smaller proportion of the overall length of the complex sentence than final adverbial clauses, i.e., adverbial clauses that precede the main clause are shorter than adverbial clauses that follow it; but since the difference was relatively small, length had only a small effect on the positioning of the adverbial clause. In the conjunction-specific analyses, *once*- and *until*-clauses were the only adverbial clauses for which the length ratio was a significant predictor.

Why do these factors influence the positioning of temporal adverbial clauses? I suggest that all of the factors examined in this study are relevant for clause order because they influence the processing of complex sentences. Specifically, I claim that iconicity of sequence, which is commonly characterized as a semantic principle, can be interpreted as a processing principle that contributes to the overall processing load of a complex sentence construction because a non-iconic clause order is difficult to plan and to interpret. As Givón (1985: 189) put it: "All other things being equal, a coded experience is easier to *store, retrieve* and *communicate* if the code is maximally isomorphic to the experience" (emphasis is the original). There are several experimental studies supporting this view. For instance, Ohtsuka and Brewer (1992) found that iconic sentences combined by *next* are easier to understand and to remember than non-iconic sentences combined by *before*, and Clark (1971) found that English-speaking children have fewer difficulties to understand *before*- and *after*-clauses if clause order is iconic (see also Carni and French 1984; Clark 1973; Coker 1978; Diessel 2004; Ferreiro and Sinclair 1971; Trosborg 1982). Assuming that non-iconic orders are difficult to plan and to interpret, it is a plausible hypothesis that complex sentences tend to be iconic because speakers prefer linguistic structures that are easy to process.

Like iconicity, the meaning of the adverbial clause is relevant for the processing of the complex sentence. In particular, conditional clauses put a particular constraint on the processing of complex sentences. As I have argued in Diessel (2005), conditional clauses provide a particular conceptual framework for the interpretation of the semantically associated clause. More precisely, the conditional clause indicates that the main clause is a hypothetical statement that is contingent on the realization of the event expressed in the subordinate clause. If the conditional clause precedes the main clause, it is immediately obvious that the sentence describes a hypothetical situation, but if the conditional clause follows the main clause the hearer may at first misinterpret it as a factual statement. Since the reanalysis of previous clauses is difficult to process, conditional clauses tend to occur at the beginning of the sentence or their occurrence is announced in the initial main clause by intonation or a subjunctive verb form.

In addition to the meaning, the pragmatic function can influence the positioning of adverbial clauses. As has been repeatedly argued in the literature, initial and final adverbial clauses serve different discourse-pragmatic functions. While final adverbial clauses are commonly used to provide new information or to spell out information that was pragmatically presupposed in the preceding main clause, initial adverbial clauses are commonly used to provide a thematic ground that facilitates the semantic processing of subsequent clauses (see Section 1.1. for relevant references). Moreover, we may assume that causal clauses typically follow the main clause because causal clauses are commonly used to back up a previous statement, i.e., the final occurrence of causal clauses is a consequence of the fact that causal clauses are often embedded in a particular discourse routine (cf. Diessel 2006; see also Diessel 2004: Ch 7, who discusses the discourse function of causal clauses in early child language).

Finally, length is an important factor for the processing of complex sentences because the length of constituents defines the recognition domain (see above). Adopting Hawkins' parsing theory, we may assume that final adverbial clauses are easier to parse than initial adverbial clauses because complex sentences with final adverbial clauses have a shorter recognition domain than complex sentences with initial adverbial clauses. This explains the predominance of final adverbial clauses in English. Note that in left-branching languages like Japanese adverbial clauses are often consistently placed before the main clause because in this language type complex sentences are easier to process if the adverbial clause occurs at the beginning of the sentence (cf. Diessel 2001, 2005). However, in right-branching languages like English, final position is the default and the initial occurrence of adverbial clauses is motivated by competing processing forces.

Adopting an incremental model of sentence comprehension in which the overall processing load of linguistic structures is determined by the cumulative effect of syntactic, semantic, and other processing constraints (cf. MacDonald et al. 1994), we may assume that speakers tend to avoid structures in which the overall processing load exceeds a certain level. This may explain why iconicity of sequence exerts a particularly strong effect on complex sentences with initial adverbial clauses. Since the combined effect of the initial position of the adverbial clause (which is difficult to parse) and the occurrence of a non-iconic clause order (which is difficult to conceptualize) can raise the overall processing load to a very high level, speakers seek to avoid the use of non-iconic clause orders in complex sentences with initial adverbial clauses. Put differently, if the adverbial clause follows the main clause there is less processing pressure to use an iconic clause order because complex sentences with final adverbial clauses are easier to parse; there is thus more tolerance in complex sentences with final adverbial clauses for the increased processing load that arises from the violation of the iconicity principle.

In sum, this paper has shown that the positional patterns of temporal adverbial clauses are consistent with the hypothesis that clause order in complex sentences is usually iconic. While iconicity of sequence is often characterized as a semantic factor, it can be seen as a processing principle that is especially relevant for complex sentences with initial adverbial clauses because these structures are difficult to parse, so that speakers seek to limit the overall processing load by using an iconic clause order.

Received 5 July 2007 *University of Jena, Germany*
Revision received 11 January 2008

Appendix

Table 7. *Position, length, conceptual order, and implicit meaning*

		CONCEPT ORDER		MEANING			LENGTH MEAN PROP.
		+prior	−prior	temp.	caus.	cond.	
WHEN	initial	15	36	31	—	20	0.425
	final	11	127	95	4	39	0.472
AFTER/BEFORE	initial	27	6	32	2	—	0.388
	final	70	81	128	20	2	0.412
ONCE/UNTIL	initial	77	5	24	—	57	0.359
	final	21	94	78	28	10	0.498

References

Altenberg, Bengt
    1984   Causal linking in spoken and written English. *Studia Linguistica* 38, 20–69.
Backhaus, Klaus, Bernd Erichson, Wulff Plinke, and Rolf Weiber
    2006   *Multivariate Analysemethoden. Eine anwendungsorientierte Einführung.* Berlin: Springer. [11th. edition].
Behaghel, Otto
    1932   *Deutsche Syntax. Eine geschichtliche Darstellung.* Vol. IV. *Wortstellung, Periodenbau.* Heidelberg: Winter.
Biber, Douglas, Stig Johansson, Geoffrey Leech, Susan Conrad, and Edward Finegan
    1999   *Longman Grammar of Spoken and Written English,* London: Longman.
Carni, Ellen and Lucia A. French
    1984   The acquisition of *before* and *after* reconsidered: What develops? *Journal of Experimental Psychology* 37, 394–403.
Chafe, Wallace
    1984   How people use adverbial clauses. *Berkeley Linguistics Society* 10, 437–49.
Clark, Eve V.
    1971   On the acquisition of the meaning of *after* and *before. Journal of Verbal Learning and Verbal Behavior* 10, 266–75.
    1973   How children describe time and order. In Charles A. Ferguson and Dan I. Slobin (eds.), *Studies of Child Language Development.* New York: Holt, Rinehart and Winston, 585–606.
Coker, Pamela L.
    1978   Syntactic and semantic factors in the acquisition of *after* and *before. Journal of Child Language* 5, 261–77.
Crawley, Michael J.
    2005   *Statistics. An Introduction into R.* John Wiley and Sons, Ltd.
Croft, William
    2003   *Typology and Universals.* Cambridge: Cambridge University Press.
Dancygier, Barbara
    1998   *Conditionals and Prediction. Time, knowledge, and causation in conditional constructions.* Cambridge: Cambridge University Press.

Dancygier, Barbara and Eve Sweetser
    2000   Constructions with *if, since* and *because:* causality, epistemic stance, and clause order. In Elizabeth Couper-Kuhlen and Bernd Kortmann (eds.), *Cause, Condition, Concession, Contrast: cognitive and discourse perspectives.* Berlin: Mouton de Gruyter, 111–42.

Diessel, Holger
    1996   Processing factors of pre- and postposed adverbial clauses. *Berkeley Linguistics Society* 22, 71–82.
    2001   The ordering distribution of main and adverbial clauses: A typological study. *Language* 77, 343–65.
    2004   *The Acquisition of Complex Sentences.* Cambridge: Cambridge University Press.
    2005   Competing motivations for the ordering of main and adverbial clauses. *Linguistics* 43, 449–70.
    2006   Causal and conditional constructions. Paper presented at the Second International Conference of the German Cognitive Linguistics Association. Munich.

Dik, Simon
    1989   *The Theory of Functional Grammar: Part 1: The structure of the clause.* Dordrecht: Foris.

Dressler, Wolfgang U.
    1995   Interactions between iconicity and other semiotic parameters in language. In Raffaele Simone (ed.), *Iconicity in Language.* Amsterdam: John Benjamins 1995, 212–37.

Fenk-Oczlon, Gertraud
    1991   Frequenz und Kognition—Frequenz und Markiertheit. *Folia Linguistica* 25, 361–94.

Ferreiro, Emilia and Hermina Sinclair
    1971   Temporal relationships in language. *International Journal of Psychology* 6, 39–47.

Ford, Cecilia E.
    1993   *Grammar in Interaction. Adverbial clauses in American English conversations.* Cambridge: Cambridge University Press.

Givón, Talmy
    1985   Iconicity, isomorphism and nonarbitrary coding in syntax. In John Haiman (ed.), *Natural Syntax.* Amsterdam: John Benjamins, 187–220.
    1990   *Syntax. A functional-typological introduction.* Vol. II. Amsterdam: John Benjamins.
    1991   Isomorphism in the grammatical code: cognitive and biological considerations. *Studies in Language* 15, 85–114.

Greenberg, Joseph H.
    1963[1966]   Some universals of grammar with particular reference to the order of meaningful elements. In Joseph H. Greenberg (eds.), *Universals of Grammar* [2nd edition]. Cambridge, Mass.: MIT Press. [1st edition 1963], 73–113.

Haiman, John
    1978   Conditionals are topics. *Language* 54, 564–89.
    1980   The iconicity of grammar. *Language* 56, 515–40.
    1983   Iconic and economic motivations. *Language* 59, 781–19.
    1985   *Iconicity in Syntax.* Amsterdam: John Benjamins.

1994	Iconicity. In R. E. Asher (ed.), *The Encyclopedia of Language and Linguistics*. Oxford: Pergamon Press, 1629–33.
2006	Iconicity. In Keith Brown (ed.), *Encyclopedia of Language and Linguistics*. Vol. V. [2nd edition]. Amsterdam: Elsevier, 457–461.

Haspelmath, Martin.
2008   Frequency vs. iconicity in explaining grammatical asymmetries. *Cognitive Linguistics* 19, 1–33.

Hawkins, John A.
1994   *A Performance Theory of Order and Constituency*. Cambridge: Cambridge University Press.
2004   *Efficiency and Complexity in Grammars*. Oxford: Oxford University Press.

Hengeveld, Kees
1989   Layers and operators in Functional Grammar. *Journal of Linguistics* 25, 127–57.

Hetterle, Katja
2007   Causal clauses in cross-linguistic perspective. Unpublished Manuscript. University of Jena.

Itkonen, Esa
2004   Typological explanation and iconicity. *Logos and Language* 5, 21–33.

Jakobson, Roman
1965[1971]   Quest for the essence of language. In Roman Jakobson (ed.), *Selected Writings*. Vol. II. The Hague: Mouton. [Originally published in Diogenes 51(1965)], 345–59.

Lehmann, Christian
1974   Prinzipien für ‚Universal 14'. In Hansjakob Seiler (ed.), *Linguistic Workshop* II. Munich: Wilhem Fink, 69–97.

MacDonald, Maryellen C., Neal J. Pearlmutter, and Mark S. Seidenberg
1994   The lexical nature of syntactic ambiguity resolution. *Psychological Review* 191, 676–703.

Ohtsuka, Keisuke and William F. Brewer
1992   Discourse organization in the comprehension of temporal order in narrative texts. *Discourse Processes* 15, 317–336.

Plank, Frans
1979   Ikonisierung und De-Ikonisierung als Prinzipien des Sprachwandels. *Sprachwissenschaft* 4, 121–158.

Quirk, Randolph, Sidney Greenbaum, Geoffrey Leech, and Jan Svartvik
1985   *A Comprehensive Grammar of the English Language*. London: Longman.

Ramsay, Violetta
1987   The functional distribution of preposed and postposed *if* and *when* clauses in written discourse. In Russell Tomlin (ed.), *Coherence and Grounding in Discourse*. Amsterdam: John Benjamins, 383–408.

Schmidtke, Karsten
in press   A typology of purpose clauses.

Tabachnick, Barbara G. and Linda S. Fidell
2004   *Using Multivariate Statistics*. New York: Harper Collins. [3rd edition].

Tabakowska, Elżbieta, Christina Ljungberg, and Olga Fischer (eds.)
2007   *Insistent Images*. Amsterdam: John Benjamins.

Taylor, John
2002   *Cognitive Grammar*. Oxford: Oxford University Press.

Thompson, Sandra A.
 1985 Grammar and written discourse. Initial and final purpose clauses in English. In Talmy Givón (ed.), *Quantified Studies in Discourse.* Special issue of *Text* 5, 55–84.
 1987 'Subordination' and narrative event structure. In Russell Tomlin (ed.), *Coherence and Grounding in Discourse*. Amsterdam: John Benjamins, 435–54.
Thompson, Sandra A. and Robert E. Longacre
 1985 Adverbial clauses. In Timothy Shopen (ed.), 1985. *Language Typology and Syntactic Description.* Vol. II, Cambridge: Cambridge University Press, 171–234.
Trosberg, Anna
 1982 Children's comprehension of *before* and *after* reinvestigated. *Journal of Child Language* 9, 381–402.
Verstraete, Jean-Christophe
 2004 Initial and final position of adverbial clauses in English: the constructional basis of the discoursive and syntactic differences. *Linguistics* 42, 819–853.
Wasow, Thomas
 2002 *Postverbal Behavior.* Stanford: CSLI Publications.

Eline Zenner, Dirk Speelman and Dirk Geeraerts
Cognitive Sociolinguistics meets loanword research: Measuring variation in the success of anglicisms in Dutch

Abstract: This paper introduces a new, concept-based method for measuring variation in the use and success of loanwords by presenting the results of a case-study on 149 English person reference nouns (i.e. common nouns used to designate people, such as *manager*) in Dutch. With this paper, we introduce four methodological improvements to current quantitative corpus-based anglicism research, based on the general tenets of Cognitive Sociolinguistics (Geeraerts 2005; Kristiansen and Geeraerts 2007; Geeraerts 2010; Geeraerts et al. 2010): (1) replacing raw frequency as a success measure by a concept-based onomasiological approach; (2) relying on larger datasets and semi-automatic extraction techniques; (3) adding a multivariate perspective to the predominantly structuralist orientation of current accounts; (4) using inferential statistical techniques to help explain variation. We illustrate our method by presenting a case-study on variation in the success of English person reference nouns in Dutch. Generally, this article aims to show how a Cognitive Sociolinguistic perspective on loanword research is beneficial for both paradigms. On the one hand, the concept-based approach provides new insights in the spread of loanwords. On the other hand, attention to contact linguistic phenomena offers a new expansion to the domain of cognitive linguistic studies taking a variationist approach.

Keywords: Cognitive Sociolinguistics, lexical borrowing, onomasiology, semantics

---

Eline Zenner: E-mail: eline.zenner@arts.kuleuven.be

---

1 The success of foreign lexical material

In this paper, a new concept-based method for measuring variation in the use and success of loanwords is introduced. We present the results of a case-study on 149 English person reference nouns (i.e. common nouns used to designate people, such as *manager*) in Dutch, arguing that the success of the loanwords is a multifactorial phenomenon, with success being determined simultaneously by processing factors, usage factors, structural factors, and cultural factors. In the present section, we position our study against the background of contact linguistics. Section 2 situates it in the context of Cognitive Sociolinguistics, with a special focus on the methodological requirements. Section 3 introduces the data and Section 4 presents the multivariate analyses to which we subjected the data. Section 5 formulates our conclusions.

Like the study of lexical borrowing in general (Whitney 1881; Haugen 1950; van Coetsem 1988; Field 2002; Haspelmath and Tadmor 2009), anglicism research has a longstanding tradition in (historical) linguistics, with a notable rise in attention for the topic in the late nineteenth and early twentieth century (e.g. Dunger 1899; De Vooys 1925). Today, anglicism research is still very much in fashion. Especially in weak contact settings like Western Europe, where contact with English is typically remote and primarily mediated through the media (Onysko 2009: 58), English loanwords are often subject to much (heated) debate.

Most studies on anglicisms (in weak contact situations) center around one of four issues. A first goal is to provide a precise definition of what an anglicism is (Nettmann-Multanowska 2003; Onysko 2007; Fischer 2008), making the necessary distinctions between different transfer types (e.g. Haugen's [1950] loanword, loanblend and loanshift). Second, many studies devote attention to the different degrees of nativization a loanword may be subject to on the morphological, phonological, orthographic or (more rarely) semantic level (Filipovic 1977; Carstensen 1965; Rodriguez Gonzalez 1999; Winter-Froemel 2011). Third, this information on nativization and adaptation is often also included in lexicographical approaches (Carstensen and Busse 1994; Van der Sijs 1996; Görlach 2001).

These first three topics are primarily developed in qualitative accounts. However, the final topic, which the present paper addresses, is more often dealt with in quantitative accounts. It tackles the question what type or class of English lexical material (e.g. what part of speech) is the most successful source of borrowing. This question is developed from two different and often co-occurring perspectives (see Van Hout and Muysken 1994: 44): the first emphasizes the number of different anglicisms borrowed (types); the second pays attention to the frequency of these anglicisms (tokens).

The first, type-based perspective focuses on identifying features that influence the likelihood that a certain lexeme A is transferred from donor language X (in our case English) to recipient language Y (in our case Dutch). This emphasis on "the ease with which a lexical item or a category of lexical items can be borrowed" (Van Hout and Muysken 1994) originates in typological studies aimed at finding a universal scale of receptivity to foreign material (Whitney 1881;

Field 2002; Haspelmath and Tadmor 2009). In anglicism research, such theoretical claims about borrowability and universality are hardly ever made (but see Onysko 2007: 49–51) and references to typological studies are equally scarce. Nevertheless, in finding out which class of words is most receptive to anglicisms, both typology and anglicism research primarily and often exclusively focus on structural linguistic categorizations such as part of speech. The second, token-based perspective focuses on variation in the success of lexical items once they are transferred, i.e. on variation in the degree of penetration of loanwords in a given receptor language. The main aim is to find out what class of anglicisms (e.g. nouns, verbs or adjectives) has the highest token counts and can hence be considered to be most successful.

In most corpus-based studies, type and token counts are presented together. In this paper, we focus solely on token counts, as our main aim is to problematize the use of raw token frequency as a success measure. Situated within the framework of Cognitive Sociolinguistics (e.g. Geeraerts et al. 2010), we introduce several additional methodological innovations to current quantitative corpus-based anglicism research. We discuss these innovations in more detail below. Next, we describe the design and results of a case-study on variation in the success of English person reference nouns in Dutch.

2 Towards a Cognitive Sociolinguistic perspective on lexical borrowing

Cognitive Sociolinguistics (Geeraerts 2005; Kristiansen and Geeraerts 2007; Kristiansen and Dirven 2008; Croft 2009; Geeraerts 2010; Geeraerts et al. 2010) aims at a convergence between cognitive linguistics and existing traditions of variationist language research and advocates cross-fertilization of the two disciplines (see Hollmann and Siewierska 2011). Specifically, it argues for the importance of introducing semantics in the variationist paradigm, either by studying meaning variation per se, or by analyzing the role of semantics in the demarcation of formal variables. In line with the tradition of sociolinguistics, it emphasizes the importance of methodology in understanding linguistic variation, defining the following requirements for variationist studies in Cognitive Linguistics: (1) providing a precise and reliable definition of the measurements used to trace variation in the phenomenon under scrutiny; (2) relying on sound empirical data for conducting these measurements; (3) explaining the attested variation by inquiring into the combined effect of structural, conceptual and sociolectal parameters; (4) using state-of-the art analytical techniques to assess the importance of each of these parameters. These four methodological requirements form the cornerstones of the design of our study on variation in the use and success of loanwords. Below, we discuss the application of each of these four requirements to loanword research in more detail.

2.1 Reliable success measure

Corpus-based anglicism research largely relies on token frequencies to describe linguistic patterns (e.g. Van Iperen 1980; Viereck 1980; Yang 1990; Fink 1997; and Muhr 2009 for an overview of different studies). Typically, raw frequencies are provided for single lexical items or, more frequently, in the form of aggregate counts for different categories (e.g. total amount of anglicisms per part of speech). The main aim of these counts is to provide detailed and comprehensive inventories of anglicism use. However, when aiming to assess variation in the success of different types of loanwords, several issues with the use of raw frequency need to be raised.

In lexical borrowing research, such criticism with regard to raw frequency has been voiced by Van Hout and Muysken (1994), who focus on the use of raw frequencies for establishing borrowability hierarchies. They state that token counts of (a set of) borrowed items only become meaningful when these are compared to something else: "set-external comparison is called for, involving either the recipient or the donor language." (Van Hout and Muysken 1994: 45). Specifically, the authors propose to take the distribution of the borrowed elements in the source language as a point of departure. However, using this type of set-external proof requires parallel corpora. As these are harder to come by than traditional corpora, the general applicability of the method can be questioned.

In Cognitive Sociolinguistics, and more particulary in the domain of sociolexicology (Grondelaers et al. 2007; Geeraerts and Speelman 2010), similar claims have been made concerning the importance of set-external proof. Most importantly, Speelman et al. (2003) note that the frequency of a word should not be treated "as an autonomous piece of information". Their main concern is that the thematic bias inherent to text corpora can distort the reliability of results relying on raw frequency. When comparing anglicisms in two time periods for example, differences in raw frequencies cannot be unambiguously interpreted. Even given two equally sized corpora, a rise in the token frequency of a given anglicism, say *manager*, does not necessarily mean that this lexical item has become more entrenched in the receptor language vocabulary. It could also simply indicate that the more recent corpus contains disproportionately more articles on business and economy than the older corpus. In anglicism research, the possible distortion caused by thematic bias is noted by only a handful of authors (e.g. Chesley and Baayen 2010; Rando 1973: 77; Poplack et al. 1988: 95).

Like Van Hout and Muysken (1994), Speelman et al. (2003) propose to incorporate set-external proof, in this case by taking an onomasiological perspective on lexical variation. This onomasiological approach to lexical variation received a first formulation within the field of Cognitive Linguistics in Geeraerts et al. (1994), Geeraerts (1997) and Geeraerts et al. (1999). It entails shifting the focus from lexical items towards concepts, by verifying and quantifying which lexical expressions are used to name a particular concept. Applying the onomasiological approach to loanwords, we propose to not only take the frequency of a loanword (e.g. *jeans*) into consideration, but also that of recipient language lexemes used to express the same concept (e.g. Dutch *spijkerbroek*): the recipient language alternatives serve as set-external proof.

The precise quantitative implementation of the concept-based approach taken by Speelman et al. (2003) entails creating so-called onomasiological profiles, which "in a particular source is the set of synonymous names for that concept in that particular source, differentiated by relative frequency" (Geeraerts 2010: 831). For example, in Dutch, the concept JEANS can be expressed by the anglicism *jeans*, the hybrid compound *jeansbroek* and the Dutch alternative *spijkerbroek*. Assuming that in a fictional corpus, *jeans* occurs 130 times, *jeansbroek* 40 times and *spijkerbroek* 55 times, then the onomasiological profile is ⟨*jeans*: 58%; *jeansbroek*: 18%; *spijkerbroek*: 24%⟩ (see Table 1).

The success of a loanword is defined as the relative preference for the anglicism vis-à-vis existing synonymous expressions, giving a 58% success rate for *jeans*. As such, low frequency is not necessarily equated with low success: "[i]f a particular form covers the majority of realizations of a particular concept, it is the preferred choice of expression, even if its absolute frequency is relatively low" (Hoffmann 2004: 190). Once these success rates are gathered for a number of anglicisms, the question is how variation in these success rates (e.g. 58% for *jeans* vs. 90% for *babysit*) can be explained. This issue will be discussed further below.

lexicalizations for JEANS	token frequency	relative frequency
jeans	130	130/(130+40+55) = 0.58
jeansbroek	40	40/(130+40+55) = 0.18
spijkerbroek	55	55/(130+40+55) = 0.24

Table 1: Profile for concept *JEANS*

Summarizing, the profile-based success measure for English loanwords presented here forms the first methodological innovation we wish to introduce to current anglicism research: it provides us with a precise and reliable operationalization of the phenomenon under scrutiny. In lexicology, such an onomasiological approach has previously been introduced in several corpus-based and survey-based studies (De Wolf 1996; Blank 2003; Diaz Vera 2005; Nadasdi et al. 2008; Bednarek 2009), though often without much attention for reliable quantifications. In Cognitive Linguistics, onomasiological profiling has not only been used in sociolexicology, but also in Cognitive Grammar. Hoffmann (2004: 190) stresses the importance of working on a concept-based level when studying grammaticalization. Boyd and Goldberg (2011) and Goldberg (2011) take an onomasiological perspective for their definition and operationalization of statistical preemption, i.e. "a particular type of indirect negative evidence that results from repeatedly hearing a formulation, B, in a context where one might have expected to hear a semantically and pragmatically related alternative formulation, A" (Boyd and Goldberg 2011: 60). In contact linguistics, by contrast, quantitative onomasiological studies are to our knowledge absent. Despite this lack of quantitative studies, the general importance of receptor language alternatives has been noted, ensuring the validity of introducing them as set-external proof. The most extensive comments on native alternatives have been made by Myers-Scotton (2002), who distinguishes between core borrowings and cultural borrowings: the former are words which duplicate already existing words, the latter are words for new non-lexicalized concepts. A similar distinction has been proposed by Rohde et al. (1999). Grzega (2003) uses the notion to propose a new definition of loanwords (and see Whitney 1881; Hock and Joseph 1996; Gómez Rendón 2008; Haspelmath 2008). Focusing specifically on anglicism research, the distinction between luxury and necessary anglicisms (discussed in more detail further below) largely coincides with that between core and cultural borrowings. Also, some studies give a brief qualitative discussion of a set of anglicisms with recipient language alternatives (Rando 1973: 79; Graedler and Kvaran 2010: 39–40; Humbley 2008), occasionally providing basic quantifications for a handful of concepts. However, systematic quantitative analyses taking an onomasiological perspective have to our knowledge not yet been conducted.

2.2 Large corpora

Given the relatively low average frequency of individual content words (as opposed to function words like pronouns or grammatical structures like causatives), the study of lexical variation ideally relies on large corpora (see Geeraerts 2010). However, in contact linguistic studies it is often stressed that finding sufficient data is difficult, because the linguistic community under scrutiny is either limited in size and hardly produces written material, or because the contact phenomena under scrutiny are typical of spoken language (see Backus 1996). However, neither of these arguments can be extended to anglicism research.

In anglicism research for weak contact situations, working with spoken material (see Sharp 2001; Sagmeister-Brandner 2008) is more the exception than the rule. Most studies rely on print media by analyzing the use of anglicisms in a handful of issues of a given magazine or newspaper (Viereck 1980; Fink 1997), or rely on written material from more specific registers (e.g. Piller 2001 and Martin 2006 for advertising; Posthumus 1991 and Van Iperen 1980 for sports). Also, some studies are based on the inclusion of anglicisms in dictionaries instead of on naturally occurring data. Finally, a surprisingly large group of researchers discuss only a set of casual personal observations, usually without being clear on their sources.

When corpora are used, they usually do not exceed the one million word boundary (but see Onysko's 2007 five million word corpus). Though these collections are reasonably sized when compared to average corpora of spoken language, quantitative lexical variation studies require larger corpora. Given the number of billion word print media corpora that have been made available over the last decades for most Western European languages, why then do anglicism researchers not take advances of these resources? The main reason is a methodological bottleneck in anglicism extraction: on the one hand, researchers show a strong desire for exhaustive inventorization, aiming to list every single anglicism used in a corpus. On the other hand, the identification of anglicisms in the corpus is done manually, even in rare cases where more advanced tools (e.g. concordance software) are used (Onysko 2007). Combined, these two features pose a severe limit on what can be considered to be manageable corpus size.

Consequently, in order to use the available billion word corpora and to meet the requirements of lexical variation studies set out by Geeraerts (2010), two steps need to be taken. First, analyses need to be automated as much as possible, reducing time-consuming manual analyses to a minimum. Precision and recall of existing algorithms for the automatic extraction of anglicisms (Hanon 1973; Andersen 2005; Alex 2008) are however not yet high enough to serve as a reliable basis for lexical variation studies. Hence, a second step is to let go of the ideal of exhaustive inventories: we suggest studying only a subset of the anglicisms used in a corpus, this way prioritizing the use of large corpora and sufficient data for the lexemes under scrutiny over exhaustive inventorization.

2.3 A multivariate approach

Corpus counts retrieved from the data are mainly used to find out what class of (loan)words contains the most successful (so far measured as the most frequent) anglicisms. From a Cognitive Sociolinguistic perspective, dealing with variation implies taking a multivariate approach: instead of focusing on one specific parameter to explain the attested variation, the combined effect of structural, sociolectal, conceptual and stylistic features needs to be assessed.

In contrast, analyses in quantitative anglicism research are mainly univariate, with a focus on structural features. Like in typological studies on borrowability (Gómez Rendón 2008; Haspelmath and Tadmor 2009), attention is mainly paid to tracing the impact of part of speech on variation in the success of anglicisms (Poplack et al. 1988; Fink 1997; Sharp 2001; Pulaczewska 2008). Aggregate counts for both types and tokens of the amount of anglicisms per part of speech consistently show a predominance of borrowed nouns. Next, aggregate counts are often also provided for different transfer types (e.g. loanword, loanblend or loanshift). Finally and less frequently, the impact of two non-structural features is often quantified. First, studies on the diachronic evolution in the use of anglicisms typically show a clear increase over time (Yang 1990: 26; Onysko 2007). Second, researchers study which lexical field holds most anglicisms by providing aggregate counts for different semantic classes (Yang 1990: 89–92) or tallies for each subsection of the newspaper or magazine analyzed (Rando 1973: 75; Fink 1997; and see Muhr 2009 for an overview).

Qualitative anglicism research discusses a wider variety of features. However, how important these features are in explaining variation in the use of anglicisms is unclear, as they are often not defined objectively and as their impact has not been empirically tested. Features typically included are speech economy (anglicisms are successful because they are short) (Galinsky 1967: 48–58; Chesley and Baayen 2010), the age of borrowing (more anglicisms are borrowed after World War II) (Rando 1973: 73; Crystal 2003; Berns 1988: 38–39, Van der Sijs 1996: 303), source language variety (American English loanwords do better than British English loanwords) (Netmann-Multanoswka 2003: 18–20), and the distinction between necessary anglicisms (introduced to fill a lexical gap) and luxury anglicisms (introduced as alternative for already lexicalized concepts) (Onysko and Winter-Froemel 2011; Androutsopoulos forthcoming). Attention is also paid to cross-linguistic and regional variation, comparing the use of anglicisms in different languages (Görlach 1994; Filipovic 1977; Nettmann-Multanowska 2003), or in different national varieties of the same language (i.e. pluricentric variation; Rodriguez Gonzalez 1999: 109; Muhr 2004, Nettmann-Multanowska 2003). A minority of studies also provide quantifications for these regional patterns (Viereck

1980; Gerritsen et al. 2007). Recently, some individual attempts have been made to introduce discourse perspectives as well (Androutsopoulos forthcoming; Leppänen and Nikula 2007). Finally, despite some isolated comments on the use of anglicisms in specific social groups (e.g. youth language) (Rodriguez Gonzalez 1999: 116), attention for social variation is largely absent (though note Poplack et al. 1988).

2.4 Inferential statistics

In assessing the impact of parameters like part of speech on the success of anglicisms, typically only descriptive statistics are provided. These mainly come in the form of the aggregations described above, occasionally complemented with basic proportions. When taking a multivariate approach to variation, verifying the impact of each predictor separately does not suffice: more advanced analytical tools are needed to identify the individual importance of a given predictor when taking the combined effect of all predictors into account. So far, inferential statistics are virtually absent in quantitative anglicism research. One notable exception is the work of Chesley and Baayen (2010), who use multiple (linear and logistic) regression analyses to assess the impact of a number of predictors (sense pattern, length, frequency) on the viability of an anglicism. Viability is measured by comparing the frequency of a set of new anglicisms (neologisms) at an earlier period with their frequency at a later period. Despite showing attention for multivariate analyses, their study still relies on raw frequency to measure success. For anglicisms in intense contact situations, it is also important to note the study of Poplack et al. (1988), which is groundbreaking in modeling lectal variation in anglicism use: attention is paid to differences in the amount of loanwords and the degree to which these are integrated in the receptor language according to social class, region and language proficiency. Moreover, ANOVA, a well-known multivariate statistical analysis, is used to analyze the data, which allows the researchers to rank the importance of the different lectal features under scrutiny. Nevertheless, the analyses are predominantly based on raw frequencies, and only limited attention is paid to receptor language alternatives.

3 Presenting the Case-Study: English person reference nouns in Dutch

Having discussed the main improvements we wish to introduce to anglicism research, we now present a practical application of the proposed method. As explained above, we let go of the idea of exhaustive inventorization, scrutinizing only a subset of anglicisms occurring in Dutch. Specifically, we focus on English person reference nouns, i.e. common nouns used to designate people (*designer, bully, babysitter, mother*). Choosing this subset of the lexicon, which only contains nouns, may seem like imposing a limitation to the study, as it excludes the possibility of studying part of speech. However, as the impact of part of speech on borrowability has already received considerable attention and as it seems established that nouns are most borrowable, a more interesting question is what features explain variation in borrowability and success of loanwords *within* the class of nouns. Person reference nouns have the added advantage that they are similar enough to be compared, yet come from a variety of different semantic fields. The design of our case-study consists of the following four steps: (1) choosing a corpus big enough for lexical variation studies; (2) building a set of onomasiological profiles by selecting English person reference nouns, finding Dutch synonymous expressions, retrieving token counts from the corpus and calculating the success rates for the anglicisms; (3) defining features which may influence variation in the success rates; (4) choosing appropriate statistical techniques to model the attested variation.

3.1 Corpus

Having two national varieties, Dutch is considered to be a pluricentric language (Clyne 1992). Belgian Dutch, one of the three official languages of Belgium, is spoken in Flanders (the northern part of the country). Netherlandic Dutch is the only official language of the Netherlands. For both varieties, we have a large newspaper corpus. LeNC contains all articles printed in the 6 national Belgian newspapers written in Dutch in the period of 1999 to 2005. The diachronic span of TwNC, which holds all articles from the 5 national newspapers of the Netherlands, is smaller, ranging from 1999 to 2002. The corpora, which are each syntactically parsed and lemmatized, together consist of over 1.6 billion words. As they contain data from both qualitative and popular newspapers, the corpora also allow us to study register variation.

3.2 Building the profiles

3.2.1 Selecting anglicisms

Adopting the profile-based method of onomasiological variation, we define the success of an anglicism as the relative preference for the anglicism vis-à-vis existing synonymous expressions. Below, we describe in more detail which steps need to be taken to acquire these profile-based success rates for a set of 149 English person reference nouns in Dutch. The first step is selecting this set of English loanwords. To this end, both a theoretical and practical issue need to be addressed.

Theoretically, the main issue is to provide a definition of anglicisms. Many different definitions are available for both *loanword* in general and for *anglicism* in particular, ranging from highly inclusive (incorporating all transfer types) (e.g. Poplack et al. 1988) to more restrictive (limited to specific transfer types) (e.g. Görlach 2001; Chesley and Baayen 2010). We take a more restrictive approach by only considering those anglicisms which are structurally recognizable as English to a native speaker of Dutch "due to the fact that they largely retain their English graphemic-phonemic correspondence" (Onysko 2007: 10). The main reason for this approach is that we are trying to find out what triggers language users to opt for the loanword and not for a (or any of a set of) possible alternative(s), because "the non-Dutch character of a word can only exert influence on the language user's behavior when the expression at issue is identifiable as a non-Dutch word" (Geeraerts and Grondelaers 2000: 56). Loan translations (*kettingroker* for *chain smoker*), neoclassical forms coined in English and pronounced in a Dutch way once borrowed (*animator*) and English words that are fully concordant to Dutch orthography and phonology (and to the mapping between both) are therefore excluded from this study. For the latter case, compare *film* and *manager*. Both are English loans, but whereas a naive Dutch pronunciation of the written form *film* sounds very close to English, a naive Dutch pronunciation of *manager* would sound more like /mɑ'nɑ: jər/. Finally, hybrids (*showbink* for *showmaster*) are also not considered, because they are "loan-based creations" originating in the receptor language (Haspelmath 2008: 39). On the other hand, we do include words which are structurally English but not necessarily very common in English (*ghostwriter*).

Practically, we need to draft a list of English person reference nouns occurring in Dutch. To this end, we combine Dutch and English sources. First, using Python scripts (Lutz 2007), we automatically match all hyponyms of *person* from English WordNet with the token frequency list of the Dutch corpora, and then manually remove noise like cognates (*man*), proper nouns (*Russian*), and loans from other languages (*minister*). Next, we search Van Dale (the main Dutch descriptive dictionary) (Den Boon and Geeraerts 2005) for entries with an etymological link to English which contain the cues *iem.* (*iemand* "someone") or *persoon* ("person") in the semantic description. Finally, we consult the online database 2400x Liever Nederlands ("Dutch preferred 2400 times"), a list of English items and suggested Dutch alternatives created by Stichting Nederland (see also

Koops et al. 2009). Of all retrieved items, we only include those which follow the theoretical criteria set out above and which occur at least ten times in the Dutch corpora (see Martel 1984: 183). Items with unclear etymology (*deviationist*, borrowed from English or French), multi-word units (*big spender*) and collectives (*team*) are excluded. Note that not all anglicisms in the resulting list have only one meaning: some are not exclusively used as person reference noun (*single*), others can refer to several different types of people (*user*). In a concept-based approach these meanings need to be separated: when calculating the success rate of *single* ("person not involved in an intimate relationship"), we do not want to take into account those cases of *single* that refer to vinyl records. We hence indicate the number of meanings for each anglicism based on Dutch and English dictionaries and on an analysis of a sample of tokens from the corpora. In a later stage (see below), polysemous items are disambiguated. After grouping English synonyms (e.g. *goalie* and *keeper*) together, the next step is to find all synonymous expressions available in Dutch for each of the different English person reference nouns.

3.2.2 Selecting synonyms

For the English person reference nouns retrieved in the previous step, we now need to identify all synonyms available in our Dutch corpora. As such, an important theoretical presupposition of this paper is that synonymy exists. Taking a strict definition of synonymy, which requires that two words can replace each other in any given context without changing the propositional content of the sentence they are used in (see Edmonds and Hirst 2002: 107), claiming that true synonymy exists in natural language is hardly tenable. For near-synonyms, which are much more frequent (see e.g. Divjak and Gries 2006; and Levshina et al. in press), Edmonds and Hirst (2002) (based on Cruse 1986) claim that these can differ semantically in four different ways: denotationally, stylistically, expressively or structurally. The main goal of our approach is not to identify true synonyms, but to identify those contexts for those near-synonyms which are maximally equivalent with a given English person reference noun on each of these four levels. Below, we discuss this approach in more detail.

Though their paper is primarily directed towards automating lexical choice between near-synonyms, we follow some of the core ideas of Edmonds and Hirst (2002). Specifically the theoretical notion of granularity of meaning and the idea of a two-tiered model of lexical choice are particularly helpful for our analyses. By granularity of meaning, the authors mean "the level of detail used to describe or represent the meanings of a word. A fine-grained representation can encode subtle distinctions, whereas a coarse-grained representation is crude and glosses over variation" (Edmonds and Hirst 2002: 116). This distinction leads them to propose a two-tiered model of lexical choice. At the conceptual, coarse-grained level, near-synonyms have the same meaning, and are hence clustered under one shared concept. At the sub-conceptual, stylistic level, the four different types of semantic variation (denotational, stylistic, expressive and structural) come into play, serving as the basis for lexical choice. Using this model, we work in two steps in detecting synonyms for our English person reference nouns (compare Onysko and Winter-Froemel 2011). First, on the coarse-grained level, we track down all *potential* synonyms of a given English person reference noun. Second, we determine which of these lexical items in which contexts are similar enough to the anglicism at all four levels of variation to be included in the onomasiological profile. This second step is especially important for luxury anglicisms. For necessary anglicisms (which fill a lexical gap), receptor language synonyms are mainly introduced as an alternative to the anglicism and hence mainly serve the purpose of allowing language users to avoid using foreign material. As a result, these are usually semantically very similar to the anglicism. For luxury anglicisms, where the anglicism serves as an additional lexicalization of a concept, this reasoning does not hold and hence, more semantic differences between the anglicism and other lexicalizations can be expected (see Rohde et al. 1999).

In practice, we start our search for synonyms by combining information from different sources. First, we rely on Dutch and English lexicography, consulting general descriptive dictionaries, specialized dictionaries for semantic relations and thesauri. As our aim is to draft a list of all *potential* synonyms, we also include the synonyms of the synonyms. The same holds true for the list of lexemes extracted from our second source, results from automatic synonym detection by means of Word Space Models. Specifically, we use the output of the best working algorithm defined in Peirsman et al. (2007).

From the resulting list of potential synonyms, we now have to select the actual synonyms, by paying attention to denotational, stylistic, expressive and structural differences between the English person reference nouns and the suggested alternatives. On the **DENOTATIONAL LEVEL**, the focus lies on finding referential differences between the near-synonyms (Edmonds and Hirst 2002: 109–110/123), for which we rely on the definition of these items in dictionaries and on a manual analysis of random samples of 200 corpus examples per lexeme, complemented where needed with information from encyclopedic sources. Alleged synonyms which upon closer inspection appear to be hyperonyms (*gebruiker* "user" for *drug addict*), hyponyms (*naaldgast* "needle guy" for *addict*), co-hyponyms (e.g. *koffiehuishouder* "coffee shop tenant" for *barkeeper*) or which are so referentially different from the anglicism that they cannot even be considered to be *near*-synonyms (*pechvogel* "unlucky person" for *underdog*) are not included in the onomasiological profiles. Next, when a concept includes semantically vague items (*manager*), the entire concept (i.e. the anglicism and all alternatives) is excluded from the analyses, as reliably demarcating different meanings of vague items without a thorough (and time-consuming) semantic analysis of all tokens is hardly feasible (Geeraerts 2007). For polysemous and homonymous items (*single*), disambiguating between different meanings should not pose too many problems. Hence, these concepts are included in the analyses, and the ambiguous lexemes will be subject to disambiguation at a later stage. Finally, monosemous items which are referentially (nearly) identical to the English noun are also included in the profile (*kinderoppas* for *babysitter*).

Next, we focus on **STYLISTIC** differences between the English noun and the proposed alternatives. Contrary to Edmonds and Hirst (2002: 124), who tackle this issue *a priori*, we track down stylistic variation between the lexical items *a posteriori* by verifying whether the success rate of a specific anglicism differs depending on the register of the corpus (see below). We do take **EXPRESSIVE DIFFERENCES** into account at this stage, only including items which are equivalent with respect to the speaker's attitude towards the person referred to. To this end, we follow the three-way distinction between favorable, neutral and pejorative attitudes put forward by Edmonds and Hirst (2002). For example, though Dutch *homo* is listed as a potential synonym of *fag*, we do not include it in the profile, as *homo* is a neutral expression, whereas *fag* has negative connotations. Finally, like Edmonds and Hirst (2002), we pay less attention to differences on the **STRUCTURAL LEVEL** (combinatorial preferences) in our analyses. We do exclude lexicalized compounds and longer stretches of English, which we discuss in more detail below.

Finally, in building the profiles, we strive for an equal distribution of the concepts over five different lexical fields (which will be presented in detail further on in this paper). As such, our definite selection contains 129 concepts and 358 different lexemes (149 of which are English).

Table 2 contains examples of the profiles, a full list of all profiles can be found in the appendix. As becomes apparent, some concepts can only be expressed by the English person reference noun: either no alternatives were found in the reference material at all, or the suggested alternatives did not occur (e.g. *voorjuichster* for *cheerleader*). Because of the design of this study, the third theoretical option, i.e. concepts which can only be expressed by a Dutch person reference noun, do not occur in the dataset. The table also shows how some lexemes have several meanings and hence need to be disambiguated before we can calculate the success rates. How we dealt with polysemy and other types of noise is discussed in the following section.

concept	description	English PRN	alternatives
BABYBOOMER	someone born during the baby boom in the 1950s	babyboomer, boomer	geboortegolver
BACKPACKER	someone who likes to travel from place to place on low budget, with a backpack	backpacker	rugzakker, rugzaktoerist
BITCH	a highly negative term used to address or talk about a woman who you dislike very much	bitch, cunt	teef, kreng, feeks, kutwijf, secreet
FOODIE	someone fond of good food	foodie	culi
FREAK[FAN]	someone who is very fond of and devoted to something, obsessing over it	freak	fanaat, fanaticus, fanatiekeling
FREAK[WEIRDO]	someone who has a hard time fitting in because of his abnormal behavior	freak, weirdo	zonderling, excentriekeling
GOALGETTER	someone who plays sports and is very good at scoring goals	goalgetter	goaltjesdief, doelpuntenmachine
HACKER	someone who illegally breaks into computer systems	hacker	computerkraker
MERCHANDISER	someone studying the market and consumers in order to improve turnover and production	merchandiser	verkoopadviseur, verkoopstrateeg
JOBHOPPER	someone who changes jobs very frequently	jobhopper	/
CHEERLEADER	someone who leads cheering at a sports event	cheerleader	/

Table 2: Examples of profiles

3.2.3 Retrieving token counts

Given the size of our corpus, we extract the tokens for the lexicalizations of the concepts automatically. As the algorithm behind the lemmatizer of the corpora (Alpino, designed specifically for Dutch) underperforms for foreign elements, we start off with a very exhaustive search to minimize the risk of missing tokens. Next, post-processing steps are taken to remove noise from this first database which contains roughly 840,000 tokens, approximately 220,000 of which are English: proper names, codeswitches and irrelevant meanings of polysemous items need to be excluded from the database.

As a considerable number of our (English) person reference nouns occur as (part of) a proper name, we first turn to the exclusion of **PROPER NAMES**, which is done automatically. In excluding proper names we did not follow the lemmatization of the corpus, which underperforms for foreign words. Instead, we created an algorithm specific for single nouns, based on capitalization and sentence position.

Next, we semi-automatically remove **LONGER STRETCHES OF ENGLISH** from the database. We exclude (1) lexicalized compounds (*management consultant* vs. *consultant*) and (2) codeswitches and borrowed phraseology, i.e. cases where the English noun is embedded in a longer grammatical English structure (see Ortigosa and Otheguy 2007). As concerns codeswitches, it is important to note that the phenomenon is very rare in Dutch newspapers and primarily occurs in direct quotes (compare Onysko 2007):

(1) Dat er geweldige kleren te zien waren bij de show van Viktor and Rolf, daar was de internationale modepers het roerend over eens. De International Herald Tribune noemde het een "triumph" en schreef "this show saw the *designers* maturing in a delightful way."

"International fashion press complete agree that some fabulous outfits were on display at the Viktor and Rolf show. The International Herald Tribune called it a 'triumph' and wrote 'this show saw the *designers* maturing in a delightful way.'"
(TwNC, *Het Parool* 21 March 2001)

To exclude these cases, we designed a language guesser based on 216 grammatical words selected from a reference book on English grammar (Quirk et al.; Leech 1985).

Finally, we tackle the issue of **POLYSEMY**: only observations with the correct meaning can be considered when building onomasiological profiles. As existing algorithms are not sufficiently accurate (but see current advances made by Heylen and Speelman 2011), we do not rely on automatic word sense disambiguation. For low-frequent types (token frequency under 3500), disambiguation is performed manually, which is too time-consuming for items with a higher token frequency. In these cases, we analyze a sample of 1000 tokens and look for context cues which can be used in (semi-)automatic disambiguation. If such cues cannot be found, reliable disambiguation is not possible and consequently the concept is discarded from the analyses. The practical consequence is that polysemy might be underrepresented for the highly-frequent lexemes in our analyses. We will come back to this when discussing the results of our analyses.

3.2.4 Calculating success rates

Once noise is removed, we rely on the clean token counts to calculate the success rates of the anglicisms. Examples are listed in Table 3.

concept	concept frequency	English PRN[1]	frequency of English PRN	success rate anglicism
BABYBOOMER	1683	babyboomer	1611	1611/1683 = 95%
BABYBOOMER	1683	boomer	37	37/1683 = 2%
BACKPACKER	1366	backpacker	425	425/1366 = 31%
BITCH	2507	bitch	1048	1048/2507 = 42%
BITCH	2507	cunt	13	13/2507 = 1%
GOALGETTER	5353	goalgetter	4163	4163/5353 = 78%
HACKER	29904	hacker	4984	4984/29904 = 17%
CHEERLEADER	978	cheerleader	978	978/978 = 100%

Table 3: Examples success rates for *LeNC + TwNC*

Of the 149 English person reference nouns included in our study, 18 occur as the only lexicalization for the concept (e.g. *jogger, interviewer, cheerleader, spammer*). The technical difficulties these items pose for the analysis will be discussed below.

3.3 Defining and coding possibly influential features

Table 3 clearly shows variation in the success rates of anglicisms, which raises the question how this variation can be explained. To this end, we define nine possibly influential features, based on reasons for the success of anglicisms found in existing literature. Most of these suggested reasons have so far not been empirically tested and have not yet been operationalized.

Qualitative studies on the use of anglicisms often claim that English loanwords are popular because they are short, with shortness typically mentioned as an absolute property of a word. Taking a relative perspective ("shorter than") however offers a more reliable and straightforward way to assess the impact of **SPEECH ECONOMY**: the question then becomes whether or not the English word is the shortest of the possible lexicalizations of a concept and whether this quality influences its success rate (Poplack et al. 1988; Winter-Froemel 2008; and Sagmeister-Brandner 2008). Comparing the number of syllables of all lexicalizations of a concept (cf. Chesley and Baayen 2010), our hypothesis implies that if the anglicism is the shortest lexicalization for a concept, it will have a higher success rate than anglicisms which are not. In our dataset, 53 anglicisms are shorter

---

[1] Henceforth, we use "PRN" as abbreviation for "person reference nouns".

than any of the alternatives, 78 are not, and 18 form the only lexicalization of the concept expressed.

Another frequently mentioned factor is **LEXICAL FIELD**. As we zoom in on a subset of the lexicon, we do not rely on existing classifications (e.g. Haspelmath and Tadmor 2009), but define five categories specific to our person reference nouns: (1) 29 loanwords are related to media and IT (*cartoonist, spammer*); (2) the category "sports and recreation" contains 28 loanwords (*golfer, backpacker*); (3) 31 items are related to business, economy and other legal ways of making money (*businessman, trucker*); (4) 26 loanwords are used for the neutral or positive social categorization of people (*babyboomer, soulmate*); (5) 35 loanwords are referred to as *deviance* items, i.e. words naming illegal occupations and swearwords (*hitman, motherfucker*). Several hypotheses are at play concerning the anticipated effect of lexical field. First, we believe that the most successful borrowings will be found in those fields which are strongly influenced by the Anglo-American world, like information technology, mass media and sports (Zandvoort 1964: xi; Posthumus 1991: 165; Rodriguez Gonzalez 1999: 105; Crystal 2003: 91–103/114–120). Second, we expect loanwords in the deviance class to be more successful than others, because of two opposing hypotheses. On the one hand, loanwords are alleged to have a euphemistic effect (Galinsky 1967: 47–48; Hock and Joseph 1996: 231–236; Yang 1990: 131–133; Berns 1988: 45). This could lead to a higher than average success for anglicisms in the deviance group, because they are felt to be less insulting than the Dutch items (using *bitch* is softer than using *kutwijf*). In contrast, loanwords are also said to be stylistically marked. As a result, anglicisms in the deviance class could be selected for their dysphemistic instead of their euphemistic effect (using *bitch* is more marked than using *kutwijf*). Again, this would result in a higher success rate for loanwords in the deviance group.

Given the spread of Anglo-American culture in Western Europe after the end of World War II (Di Scala 2004: 478/674), 1945 forms a clear benchmark for the amount of English loanwords borrowed. The question is whether **ERA OF THE BORROWING EVENT** (as an indication of the age of the borrowed item) also influences the success of these loanwords. Two (potentially conflicting) hypotheses can be put forward. A *cultural hypothesis* states that close contact with Anglo-American culture in the aftermath of World War II not only led to more loanwords, but also to more successful loanwords; a *structural hypothesis* holds that older loanwords are more successful, because they have had more time to establish themselves in the receptor language (Fischer 2008: 8; Haspelmath and Tadmor 2009: 13; Gómez Rendón 2008: 271). To verify the hypotheses, we date our anglicisms as accurately as possible, consulting over fifty different lexicographical sources from three different groups. The most reliable group provides dates of first entry. As these sources do not contain information on all anglicisms, we also check all editions of a set of authoritative Dutch dictionaries, relying on the year of publication of the first edition in which the loanword appears. The older descriptive dictionaries however tend to have purist entry policies, and younger descriptive dictionaries only include words once they reach a certain degree of entrenchment in general language. To factor in this possible time-lag in the first entry dates of words in these dictionaries vs. their actual first occurrence, we also select a set of prescriptive style guides and neologism dictionaries, which typically also include (new) foreign words. For example, *foodie* is only mentioned in the 2005 edition of Van Dale (Den Boon and Geeraerts 2005), but De Coster (1999) dates its entrance in Dutch back to 1985. Based on this information, we group all loanwords in three categories: borrowed up to 1945 (29 loanwords), borrowed between 1945 and 1989 (67 loanwords), and borrowed after 1989 (53 loanwords). The 1989-benchmark is chosen because "[o]nce the Cold War had ended (...) the tight bound with America was relaxed, and Europe developed an internal focus" (Wakeman 2003: 147), which may lead to a decrease in the success of anglicisms.

One exception to the lack of onomasiological approaches to loanwords is the often-made distinction between **LUXURY AND NECESSARY LOANS**. As the subjective terminology suggests, the distinction is primarily used in prescriptive accounts (see Rodriguez Gonzalez 1999 and comments in Onysko 2009; Onysko and Winter-Froemel 2011; Androutsopoulos forthcoming): using necessary anglicisms is allowed, as they fill a lexical gap (they are used to name a new, non-lexicalized concept, e.g. *webmaster*), but it is advised to avoid using luxury anglicisms, which are introduced as an alternative name for an already lexicalized concept (e.g. *soulmate* for Dutch *zielsvriend*). Recently, attempts have been made to formalize the distinction (Onysko and Winter-Froemel 2011; Rohde et al. 1999), but the actual difference in success of luxury and necessary anglicisms has not been quantified. For our study, we measure the influence of the status of a loanword at the moment it was borrowed on its success in our corpora. The hypothesis is that English words introduced as necessary loanwords are more successful than those introduced as luxury loanwords. Even if, over time, alternative expressions are introduced for necessary anglicisms (*voetbalvandaal* for *hooligan*), we believe that the fact that the anglicism was the first word to lexicalize the concept has a lasting effect on its success; luxury anglicisms have a harder time establishing themselves in the receptor language, as they have to compete with older and hence more entrenched lexicalizations of the concept expressed. To operationalize the distinction, we date all words in the profile according to the method described above. If the loanword is the oldest of the lexicalizations, we consider it to be a necessary anglicisms (69 cases), in all other cases, it is considered to be a

lexicalizations for LINESMAN_FOOTBALL	introduced in Dutch in
grensrechter	1909
linesman	**1914**
lijnrechter	1976
assistent-scheidsrechter	1999

Table 4: Operationalizing the distinction between necessary and luxury anglicisms

luxury anglicism (80 cases; see example Table 4). Of course, there is a possibility that some alternative expressions existed at a certain stage in the life of the concept, but are not currently in use. As such, our operationalization is not completely reliable, yet it forms a good general approximation.

The importance of **SOURCE LANGUAGE FREQUENCY** is also often mentioned in typological studies, but is to our knowledge not included in anglicism research. The more language users are exposed to a lexeme in their contact with the source language, the more likely it is they will introduce it in the receptor language and, once borrowed, the more frequent they will use it (Van Hout and Muysken 1994: 52). Several issues need to be raised concerning source language frequency, the most important being that word frequency is not a static phenomenon. Which has the highest impact on the success of a loanword at time X: source language frequency at the time that the loanword was introduced (e.g. early nineteenth century for *jockey*, borrowed in 1811) or source language frequency at the time of measurement (in our case 1999–2005)? Ideally, we could empirically test which of both has the strongest impact on loanword success, but finding reliable frequency counts for the time of introduction poses a problem for older loanwords. Only focusing on frequency at the time of measurement however also poses problems: given the plethora of different varieties of English used today, how can we assess which of these Englishes (ELF English in the workplace, American English on television, all sorts of vernaculars in hip hop, any possible variety on the internet) serves as prime source for contact? Clearly, the choice of corpus has an undeniable impact on frequency counts (simply imagine comparing the frequency per million words of *bitch* in the newspaper section of BNC with its frequency in a corpus of hip hop lyrics). Moreover, in weak contact situations (like the influence of English on Dutch), source language exposure is primarily indirect (through mass media), making source language frequency a less relevant factor. As a result, we did not include source language frequency in our analyses.

RECEPTOR LANGUAGE FREQUENCY is also mentioned more frequently in typological studies than in anglicism research. When Haspelmath (2008) states that high frequency words will be "resistant to borrowing, because it is well known that high-frequency items are resistant to other types of language change such as analogy," it is not entirely clear what he exactly means. At least three interpretations are possible: (1) high frequency items are not borrowed; (2) high frequency items are not borrowed and do not allow for the introduction of a borrowed alternative; (3) high frequency items are not borrowed and do not allow for *successful* borrowed alternatives. Van Hout and Muysken (1994: 52–53) include a radically different fourth possibility, stating that frequent words might not show more resistance, but more acceptance to borrowed alternatives. Though Van Hout and Muysken (1994) do not take an onomasiological approach themselves, they stress its importance in testing the impact of receptor language frequency and in defining which of the options given above is actually measured. We propose to include such an onomasiological perspective by measuring the receptor language frequency of *concepts* rather than of *lexemes*. To form a hypothesis we fall back on a link between frequency and entrenchment of the concept (Langacker 1987, but see e.g. Schmid 2010 for a critical note), which is "the degree to which it is conventionalized both for the individual speaker (i.e. how routinized it is cognitively) and the speech community (i.e. the degree to which it is shared across speakers)" (Rohde et al. 1999: 266). The idea is that the higher the entrenchment of a concept, the more it can be considered to be part of our core vocabulary, and the more resistance will occur to using foreign language material to lexicalize the concept (e.g. Hock and Joseph 1996: 257). Of course, the impact of this predictor might be crucially different for luxury and necessary loanwords. We can also again raise the question whether concept frequency is important at the time of introduction of the loanword or at time of measurement. Ideally, we would be able to measure both, but this is hardly feasible in practice. Hence, our current operationalization of concept frequency is limited to time of measurement, summing the frequencies of all lexicalizations of a given concept in the corpus and logging the number to neutralize extremes (e.g. for HOOLIGAN: $\log(hooligan + voetbalvandaal) = \log(10103+642) = 9.28$). Finally, we wish to note that concept dispersion (the amount of different newspaper articles in which the concept is mentioned (Chesley and Baayen 2010) forms an interesting alternative operationalization for concept frequency, to be developed in follow-up research.

The final three predictors are related to the structure of our corpora: "a variational analysis is unavoidable to factor out lectal variation from the corpus data, but it is also a necessary and natural part of Cognitive Linguistics, to the extent that lectal variation underlies a specific form of linguistic meaning." (Geeraerts 2005: 182). Below we discuss the methodological steps which need to be taken to factor in these predictors for the analyses; here we briefly present the three variables. First, we verify whether we can find a **DIACHRONIC PATTERN** in the success of English nouns in our corpus, expecting to find a rise in success (e.g.

Crystal 2003). Of course, given the limited time-span of the corpus (1999–2005), it might be hard to pick up any patterns. Next, we compare the success of the English nouns in popular versus quality newspapers, in order to trace possible **REGISTER VARIATION**. There are two possible outcomes: some sources claim that using foreign language material presupposes a certain education level of the readership (Viereck 1980: 12; Cheshire and Moser 1994: 454–455), which would imply more success for anglicisms in the quality newspapers. On the other hand, as the use of English is often seen as a prime feature of youth language (Androutsopoulos 2005), we could expect more English in the popular papers. Finally and most important, we look for **REGIONAL VARIATION**. We focus on pluricentric variation by comparing the success of anglicisms in Belgian Dutch and Netherlandic Dutch (Clyne 1992). Variation in the use of foreign language material in the two national varieties of Dutch has so far largely been ignored (but see van Bezooijen and Gerritsen 1994; Van de Velde and Van Hout 2002; Geeraerts and Grondelaers 2000), although the cultural-linguistic history of Flanders and the Netherlands provides us with good reasons to inquire into the degree of variation in the use of English in the two varieties. The Netherlands is generally known for its open attitude towards foreign languages in general and towards English in particular (Booij 2001). For Flanders, the situation is more complex. Belgian Dutch is characterized by a longstanding ambivalent relationship with French: the language of the Flemish ruling class and social elite and of public life was French throughout the most part of the 18th and 19th centuries. On the one hand, this slowed down the standardization process of Dutch, as standardization typically results from a desire for more homogeneity in public and cultural emancipation. On the other hand, it caused a massive influx of French loanwords in Belgian Dutch. When in the 1960s the standardization process was eventually speeded up, language policy was directed towards assimilation with the Netherlandic Dutch standard, which had been developing since the 16th century and did not undergo any major impact of French. Hence, "the struggle for recognition of Dutch as the official language in Belgium often materialized as a competition with the French standard" (Geeraerts and Grondelaers 2000: 53), leading to an ardent rejection of French loanwords (Geerts 1992). We propose two conflicting hypotheses concerning the use of English in Dutch. First, the rejection of French loanwords could form the basis of a more general Belgian Dutch purism, which also affects the use of English. In this case, English loans will be more successful in Netherlandic Dutch than in Belgian Dutch (Geerts 1992: 85). Second, the use of English in both regions could be highly comparable, as English loanwords did not have the impeding effect on standardization French loanwords had. An extra argument for this hypothesis is the similar, firm position English holds in the media in both regions (Booij 2001).

3.4 Measuring the impact of the features: mixed modeling

When simultaneously inquiring into the effect of the nine predictors, inferential statistical analyses are necessary to acquire a reliable view on the effect of each of these predictors. In our study, we use linear regression analyses. In this respect, some comments need to be made.

First, up to this point, we described our method as relying on one measuring point per anglicism. However, if we want to take possible lectal and diachronic variation in the success of the person reference nouns into account, we cannot rely on just one measuring point per anglicism for the entire corpus, but instead we need different measuring points for each subcorpus. In the present case, this entails having six measuring points (see Table 5). Note that The Netherlandic Dutch corpus has a smaller diachronic span than the Belgian Dutch corpus, which explains the lack of Netherlandic Dutch measuring points for 2003–2005. An added practical advantage of using multiple measuring points is that they provide us with more observations (in principle 6*149 anglicisms) to use when building the inferential statistical models. Henceforth, we work with this extended dataset.

Second, we introduce the concept-based success measure as a percentage (i.e. we divide the frequency of the English item by the concept frequency * 100; see Table 5), which forms the most intuitive way of presenting the calculation. However, for parametric statistical tests, percentages are far from the ideal quantification. Being capped at 0 and 100, percentages often pose technical difficulties when introduced as response variable in linear regression analyses (residuals sometimes are far from normally distributed, heteroscedasticity often occurs and sometimes the model predicts impossible values). Two transformations of the response variable can help deal with this issue, each with its own benefits and

Subcorpus			frequency *hacker*	concept frequency	success rate *hacker* (%)
Belgian Dutch	1999–2002	popular	1000	1099	91.0%
Belgian Dutch	1999–2002	qualitative	1343	1421	94.5%
Belgian Dutch	2003–2005	popular	335	365	91.8%
Belgian Dutch	2003–2005	qualitative	619	646	95.8%
Netherlandic Dutch	1999–2002	popular	767	833	92.1%
Netherlandic Dutch	1999–2002	qualitative	578	620	93.2%

Table 5: Six measuring points for *hacker*

drawbacks. First, we can rely on odds instead of percentages (i.e. dividing the amount of times the concept is named with the anglicism by the times it is *not* named by the anglicism). The aforementioned technical difficulties are often best overcome by working with log-transformed odds instead of simply taking the odds. The most important limitation of this transformation is that it cannot be used for items without variation: odds corresponding to 100% success entail dividing by 0 (which of course is not possible) and odds corresponding to 0% success are 0, which when logged equal negative infinity (which cannot be implemented in linear regression analyses). Practically, this means that all measuring points with 0 or 100% success have to be excluded from the analyses. The second option is to let go of a continuous response variable and to work with an ordinal variable, e.g. with three categories: "not successful" (0 to 33% success), "somewhat successful" (33 to 66% success), "very successful" (66 to 100% success). The major advantage here is that no observations have to be deleted: also measuring points without variation can be included. The main drawbacks are the loss of information (because of the transformation from numeric to categorical), the reduction of statistical power and the less intuitive interpretation. Working with more than three levels for an ordinal response variable is also not a very attractive option, as the interpretative difficulties expand greatly.

Here we opt for the first solution. As a practical consequence, we create a subset of the database which excludes all measuring points with a success rate of 0% or 100%. Although our dataset only consists of concepts which can be expressed by English lexical items in Dutch, it is not hard to see how a 0% success rate can occur once multiple measuring points are introduced (Table 6). Another limitation imposed on the new database is that all measuring points should be based on at least ten observations. Finally, we require that each concept has at least three reliable measuring points (i.e. based on at least ten tokens, and

subcorpus			frequency *winger*	concept frequency	success rate *winger* (%)
Belgian Dutch	1999–2002	popular	26	267	9.7%
Belgian Dutch	1999–2002	qualitative	5	38	13.2%
Belgian Dutch	2003–2005	popular	28	249	11.2%
Belgian Dutch	2003–2005	qualitative	0	66	0.0%
Netherlandic Dutch	1999–2002	popular	0	420	0.0%
Netherlandic Dutch	1999–2002	qualitative	0	315	0.0%

Table 6: Success rates for *winger*

success rate not equal to 0 or 100%). The resulting database consists of 641 measuring points for 115 English lexemes taken from 95 concepts.

As a final comment, we would like to note that mixed effect regression modelling instead of traditional fixed effect models will be used, in order to take into account that we have several measuring points per concept (see Galwey 2006; Baayen 2008; and Everitt and Hothorn 2010). We take the concept expressed as the random variable: as the data points for each concept will most likely be correlated, considering each of them as a separate observation could lead to overfitting. Including the random variable allows the algorithm to take the specific nature of each of the concepts into account in determining the overall effect of the predictors.

4 Results

Given that the number of diagnostic tests available for mixed effect regression modeling is limited, we start our analyses by building a fixed effects only model, which we then use as input for the mixed model. In building the fixed model, we rely on forward stepwise selection of the variables, cross-verified with a bootstrapping algorithm. After thoroughly verifying the diagnostics of this fixed effects model, we introduce *concept* as a random variable. Both a main model and an interaction model are built, the latter containing only those interactions which are reasonably important in an ANOVA analysis of the fixed effect model and theoretically relevant. The resulting effects are presented below, with main effects from the mixed model presented in Table 7 and the effects for the mixed model with interactions presented in Table 8. For ease of argumentation, we first

	estimate	std.error	z-value	p-value
(intercept)	5.171	0.990	5.222	0.000***
log(concept frequency)	−0.617	0.131	−4.715	0.000***
luxury anglicism	−0.498	0.294	−1.693	0.091
era borrowing-age group 1 (helmert)	−0.012	0.224	−0.052	0.959
era borrowing-age group 2 (helmert)	−0.492	0.125	−3.928	0.000***
lexical field-sports and recreation	−0.299	0.734	−0.408	0.684
lexical field-legal moneymaking	−1.514	0.671	−2.257	0.024*
lexical field-social life	−1.580	0.665	−2.376	0.018*
lexical field-deviance	−1.608	0.651	−2.469	0.014*
speech economy-anglicism not shortest	−0.494	0.275	−1.795	0.073

Table 7: Main effects model (mixed)

describe the results based on the main effects only model. Next, we attenuate these results based on the more complex interaction model and on a set of extra analyses. Note that in theory, it would also be possible to build several regression models which can then be compared (e.g. comparing a model for the necessary loanwords vs. the luxury loanwords). In practice, this would however lead to data sparseness.

4.1 Main model

For the fixed main effects model, all variables except region, register and diachronic period are selected by the forward stepwise selection algorithm and are retained in bootstrapping. The model explains a reasonable 35% of the attested variation (expressed in the R^2-measure), and the diagnostics indicate a good fit. For the mixed model, we calculate the reduction in standard deviation around the blups (best linear unbiased predictors for the random variable; i.e. the random effect counterpart of estimates for fixed effects) for the fitted model versus an intercept only model (Baayen 2008), both containing *concept* as random variable. For our model, the standard deviation is reduced by 22%, indicating a reasonably good fit, which is also indicated by the normal distribution of the blups (verified by the Shapiro Wilk test) and by the standard errors, which are all well under two. Table 7 shows the estimates for our variables in the mixed model, ranked according to their relative importance in an ANOVA of the fixed effects only model. Below, we discuss the impact of each of these variables in turn, showing how the model contains intuitive patterns and is overall highly interpretable.

The first variable, **CONCEPT FREQUENCY**, is the only numeric predictor in our model. For numeric predictors, the sign of the estimate shows the direction of the correlation with the numeric response variable and the p-value shows the significance of this correlation. In this case we find a highly significant negative correlation between concept frequency and the success of the anglicism. We indicated above that high frequency concepts can be considered to be more entrenched. In turn, more entrenched concepts can be considered to be part of our core vocabulary, which makes them more resistant to successful borrowed alternatives. Put differently, the more frequent the concept, the less success the anglicism will have, which is the pattern we see in Table 7. However, as is noted by Chesley and Baayen (2010: 20–21), a diachronic perspective on entrenchment is needed to fully grasp the potential link between entrenchment and borrowability. Also, the link between concept frequency and success of the loanwords cannot be overstated, as the degree of polysemy of the items in the concept might be a confounding variable at this point. As was mentioned above, concepts with highly-frequent polysemous items were only included in our analyses if (semi-)automatic disambiguation of the lexical items is possible. For items with low frequency, no restrictions were imposed. As such, chances are that the current dataset shows an underrepresentation of polysemous highly-frequent lexemes. Consequently, the pattern found for concept frequency might in part be influenced by the fact that the low frequency concepts contain more polysemous items than the high frequency concepts.

For our next predictor, which distinguishes between **LUXURY AND NECESSARY ANGLICISMS**, Table 7 shows the estimated success of luxury anglicisms compared to the estimated success of necessary anglicisms. As the latter functions as the reference value, its behavior is captured in the intercept. The negative sign of the estimate for luxury anglicisms indicates lower average success for luxury anglicisms than for necessary anglicisms, which fits with the expectation that anglicisms which are introduced to fill a lexical gap will have an easier time establishing themselves as a successful lexicalization for a concept (even when source language competitors are introduced over time) than anglicisms which are introduced as alternative lexicalization for an already lexicalized concept and which hence have to compete with an already established lexeme. With a p-value of 0.09, this effect is however only borderline significant.

In modeling the effect of **ERA OF BORROWING**, we use reverse Helmert coding and take the oldest group (anglicisms borrowed up to 1945) as the reference value. We learn from the model that no significant difference can be found in the success rates in our corpus (i.e. 1999–2005) of words borrowed in the period of 1945 to 1989 (age group 1) and the oldest group. The estimate for age group 2 captures the difference in success of anglicisms borrowed after 1989 with those borrowed before 1989 (i.e. the two previous groups taken together), showing a significantly lower success for anglicisms from the youngest group. This means that we find evidence for the structural hypothesis, which states that loanwords need time to establish themselves in the language, making it harder for young loanwords to become successful lexicalizations of a concept. Tentatively, we could consider the absence of this effect when comparing words borrowed before 1945 and words borrowed between 1945 and 1989 as proof for the cultural hypothesis. If only the structural effect were at play, words borrowed between 1945 and 1989 would be significantly less successful than words borrowed before 1945. The lack of such difference might be explained by a positive post World War II effect on the words borrowed between 1945 and 1989. Of course, more evidence is needed to reliably draw such conclusions. Furthermore, it should be verified to what extent the effect of era of borrowing is dependent on whether or not the anglicism is a luxury or a necessary loanword, which will be discussed in the next section of this paper.

Media and IT serves as the reference value for measuring the impact of **LEXICAL FIELD**, as we expect to find most anglicisms there. The results show that the success rates of the English person reference nouns from the fields of media and IT items and sports and recreation are not significantly different from each other, and that (as expected) both are more successful than anglicisms from any of the other fields. The estimates for the remaining three lexical fields lie very closely together, with least success found for anglicisms from the class of deviance items: our analyses therefore do not support the alleged euphemistic or dysphemistic effect of anglicisms. However, an in-depth contextual analysis is needed to be able to provide conclusive evidence of the pragmatic effect of the anglicisms under scrutiny. Moreover, concepts from the deviance class can typically be expressed by more lexical equivalents than concepts from the other lexical fields (see appendix), which can also explain the more limited success of "deviance" anglicisms.

Finally, for the effect of **SPEECH ECONOMY**, we take anglicisms which are the shortest lexicalization of the concept (measured in syllables) as reference point, again because we expect this group to have the most successful anglicisms, which is confirmed by the model. The effect is however not very strong, the result being only borderline significant.

4.2 Attenuating the analyses

The interpretations provided above need to be attenuated. To this end, we mainly rely on a more complex interaction model (see Table 8). The fixed effects only interaction model explains 40% of the attested variation, and the diagnostics indicate a good fit. For the mixed model, the reduction in standard deviation around the blups for the random variable is 23%. The blups are normally distributed and all standard errors are below two. As reading the output of the interaction model is rather complex, we provide graphical representations of the interactions based on descriptive data to make analyses of the patterns more intuitive.

The main model showed a clear negative correlation between concept frequency and the success of an anglicism. In Figure 1, we see how this negative effect of the frequency (and, hence, entrenchment) of a concept is conditional to the relative length of the anglicism.

The left pane shows the effect of concept frequency on the success rates of anglicisms which are the shortest lexicalization of a concept, the right pane shows the effect for anglicisms which are not. The dotted lines show the fit for separate simple regression models regressing success on concept frequency, with a non-significant model in the former case, and an R^2 of 27% in the latter case. It

	estimate	std.error	z-value	p-value
(Intercept)	5.890	1.171	5.032	0.000***
log(concept frequency)	−0.830	0.149	−5.586	0.000***
luxury anglicism	0.046	0.312	0.147	0.883
era borrowing-age group 1 (helmert)	1.554	0.323	4.806	0.000***
era borrowing-age group 2 (helmert)	−0.216	0.216	−0.999	0.318
lexical field-sports and recreation	−0.652	0.727	−0.897	0.370
lexical field-legal moneymaking	−1.725	0.672	−2.566	0.010*
lexical field-social life	−1.720	0.662	−2.598	0.009**
lexical field-deviance	−1.695	0.658	−2.574	0.010*
speech economy-anglicism not shortest	−5.097	1.508	−3.380	0.001***
log(concept frequency): speech economy-anglicism not shortest	0.781	0.204	3.829	0.000***
luxury anglicism: era borrowing-age group 1 (helmert)	−2.118	0.323	−6.551	0.000***
luxury anglicism: era borrowing-age group 2 (helmert)	−0.209	0.221	−0.947	0.344

Table 8: Interaction model (mixed)

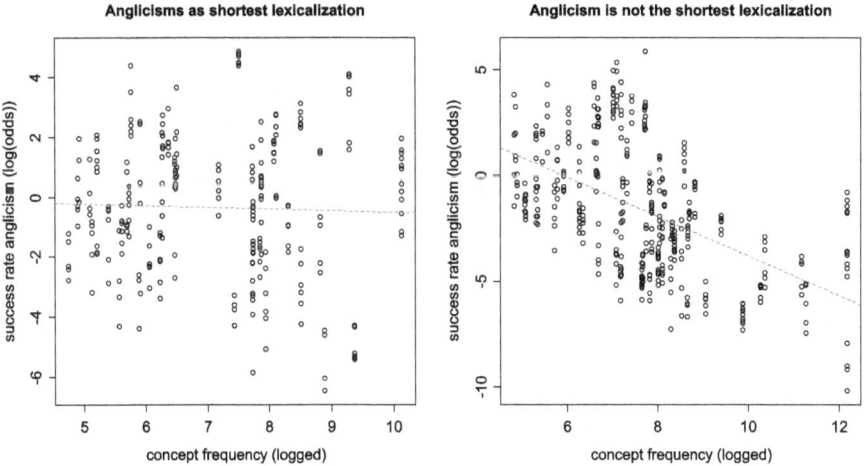

Fig. 1: Interaction concept frequency and speech economy

appears that speech economy clearly restricts concept frequency as a factor: if an anglicism is the shortest lexicalization, concept frequency does not have any impeding effect on the success of the anglicism.

For the interaction between era of borrowing and the distinction between luxury and necessary anglicisms, it is again important to remember that reverse

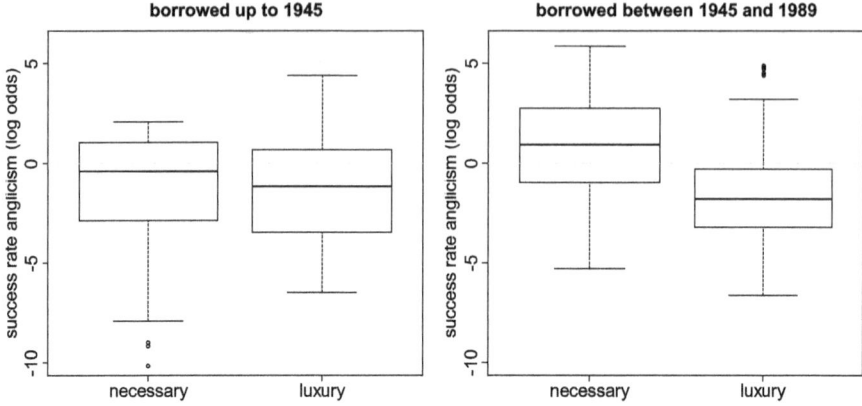

Fig. 2: Interaction era of borrowing and luxury/necessary: age group 1

Helmert coding was used for era of borrowing, which means that we first compare the words borrowed up to 1945 with words borrowed between 1945 and 1989, and that next, we take these two groups together and compare them to words borrowed after 1989. Within each age group, we set the behavior of luxury and necessary anglicisms side by side.

Figure 2 shows the first comparison. In the main model presented in the previous section, the difference in success between luxury and necessary loanwords was only borderline significant. Apparently, this is partly due to the interaction with era of borrowing: the difference in success in our present day corpus between luxury and necessary anglicisms is not significant for the oldest group of loanwords, but becomes highly significant for words borrowed between 1945 and 1989. Also, we see that luxury anglicisms follow the structural hypothesis: older loanwords are more successful, as they have had more time to establish themselves in the receptor language. In contrast, necessary anglicisms behave differently: older necessary anglicisms are less successful in our present day corpus than younger necessary anglicisms. Upon closer inspection, this pattern is highly intuitive. Luxury anglicisms are introduced as an alternative for an established lexicalization of a given concept, and hence need time to become a worthy competitor of this established lexeme. The older the luxury anglicism, the more time it has had to establish itself as alternative lexicalization, the more success it will have in our corpus. For necessary anglicisms, the situation is reversed. Given the restrictions to our dataset, all necessary anglicisms studied in this paper have at least one competitor. In these cases, the necessary anglicism is the first and most established lexicalization of the concept, which can gradually lose ground to the upcoming alternative(s). The older the necessary anglicism, the more time

	borrowed up to 1945	borrowed between 1945 and 1989	borrowed after 1989
necessary anglicism	5	24	12
luxury anglicism	17	30	27

Table 9: Number of anglicisms for luxury/necessary per time period

Fig. 3: Interaction era of borrowing and luxury/necessary: age group 2

competing lexemes have had to become worthy alternative lexicalizations of the concept expressed, and the less success the anglicism will have in our corpus. In sum, the older the loanwords, the more similar the success rates of luxury and necessary anglicisms. However, Table 9 shows that we should not overstate the importance of this interaction, as our database contains only 5 necessary anglicisms borrowed before 1945 (*barkeeper, catcher, gangster, goalkeeper* and *scriptgirl*).

Focusing on the second comparison (see Figure 3), we see very similar behavior for words from the two age groups, which is reflected in the lack of a significant pattern for both the main effect and the interaction effect of age group 2. For both age groups, necessary anglicisms outperform luxury anglicisms. Also, the higher success for younger necessary anglicisms attested in Figure 2, is not present here. To fully understand this pattern, a more fine-grained classification than the binary distinction between luxury and necessary anglicisms, which takes the amount of years between the first and alternative lexicalizations into account, is needed.

Next, apart from the interaction model, two more comments need to be made to attenuate the results described in the previous section. Firstly, an association

	media and IT	sports and recreation	legal money-making	social life	deviance
necessary anglicism	0.652	0.500	0.240	0.250	0.226
luxury anglicism	0.348	0.500	0.760	0.750	0.774

Table 10: Proportion of luxury/necessary per lexical field

exists between lexical field and the distinction between necessary and luxury loanwords (see Table 10). Though the association is not strong enough to jeopardize the results and interpretations from the main model, it is interesting to note the pattern. Clearly, the anglicisms related to media and IT (the most "successful" lexical field) are typically introduced in Dutch to fill a lexical gap. Anglicisms related to business, social life, and deviance items, are in contrast more often introduced as alternative lexicalization for a concept. This pattern has already been noticed by Poplack et al. (1988: 61), who note that "many of the borrowings apparently motivated by need are concentrated in certain semantic fields." Although the association in Table 10 can help explain the higher success of media and IT anglicisms, the pattern is not strong enough to cancel out an individual effect of lexical field.

Finally, we address the absence of the lectal and diachronic parameters in the two regression models. The lack of differences in the success rates of the person reference nouns in the 1992–2002 subcorpora and the 2002–2005 subcorpora does not come as a surprise: the time-span of our corpus is too limited to trace diachronic evolution in the overall use of English. For register variation, we believe that the absence of patterns can be explained by the fact that most of our loanwords are already established in Dutch. Hence, not that much proficiency is required to understand them. Also, the register differences between quality and popular newspapers is rather limited for the newspapers investigated, as no real tabloids are part of the corpus. Finally, the lack of regional variation might be linked to register, as there are not that many differences between Standard Belgian Dutch and Standard Netherlandic Dutch (compared to more colloquial varieties). On the other hand, strong regional differences in the success of English which might creep up for specific concepts may have been leveled out in the aggregate analyses. To this end, we compare the success rates of all English person reference nouns in Belgian Dutch and Netherlandic Dutch in Figure 4. The figure provides a scatterplot, with the Belgian Dutch success rates on the x-axis and the Netherlandic Dutch success rates on the y-axis: the closer the lexeme is to the diagonal, the closer the success rates lie together. This again illustrates that the differences between the regions in the success of the loanwords studied is limited. More complex analyses, in which we compare the blups for the random

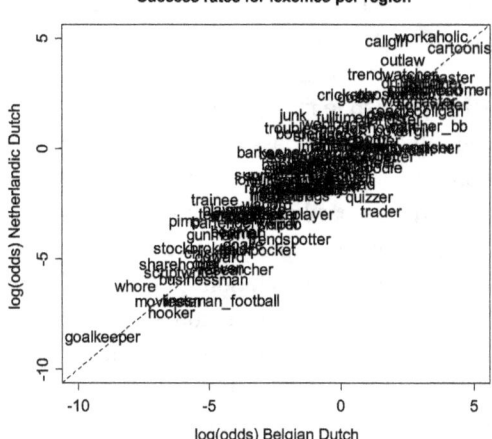

Fig. 4: Looking for regional differences

variable in a mixed model where the random variable *concept* is nested in the predictor *region* (see Baayen 2008), do not indicate any striking differences between the regions. The consistent lack of regional patterns indicates that the basic hypothesis that Belgian Dutch has a stronger purist background than Netherlandic Dutch does not hold. Either this hypothesis is generally outdated, and the use of foreign languages runs parallel in both regions, or it is not applicable to English influence specifically.

5 Conclusion

In this paper, we presented a new concept-based approach to measuring and explaining variation in the success of English loanwords in Dutch. Our results show that the English person reference nouns studied in our database are more successful (1) if the anglicism is the shortest lexicalization of the concept; (2) if it is used to express a low-frequency concept (given that shorter lexicalizations exist); (3) if the loanword is introduced in Dutch as a necessary loan for which a Dutch alternative was only coined later, which is especially true for younger loanwords; (4) if the loanword is used to lexicalize a concept from a lexical field closely related to or originating in Anglo-American culture. As such, this paper contributes to the field of anglicism research by providing in-depth empirical analyses, based on a large database and on new measuring techniques, of a number of hypotheses about the use and spread of English which have previously been raised in studies using a qualitative method, but which have hitherto largely remained untested in a quantitative, statistically reliable sense. Overall, our results provide empirical proof to substantiate most of these hypotheses. Nevertheless, two important nuances need to be made. First, we do not find any patterns proving the allegedly euphemistic effect of using English loanwords. In contrast, the person reference nouns in the connotationally marked class of words (swearwords and words describing illegal professions) are significantly less successful than all other anglicisms in our study. Although this is partly due to the fact that a disproportionate amount of the items in this class are luxury anglicisms, the diagnostics of the regression models ensure us that the association is not so strong as to cancel out an individual effect of lexical field. However, a more in-depth pragmatic analysis is needed before drawing any conclusions. Second, no regional variation is found in our dataset. After performing more advanced, fine-grained analyses of the success of individual person reference nouns, we were able to conclude that the puristic background of Flanders (the northern part of Belgium), which is well attested for the influence of French, does not have any notable effect on the use of English. Of course, follow-up studies relying on larger sets of concepts will need to corroborate these results.

On a more general level, the main purpose of this paper is to show how an application of the insights from Cognitive Sociolinguistics to loanword research is beneficial for both cognitive linguistics and contact linguistics. Specifically, we propose a new way of analyzing variation in the use of loanwords in which we follow the guidelines of Cognitive Sociolinguistics: we aim at a convergence between cognitive linguistics and existing traditions of variationist language research by stressing the importance of introducing semantics in the variationist paradigm in general and in the demarcation of our response variable in particular (compare Hollmann and Siewierska 2011). Most important we introduce *a concept-based onomasiological approach to measuring the success of loanwords* in which the existence of alternative lexicalizations for the concept denoted by the loanword is taken into account.

From a contact linguistic point of view, then, it has become clear that this method, which can easily be expanded to other contact situations than the one presented in this paper, not only helps us to acquire a more reliable view on the success and spread of loanwords, it also helps us to provide more *objective operationalizations* for features which influence variation in these success rates. Most important, it allows us to propose a clear strategy to differentiate between the so far subjectively defined notions of necessary or cultural loanwords on the one hand and luxury or core loanwords on the other hand.

From a cognitive linguistic perspective, we may note that usage-based, cognitive linguistic approaches to contact linguistic phenomena, like the one presented in this paper, are still surprisingly scarce (but see e.g. Backus 1996; Dogruoz and

Backus 2009; and Winter-Froemel 2011). As such, the overall contribution of our approach it is to provide a new and theoretically promising expansion of the current scope of cognitive (socio-)linguistics to the study of contact linguistic phenomena. From a theoretical point of view, our analysis of contact phenomena corroborates the *multifactorial nature of linguistic phenomena* that comes to the fore so clearly in the context of a usage-based approach: in a non-modular way, the success of borrowing processes turns out to be determined simultaneously by processing factors (the relative length of the loan word), by usage factors (the frequency of the concept), by conceptual factors (the presence of a lexical gap), and by cultural factors (the link with global Anglo-American culture).

References

Alex, Beatrice. 2008. *Automatic detection of English inclusions in mixed-lingual data with an application to parsing*. PhD at ICCS, University of Edinburgh.

Andersen, Gisle. 2005. Assessing algorithms for automatic extraction of anglicisms in Norwegian texts. Paper presented at the *Corpus Linguistics Conference*, July 2005, Birmingham.

Androutsopoulos, Jannis. 2005. . . . und jetzt gehe ich chillen: Jugend- und Szenesprachen als lexikalische Erneuerungsquellen des Standards. In Ludwig Eichinger & Werner Kallmeyer (eds.), *Standardvariation. Wie viel Variation verträgt die deutsche Sprache?* Berlin/New York: Walter de Gruyter, 171–206.

Androutsopoulos, Jannis. forthcoming. English 'on top': Discourse functions of English resources in the German mediascape. *Sociolinguistic Studies* [Accepted, April 2011].

Baayen, Harald R. 2008. *Analyzing linguistic data. A practical introduction to statistics using R*. Cambridge: Cambridge University Press.

Backus, Ad. 1996. *Two in one. Bilingual speech of Turkish immigrannts in The Netherlands*. Tilburg: Tilburg University Press.

Bednarek, Adam. 2009. *Studies in Canadian English: Lexical variation in Toronto*. Cambridge: Cambridge Scholars Publishing.

Berns, Margie. 1988. The cultural and linguistic context of English in West Germany. *World Englishes* 7(1): 37–49.

Blank, Andreas. 2003. Words and concepts in time: towards diachronic cognitive onomasiology. In R. Eckardt (ed.), *Words in time: diachronic semantics from different points of view*. Berlin/New York: Mouton De Gruyter, 37–66.

Booij, Geert. 2001. English as the Lingua Franca of Europe: A Dutch Perspective. *Lingua e Stile* 36(2), 347–357.

Boyd, Jeremy K. & Adele E. Goldberg. 2011. Learning what NOT to say: The role of statistical preemption and categorization in *a*-adjective production. *Language* 87(1), 55–83.

Carstensen, Broder. 1965. *Englische Einflüsse auf die deutsche Sprache nach 1945*. Heidelberg: Carl Winter Universitätsverlag.

Carstensen, Broder & Ulrich Busse. 1994. *Anglizismen-Wörterbuch: Der Einfluss des Englischen auf den deutschen Wortschatz nach 1945*. Berlin/New York: De Gruyter.

Cheshire, Jenny & Lise-Marie Moser. 1994. English as a cultural symbol: The case of advertisements in French-speaking Switzerland. *Journal of Multilingual and Multicultural Development* 15(6), 451–469.

Chesley, Paula & Harald R. Baayen. 2010. Predicting new words from newer words: lexical borrowing in French. *Linguistics* 48(4), 1343–1374.

Clyne, Michael. 1992. *Pluricentric languages: differing norms in different nations*. Berlin/New York: Mouton de Gruyter.

Croft, William. 2009. Toward a social cognitive linguistics. In V. Evans & S. Pourcel (eds.), *New directions in cognitive linguistics*. Amsterdam: John Benjamins, 395–420.

Cruse, Alan D. 1986. *Lexical semantics*. Cambridge: Cambridge University Press.

Crystal, David. 2003. *English as a global language. Second edition*. Cambridge: Cambridge University Press.

De Coster, Marc. 1999. *Woordenboek van neologismen: 25 jaar taalaanwinsten*. Amsterdam: Contact.

De Vooys, Cornelis G. N. 1925. *Engelse invloed op het Nederlands*. Groningen/Den Haag: J.B. Wolters.

De Wolf, Gaelan Dodds. 1996. Word choice: lexical variation in two Canadian surveys. *Journal of English Linguistics* 24, 131–155.

Den Boon, Ton & Dirk Geeraerts. 2005. *Van Dale groot woordenboek van de Nederlandse taal*. 14th edition. Utrecht/Antwerpen: Van Dale Lexicografie.

Diaz Vera, Javier E. 2005. Onomasiological variation and change in the older Scots vocabulary of marriage. *Scottish Language* 24, 1–12.

Di Scala, Spencer M. 2004. *Twentieth century Europe: Politics, society, culture*. Boston: McGraw-Hill.

Divjak, Dagmar & Stefan Th. Gries. 2006. Ways of trying in Russian: clustering behavioral profiles. *Corpus Linguistics and Linguistic Theory* 2(1), 23–60.

Dogruoz, Seza & Ad Backus. 2009. Innovative constructions in Dutch Turkish: an assessment of ongoing contact-induced change. *Bilingualism: Language and Cognition* 12(1): 41–63.

Dunger, Hermann. 1899. Wider die Engländerei in der deutschen Sprache. *Zeitschrift des allgemeinen deutschen Sprachvereins* 14(12), 241–251.

Edmonds, Philip & Graeme Hirst. 2002. Near-synonymy and lexical choice. *Computational Linguistics* 28(2), 105–144.

Everitt, Brian S. & Torsten Hothorn. 2010. *A handbook of statistical analyses using R*. Boca Raton: Taylor and Francis Group.

Field, Fredric W. 2002. *Linguistic borrowing in bilingual contexts*. Amsterdam: John Benjamins.

Filipovic, Rudolf. 1977. English words in European mouths and minds. *Folia Linguistica* 11, 195–206.

Fink, Hermann. 1997. *Von Kuh-Look bis Fit for Fun: Anglizismen in der heutigen deutschen Allgemein- und Werbesprache*. Frankfurt am Main: Peter Lang.

Fischer, Roswitha. 2008. Introduction. Studying anglicisms. In R. Fischer & H. Pulaczewska (eds.), *Anglicisms in Europe. Linguistic diversity in a global context*. Cambridge: Cambridge Scholars Publishing, 1–14.

Galinsky, Hans. 1967. Stylistic aspects of linguistic borrowing. A stylistic view of American elements in modern German. In B. Carstensen & H. Galinksky (eds.), *Amerikanismen der deutschen Gegenwaltsprache: Entlehnungsvorgänge und ihre stilistischen Aspekte*. Heidelberg: Winter, 35–72.

Galwey, Nicholas W. 2006. *Introduction to mixed modelling: beyond regression and analysis of variance*. Chichester: Wiley.

Geeraerts, D. 1997. *Diachronic prototype semantics: a contribution to historical lexicology*. Oxford: Clarendon.

Geeraerts. 2005. Lectal variation and empirical data in Cognitive Linguistics. In F. J. Ruiz De Mendoza Ibanez & M. Sandra Pena Cerval (eds.), *Cognitive Linguistics: Internal dynamics and interdisciplinary interaction*. Berlin/New York: Mouton de Gruyter, 163–189.

Geeraerts, Dirk. 2007. Vagueness's puzzles, polysemy's vagaries. In P. Hanks (ed.), *Lexicology: critical concepts in linguistics*. London: Routledge, 282–327.

Geeraerts, Dirk. 2010. Lexical variation in space. In P. Auer & J. E. Schmidt (eds.), *Language in space. An international handbook of linguistic variation. Volume 1: Theories and methods*. Berlin/New York: Mouton de Gruyter, 821–837.

Geeraerts, Dirk & Stefan Grondelaers. 2000. Purism and fashion. French influence on Belgian and Netherlandic Dutch. *Belgian Journal of Linguistics* 13, 53–68.

Geeraerts, Dirk, Stefan Grondelaers & Peter Bakema. 1994. In R. Dirven & R. W. Langacker (eds.), *The structure of lexical variation. Meaning, naming and context*. Berlin/New York: Mouton de Gruyter.

Geeraerts, Dirk, Stefan Grondelaers & Dirk Speelman. 1999. *Convergentie en divergentie in de Nederlandse woordenschat. Een onderzoek naar kleding- en voetbaltermen*. Amsterdam: Meertens Instituut.

Geeraerts, Dirk, Gitte Kristiansen & Yves Peirsman (eds.). 2010. *Advances in Cognitive Sociolinguistics*. Berlin/New York: Mouton De Gruyter.

Geeraerts, Dirk & Dirk Speelman. 2010. Heterodox concept features and onomasiological heterogeneity in dialects. In D. Geeraerts, G. Kristiansen & Y. Peirsman (eds.), *Advances in Cognitive Sociolinguistics*. Berlin/New York: Mouton de Gruyter, 23–39.

Geerts, Guido. 1992. Dutch. In M. Clyne (ed.), *Pluricentric languages: differing norms in different nations*. Berlin/New York: Mouton de Gruyter, 71–92.

Gerritsen, Marinel et al. 2007. English in product advertisements in Belgium, France, Germany, the Netherlands and Spain. *World Englishes* 26(3), 291–315.

Goldberg, Adele E. 2011. Corpus evidence of the viability of statistical preemption. *Cognitive Linguistics* 22(1), 131–153.

Gómez Rendón, Jorge Arsenio. 2008. *Typological and social constraints on language contact: Amerindian languages in contact with Spanish*. Utrecht: LOT.

Görlach, Manfred. 1994. A usage dictionary of anglicisms in selected European languages. *International Journal of Lexicography* 7(3), 223–246.

Görlach, Manfred. 2001. *A dictionary of European anglicisms: a usage dictionary of anglicisms in sixteen European languages*. Oxford: Oxford University Press.

Graedler, Anne-Line & Gudrún Kvaran. 2010. Foreign influence on the written language in the Nordic language communities. *International Journal of the Sociology of Language* 204, 31–42.

Grondelaers, S., D. Speelman & D. Geeraerts. 2007. Lexical variation and change. In D. Geeraerts & H. Cuyckens (eds.), *The Oxford Handbook of Cognitive Linguistics*. Oxford: Oxford University Press, 988–1011.

Grzega, Joachim. 2003. Borrowing as a word-finding process in cognitive historical onomasiology. *Onomasiology Online* 4, 22–42.

Hanon, Suzanne. 1973. The study of English loan-words in modern French. *Computers and the Humanities* 7(6), 389–398.

Haspelmath, Martin. 2008. Loanword Typology: steps toward a systematic cross-linguistic study of lexical borrowability. In T. Stolz, D. Bakker & R. Salas Palomo (eds.), *Aspects of language contact: New theoretical, methodological and empirical findings with special focus on Romancisation processes*. Berlin/New York: Mouton de Gruyter, 43–62.

Haspelmath, Martin & Uri Tadmor. 2009. *Loanwords in the world's languages: a comparative handbook*. Berlin/New York: Mouton de Gruyter.

Haugen, Einar. 1950. The analysis of linguistic borrowing. *Language* 26(2), 210–231.

Heylen, Kris & Dirk Speelman. 2011. Token vector space demo. ⟨https://perswww.kuleuven.be/~u0038536/VSVIS/⟩ [Accessed 3 November 2011].

Hock, Hans Henrich & Brian D. Joseph. 1996. *Language history, language change, and language relationship: an introduction to historical and comparative linguistics*. Berlin/New York: Mouton De Gruyter.

Hoffmann, Sebastian. 2004. Are low-frequency complex prepositions grammaticalized? On the limits of corpus data and the importance of intuition. In H. Lindquist & C. Mair (eds.), *Corpus approaches to grammaticalization in English*. Amsterdam/Philadelphia: John Benjamins, 171–210.

Hollman, Willem B. & Anna Siewierska. 2011. The status of frequency, schemas, and identity in Cognitive Sociology. *Cognitive Linguistics* 22(1), 25–54.

Humbley, John. 2008. How to determine the success of French language policy on Anglicisms – some methodological considerations. In R. Fischer & H. Pulaczewska (eds.), *Anglicisms in Europe. Linguistic civersity in a global context*. Cambridge: Cambridge Scholars Publishing, 85–105.

Koops, Bert-Jaap, Pim Slop, Paul Uljé, Kees Vermeij & Dick van Zijderveld. 2009. *Funshoppen in het Nederlands: woordenlijst onnodig Engels*. Amsterdam: Bakker.

Kristiansen, Gitte & René Dirven. 2008. *Cognitive sociolinguistics: Language variation, cultural models, social systems*. Berlin/New York: Mouton De Gruyter.

Kristiansen, Gitte & Dirk Geeraerts. 2007. On non-reductionist intercultural pragmatics and methodological procedure. In I. Kecskes & L. R. Horn (eds.), *Explorations in pragmatics: linguistic, cognitive and intercultural aspects*. Berlin/New York: Mouton de Gruyter, 257–286.

Langacker, Ronald W. 1987. *Foundations of cognitive grammar, Vol. I: Theoretical prerequisites*. Stanford/California: Stanford University Press.

Leppänen, Sirpa & Tarja Nikula. 2007. Diverse uses of English in Finnish society: Discourse-pragmatic insights into media, educational and business contexts. *Multilingua* 26(4), 333–380.

Levshina, Natalia, Dirk Geeraerts & Dirk Speelman. in press. Dutch causative constructions with doen and laten: Quantification of meaning and meaning of quantification. In D. Glynn & J. Robinson. *Polysemy and synonymy: corpus methods and applications in Cognitive Linguistics*. Amsterdam/Philadelphia: John Benjamins.

Lutz, Mark. 2007. *Learning Python*. Sebastopol (CA): O'Reilly.

Martel, Pierre. 1984. Les variables lexicales sont-elles sociolinguistiquement intéressant? *ACILR XVII*(5), 183–193. Aix-en-Provence.

Martin, Elizabeth. 2006. *Marketing identities through language: English and global imagery in French advertising*. New York: Palgrave Macmillan.

Muhr, Rudolf. 2004. Anglizismen als Problem der Linguistik und Sprachpflege in Österreich und Deutschland zu Beginn des 21. Jahrhunderts. In R. Muhr & B. Ketteman (eds.), *Eurospeak*.

Der Einfluss des Englischen auf europäische Sprachen zur Jartausendwende. Frankfurt am Main: Peter Lang, 9–54.

Muhr, Rudolf. 2009. Anglizismen und Pseudoanglizismen im Österreichischen Deutsch: 1945–2008. Ein Bericht. In F. Pfalzgraf (ed.), *Englischer Sprachkontakt in den Varietäten des Deutschen/English in Contact with Varieties of German*. Frankfurt am Main/New York: Peter Lang, 123–169.

Myers-Scotton, Carol. 2002. *Contact linguistics: bilingual encounters and grammatical outcomes*. Oxford: Oxford University Press.

Nadasdi, Terry, Raymond Mougeon & Katherine Rehner. 2008. Factors driving lexical variation in L2 French: A variationist study of automobile, auto, voiture, char and machine. *French Language Studies* 18, 365–381.

Nettmann-Multanowska, Kinga. 2003. *English loanwords in Polish and German after 1945: Orthography and morphology*. Frankfurt am Main/New York: Peter Lang.

Onysko, Alexander. 2007. *Anglicisms in German. Borrowing, lexical productivity and written codeswitching*. Berlin/New York: Walter de Gruyter.

Onysko, Alexander. 2009. Divergence with a cause? The systemic integration of anglicisms in German as an indication of the intensity of language contact. In F. Pfalzgraf (ed.), *Englischer Sprachkontakt in den Varietäten des Deutschen/English in contact with varieties of German*. Frankfurt am Main/New York: Peter Lang, 53–74.

Onysko, Alexander & Esme Winter-Froemel. 2011. Necessary loans – luxury loans? Exploring the pragmatic dimension of borrowing. *Journal of Pragmatics* 43(6), 1550–1567.

Ortigosa, Ana & Ricardo Otheguy. 2007. Source language patterns as determinants of borrowing behavior: single and collocation borrowings in Spanish in New York. *Southwest Journal of Linguistics* 26(1), 61–79.

Peirsman, Yves, Kris Heylen & Dirk Speelman. 2007. Finding semantically similar words in Dutch. Co-occurrences versus syntactic contexts. In M. Baroni, A. Lenci, M. Sahlgren (eds.), *Proceedings of the CoSMO workshop, Roskilde, Denmark*, 9–16.

Piller, Ingrid. 2001. Identity constructions in multilingual advertising. *Language in Society* 30(2), 153–186.

Poplack, Shana, David Sankoff & Chris Miller. 1988. The social correlates and linguistic processes of lexical borrowing and assimilation. *Linguistics* 26, 47–104.

Posthumus, Jan. 1991. De acceptatie van Engelse leenwoorden in het Nederlands. *Terminologie et Traduction* 1, 163–193.

Pulaczewska, Hanna. 2008. Anglicisms in German and Polish hip-hop magazines. In R. Fischer & H. Pulaczewska. *Anglicisms in Europe. Linguistic civersity in a global context*. Cambridge: Cambridge Scholars Publishing, 222–246.

Quirk, Randolph, Sidney Greenbaum & Geoffrey Leech. 1985. *A comprehensive grammar of the English language*. London: Longman.

Rando, Gaetano. 1973. A quantitative analysis of the use of anglicisms in written Standard Italian during the 1960s. *Italica* 50, 73–79.

Rodriguez Gonzalez, Felix. 1999. Anglicisms in contemporary Spanish. An overview. *Atlantis* XXI, 103–139.

Rohde, Ada, Anatol Stefanowitsch & Suzanne Kemmer. 1999. Loanwords in a usage-based model. *CLS 35: The Main Session*, 265–275.

Sagmeister-Brandner, Sonja. 2008. *Breaking news: so kommen englische Wörter ins Radio und Fernsehen: eine empirische Studie österreichischer Nachrichten zwischen 1967–2004*. Frankfurt: Peter Lang.

Schmid, Hans-Jörg. 2010. Does frequency in text instantiate entrenchment in the cognitive system? In D. Glynn (ed.), *Quantitative Cognitive Semantics: Corpus-driven approaches*, Berlin/New York: Mouton De Gruyter, 101–135.
Sharp, Harriet. 2001. *English in spoken Swedish. A corpus study of two discourse domains.* Stockholm: Almqvist and Wiksell.
Speelman, Dirk, Stefan Grondelaers & Dirk Geeraerts. 2003. Profile-based linguistic uniformity as a generic method for comparing language varieties. *Computers and the Humanities* 37, 317–337.
van Bezooijen, Renée & Marinel Gerritsen. 1994. De uitspraak van uitheemse woorden in het Standaard-Nederlands: een verkennende studie. *De Nieuwe Taalgids* 87(2), 145–160.
van Coetsem, Frans. 1988. *Loan phonology and the two transfer types in language contact.* Dordrecht: Foris.
Van de Velde, Hans & Roeland Van Hout. 2002. Loan words as markers of differentiation. *Linguistics in the Netherlands* 19, 163–173.
Van der Sijs, Nicoline. 1996. *Leenwoordenboek: de invloed van andere talen op het Nederlands.* Den Haag: Sdu.
Van Hout, Roeland & Pieter Muysken. 1994. Modeling lexical borrowability. *Language Variation and Change* 6(1), 39–62.
Van Iperen, Art. 1980. Van kick-off tot aftrap. *Le langage et l'homme* 44, 62–70.
Viereck, Karin. 1980. *Englisches Wortgut, seine Häufigkeit und Integration in der österreichischen und bundesdeutschen Pressesprache.* Frankfurt: Peter Lang.
Wakeman, Rosemary. 2003. European mass culture in the media age. In *Themes in Modern European History*, ed. Rosemary Wakeman, London: Routledge, 142–166.
Whitney, William D. 1881. On mixture in language. *Transactions of the American Philological Association* 12, 5–26.
Winter-Froemel, Esme. 2008. Unpleasant, unnecessary, unintelligible? Cognitive and communicative criteria for evaluating borrowings and alternative strategies. In R. Fischer & H. Pulaczewska (eds.), *Anglicisms in Europe. Linguistic diversity in a global context.* Cambridge: Cambridge Scholars Publishing, p. 16–41.
Winter-Froemel, Esme. 2011. *Entlehnung in der Kommunikation und im Sprachwandel. Theorie und Analysen zum Französischen.* Berlin/Boston: Walter de Gruyter.
Yang, Wenliang. 1990. *Anglizismen im Deutschen.* Tübingen: Max Niemeyer Verlag.
Zandvoort, Reinard Willem. 1964. *English in the Netherlands: a study in linguistic infiltration.* Groningen: Wolters.

Appendix: concepts by lexical field
(items in italics did not occur in the corpus)

media & IT

BLOGGER	blogger, weblogger
CARTOONIST	cartoonist, cartoontekenaar
COPYWRITER	copywriter, tekstschrijver
COVERGIRL	covergirl, hoezenpoes, *omslagmeisje*
CROONER	crooner

E-TAILER	e-tailer, webwinkelier, internetwinkelier
GHOSTWRITER	ghostwriter, schaduwschrijver, nègre, spookschrijver
HACKER	hacker, computerkraker
INTERVIEWER	interviewer
MOVIESTAR	moviestar, filmster
PIN-UP	pin-up, playmate, prikkelpop, *prikkelpoes, punaisepoes*
ROADIE	roadie, roadmanager, *tourneeassistent, tourneetechnicus*
ROYALTYWATCHER	royaltywatcher, hofverslaggever, hofkenner, royaltyverslaggever, *vorstenhuisdeskundige*
SCRIPTGIRL	scriptgirl, regieassistente
SCRIPTWRITER	scriptwriter, scriptschrijver, scenarist, scenarioschrijver
SHOWGIRL	showgirl, revuemeisje
SONGWRITER	songwriter, songschrijver, liedjesschrijver
SPAMMER	spammer
SPEECHWRITER	speechwriter, toesprakenschrijver, *redeschrijver*
SPINDOCTOR	spindoctor, spindokter, mannetjesmaker
STARLET	starlet, sterretje
TELEVOTER	televoter, *telefoonstemmer, telestemmer*
TRENDWATCHER	trendwatcher, trendspotter, trendvolger, trendwaarnemer
WEBMASTER	webmaster, webbeheerder, webmeester, webstekbeheerder, websitebeheerder
UNDERSTUDY	understudy, doublure

sports & recreation

BACKPACKER	backpacker, rugzakker, rugzaktoerist
FOODIE	foodie, culi
GLOBETROTTER	globetrotter, wereldreiziger
QUIZZER	quizzer, quizspeler, quizdeelnemer, quizkandidaat
QUIZMASTER	quizmaster, quizleider, quizvoorzitter
WEIGHTWATCHER	weightwatcher
CATCHER_BB	catcher, achtervanger, vanger, *vangman*
CATCHER_WRESTLE	catcher, vrijworstelaar
CHEERLEADER	cheerleader, *voorjuichster*
CRICKETER	cricketer, cricketspeler
GOALGETTER	goalgetter, goaltjesdief, doelpuntenmachine
GOLFER	golfer, golfspeler
GROUNDSMAN	groundsman, terreinknecht
HANDBIKER	handbiker, rolstoelwheeler, *rolstoelfietser*
HOOLIGAN	hooligan, voetbalvandaal
JOCKEY	jockey, rijknecht
JOGGER	jogger,
KEEPER	keeper, goalie, goalkeeper, doelman, doelverdediger, doelwachter, kiep
LINESMAN_FOOTBALL	linesman, lijnrechter, grensrechter, assistent-scheidsrechter
OUTFIELDER	outfielder, verrevelder, buitenvelder
PITCHER	pitcher, werper

QUARTERBACK	quarterback, *kwartback*
SKYDIVER	skydiver, vrijevaller
SNOWBOARDER	snowboarder, sneeuwplankglijder, *plankskiër, sneeuwplanker*
WICKETKEEPER	wicketkeeper,
WINGER_SOCCER	winger, vleugelspeler, buitenspeler

legal moneymaking

BABYSIT	babysit, babysitter, kinderoppas
BARMAN	barman, bartender, barkeeper, barbediende
BEAR	bear, baissier, baissespeculant, *contramineur*, beer
BELLBOY	bellboy, piccolo
BROKER	broker, stockbroker, effectenmakelaar, fondsenhandelaar
BULL	bull, haussier, stier
BUSINESSMAN	businessman, zakenman
FREELANCER	freelancer,
FULLTIMER	fulltimer, voltijder, voltijdwerker, voltijdmedewerker, fulltimemedewerker
HALFTIMER	halftimer, *halftijder, halftijdwerker, halftijdmedewerker,* halftimemedewerker
HEADHUNTER	headhunter, koppensneller, *kaderwerver, kaderjager, breinronselaar*
JOBHOPPER	jobhopper
MARKETEER	marketeer, marketingman, markt(des)kundige, markstrateeg, marketier, marktanalist, marktonderzoeker
MERCHANDISER	merchandiser, verkoopadviseur, verkoopstrateeg
NANNY	nanny, kinderjuffrouw
PARTTIMER	parttimer, deeltijder, deeltijdwerker, deeltijdmedewerker, parttimemedewerker
RESEARCHER	researcher, onderzoeker, vorser, navorser
SANDWICHMAN	sandwichman
SHAREHOLDER	shareholder, aandeelhouder, participant, *actionaris*
SHRINK	shrink, zielenknijper, psych
TAILOR	tailor, kleermaker, snijder, tailleur
TRADER	trader, beurshandelaar
TRAINEE	trainee, stagiair
TROUBLESHOOTER	troubleshooter, probleemoplosser
TRUCKER	trucker, vrachtrijder, truckchauffeur, vrachtwagenchauffeur
TUTOR	tutor, repetitor, studiebegeleider, studieadviseur
WORKAHOLIC	workaholic, werkverslaafde, *arbeidsmaniak*

social life

BABYBOOMER	babyboomer, boomer, geboortegolver
BORDERLINER	borderliner, borderlinepatiënt
CAVEMAN	caveman, holbewoner, troglodiet
DANDY	dandy, fat, saletjonker
FREAK_FAN	freak, fanaat, fanaticus, fanatiekeling
GENDERBENDER	genderbender, *uniseksser*

GROUPIE	groupie
HARDLINER	hardliner, extremist, ultra, fundamentalist
HAVE-NOT	have-not, bezitloze, berooide, pauper, niet-hebber
IMAGEBUILDER	imagebuilder, imagovormer, imagobouwer, *reputatiebouwer*, beeldvormer
LONER	loner, eenling, einzelgänger, eenzelvige, eenzaat
OUTCAST_SOC	outcast, paria, vertrappeling, verworpene/-eling, uitgestotene, verschopte/-eling, verstotene/-eling
REDHEAD	redhead, roodharige, rooie
SHOPAHOLIC	shopaholic, koopverslaafde
SOULMATE	soulmate, zielsgenoot, zielsvriend, zielsverwant, hartsvriend, boezemvriend
SUFFRAGETTE	suffragette
SURVIVOR_EXPEDIT	survivor, overlever
SURVIVOR_LITERAL	survivor, overlevende, overlever
SURVIVOR_METAPH	survivor, overlever
SURVIVOR_COURAGE	survivor, overlever, doorzetter, volhouder
TEAMPLAYER	teamplayer, teamspeler, samenwerker, groepsspeler
TEENAGER	teenager, tiener
TOMBOY	tomboy, jongensmeisje
TWEN	twen, twintiger
UNDERDOG	underdog

deviance

BITCH	bitch, cunt, teef, kreng, feeks, kutwijf, secreet
CALLGIRL	callgirl, luxeprostituee, luxehoer, belprostituee, *sekshostess*
CHICKEN	chicken, coward, bangschijterd, schijtlaars, angsthaas, bangerd, bangerik, lafaard, *bloodaard*
COPYCAT	copycat, nabootser, na-aper
DRUGSRUNNER	drugsrunner, pusher, *gebruiksronselaar, gebruikswerver*
FREAK_DRUGS	freak, harddrugsgebruiker
FREAK_SOCIETY	freak, weirdo, zonderling, excentriekeling
GANGSTER	gangster, bendelid
GUNMAN	gunman, hitman, huurmoordenaar, beroepsmoordenaar, *bravo*
HOOKER	hooker, whore, prostituee, hoer
JOYRIDER	joyrider, joyrijder, sluikrijder, *jatrijder, roofrijder*
JUNK_DRUGS	junk, junkie, drugsverslaafde
KIDNAPPER	kidnapper, ontvoerder
LOSER	loser, mislukkeling
MOTHERFUCKER	motherfucker, asshole, klootzak, lul, smeerlap, rotzak
NIGGER	nigger, nikker, neger, zwartjoekel
OUTLAW	outlaw, vogelvrijverklaarde
PICKPOCKET	pickpocket, zakkenroller, *escomateur*
PIMP	pimp, pooier, souteneur, bikker
REDNECK	redneck
SNIPER	sniper, sluipschutter, scherpschutter

STALKER	stalker, dwangvolger
STREAKER	streaker, flitser
WARLORD	warlord, krijgsheer
WISEGUY	wiseguy, betweter, wijsneus, pedant
SKINHEAD	skinhead, skin

Acknowledgements

The authors wish to thank two anonymous reviewers for their useful suggestions. They would also like to thank Jack Grieve for proof-reading the paper. This study was supported by a personal grant by FWO Flanders.

What constructional profiles reveal about synonymy: A case study of Russian words for SADNESS and HAPPINESS

*Laura A. Janda and Valery D. Solovyev**

Abstract

We test two hypotheses relevant to the form-meaning relationship and offer a methodological contribution to the empirical study of near-synonymy within the framework of cognitive linguistics. In addition, we challenge implicit assumptions about the nature of the paradigm, which we show is skewed in favor of a few forms that are prototypical for a given lexical item. If one accepts the claim of construction grammar that the construction is the relevant unit of linguistic analysis, then we should expect to find a relationship between the meanings of words and the constructions they are found in. One way to investigate this expectation is by examining the meaning of constructions on the basis of their lexical profile; this line of research is pursued in collostructional analyses. We have taken a different approach, examining the meaning of near-synonyms on the basis of what we call their "constructional profile". We define a constructional profile as the frequency distribution of the constructions that a word appears in. Constructional profiles for Russian nouns denoting SADNESS *and* HAPPINESS *are presented, based upon corpus data, and analyzed quantitatively (using chi square and hierarchical cluster analysis). The findings are compared to the introspective analyses offered in synonym dictionaries.*

Keywords: synonymy; Construction Grammar; corpus data; Russian.

1. Introduction

There are many ways to investigate the relationship between form and meaning. This study explores the relationship between the meaning of a

---

*   Correspondence address: Laura A. Janda, University of Tromsoe, Institutt for språkvitenskap, UiT, 9037 Tromsø, Norway. Authors' e-mails: ⟨laura.janda@uit.no⟩; ⟨maki.solovyev@mail.ru⟩.

noun and both the range and frequency of constructions that a noun appears in. We introduce the term "constructional profile" to describe the distribution of constructions associated with a given noun. There are two hypotheses: 1) Each noun will have a unique constructional profile, and 2) Similarity of meaning is correlated with similarity of constructional profile. The second hypothesis entails the expectation that closer synonyms will have constructional profiles that are more similar than synonyms that are further apart, and synonyms will have more similar constructional profiles than semantically unrelated words.

The grammar of a case language (in which case is obligatory and morphologically marked in noun phrases) facilitates the operationalization of the hypotheses by providing objective measures to distinguish constructions, namely case markings and prepositions. Corpus data can be used to determine the distribution of constructions, and quantitative techniques can be applied to analyze these measures. Thus this study fulfills the criteria for "state of the art" corpus-oriented usage-based linguistics (Geeraerts 2005; Tummers et al. 2005).

Both the focus on morphology and the focus on the noun phrase set the present study apart from most work that has been done on meaning and constructions. Feldman (2006: 260–261, 318) notes that, aside from intonation and gesture, there are three mechanisms for conveying semantic relations in language, and they are: 1) words, 2) word order, 3) word form (inflection). Feldman points out that work in linguistics has been preponderantly based on English, and "this helps explain why much less attention has been paid to morphology as a source of meaning than to words and word order". Feldman's comment about the bias toward non-inflected languages is applicable to work in construction grammar, though there are some notable exceptions (Barðdal 1999 and 2006; Fried 2005). While Goldberg's work involves verb phrases and indeed most work in construction grammar is restricted to verb phrases, Goldberg (2006: 5, 221) acknowledges that "[a]ll levels of grammatical analysis involve constructions" and that constructions can profile units other than verbs. By using constructional profiles to probe the behavior of synonyms, this study also departs from the tradition of relying on lexical collocations to examine related meanings (cf. Kilgarriff 1997; Ide and Véronis 1998; Kobricov 2004; and Budanitsky et al. 2006).

We use emotion terms to test the "constructional profile" method for a number of reasons. One reason is that emotion terms are abstract and thus should be less prone to select the constructions they appear in based on ontological types. A concrete noun denoting a SURFACE, for example, would be predisposed to occur in constructions for 'onto', 'on' and 'off of'[1]. Emotion terms lack direct physical correlates that would limit the data in this way, presenting more complex constructional profiles. Secondly, emotion words have traditionally been a focus of attention in both cognitive linguistics and Slavic linguistics (Apresjan 1993; Dziwirek forthcoming; Dziwirek and Lewandowska-Tomaszczyk 2003; Kövecses 2001; Lakoff and Johnson 1980; Levontina and Zalizniak 2001; Mostovaja 1998; Radden 1998; Wierzbicka 1998 and 1999), primarily due to their metaphorical nature and the various ways they are understood in different languages. Finally, there is some disagreement among synonym dictionaries (Abramov 1994; Aleksandrova 1989; Apresjan et al. 1997; Evgen'eva 2001; Švedova 2003) concerning the grouping of the Russian 'sadness' terms. The various proposals in these sources constitute hypotheses that can be tested using constructional profiles as a measure.

Russian lacks an umbrella term that would be equivalent to the English word *sadness*, relying instead on a series of synonyms: *grust'*, *melanxolija*, *pečal'*, *toska*, *unynie*, and *xandra*. There are clearly differences among the meanings of these words for 'sadness', since it is possible for native speakers to produce sentences like this one:

Uxodiš', i ja gljažu vsled tebe s grust'ju, no bez toski.[2]
[Depart, and I-Nom look following you-Dat with sadness-Inst, but without sadness-Gen.]
'You leave and I watch you go with sadness$_{grust'}$, but without sadness$_{toska}$.'

As this example suggests, SADNESS$_{grust'}$ is the kind of sadness that is associated with grief, whereas SADNESS$_{toska}$ is the sadness associated with yearning. However, such contrastive examples are rare, and conclusions of this sort are subjective and introspective. This study uses constructional profiles of the Russian SADNESS terms as an objective measure to probe the relationships among synonyms. The behavior of the SADNESS terms is further compared with that of a series of antonyms denoting HAPPINESS: *likovanie*, *naslaždenie*, *radost'*, *udovol'stvie*, and *vostorg*.

This article is organized as follows. Section 2 gives an overview of relevant scholarly contributions to synonymy and the relatedness of word meanings, both outside of and within the framework of cognitive linguistics. Section 3 addresses the theoretical assumptions made on the basis of construction grammar and defines the term "constructional profile". The

---

1. The constructional profile of the SURFACE noun *stul* 'chair' suggests that it does indeed occur predominantly in precisely these constructions, cf. Section 4.3.
2. A. A. Bestužev-Marlinskij. *On byl ubit.* (1835–1836). All examples are cited from the Russian National Corpus (www.ruscorpora.ru).

methodology is presented in Section 4, along with illustrative examples of constructional profiles. Section 5 undertakes the analysis of the constructional profiles for the Russian SADNESS terms, and compares them to those of the HAPPINESS antonyms. Conclusions and possible additional uses for constructional profiles are offered in Section 6, which is followed by an Appendix presenting the data used in the quantitative analyses.

2. Approaches to synonymy and relatedness of meanings

Of course the idea that a word's use is indicative of its meaning is not new, since it can be traced to the works of many linguists (among them Meillet, Bloomfield, and Harris, cf. Ide and Véronis 1998: 23 and others cited below). This section presents a brief overview of relevant scholarly works on synonymy and related problems (polysemy, acquisition of word meanings). For the sake of organization, the discussion is broken down into three sections representing different linguistic approaches, although there is some overlap among them. This discussion is intended to be representative rather than exhaustive.

2.1. Computational linguistics

Computational linguists have developed an impressive array of programs designed to detect and even "learn" how to disambiguate polysemous words and recognize synonyms (two closely related problems in Word Sense Disambiguation, WSD). The majority of work in WSD has followed Firth's (1957: 11) maxim "You shall know a word by the company it keeps", thus focusing on word co-occurrence data to determine word senses and their relative "distance". Such algorithms typically look at a node word and the window of x words (for example, if $x = 3$, the window would include three words to the left and three to the right) that surround it in all its occurrences in a corpus and then compare this measure to that of other words. In most WSD studies, grammatical information (syntax, morphology, word order) is not taken into account, although there is some indication that the algorithms are sensitive to grammatical facts such as word class (Burgess et al. 1998). Where grammatical information has been included, this has typically been limited to identification of part of speech (Ide and Véronis 1998: 20). Latent Semantic Analysis (LSA; Landauer et al. 1998) computes the aggregate of all the contexts that a given word appears and does not appear in and represents this as a high-dimensional "semantic space". LSA is a significant improvement over many earlier methods which relied on dictionaries and manually-crafted semantic networks; its only input is raw text parsed into words and passages. Though LSA can mimic some human activities (synonymy and word relatedness tests), it also makes some odd judgments (e.g., that English *verbally* and *sadomasochism* are closely related). Burgess et al. (1998) offer the Hyperspace Analogue to Language (HAL), which likewise computes the statistical co-occurrence patterns of words, depicted as multidimensional scaling solutions, and one of the conclusions is that synonyms do indeed occur in the same contexts. Dagan (2000) offers another solution, one that features semi-automatic thesaurus construction procedures based on corpus statistics. Like LSA and HAL, Dagan's model is based entirely on word co-occurrence vectors; it is claimed that there is no adequate parser that would make it possible to include grammatical information (Dagan 2000: 462). Turney (2002, 2005) has worked on two further options, Pointwise Mutual Information (PMI) and Latent Relational Analysis (LRA), which have been tested against items from the TOEFL and SAT tests, respectively. Though the LRA has a grammatical component, both are based primarily on word co-occurrence data. Kilgarriff (1997), Ide and Véronis (1998), Kobricov (2004), and Budanitsky et al. (2006) provide overviews of the trajectory of research in WSD. Their conclusions are rather disappointing, despite the variety and computational sophistication of the models devised. Nouns in particular have been most resistant to WSD (Ide and Véronis 1998: 21). Both Kilgarriff (1997) and Ide and Véronis (1998) make the point that despite computational advances, one of the crucial theoretical issues, namely defining what a word sense is, remains unresolved, and this has severely hampered progress, particularly since the underlying assumption is usually that word senses are discrete and independent of corpora. Kilgarriff (1997) and Budanitsky et al. (2006) cite work on polysemy and metaphor (specifically Apresjan 1974; Lakoff and Johnson 1980; and Lakoff 1987), arguing that if word senses do not behave as classical categories, and can also be influenced by ad-hoc categories, then it is very unclear how such "semantic relationships could be quantified in any meaningful way, let alone compared with prior quantifications of the classical and nonclassical relationships" (Budanitsky et al. 2006: 45). Ide and Véronis (1998: 27) conclude that "relatively little progress seems to have been made in nearly 50 years" and "it appears that we may have nearly reached the limit of what can be achieved in the current framework". Kobricov's (2004) evaluation is nearly identical, stating that even when good accuracy has been achieved, it applies only to a very small group of words, and that the best descriptor for the state of the art is "stagnation".

In sum, computational approaches to synonymy and polysemy are invested primarily in observing lexical collocations, largely to the exclusion of syntactic information. These approaches have achieved limited results, and have proved least useful in work on nouns.

2.2. Bootstrapping and frames

Bootstrapping approaches (Gleitman and Gillette 1995; Lidz et al. 2001) are concerned with how the meanings of words are acquired and stored and what role syntactic information plays in this process. At issue is the fact that verbs are relatively abstract: you often can't point to a real-world action, and the uses of verbs are often asynchronous with corresponding actions (Gleitman and Gillette 1995: 415). Furthermore, many verbs are synonymous, and speakers are able to distinguish among near-synonyms. The hypothesis is that syntactic range information makes it possible for learners to fix the meaning of novel verbs. Syntactic range information specifies what types of constructions a verb typically appears in, without reference to relative frequency. Two series of psycholinguistic experiments (Gleitman and Gillette 1995; Lidz et al. 2001) support this hypothesis, with evidence that both children and adults use systematic structural information in order to interpret English verbs. Dąbrowska (forthcoming) further argues, on the basis of experiments with English verbs of walking and running, that syntactic range information is supplemented by speaker's knowledge of collocational patterns in distinguishing the meanings of close synonyms.

The lexicographic research that serves as the basis for FrameNet has developed a sophisticated means of analyzing semantic frames, linking "the meaning of words very explicitly to the syntactic contexts in which those words occur" (Atkins et al. 2003: 253). This approach, like bootstrapping, focuses on identifying the range of syntactic constructions in which a word occurs, in addition to the collocational preferences. Frame elements focus mostly on the behavior of verbs and can yield subtle analyses of synonyms.

2.3. Behavioral profiles and collostructions

Karlsson (1985, 1986) observed, on the basis of Finnish data, that in a language with complex inflectional morphology, the majority of forms in a given paradigm are unattested or of very low frequency in a corpus. Most paradigms are instantiated by a fairly small number of stereotypic forms that are the "morphological analogues of the prototypes in Rosch's theory of word meaning" (Karlsson 1985: 150). This observation has important implications, since most theories (cf. Karlsson's overview 1985: 137) assume that a paradigm is normally fully populated, and rule-based theories assume that all forms in a paradigm are generated by rules in an equiprobable fashion. The skewed frequency profiles found in Finnish led Karlsson (1986: 28) to assert that speakers probably use a combination of lexical storage and "rules" in relation to paradigms, a conclusion that comports well with the basic tenets of cognitive linguistics (cf. Dąbrowska 2004: 7–27; Croft and Cruse 2004: 291–327). Though Karlsson (1986: 27) does claim that the Finnish data show "how meaning properties are reflected in the use of forms", his conclusions are restricted to differences among broad classes of words. According to Karlsson, for example, mass nouns, count nouns, and proper nouns behave differently from each other as groups, but verbs are fairly homogeneous. Whereas Karlsson stopped short of implying that frequency profiles might provide finer-grained distinctions within types of nouns or synonyms, Arppe, also working on Finnish data (but with a larger corpus and more sophisticated software), has found that there are indeed differences among different types of mass nouns (Arppe 2001), and there are differences even among the near-synonyms meaning THINK (Arppe 2005).

Synonyms have been the focus of attention in the use of behavioral profiles (Atkins 1987; Hanks 1996), which can combine a variety of types of information, not limited to collocational and syntactic preferences. Geeraerts (1988) pioneered synonymy research in cognitive linguistics, comparing 19th century uses of two Dutch verbs meaning DESTROY. Geeraerts' study incorporates collocational, constructional, semantic and metaphorical data and uses corpus data to corroborate introspective analyses found in synonym dictionaries. Divjak and Gries (Divjak 2006; Divjak and Gries 2006; and Gries and Divjak forthcoming) tagged 87 variables (morphosyntactic, syntactic and semantic) in order to establish the behavioral profiles of Russian verbs meaning TRY and calculate the "distances" among near-synonyms. Glynn (forthcoming) applies a similar approach to investigate the semantic relationships within the polysemy of a single word ("parasynonyms" of English *hassle*), tagging corpus examples and performing a quantitative analysis. Collostructional analysis (Stefanowitsch and Gries 2003, 2005) takes the construction as the point of departure, investigating the range and frequency of words that appear in the construction. A related strategy is metaphorical pattern analysis (Stefanowitsch 2006 a and b; Svanlund 2007), which can compare the metaphorical uses (based on the constructions) that near-synonyms appear in.

2.4. *Relationship of constructional profiles to previous research*

Most previous studies of synonyms focus on verbs, whereas the present study examines nouns. Unlike the approaches undertaken in computational linguistics, we define comparisons syntactically, in terms of constructions, instead of lexically, in terms of collocated words. Our approach can be understood as a reversal of the perspective of collostructional analysis, an option that has been proposed for future research (Stefanowitsch and Gries 2003: 237), but not yet pursued. This fresh perspective is facilitated by the fact that Russian is a case-marking language, making it possible to collect data with no subjective tagging component, based on the objective presence of morphological features. Bootstrapping and frame approaches focus on the range of syntactic contexts that a word appears in; our study additionally presents the frequencies of occurrence for relevant syntactic contexts.

3. Construction Grammar

We use the term *construction* in a way that is compatible with current usage in cognitive linguistics, in other words as used by Langacker (1987, 1990, 1991), Croft (2001), Goldberg (1995 and 2006), and Fillmore (Fillmore 1985; Kay and Fillmore 1999; Fillmore et al. forthcoming). Although some differences in the usage of *construction* among these scholars must be acknowledged (cf. Langacker 2003; and Goldberg 2006: 213–226), these points are less relevant to our analysis than the ideas that all three share, so we will focus on their common ground, ignoring minor discrepancies.

Our definition of construction is: "a conventionalized pairing of form and meaning in a language". This definition is closest in its phrasing to Goldberg's (2006: 3), yet consistent in spirit with Langacker's (1987: 58) "symbolic unit" which pairs form (phonological pole) with meaning (semantic pole).

Our constructions are of the form: "$[(preposition)\ [\underline{NOUN}]_{case}]$". This formula states that case is obligatory in all constructions, but only some constructions also involve a preposition. This formula states that the noun elaborates (Langacker 1987: 68; 304–305) the construction that is schematically specified by the case and preposition by filling the placeholder for the noun. Because the noun is the variable part of the construction, we often use a short-hand formula, stating the components "*case*" or "*preposition + case*". For each construction, this form is paired with a meaning that is only partially determined by the meanings of the components. The meaning of each construction is emergent (Langacker 1991: 5–6, 534; Bybee and Hopper 2001: 2, 10; MacWhinney 2001), motivated by the patterns of uses over the various nouns that appear in the construction, and also by the larger (clause-level) constructions that these noun phrase constructions appear in. Our analysis gives empirical substance to the claims made by Raxilina (2000) that Russian nouns can serve as constructional cores, and that the meaning of a noun is partly a function of the constructions it is found in. This analysis is also in harmony with the traditions of the Moscow semantic school (Apresjan 1995; Mel'čuk 2001) and the school of "Logical Analysis of Language" (Arutjunova 2007), which likewise assert that combinatorial properties of nouns reveal the cognitive structure of nominal semantics.

It is unlikely that speakers store all uses of given words and constructions, but there is evidence that people use generalizations about the frequency of word use (Goldberg 2006: 62, 46). These generalizations can serve as the basis for creating abstract schemas for constructions, establishing correlations between form and meaning. Goldberg (2006: 104–119) argues that constructions have strong associations with meaning by virtue of their advantages in terms of both cue validity and category validity. Cue validity refers to the likelihood that a given meaning will be present given the presence of a certain item. In a study comparing the cue validity of words (verbs) with constructions, Goldberg found that words and constructions have roughly equal cue validity, which means that knowing that a linguistic unit contains a given word gives you about the same predictive information as knowing that a linguistic unit occurs in a given construction. However, because there are far fewer constructions than lexical items in a language, constructions are far more available in terms of determining meaning. Category validity is the likelihood that a certain item will be present when the meaning is already given. In Goldberg's studies the category validity of constructions is found to be far higher than that of words (verbs). In other words, if you know that a unit expresses a certain meaning, it is much easier to predict what construction might be present than to predict what word the unit might contain. Goldberg has thus empirically established the connections between constructions, frequency and meaning. Although Goldberg's work focuses on verbs as construction cores, we argue that her conclusions are applicable to noun phrases, particularly in languages that mark case.

The morphological marking on Russian nouns makes them much more information-rich in terms of specifying what construction is present than English nouns. Kempe and MacWhinney (1999) have established, based on psycholinguistic data, that case in Russian has high cue validity and high cue availability, even relative to another case-marking language (German), and that Russian speakers do rely on case in on-line sentence interpretation. On this basis we assert that Goldberg's claims for the relationships between constructions and verbs in English are applicable to nouns in Russian as well.

3.1. Constructional profiles

A *constructional profile* is a property of a word. *Constructional profile* can be defined as: "the relative frequency distribution of constructions that a given word appears in". In other words, let us say that the word LEXEME can appear in constructions $C_1 \ldots C_n$. In order to arrive at LEXEME's constructional profile, it is necessary to gather data on the frequency of LEXEME's occurrence in each of the constructions $C_1 \ldots C_n$ and to compare those frequencies as percentages of LEXEME's overall occurrence (a.k.a. the "reliance" metric, cf. Schmid 2000: 54). LEXEME's constructional profile is thus a chart showing that LEXEME occurs X% of the time in construction C_1, Y% of the time in construction C_2, Z% of the time in construction C_3, etc. through C_n. Each percentage indicates how frequent the given construction is for the given word in a particular corpus, and the aggregate of percentages indicates the degree to which that noun is associated with that particular pattern. Constructional frequency data is extracted from corpora that are designed to reflect the parameters of a given language. In practice, there are often many constructions associated with a given word, and most occur at very low frequencies. Based on the data in our study, usually only 6–10 constructions are needed to accurately represent the constructional profile of a word.

Constructional profiles can be likened to flavors. Flavors are composite values of the variables that our tongue and nose can perceive (Churchland 1995). In other words, a flavor such as apricot is a collection of peaks with various values that differs from other collections of peaks such as the one associated with peach. A word's constructional profile is probably unique and representative of its meaning, though there are certainly other factors, such as: the embodied contexts in which a word is used, the knowledge structures (frames; cf. Fillmore 1982) it is associated with, its collocational patterns, and transparent etymological or derivational relationships to other words in the lexicon.

It is tempting to consider a possible relationship between constructional profiles and entrenchment, given assumptions that have been made about increases in neural connections as a function of frequency (Langacker 1987: 59–60, 100, 380; Langacker 1991: 45; Bybee and Hopper 2001: 9; Taylor 2002: 276; Dąbrowska 2004: 213, 223; Feldman 2006: 105). This connection is expressed most explicitly in Schmid's (2000: 39) From-Corpus-To-Cognition Principle: "Frequency in text instantiates entrenchment in the cognitive system". Some recent work (Schmid 2007, forthcoming; Gilquin 2007a and b) has pointed out that corpus frequency may be an imperfect measure of entrenchment. Given these reservations, we remain agnostic and make no claims concerning a connection between constructional profiles and entrenchment.

Russian has six cases marked by means of synthetic inflectional endings: Nominative (Nom), Accusative (Acc), Dative (Dat), Instrumental (Inst), Genitive (Gen), and Locative (Loc). Since every noun phrase obligatorily expresses one of these cases[3], a noun phrase will always carry with it the syntactic and semantic information associated with the given case. The Russian cases present a complex system with dozens of submeanings. However, Janda and co-authors (Janda 1993, 1999, 2000, 2002 a–d, 2004, forthcoming; Janda and Clancy 2002; Divjak and Janda 2008) have established that each Russian case forms a coherent semantic whole. In keeping with the above-cited research on Russian case, we will assume that case is the primary marker of the meaning of a syntactic relationship and that prepositions, where present, elaborate those meanings, forming a composite structure that shows conceptual integration (Langacker 2003). All of the Russian cases can appear with various prepositions and five of them can appear without a preposition. The various combinations of case with and without prepositions yield seventy potential constructions of the form *[(preposition) [NOUN]$_{case}$]* for any given noun in Russian (Janda and Clancy 2002).

4. Methodology

The corpora from which data were extracted and the methodology used in the process are described below, illustrated by an example of the results and how they are presented in this article.

4.1. *Corpora*

Our study extracted data from two corpora, the Russian National Corpus (http://www.ruscorpora.ru; henceforth RNC) with over 120 million words, and the Biblioteka Maksima Moškova (http://lib.ru/; henceforth BMM) with over 600 million words. Both corpora consist exclusively of authentic texts produced by and for native speakers, and their contents have been edited for typographical accuracy. One major difference between the two corpora is that the RNC has been designed to reflect a greater range of genres, including samples of popular written and spoken

---

3. Some indeclinable nouns, such as *kino* 'cinema' constitute an exception to this rule, though all numerals, adjectives, determiners and pronouns that modify such nouns bear the appropriate case marking. This indicates that for such nouns case is present, though the entire paradigm may be syncretic.

Russian, whereas the BMM is literally an electronic library of primarily literary works.

A pilot study was conducted to determine how many sentences would be needed for constructional profiles and to compare results across and within corpora. That study indicated that 500 sentences for each noun would yield sufficient results that were reliably stable for the corpora (the vast majority of data differed by a fraction of a percentage point or less, with the ceiling of differences at about two percentage points).

4.2. *Data extraction*

500 sample sentences were extracted for each word in the study in order to determine each noun's constructional profile. The pertinent noun phrase construction (the one containing the queried word) in each sentence was analyzed manually, and the case of every queried noun was recorded along with the identity of any associated preposition. The analyses were conducted by students in the Linguistics Department at the University of Kazan'. In principle it would be possible to have the analysis done by machine, but there is no automatic parser of Russian at present with sufficient accuracy. This does not mean, however, that any subjective judgments were involved. On the contrary, the identity of the case a noun appears in is unambiguous in Russian despite a small amount of paradigmatic syncretism. In rare instances where there might be some confusion, a native speaker can easily recover the case by asking the relevant Who?/What? question, which gives a unique answer for each case (*Kto?*/*Čto?* for Nominative, *Kogo?*/*Čto?* for Accusative, etc.). The task was simple and objective, the analyses were carried out by linguists in training on their native language, and the results were virtually error-free.

Once the data was collected and analyzed, the scope of the search could be narrowed down to target the most valuable results. A given noun can usually appear in a fairly large number of constructions, but most of these are of such low frequency (<1%) that they contribute little information about the noun's overall constructional profile. On the other hand, there are some constructions that appear in fairly high frequencies (e.g., Nominative subject, adnominal Genitive), but do not give much information about aspects of a noun's constructional profile because virtually any noun can appear in those constructions. The search was thus narrowed to those sentences in which the noun appeared as a non-subject argument of the verb or as an adverbial. This made it possible to focus on the noun phrase constructions that were most relevant to the verb. Thus from the original 500 sentences, only the sentences where the queried word appeared as a non-Nominative argument or adverbial were analyzed further, and all frequencies are based upon the remaining number of sentences for a given word (usually in excess of 70% of the original 500). From these data it is possible to pinpoint which constructions are most representative of a word's constructional profile to present their frequencies. The Direct Object construction is fairly frequent for most nouns, and data on that construction is included in calculations, but not in figures, to highlight the constructions that are most relevant.

4.3. *Sample analysis*

Figure 1 gives the constructional profiles of one SADNESS noun, *pečal'* and three non-synonymous nouns: *stul* 'chair', *utka* 'duck', and *mečta* 'dream' (data is presented in tables in the Appendix).

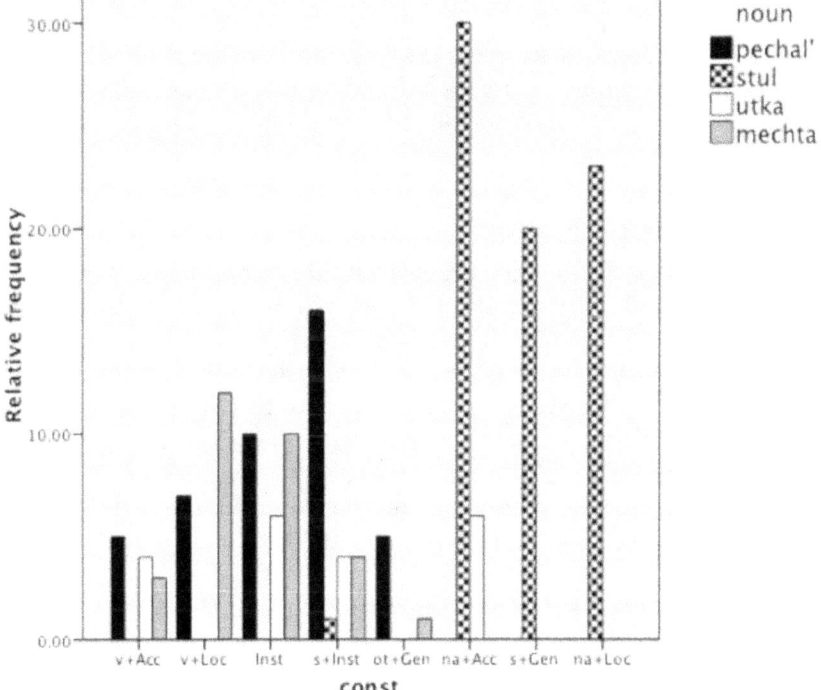

Figure 1. *Constructional profiles of non-synonyms*

We see that the both the range and relative frequencies of the constructions associated with these nouns differ. The relevant constructions can be paraphrased as follows: *v*+Acc 'into/at', *v*+Loc 'in(side)', Inst 'by means of/as', *s*+Inst 'with', *ot*+Gen '(away) from', *na*+Acc 'onto', *s*+Gen 'off of', *na*+Loc 'on'. The two abstract nouns, *pečal'* and *mečta*, share the range of constructions, appearing in the first five constructions (though in different frequencies), but not in the last three. *Utka* 'duck' is found in the *v*+Acc, Inst, *s*+Inst, and *na*+Acc constructions. *Stul* 'chair' is dominated by *na*+Acc, *s*+Gen and *na*+Loc. The chi square value of 1014.8 is highly significant (p < 0.0001 for df = 27), indicating that these differences cannot be attributed to chance. Furthermore, the Cramer's V (indicating the strength of the chi square effect) is 0.495, which qualifies as a large effect (cf. King and Minium 2008).

5. Case studies

The constructional profiles of the Russian nouns for SADNESS and HAPPINESS are presented in figures and subjected to statistical analyses. Chi square results ensure that the effects are not the result of chance and hierarchical cluster analysis measures the "distances" between words, indicating which near-synonyms are closer and which are farther apart. The latter results can be used to corroborate the groupings found in synonym dictionaries.

5.1. *Russian nouns for* SADNESS

Russian synonym dictionaries struggle with this set of nouns. Most often, *pečal'*, *toska*, and *grust'* are placed in one group, characterized as denoting the unpleasant feeling one has when one wants something one doesn't have and doesn't believe one can get it' (Apresjan et al. 1997). *Melanxolija* and *xandra* are listed as another group, and then there is disagreement over what to do with *unynie*. Apresjan et al. (1997) groups *unynie* with *pečal'*, Aleksandrova (1989) puts *unynie* with *xandra* and Evgen'eva (2001) puts *unynie* with both *grust'* and *xandra*, claiming that it has two meanings. Švedova (2003) unites *unynie* with *grust'*, *xandra* and *melanxolija*.

The constructional profiles of these words both confirm the overall pattern suggested in synonym dictionaries and explain why there is a problem with *unynie*. Figure 2 shows the constructional profiles for the SADNESS nouns.

The relevant constructions are: *v*+Acc 'into/at', *v*+Loc 'in(side)', Inst 'by means of/as', *s*+Inst 'with', *ot*+Gen '(away) from'. The constructional profiles provide a variety of information on the behavior of the SADNESS synonyms. To begin with, these six nouns all show the same range of constructions in their profiles, which was not the case for the non-synonymous nouns in Figure 1. Though the range is shared, the dis-

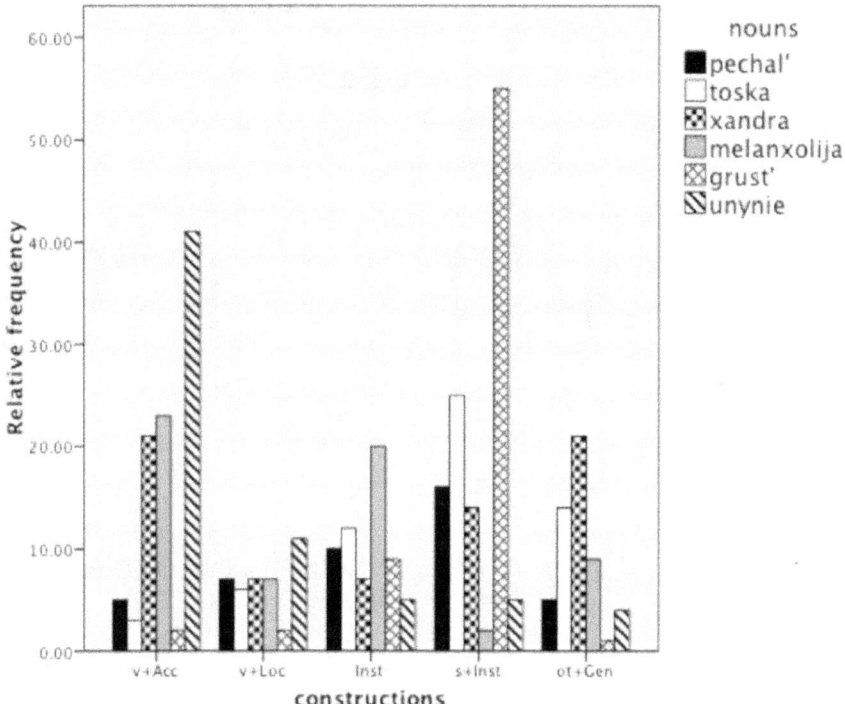

Figure 2. *Constructional profiles of* SADNESS *nouns*

tributions within this range are significantly different, as demonstrated by the chi square value which is 730.35, and the Cramer's V of 0.305 which qualifies as a moderate effect (p < 0.0001, df = 30 for both values). If we compare these results to the results for the non-synonyms, we see that though nouns in both groups are significantly different from each other, the chi square and effect values are greater for the non-synonyms than for the synonyms.

Next we notice patterns within the data: *pečal'* and *toska* have similar values for the first three constructions, but dissimilar ones for the last two. *Xandra* and *melanxolija* have similar values for the first two constructions, but dissimilar values for the last two. *Grust'* and *unynie* look like outliers: *grust'* is dominated by the *s*+Inst 'with' construction, whereas *unynie* gives the highest values in the group for the *v*+Acc 'into/at' and *v*+Loc 'in(side)' constructions.

The suggestion that some near-synonyms are closer to each other than others can be tested mathematically, using hierarchical cluster analysis to measure this pheonomenon in terms of squared Euclidian distances (cf. proximity table in the Appendix). By this metric, the closest SADNESS

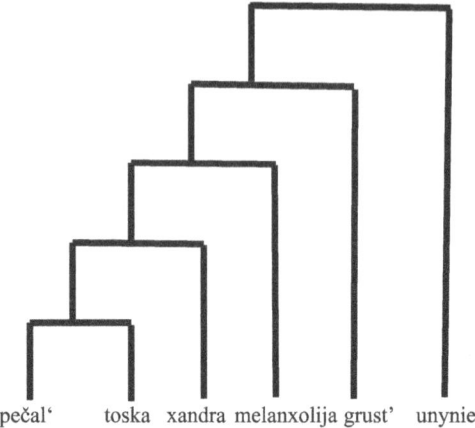

pečal'   toska xandra melanxolija grust'   unynie

Figure 3.   *Hierarchical cluster of* SADNESS *nouns*

synonyms are *pečal'* and *toska* (separated by 5.844), the next closest item is *xandra* (7.968), followed closely by *melanxolija* (8.041). *Grust'* (11.705) joins the group next, followed by *unynie* (12.798). These proximity values yield the hierarchical cluster in Figure 3.

In comparing the constructional profiles with the groupings in synonym dictionaries, we see that the grouping of *pečal'* with *toska* and *melanxolija* with *xandra* is well-justified. The difficulty with *unynie* is unsurprising, since it is indeed the most extreme outlier in the group.

5.2. Russian nouns for HAPPINESS

Antonyms are words that are virtually identical to each other in terms of what domain they refer to and what they profile within that domain, but have opposite values for some part of their meaning (Croft and Cruse 2004: 164–192). Both SADNESS and HAPPINESS are states involving human emotions evaluated on a scale of wellbeing, so their meanings are in many ways similar. In Russian, it turns out that the same set of constructions is most relevant for both groups of synonyms, making it easy to compare these groups of nouns.

Synonym dictionaries are less clear in making distinctions among these nouns. Where distinctions are made, it appears that *vostorg* is treated as the outlier: Aleksandrova (1989) defines all the other happiness nouns in terms of each other while setting *vostorg* apart, whereas Švedova 2003 places *naslaždenie, radost'*, and *udovol'stvie* in one group and *likovanie* and *vostorg* in another.

Figure 4 presents the constructional profiles of the HAPPINESS nouns.

What constructional profiles reveal about synonymy 311

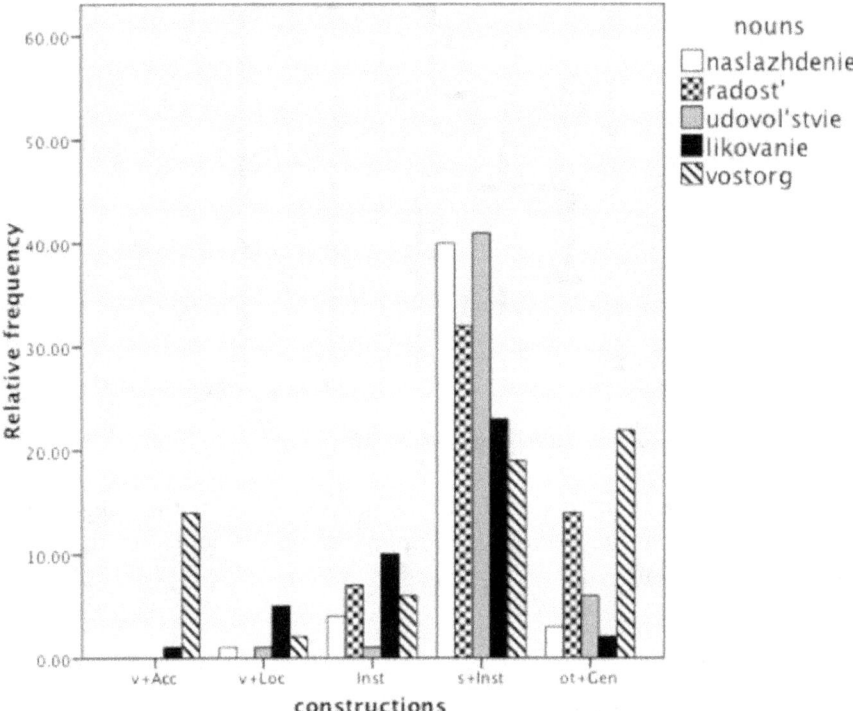

Figure 4. *Constructional profiles of* HAPPINESS *nouns*

The chi square value of 469.4, Cramer's V of 0.264 (p < 0.0001, df = 24) indicate that these nouns are significantly different from each other, though the effect is slightly less than for the SADNESS nouns. The constructional profiles corroborate the patterns in the synonym dictionaries. *Naslaždenie*, *radost'*, and *udovol'stvie* do indeed pattern similarly, with zero or low values for the first three constructions, a peak at the fourth and lower values again for the last construction. *Vostorg* behaves like an outlier, with high values for the first, fourth, and fifth construction. *Likovanie* appears to fall somewhere between the first group and *vostorg*, for it is the only other noun with a non-zero value for the first construction, has its peak with the fourth construction and then a low value for the last one. This grouping is also confirmed by the hierarchical cluster analysis (cf. proximity table in Appendix), which finds *naslaždenie* and *radost'* as the closest synonyms (separated by 3.512), closely followed by *udovol'stvie* (3.979). Further out lie *likovanie* (9.632) and finally *vostorg* (13.22). The proximity values yield the hierarchical cluster in Figure 5.

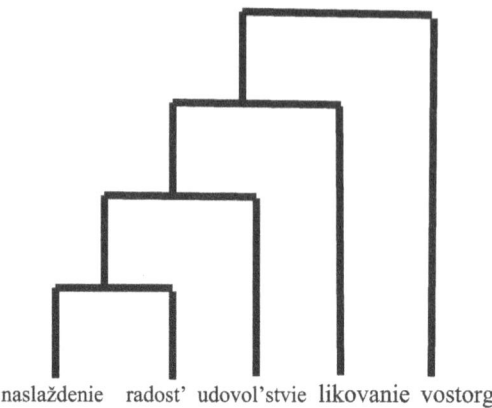
naslaždenie   radost'   udovol'stvie   likovanie   vostorg

Figure 5. *Herarchical cluster of* HAPPINESS *nouns*

Once again, the constructional profiles largely confirm the suggestions made by synonym dictionaries while pinpointing the source of disagreements among them.

6. Conclusions

We present the constructional profile, the relative frequencies of constructions a word appears in, as a possible measure of a word's meaning. The constructional profile patterns of synonyms are shown to share a small group of constructions that they appear in most frequently. Differences in frequencies correspond to differences in "distance" between synonyms. Constructional profiles largely confirm the introspective judgments of dictionary authors, and in addition pinpoint where the differences among synonyms lie. Antonyms largely share the set of constructions they appear in and may show overlap in constructional profile patterns. Unrelated words share neither property. Constructional profiles provide an opportunity for empirical verification of hypotheses relevant to a usage-based approach to linguistics.

Constructional profiles may have potential use in exploring the metaphorical behavior of words, thus building upon current work on metaphorical pattern analysis (Stefanowitsch 2006 a and b; Svanlund 2007). It would be possible to compare the constructional profiles of concrete source domain nouns and corresponding nouns in a metaphorical target domain. The CONTAINER metaphor is often cited as relevant for the domain of emotions (Lakoff and Johnson 1980: 31–32; Kövecses 2001: 37), and constructions with verbs involving 'entering into' (usually by means of 'falling' or 'sinking into') an emotional state have been associated with SADNESS nouns in both Russian and Polish (Wierzbicka 1998: 11). It would be possible to test this connection empirically by finding the constructional profiles of a group of CONTAINER nouns and comparing them to the constructional profiles of emotion terms. The data here suggest that different nouns may behave differently in terms of their metaphorical extensions. Two constructions relevant for CONTAINERS, *v*+Acc 'into/at' and *v*+Loc 'in(side)' are more prominent among the SADNESS nouns, particularly *unynie*, followed by *melanxolija* and *xandra*, than among the HAPPINESS nouns, where they are relevant for *vostorg*. Indeed, these appear to be the emotions in Russian that one can get into or be in. Curiously, the corresponding construction for leaving a CONTAINER, namely *iz*+Gen 'out of', is absent from the constructional profiles of the SADNESS and HAPPINESS nouns (though isolated examples can be found in a corpus). The only conventional means for departing these emotional states seems to involve a DISEASE metaphor using the *ot*+Gen '(away) from' construction, as in this example:

Samoe lučšee lekarstvo <u>ot xandry</u> èto čtenie.[4]
[The best medicine-Nom <u>from sadness-Gen</u> that reading-Nom.]
'The best cure <u>for sadness</u> is reading.'

The observation that departing a state of SADNESS seems to invoke a DISEASE metaphor is something that might be tested empirically by comparing the constructional profiles of some typical DISEASE nouns with those of emotion terms. Another use of the *ot*+Gen '(away) from' construction often interprets the emotion as a metaphorical CAUSE, as in this example:

Podumajte, ètot čelovek umer <u>ot melanxolii</u>![5]
[Think, that person-Nom died <u>from sadness-Gen</u>!]
'Just imagine, that person died <u>of sadness</u>!'

Again, this observation could be tested empirically.

Other potential uses for constructional profiles involve language acquisition and the relationship between storage and rules in a usage-based grammar. Constructional profiles suggest that certain forms in a paradigm are more prototypical for a given word than others. These patterns

---

4. Paneva, A. Ja. *Vospominanija* (1889–1890).
5. Lidija Ginzburg. *Zapisnye knižki. Vospominanija. Èsse.* (1920–1943).

might correspond to order of acquisition among children and strategies for online use and interpretation among adults. Psycholinguistic experiments could test whether such correlations exist.

In sum, constructional profiles may prove to be a valuable metric for determining the relationship between meaning and use, and this metric may be used for a variety of investigations relevant to the usage-based model of cognitive linguistics.

Received 25 December 2007
Revision received 15 August 2008

University of Tromsø
University of Kazan

Appendix

The following three tables give both the raw and relative frequencies used in all the charts and calculations. "DO" stands for the Direct Object construction, and "other" stands for an aggregate of all other constructions.

Unlike nouns

	pečal' 'sadness'		*stul* 'chair'		*utka* 'duck'		*mečta* 'dream'	
v+Acc	16	5%	1	0%	16	4%	11	3%
v+Loc	22	7%	0	0%	0	0%	42	12%
Inst	32	10%	2	0%	23	6%	36	10%
s+Inst	49	16%	3	1%	15	4%	15	4%
ot+Gen	16	5%	2	0%	0	0%	4	1%
na+Acc	0	0%	108	30%	23	6%	0	0%
s+Gen	0	0%	70	20%	0	0%	0	0%
na+Loc	0	0%	82	23%	0	0%	0	0%
DO	128	41%	64	18%	246	66%	174	50%
other	52	17%	25	7%	49	13%	63	18%
Total	315	100%	358	100%	372	100%	345	100%

SADNESS nouns

	pečal'		*toska*		*xandra*		*melanxolija*		*grust'*		*unynie*	
v+Acc	16	5%	8	3%	30	21%	52	23%	6	2%	126	41%
v+Loc	22	7%	16	6%	10	7%	16	7%	6	2%	33	11%
Inst	32	10%	33	12%	10	7%	45	20%	27	9%	16	5%
s+Inst	49	16%	70	25%	19	14%	5	2%	160	55%	16	5%
ot+Gen	16	5%	39	14%	29	21%	20	9%	3	1%	14	4%
DO	128	41%	84	30%	20	14%	32	14%	50	17%	25	8%
other	52	17%	33	12%	22	16%	57	25%	38	13%	82	27%
Total	315	100%	283	100%	140	100%	227	100%	290	100%	304	100%

HAPPINESS nouns

	naslaždenie		radost'		udovol'stvie		likovanie		vostorg	
v+Acc	0	0%	0	0%	0	0%	4	1%	42	14%
v+Loc	3	1%	1	0%	4	1%	21	5%	35	12%
Inst	12	4%	21	7%	4	1%	39	10%	18	6%
s+Inst	117	40%	92	32%	165	41%	90	23%	58	19%
ot+Gen	9	3%	41	14%	24	6%	8	2%	66	22%
DO	111	38%	106	37%	171	42%	171	44%	67	22%
other	39	13%	24	8%	39	10%	59	15%	18	6%
Total	291	100%	285	100%	407	100%	392	100%	304	100%

The following two tables are proximity matrices stating the squared Euclidian distances that establish the hierarchical clusters. The relevant values are bold-faced.

SADNESS nouns

Case	Squared Euclidean Distance					
	1:grust'	2:melanx	3:pechal'	4:toska	5:unynie	6:xandra
1:grust'	0.000	14.235	11.705	12.762	27.415	13.662
2:melanx	14.235	0.000	8.041	8.226	12.798	11.715
3:pechal'	**11.705**	**8.041**	0.000	5.844	17.123	14.679
4:toska	12.762	8.226	**5.844**	0.000	23.880	7.968
5:unynie	27.415	**12.798**	17.123	23.880	0.000	19.949
6:xandra	13.662	11.715	14.679	**7.968**	19.949	0.000

HAPPINESS nouns

Case	Squared Euclidean Distance				
	1:likovani	2:naslazd	3:radost'	4:udovol's	5:vostorg
1:likovani	0.000	9.632	12.526	14.144	25.993
2:naslazd	**9.632**	0.000	3.512	3.979	20.455
3:radost'	12.526	**3.512**	0.000	8.550	13.220
4:udovol's	14.144	**3.979**	8.550	0.000	27.990
5:vostorg	25.993	20.455	**13.220**	27.990	0.000

References

Abramov, N.
    1994   *Slovar' russkix sinonimov i sxodnyx po smyslu vyraženij.* Moscow: Russie slovari.
Aleksandrova, Zinaida E.
    1989   *Slovar' sinonimov russkogo jazyka.* Moscow: Russkij jazyk.

Apresjan, Jurij D.
1974   Leksičeskaja semantika: sinonimičeskie sredstva jazyka. Moscow: Nauka.
Apresjan, Jurij D.
1993   Metafora v leksografičeskom tolkovanii èmocij. *Voprosy jazykoznanija* 3, 27–35.
Apresjan, Jurij D.
1995   Leksičeskaja semantika: Sinonimičeskie sredstva jazyka. Moskva: Jazyki russkoj kul'tury.
Apresjan, Jurij D., O. Ju. Boguslavskij, I. B. Levontina, E. V. Uryson, M. Ja. Glovinskaja, and T. V. Krylova
1997   *Novyj ob"jasnitel'nyj slovar' sinonimov russkogo jazyka,* Vyp. 1. Moscow: Jazyki russkoj kul'tury.
Arppe, Antti
2001   Focal points in frequency profiles—how some word forms in a paradigm are more significant than others in Finnish. In *Proceedings of the 6th Conference on Computational Lexicography and Corpus Research*, June 28–30, 2001, University of Birmingham, Birmingham, UK.
Arppe, Antti
2005   Morphological features as 'context' in distinguishing semantically similar words. In *Proceedings from the Corpus Linguistics Conference Series*, vol. 1, Third Biennial Corpus Linguistics 2005 Conference, July 14–17, 2005, Birmingham, UK.
Arutjunova, Nina D.
2007   *Predloženie i ego smysl*. Moscow: URSS.
Atkins, Beryl, T. S.
1987   Semantic ID tags: Corpus evidence for dictionary senses. In *Proceedings of the Third Annual Conference of the UW Centre for the New Oxford English Dictionary*, 17–36.
Atkins, Sue, Charles J. Fillmore, and Christopher R. Johnson
2003   Lexicographic relevance: Selecting information from corpus evidence. *International Journal of Lexicography* 16, 251–280.
Barðdal, Johanna
1999   Case in Icelandic—a construction grammar approach. *Tijdschrift voor Skandinavistiek* 20, 65–100.
Barðdal, Johanna
2006   Construction-specific properties of syntactic subjects in Icelandic and German. *Cognitive Linguistics* 17, 39–106.
Budanitsky, Alexander and Graeme Hirst
2006   Evaluating WordNet-based measures of lexical semantic relatedness. *Computational Linguistics* 32, 13–47.
Burgess, C., K. Livesay, and K. Lund
1998   Explorations in context space: Words, sentences, discourse. *Discourse Processes* 25, 211–257.
Bybee, Joan and Paul Hopper
2001   Introduction to frequency and the emergence of linguistic structure. In Bybee, Joan and Paul Hopper (eds.), *Frequency and the Emergence of Linguistic Structure*. Amsterdam: John Benjamins, 1–26.
Churchland, Paul M.
1995   *The Engine of Reason, the Seat of the Soul: A Philosophical Journey into the Brain*. Cambridge, MA: MIT Press.

Croft, William
    2001   *Radical Construction Grammar.* Oxford: Oxford University Press.
Croft, William and D. Alan Cruse
    2004   *Cognitive Linguistics.* Cambridge: Cambridge University Press.
Dąbrowska, Ewa
    2004   *Language, Mind and Brain.* Edinburgh: Edinburgh University Press.
Dąbrowska, Ewa
    forth-   Words as constructions. In Evans, Vyvyan and Stéphanie Pourcel (eds.),
    coming   *New Directions in Cognitive Linguistics.* Amsterdam: John Benjamins.
Dagan, Ido
    2000   Contextual word similarity. In Dale, Robert, Hermann Moisl, and Harold Somers (eds.), *Handbook of Natural Language Processing.* New York: Marcel Dekker, 459–475.
Divjak, Dagmar
    2006   Ways of intending: Delineating and structuring near-synonyms. In Gries, Stefan and Anatol Stefnaowitsch (eds.), *Corpora in Cognitive Linguistics,* vol. 2: *The Syntax-Lexis Interface.* Berlin: Mouton de Gruyter, 19–56.
Divjak, Dagmar and Stefan Th. Gries
    2006   Ways of trying in Russian: Clustering behavioral profiles. *Corpus Linguistics and Linguistic Theory* 2, 23–60.
Divjak, Dagmar and Laura A. Janda
    2008   Ways of attenuating agency in Russian. In Siewierska, Anna (ed.), *Impersonal Constructions in Grammatical Theory.* Special issue of *Transactions of the Philological Society* 106, 138–179.
Dziwirek, Katarzyna
    forth-   A folk classification of Polish emotions: Evidence from a corpus-based
    coming   study.
Dziwirek, Katarzyna and Barbara Lewandowska-Tomaszczyk
    2003   Syntax and semantics of Polish and English expressions of emotions: A corpus study. Paper presented at the American Association of Teachers of Slavic and East European Languages conference, San Diego, CA.
Evgen'eva, A. P. (ed.)
    2001   *Slovar' sinonimov russkogo jazyka.* Moscow: Astrel'.
Feldman, Jerome A.
    2006   *From Molecule to Metaphor: A Neural Theory of Language.* Cambridge, MA: MIT Press.
Fillmore, Charles
    1982   Frame semantics. In Linguistic Society of Korea (eds.), *Linguistics in the Morning Calm.* Seoul: Hanshin Publishing, 111–137.
Fillmore, Charles
    1985   Syntactic intrusions and the notion of grammatical construction. In *Proceedings of the Berkeley Linguistics Society* 11, 73–86.
Fillmore, Charles J., Paul Kay, Laura Michaelis, and Ivan Sag
    forth-   *Construction Grammar.* Stanford, CA: CSLI Publications.
    coming
Firth, John R.
    1957   A synopsis of linguistic theory 1930–1955. In Philological Society (eds.), *Studies in Linguistic Analysis.* Oxford: Blackwell, 1–32.
Fried, Mirjam
    2005   A frame-based approach to case alternations: The swarm-class verbs in Czech. *Cognitive Linguistics* 16, 475–512.

Geeraerts, Dirk
1988   Where does prototypicality come from? In Rudzka-Ostyn, Brygida (ed.), *Topics in Cognitive Linguistics*. Amsterdam: John Benjamins, 207–229.

Geeraerts, Dirk
2005   Lectal variation and empirical data in Cognitive Linguistics. In Ruiz de Mendoza Ibáñez, Francisco J., and M. Sandra Peña Cervel (eds.), *Cognitive Linguistics: Internal Dynamics and Interdisciplinary Interaction* (=Cognitive Linguistics Research 32). Berlin: Mouton de Gruyter, 163–189.

Gilquin, Gaëtanelle
2007a   To err is not all. What corpus and elicitation can reveal about the use of collocations by learners. *Zeitschrift für Anglistik und Amerikanistik*, 273–292.

Gilquin, Gaëtanelle
2007b   The cognitive reality of frequent verb-noun combinations: An empirical study. Paper presented at the International Cognitive Linguistics Conference, Krakow, Poland.

Gleitman, Lila R. and Jane Gillette
1995   The role of syntax in verb learning. In Fletcher, Paul and Brian MacWhinney (eds.), *The Handbook of Child Language*. Oxford: Blackwell, 413–427.

Glynn, Dylan
forthcoming   Polysemy, syntax, and variation. A usage-based method for Cognitive Semantics. In Evans, Vyvyan, and Stéphanie Pourcel (eds.), *New Directions in Cognitive Linguistics*. Amsterdam: John Benjamins.

Goldberg, Adele
1995   *Constructions: A Construction Grammar Approach to Argument Structure*. Chicago: Chicago University Press.

Goldberg, Adele
2006   *Constructions at Work: The Nature of Generalizations in Language*. Oxford: Oxford University Press.

Gries, Stefan Th. and Dagmar S. Divjak
forthcoming   Behavioral profiles: A corpus-based approach towards cognitive semantic analysis. In Evans, Vyvyan and Stéphanie Pourcel (eds.), *New Directions in Cognitive Linguistics*. Amsterdam: John Benjamins.

Hanks, Patrick
1996   Contextual dependency and lexical sets. *International Journal of Corpus Linguistics* 1, 75–98.

Ide, Nancy and Jean Véronis
1998   Introduction to the Special Issue on Word Sense Disambiguation: The state of the art. *Computational Linguistics* 24, 1–40.

Janda, Laura A.
1993   *A Geography of Case Semantics: The Czech Dative and the Russian Instrumental* (=Cognitive Linguistics Research 4). Berlin: Mouton de Gruyter.

Janda, Laura A.
1999   Peircean semiotics and cognitive linguistics: A case study of the Russian genitive. In Shapiro, Michael (ed.), *The Peirce Seminar Papers*. New York: Berghahn Books, 441–466.

Janda, Laura A.
2000   A cognitive model of the Russian accusative case. In R. K. Potapova, V. D. Solov'ev, and V. N. Poljakov (eds.), *Trudy meždunarodnoj konferencii Kognitivnoe modelirovanie*, No. 4, part I. Moscow: MISIS, 20–43.

Janda, Laura A.
2002a   Cases in collision, cases in collusion: The semantic space of case in Czech and Russian. In Janda, Laura A., Steven Franks, and Ronald Feldstein (eds), *Where One's Tongue Rules Well: A Festschrift for Charles E. Townsend*. Columbus, OH: Slavica, 43–61.

Janda, Laura A.
2002b   Cognitive hot spots in the Russian case system. In Shapiro, Michael (ed.), *Peircean Semiotics: The State of the Art* (=*The Peirce Seminar Papers* 5). New York: Berghahn Books, 165–188.

Janda, Laura A.
2002c   The case for competing conceptual systems. In Lewandowska-Tomaszczyk, Barbara and Kamila Turewicz (eds.), *Cognitive Linguistics Today* (=Łódź *Studies in Language* 6). Frankfurt: Peter Lang, 355–374.

Janda, Laura A.
2002d   Concepts of case and time in Slavic. *Glossos* 3 at http://www.seelrc.org/glossos/.

Janda, Laura A.
2004   Border zones in the Russian case system. In Apresjan, Ju. D. (ed.), *Sokrovennye smysly*. Moscow: Jazyki slavjanskoj kul'tury, 378–398.

Janda, Laura A.
forth-   Transitivity in Russian from a cognitive perspective. In Kustova, Galina
coming (ed.), *Dinamičeskie modeli: Slovo. Predloženie. Tekst*. Moscow: Jazyki slavjanskoj kul'tury.

Janda, Laura A. and Steven J. Clancy
2002   *The Case Book for Russian*. Bloomington, IN: Slavica.

Karlsson, Fred
1986   Frequency considerations in morphology. *Zeitschrift für Phonetik, Sprachwissenschaft und Kommunikationsforschung* 39, 19–28.

Karlsson, Fred
1985   Paradigms and word forms. *Studia gramatyczne VII. Ossolineum*, 135–154.

Kay, Paul, and Charles J. Fillmore
1999   Grammatical constructions and linguistic generalizations: the what's X doing Y? construction. *Language* 75, 1–34.

Kempe, Vera and Brian MacWhinney
1999   Processing of morphological and semantic cues in Russian and German. *Language and Cognitive Processes* 14, 129–171.

Kilgarriff, Adam
1997   I don't believe in word senses. *Computers and the Humanities* 31, 91–113.

King, Bruce M. and Edward W. Minium
2008   *Statistical Reasoning in the Behavioral Sciences*. Hoboken, NJ: John Wiley and Sons.

Kobricov, B. P.
2004   Metody snjatija semantičeskoj neodnoznačnosti. *NTI* Ser. 2, Vyp. 3, 1–30.

Kövecses, Zoltán
2001   *Metaphor and Emotion: Language, Culture, and Body in Human Feeling*. Cambridge: Cambridge University Press.

Lakoff, George
1987   *Women, Fire and Dangerous Things*. Chicago: Chicago University Press.

Lakoff, George and Mark Johnson
1980   *Metaphors We Live By*. Chicago: Chicago University Press.

Landauer, T. K., P.W. Foltz, and D. Laham
1998   Introduction to latent semantic analysis. *Discourse Processes* 25, 259–284.
Langacker, Ronald W.
1987   *Foundations of Cognitive Grammar I. Theoretical Prerequisites*. Stanford: Stanford University Press.
Langacker, Ronald W.
1990   *Concept, Image, and Symbol: The Cognitive Basis of Grammar*. Berlin: Mouton de Gruyter.
Langacker, Ronald W.
1991   *Foundations of Cognitive Grammar II*. Stanford, CA: Stanford University Press.
Langacker, Ronald W.
2003   Constructional integration, grammaticization, and serial verb constructions. *Language and Linguistics* 4, 251–278.
Levontina, Irina B. and Anna A. Zalizniak
2001   Human emotions viewed through the Russian language. In Harkins, Jean and Anna Wierzbicka (eds.), *Emotions in Crosslinguistic Perspective* (=*Cognitive Linguistics Research* 17). Berlin: Mouton de Gruyter, 291–336.
Lidz, Jeffrey, Henry Gleitman, and Lila Gleitman
2001   Kidz in the 'hood: Syntactic bootstrapping and the mental lexicon. *University of Pennsylvania Institute for Research in Congitive Science Technical Report* No. ORCS-01-01.
MacWhinney, Brian
2001   Emergentist approaches to language. In Bybee, Joan and Paul Hopper (eds.), *Frequency and the Emergence of Linguistic Structure*. Amsterdam: John Benjamins, 449–470.
Mel'čuk, Igor' A
2001   *Communicative Organization in Natural Language: The Semantic-Communicative Structure of Sentences*. Amsterdam: John Benjamins.
Mostovaja, Anna D.
1998   On emotions that one can 'immerse into', 'fall into' and 'come into': The semantics of a few Russian prepositional constructions. In Athanasiadou, Angeliki and Elżbieta Tabakowska (eds.), *Speaking of Emotions: Conceptualisation and Expression* (=*Cognitive Linguistics Research* 10). Berlin: Mouton de Gruyter, 295–329.
Radden, Günter
1998   The conceptualization of emotion causality by means of prepositional phrases. In Athanasiadou, Angeliki and Elżbieta Tabakowska (eds.), *Speaking of Emotions: Conceptualisation and Expression* (=*Cognitive Linguistics Research* 10). Berlin: Mouton de Gruyter, 273–294.
Raxilina, Ekaterina V.
2000   *Kognitivnyj analiz predmetnyx imen*. Moscow: Russkie slovari.
Schmid, Hans-Jörg
2000   *English Abstract Nouns as Conceptual Shells*. (=*Topics in English Linguistics* 34). Berlin: Mouton de Gruyter.
Schmid, Hans-Jörg
2007   Does frequency in text really instantiate entrenchment in the cognitive system? Paper presented at the International Cognitive Linguistics Conference, Krakow, Poland.

Schmid, Hans-Jörg
   forth-   Entrenchment, salience and basic levels. In Geeraerts, Dirk and Hubert
   coming   Cuyckens (eds.), *Handbook of Cognitive Linguistics*. Oxford: Oxford University Press.
Stefanowitsch, Anatol
   2006a   Corpus-based approaches to metaphor and metonymy. In Stefanowitsch, Anatol and Stefan Th. Gries (eds.), *Corpus-based Approaches to Metaphor and Metonymy* (=*Trends in Linguistics* 171). Berlin: Mouton de Gruyter, 1–16.
Stefanowitsch, Anatol
   2006b   Words and their metaphors: A corpus-based approach. In Stefanowitsch, Anatol, and Stefan Th. Gries (eds.), *Corpus-based Approaches to Metaphor and Metonymy* (=*Trends in Linguistics* 171). Berlin: Mouton de Gruyter, 61–105.
Stefanowitsch, Anatol and Stefan Th. Gries
   2003   Collostructions: Investigating the interaction of words and constructions. *International Journal of Corpus Linguistics* 8, 209–243.
Stefanowitsch, Anatol and Stefan Th. Gries
   2005   Covarying collexemes. *Corpus Linguistics and Linguistic Theory* 1, 1–43.
Svanlund, Jan
   2007   Metaphor and convention. *Cognitive Linguistics* 18, 47–89.
Švedova, N. Ju. (ed.)
   2003   *Russkij semantičeskij slovar'* v. III. Moscow: Institut russkogo jazyka RAN.
Taylor, John R.
   2002   *Cognitive Grammar*. Oxford: Oxford University Press.
Tummers, Jose, Kris Heylen and Dirk Geeraerts
   2005   Usage-based approaches in Cognitive Linguistics: A technical state of the art. *Corpus Linguistics and Linguistic Theory* 1 (2), 225–261.
Turney, Peter D.
   2002   Mining the Web for Synonyms: PMI-IR versus LSA on TOEFL. In *Proceedings of the Twelfth European Conference on Machine Learning*, 491–502.
Turney, Peter D.
   2005   Measuring semantic similarity by latent relational analysis. In *Proceedings of International Joint Conference on Artificial Intelligence*, 1136–1141.
Wierzbicka, Anna
   1998   'Sadness' and 'anger' in Russian: The non-universality of the so-called 'basic human emotions'. In Athanasiadou, Angeliki and Elżbieta Tabakowska (eds.), *Speaking of Emotions: Conceptualisation and Expression* (=*Cognitive Linguistics Research* 10). Berlin: Mouton de Gruyter, 3–28.
Wierzbicka, Anna
   1999   *Emotions across Languages and Cultures: Diversity and Universals*. Cambridge: Cambridge University Press.